Would you prefer to go straight to the bonuses?

Go to ConsciousCalculations.com and share your email address, and we will happily send them to you. You can also click on this QR code:

"Todd Langford's skill set has had a exponential impact on my personal and business strategies." TIM COOPER

"Todd is a masterful teacher. I've been learning from him since 2011. He's the most analytic number cruncher I've ever met. Todd knows his stuff! He's the poster child for numerical fluency and mathematical expertise. Todd's ability to tell stories and apply those stories to financial principles is exceptional. The way he intertwines client "life experiences" with financial calculators brings true clarity to Truth Concepts. His teaching is compelling and his mathematical proficiency is unarguable in proving financial concepts. Truth Concepts helps me prove out the numbers for clients to see. The Truth Concepts calculators are compelling evidence of why a person should have whole life insurance in their portfolio. Truth Concepts calculators have allowed me to show the real costs of market-based investments compared to whole life insurance. Using Truth Concepts, I've been able to sell more whole life policies and help more people have guarantees in their lives and in their financial portfolios."
BARRY BROOKSBY

"I have known Todd, and used his software programs since the mid-1990s. His mathematical genius, insight, and ability to paint pictures using numbers is nothing short of amazing. His unique abilities have been a real gift to the financial services industry, and I am fortunate to have known him over my career." BURTON STEWART

"Todd Langford's Truth Concepts software has been instrumental in helping me understand the mathematical reality behind financial decisions and their long term impact. His calculators bring clarity to complex concepts and have strengthened my ability to communicate meaningful financial strategies to both my own family and the families I serve. Todd's commitment to pursuing truth in the financial world is truly exceptional." KYLE FULLER

"Even after a quick look through the Table of Contents, I can already say, 'Amazing.' I have known Todd for a very long time and he is been nothing but an example of the highest level of character and integrity in the financial honesty that he exudes is beyond anything else in the financial industry. I am taken back by the continued experiences I have with others the refuse to embrace the truth that Todd exudes from all of his work is calculators and especially his dedication to providing the truth about money is unmatched." TOM YOUNG

"My experience with Todd has been completely eye-opening from the time that I met him and how he was able to help me understand what I was looking at. Todd and my father, Trent Fortner, have known each other for 30 plus years. I've always heard how amazing and incredibly talented Todd was, but once I finally got to meet him and have him help me on many different occasions, he is my go-to mentor when it comes to learning the calculations the right way. His calculators within Truth Concepts have impacted not only me but the lives of my clients to understand the truth about what's going on in reality, not just what we see at first glance. Todd is an incredible trainer who helps you understand how a calculator works, and this will become more important as time goes on, especially with the rise of AI. You can't just take AI's word for it; you must know how the calculation works and how it reached its conclusion. Others would benefit from reading this book because, in today's world of finance, most people lean on software to understand an end result. They understand their inputs and what is produced on the back end. But they don't actually know how they arrived at their current calculation results. Today's financial softwares just kick out end results and it may end up hurting the younger generation. Having Todd's guidance will be able to help understand the end result and what the process was to get there. By reading this book, my hope is that you would understand how the calculations work so that, when you have a client working through software, especially AI, you can know right away whether it's truth or not. You can then prove it and back it up with calculations through Truth Concepts. By reading this book, my hope is that you would understand how the calculations work so that, when you have a client working through software, especially AI, you can know right away whether it's truth or not. You can then prove it and back it up with calculations through Truth Concepts."
BROCK FORTNER

"I've known Todd for over 20 years. I've relied on him for his Truth Concepts calculators as well as his expertise in the financial advice world. His knowledge and practical application for people making money decisions is second to none. He's been a resource for my business and for my clients in many a ways he can never be thanked enough for." LEONARD RASKIN

"In an industry often driven by opinions and assumptions, Todd Langford stands apart by anchoring everything in truth and mathematics. His work has significantly influenced how I think, evaluate, and advise, bringing a level of clarity that is rare in financial services. *Conscious Calculations* goes beyond numbers—it helps align truth, math, and decision-making, and will elevate how both advisors and clients understand financial strategy." JOHN STEWART

"Mark Twain famously remarked that 'There are three kinds of lies: lies, damned lies and statistics.' In the financial world there seems to be a lot of 'smoke and mirrors.' Todd Langford cuts through the crap. Math is math; and he has worked for decades to bring truth to the world of the financial math through his suite of calculators to help advisors to know the truth behind the numbers and for the public to be able to compare and understand not only what the numbers mean, but how they affect their lives." MARK BERTRANG

"I've been attending Todd's in-person training and using Truth Concepts software since 2015, and it has completely changed how I see and present personal finance. Todd has a gift for turning complex math into clear conversations and teaching advisors how to explain these concepts in a way clients understand. This book will help advisors and clients see the truth behind the numbers and make better decisions." TRENT MACKEEN

"I have used Truth Concepts software and attended Todd Langford's training for several years. Todd is a master at creating calculators that help me explain financial truths to my clients. Whether I'm meeting with a married business owner with a more complicated financial picture or a single professional whose situation is more straightforward, I can count on Todd's calculators to illustrate a concept or reinforce my own understanding so I can speak more confidently about it. I encourage all Financial Professionals to read this book for their own professional growth and development." LESLEY BATSON

"Todd Langford's insights and Truth Concepts software have been a transformative influence on my business. They showed me how to use whole life insurance as a stable financial foundation. His commitment to seeking deep truths has given me the conviction to lead my practice with clarity and certainty, standing firmly on facts that only math can reveal. This is a must-read for any advisor who wants to serve clients with greater quality, clarity, and truth." DAVID ZAPATA

"I've known Todd as a teacher/trainer for over 25 years. In that time I think the most profound thing that he has said or taught financial professionals is to use calculators not to prove you are right, but to determine what is actually so, about the math behind the concept in question—the Truth. Sometimes what you thought to be true doesn't work out to be true when all of the variables and ripple effects of the calculation are considered. Truth Concepts isn't about fancy presentations intended to "wow" the client - it's about determining what is so about the calculation and how that truth may impact the choices available to the client. The industry has been greatly served by Todd's continual efforts to both quantify various concepts and to teach financial professionals the difference between selling and providing sound advice." ROSS FELDMAN

"Todd Langford has put thousands of hours into perfecting the calculators and stories that expose the truth of personal financial decision making. *Conscious Calculations* is a book that should be on everyone's desk who is serious about improving their financial outcomes. I've learned from Todd for over 30 years and will continue to do so." TRENT FORTNER

"In *Conscious Calculations*, my dear friend and mentor of many years Todd Langford has created a masterpiece. This book is a one-of-a-kind condensed, actionable guide through which anyone willing to consume it will gain great value. I've made 57 laps around the sun and on that journey lost most of my net worth more than once because I had more to learn. In seeking that knowledge I've attended the author Todd Langford's Truth Concepts basic and advanced trainings more times than I can count, perhaps more than any other advisor and will continue to do so – my clients and the clarity I seek are that important. Todd is a genius with decades of experience and this book that distills down that world of knowledge into a surprisingly easy read is an absolute gem! Advisors who stop short of mastering these calculations will continue to deliver their solutions sheepishly and their clients will sense it and avoid acting. And individuals seeking a financial future for their family that they understand, and control will benefit from this work of art just as much." GARY PINKERTON

"It's often said that math is a universal language. I didn't fully understand what that meant until I met Todd Langford and experienced his ability to reveal, clarify, and communicate truth through numbers. Todd has a rare gift: he takes what appears complex and makes it understandable. In an industry where confusion around math has too often been used to perpetuate half-truths, Todd brings clarity. He equips people to see what's real, to think critically, and to align their financial decisions with truth rather than assumption. I'm deeply grateful for Todd and his work. It has strengthened my own conviction in the financial strategies I teach and reignited my desire to help others become truly empowered with money—by understanding the math that drives it." RYAN LEE

"I want to take a moment to offer my deepest gratitude to Todd for all of his hard work and dedication. He's brought so much light into a space that can often feel confusing and blurry. Todd's efforts have given me, and countless others, the courage to step out of uncertainty and into clarity. His passion and commitment to bringing truth to every conversation have helped me grow not only professionally but also personally as I guide my clients toward a brighter, more secure future. Todd, your work is a true beacon, and I am so grateful for the difference you've made in my life and in the lives of my clients. As a financial strategist, this book has completely reshaped how I help my clients navigate their future. Todd's approach, built on what he calls 'truth training,' has given me a foundation of real clarity. It's not just about pitching a product; it's about connecting the numbers to their real-life goals. Chapter 2's five fundamental calculators gave me a solid starting point; they helped my clients see exactly where they stand today. But it's Chapter 4 that boosted my confidence like never before—those calculators gave me a precise, step-by-step roadmap, so I could guide them toward their financial goals with real conviction. And to round out this transformation, Chapter 7 gave me the framework to ensure that confidence stays with me long-term. By using these calculators, I've not only understood my own convictions but have been able to share them with a clear purpose. When I present whole life products now, I don't just offer a plan—I offer a proven, step-by-step strategy. This book has given me not just the tools, but the confidence and conviction to help my clients see how whole life products can secure their future—step by step, with absolute clarity." WADE BORTH

"Todd and his software skills is what got me committed to my financial education 26 years ago. I remember the specific example: "If what the auto dealership told you was a lie would you want to know?" He then showed beyond a shadow of doubt that a 0% loan interest rate is always more than 0%; in fact it could be more than traditional automobile financing. He then went on and showed how reducing tax rates increases tax revenues and a whole lot more. I was sold on not just thinking out of the box, but accounting for everything. Because of this introduction to key financial concepts, my CPA opinions changed 180 degrees. Todd 's work has inspired me to bring these truths to my clients personally but also in my series of books, Confessions of a CPA." BRYAN BLOOM

"Todd demonstrates a sophisticated understanding that effective financial strategy begins with a rigorous assessment of present conditions, followed by the establishment of disciplined, coherent principles to guide decision-making. From this foundation, he emphasizes the development of practical, forward-looking actions that enable clients to transition from their current financial reality to their desired long-term outcomes. His analytical tools empower advisors to cut through complexity and noise, allowing for precise identification of client challenges—their origins, characteristics, and full scope. This clarity helps build thoughtful, comprehensive strategies that are realistic and actionable. Equally notable is Todd's emphasis on action. In an environment where trust is increasingly scarce, he equips advisors not only to deliver insight but to guide clients toward meaningful, results-driven decisions. He recognizes that trust, once established, must be consistently reinforced through clarity, competence, and follow-through. His calculators represent more than simple utilities—they are precision instruments that enhance advisory discipline and elevate the standard of financial practice. For advisors committed to delivering measurable value and enduring client relationships, these tools are well worth integrating into their process."

Mike Baker (Pilot)

"When I first heard Todd Langford's name through Caleb Guilliams, I'll admit—I lumped him in with the rest of the financial services industry. I'd spent 30 years in digital marketing running billions through Google Ads, building calculators of my own, and I figured anyone selling whole life insurance was just another slick salesperson. I was dead wrong. When I sat down with Todd on my podcast, I realized he's the opposite of a salesperson—he's more like a doctor walking into a village of witch doctors. Everyone else is reading chicken bones and Ouija boards, and Todd shows up with an MRI machine. He doesn't need to sell you anything. He just turns on the light and lets the math speak. What struck me most is that Todd has a biology degree—not finance, not math—and yet he built Truth Concepts into the definitive tool for honest financial planning over nearly 40 years. That's because he understands something most people miss: the numbers don't lie, but people can be tricked when you add enough convolution. Todd strips all of that away. I come from the data side of digital marketing, and Todd comes from the math side of financial planning. We both learned the same lesson: you don't need to be a great salesperson if the truth is on your side. Todd doesn't just teach advisors how to use calculators—he gives them the confidence to tell their clients what's real, even when it's not what they want to hear. I'm honored to know Todd and to be part of the circle of people—Kim Butler, Caleb, Norman Baker—who believe that clarity and truth will always beat gimmicks and hype."

Dennis Yu

CONSCIOUS CALCULATIONS

The Truth Behind The Numbers in Personal Finance

TODD LANGFORD
with Kristen Hugins

Dedicated to all who seek the whole truth about money in personal finance.

Published in the United States of America
by the Prosperity Economics Movement.

ProsperityEconomics.org

ISBN: 979-8-9940994-6-9

Cover design by Debbi Sherman, Cimmeron Studios
Calculator images captured by David Osmond
Interior design, layout, and typography by Andrew Chapman

Special Sales

To all who seek the whole truth around the numbers in personal finance.

Disclaimer

Although this book addresses personal financial math, calculations, and standards, the authors are *not* tax professionals, attorneys, or credit specialists. This book is intended to provide a general understanding of financial math, *not* specific advice for any one individual. Each individual's financial circumstances are different, and we recommend you talk with a professional in the field who is certified and vetted in the particular area you may have a question about or decision to make regarding your (or in the case of strategists, your clients') finances.

Truth Concepts™ is software owned by Numbers Analytic, Inc., founded by Todd Langford.

All Truth Concepts (TC) calculators and tools fall under this trademark, and Asset Flow™ has its own trademark.

Most calculations in this book are from TC Version 3.00.2.45 in 2025. A few were from 2022. Thanks go to David Osmond for each of the pictures of the calculators! For current versions, go to:

http://www.truthconcepts.com

A "how to read" suggestion: During your first read, read the book through in its entirety. Then go back and read it again, chapter by chapter. Pay special attention to the Appendix. Keep the book close by and refer to it frequently as you implement the knowledge. Note Chapter 8 has a section for clients and a separate one for financial strategists. It has been said those who can't do, teach. I couldn't disagree more. The primary role of an owner is as a teacher. You want to own your skills around personal finance whether you are an individual investor or a financial strategist. Teaching others is the way you leverage your wisdom, knowledge, skills, and desire and manifest your vision. There are people all over the US and Canada who need and want to be taught.

Disclaimer

Contents

Introduction: Why Getting to the Truth Matters 1

Chapter 1: Foundational Financial Philosophies 7

Chapter 2: Five Fundamental Calculators 19

Chapter 3: Why Simplify Software? 37

Chapter 4: The Calculators—Part One 43

Chapter 5: The Calculators—Part Two 69

Chapter 6: The TC Software Tools 121

Chapter 7: Duet of Truth: Math and Principle 141

Chapter 8: Becoming a Conscious Calculator 153

Epilogue: Nothing Is Truer Than Truth 167

Appendix 175

What Is Next for You? 193

About the Authors 195

Introduction: Why Getting to the Truth Matters

The idea that "if it looks too good to be true, it is" causes limited thinking. Everything of value looked too good to be true when it was first put forth. Think about electricity, cell phones, driverless cars, etc. So if it "looks too good to be true," dig a little deeper.

At Truth Concepts™, we work from a foundation of seven core standards:

1. Use *financial math* formulas & calculators, not simple grade-school math, which ignores time.
2. Always compare strategies using *equivalent cash flows.*
3. Measure both Opportunity *Cost* (what you give up) and Opportunity *Gain* (what you earn) at a reasonable *net* cost of money.
4. Use the *actual* Internal Rate of Return (IRR) over time, *not* the misleading *averages.*
5. Consider the *ripple effects* of every financial decision - nothing exists in a vacuum.
6. Avoid *paltering* - don't let true but *irrelevant* facts lead to false conclusions.
7. Accurate strategies require both *accurate math* and the *correct formula.*

In an age where financial literacy is more crucial than ever, the landscape of personal finance is fraught with confusion and misinformation. The prevalence of misleading narratives—from sensationalized news headlines to the persuasive pitches of financial salespeople—can obscure the truths that underpin sound financial decision-making.

For instance, a recent article in *The New York Times* highlighted how misleading narratives around debt repayment often encourage individuals to liquidate their assets to eliminate liabilities, **without considering the opportunity costs involved and the consequential change in risk, due to no longer having access to cash** (Parker, "What to Do About Debt"). Such oversimplified advice can lead to significant financial setbacks, especially when consumers overlook the potential returns on their investments. This tendency to present complex financial situations as binary choices contributes to a broader culture of misunderstanding.

Moreover, social media has amplified confusion, allowing incorrect financial advice to spread rapidly. An article from *The Wall Street Journal* discussed how popular investment platforms and influencers often promote strategies that lack rigorous analysis, leading many inexperienced investors astray (Huang, "The Risk of Relying on Social Media for Financial Advice"). This phenomenon has not only fostered unrealistic expectations but has also blurred the lines between legitimate financial guidance and basic speculation.

These narratives are not merely benign misunderstandings; they can be intricately tied to the agendas of those in the financial industry who benefit from a lack of clarity. As a result, navigating the world of personal finance without a firm grasp of the underlying truths can lead to costly mistakes.

This book seeks to illuminate the complexities of financial decision-making by demystifying the mathematics at play. It is a mission driven by the urgent need for honesty, clarity, and accountability in financial advice. By equipping both strategists and consumers with a deeper understanding of financial calculations, we aim to foster conscious and informed decision-making.

My journey into the realm of personal finance began in a rather unconventional manner. Growing up, I became adept at using the HP12C, a financial calculator that has stood the test of time for over four decades. Released in 1981, the HP12C was the world's first calculator that allowed a person to determine financial math, as opposed to grade school math. It is still selling today in its original form and continues to be HP's longest and best-selling product. It served not just as a tool for calculations, but as a gateway into a world where math and finance intersect in often surprising ways. The HP12C is a symbol of reliability, and its continued popularity speaks to the foundational nature of the principles it embodies.

However, the HP12C is hard to use since it functions on Reverse Polish notation. This is why I developed five free calculators that are much easier to use. You can get access to them here: https://truthconcepts.com/five-financial-calculators. My early experiences, rooted in a background that combined biology and computer science, offered a unique perspective on financial calculations—one that emphasized logic and precision over meager convention—and valued making calculators that were both accurate and accessible.

While I was attending school (right when IBM PCs came on the market), there was a computer place in town, and I was seeking part-time work. Computers just "fit" me, and I figured them out early in their evolution. I started repairing computers at this computer shop, writing batch files for menus, and learning everything I could.

Around the same time, I met Norman Baker, an estate planner from the Nacogdoches area in Texas, who had a unique way of looking at numbers. He bought property in this small university town of 30,000 people, and ran a property and casualty insurance agency. He'd also been in the estate planning business for years. He valued having the latest and greatest technology in his field and owned several computers, IBM PCs, one with a single 5 ¼ inch floppy drive, and one with a hard drive (a whole 10 MB—you'd never have to change disks!).

As you can imagine, I was drawn to him as a tech- and finance-savvy mentor, and I spent a lot of time helping him in his office. It was 1986, and Lotus was *the* spreadsheet software to use. Norman taught me Lotus, and he would compile rudimentary spreadsheets to explain estate planning. Financial math was totally foreign to me at this time, but I picked up the spreadsheets and what was going on inside of them quickly. I learned how to modify Lotus at a basic level, and eventually I was working for both the computer shop and Norman's office. I soon transitioned to working full-time for Norman in addition to my full school schedule.

Norman Baker understood how the numbers really worked when it came to personal financial math. I came to him with a basic understanding of math, but I knew nothing about *financial* math. At one point, Norman and I were running an errand to the bank, and when we went in, his original loan was at 4% interest, but the bank was requiring him to renew the loan at 5%. He said, "You're going up by 25% on me!"

The banker said, "No, it's just a 1% increase."

He corrected them, and said, "You are raising my interest charges by 25%."

They just said, "Oh Norman, you always calculate math in such a weird way." At the time, I even questioned if his calculations were right. How could the bank be wrong? My whole life up until that point, I'd been taught to trust the bank.

In questioning him on that particular point and asking him to explain, I learned that if you convert the interest rate to actual dollars in order to see what's really going on, it actually is a 25% increase, not 1% like the banker insisted. Let's use the example of a loan with a $100,000 balance. At the original 4% interest rate, the actual annual interest cost would be $4,000. The banker said it was a 1% increase and quoted 5% for the next year. Under the new loan rate, the interest cost is $5,000. Increasing the loan cost from $4,000 to $5,000 is a 25% increase because $4000 x .25 is $1,000, which is how much the increase was in interest cost.

The fact that most people do not understand this is a huge advantage the financial institutions have. They may not know or understand this at local bank levels, but they know at the federal level. Presumably someone at the bank knows, but at the branch, the staff are often salespeople, the people-oriented people who are less numbers-oriented. But there must have been a loan officer or bank CFO in the back of the bank who knew that financial math.

When Norman brought that first 4-5% interest rate increase realization to my attention, he and I created spreadsheets (not quite software yet) to make the point and help others understand how this math worked in their world.

I definitely have developed what some call a "math brain." I have an ability to see numbers and identify immediately, right there, that the math is not right. This comes partly from working with math, computers, and calculators constantly since my school days—and great mentors like Norman Baker.

I always want all the decimal places in the equation. I don't like to have change left over. That's what I like about math; you can figure out what's right and what's wrong, and work with the numbers until you get to the exact answer without rounding.

For example, I have a problem I'm working on now that I've been working on a whole day that is seventy-five cents off! That matters to me because time and distance magnify that difference. Seventy-five cents off here will be thousands of dollars off in a hundred years, especially when time and compounding are incorporated into the mix.

Whether it's measuring gravity with a level to build a building or doing financial math, both are exacerbated by distance or time. **Like construction, there is no "about" in finance.** The building will lean, crack, or fall over time if it's off—even slightly. Like that building, money will change over time as well.

Perhaps because of this connection and commitment to exact measurements, I have found I am skilled in building things. Our family has a shed on our property for one llama that needed its own place for a while (I built it with our kids when they were teenagers). My wife, Kim, says that that shed will be there a hundred years from now because I am so careful, specific, and only do quality workmanship. It's a principle, or value, of mine that is woven into everything I do. See the picture in the back of the book if you want a smile.

Frankly, in a marriage, this value of precision can cause conflict. My wife often says, "It's good enough!" But I don't understand that phrase, good enough. Doing things too quickly has always turned into me having to do them again, and I despise redoing something. I like doing things right the first time. I consider all the variables and circumstances, whether with a new calculator or something I'm building. I ask "what if" about everything I can think of to anticipate and prepare for any scenario.

During my time at Norman's estate planning firm, I found myself at the intersection of typical personal finance and the burgeoning world of computing. I wrote spreadsheets in Lotus and learned to navigate the intricacies of financial modeling, often juxtaposing my calculations against the trusted

HP12C to ensure accuracy. This dual approach shaped my understanding of financial principles, as I realized that the interpretation of math can vary widely based on context, assumptions, and the motivations of those presenting the information.

Back in my college days when Norman taught me Lotus, I thought it was the most amazing software in the world. Since I really don't like redoing things, you can imagine how getting to copy/paste theories and do computations with the click of a button allowed me to play in a rapid way and enjoy the math side of finances without having to do redundant calculations. Instead I could focus on what was new and exciting. This is what I hope both strategists and clients can do by using my calculators.

As I developed my calculators through my company, Truth Concepts, I recognized the profound impact that clear, accurate financial tools could have on individuals and strategists alike. The essence of my work revolves around empowering users to make informed decisions by revealing the truth behind complex financial scenarios. For instance, understanding the interplay between debt costs and the opportunity value of cash assets is not just a mathematical exercise; it's a crucial insight that can drastically alter one's financial trajectory.

At the heart of *Conscious Calculations* is the idea that financial literacy is not solely about understanding numbers but also about grasping the principles that underpin those numbers. **This book is designed to empower readers to discern between absolute truths—those dictated by the mathematics of finance—and the more subjective principles that guide decision-making.** Just as an athlete must balance nutrition with exercise to achieve optimal health and peak performance, so too must individuals balance the rigors of mathematical accuracy with principled decision-making to ensure financial wellness.

As we delve deeper into the chapters ahead, we will explore the philosophies of financial growth and the accountability that strategists hold in ensuring their clients receive truthful, accurate guidance. We will examine the five fundamental calculators that serve as the bedrock of financial calculations, illustrating their applications through real-world stories. Furthermore, we will dive into all of the Truth Concepts calculators, when they are best used, and how they each help clients and strategists get to the true numbers to shape their own financial outcomes.

Ultimately, our exploration will culminate in a call to action: to become conscious calculators in our own right. This journey is about more than just numbers; it's about fostering a mindset of responsibility, integrity, and informed choice. By equipping ourselves with helpful calculators and tools, supported by the standards laid out in this book, we can navigate the complexities of personal finance with confidence and clarity.

The pursuit of truth in personal finance is not merely an academic endeavor but a vital necessity in a high-stakes world. As we embark on this journey together, may we strive to shine the light of wisdom into the shadows of confusion and misinformation, empowering ourselves and others to make decisions grounded in truth.

Chapter 1: Foundational Financial Philosophies

The number one rule of the banking strategy is that you've got to pay it back, at interest.

Personal finance is inherently complex. For most people, the world of investing, saving, and wealth-building seems like an endless sea of jargon, unfamiliar terminology and abstract concepts. Even those with financial strategists often struggle to truly grasp what's going on beneath the surface of their portfolios. This confusion can be both frustrating and paralyzing, leading individuals to either make poor financial choices or avoid making decisions altogether.

But here's the *truth*: financial clarity doesn't have to be elusive. With the right guidance, both the strategist and the client can embark on a shared journey to understand the math behind their decisions, the emotions that often drive those actions, and the consequences of each choice.

Exploring and illuminating the foundational principles that should guide every financial conversation is crucial. Accountability, transparency, and clear communication can foster stronger relationships between financial strategists and their clients, and a better understanding of the underlying math can empower clients to make smarter decisions.

Most importantly, breaking down these concepts into digestible, actionable steps can eliminate confusion and put clients on the path to achieving their financial objectives.

THE SHARED JOURNEY OF STRATEGISTS AND CLIENTS

Financial advising is not a one-way street. The client's and strategist's journey must align, and both parties must engage in a meaningful, collaborative relationship for optimal outcomes.

Trust and Vulnerability

At its core, financial advising is deeply personal. For many clients, their financial situation is an area where they feel vulnerable—whether it's the weight of debt, anxiety about retirement, or the uncertainty about how to manage wealth. Financial strategists are not merely dealing with numbers; they are working with individuals' hopes, fears, and aspirations. This emotional element requires a strategist to be not just a financial expert, but an attentive listener and grounded guide.

The client-strategist relationship is one of mutual trust. When that trust is built on transparency, clear communication, and empathy, the strategist is in a better position to recommend strategies that align with the client's objectives. Conversely, when there's a breakdown in communication, confusion often follows, and financial missteps are likely.

Misunderstandings Between Strategists and Clients

One of the most common issues clients face is a lack of clarity around the advice they receive. For instance, a strategist might suggest a financial vehicle based on a client's long-term goals, but if the client doesn't fully understand the rationale behind that strategy, they may find it hard to stick to it. Long term financial vehicles can be dangerous if the client doesn't understand the long term nature of them. With time, often comes a diminished memory of the information around the vehicle. If the explanation up front is not well understood and re-affirmed (and documented), liquidating the product prematurely often results in major losses. Or worse, they may take actions that contradict the advice, simply because they have forgotten it.

Take the case of one client, Sarah, who hired a financial strategist to help her plan for retirement. Sarah's objective was to retire early and travel the world. However, her strategist presented her with a portfolio designed for gradual, long-term growth, focusing primarily on stable investments. While the strategist's strategy was sound from a financial perspective, Sarah didn't understand the rationale behind it. She felt frustrated because she wasn't seeing the immediate returns she expected to fund her dream lifestyle and pulled her funds out early. Had the strategist spent more time getting clear about her objectives, there may not have been this disconnect. Additionally, if the strategist spent more time explaining and annually reviewing how the portfolio's slow growth would accumulate over time, Sarah might have been more patient with the process and less likely to pull her funds out prematurely.

The Importance of Objectives and Optimizing Each Financial Step

It's essential for both the strategist and client to take the time to align on a set of shared objectives, sometimes called a Financial Doctrine. One of the best questions a financial strategist can ask their clients is, "What are three things you want to accomplish financially?" This provides purpose, clarity, and focus for any future financial decisions. Those ongoing discussions are paramount for optimizing personal financial success.

It's also important that financial strategists actively engage with their clients to better understand not only their personal desires, but also their fears around money. Then the strategist can address any fears directly and educate the client on concerns such as risk, certainty, and protecting their wealth.

Once a client is in a good place with their objectives and mindset around their financial future, they can work with their strategist to optimize each financial step they take. **This is where the Truth Concepts calculators do their best work—providing calculations to make each financial step the most efficient step possible.** When both the client and strategist are aligned in terms of objectives, values, and efficient financial steps, the client's overall financial strategy has a higher chance of success.

THE MATH PRINCIPLE: RIGHT OR WRONG?

In the world of financial strategy, the math principle is often considered the foundation of all decisions. The idea is simple: given the right data, the right formulas, and the right approach, you can make decisions that are mathematically sound and predict outcomes accurately. But is this always true? Is financial decision-making always a matter of being "right" or "wrong," or is there more to it?

Money decisions, whether they involve retirement planning, investment choices, insurance decisions, or purchasing a home, all have one thing in common: they are driven by math. At the core of personal finance is a series of equations, ratios, and calculations that can be measured and understood.

Breaking Down Complex Calculations

Many financial concepts can seem intimidating at first, but breaking them down into manageable parts makes them much more accessible. For instance, instead of worrying about the entire retirement plan at once, focus on how regular contributions can accumulate over thirty years at a given rate of return.

This concept of compound interest can be understood in simple terms when using one—or any combination of—our five financial calculators:

- Time
- Rate
- Present Value
- Payment
- Future Value

Using simple calculators to demonstrate examples like the one above can help clients see the practical impact of math on their financial future. Even small, regular investments can compound significantly over time.

Examples of Financial Miscalculations

Sometimes showing extreme examples helps people understand things.

The impact of financial miscalculations is often compounded by misunderstanding the math. For instance, a common error among investors is underestimating the time it takes for the exponential curve of compound interest to pick up speed, which often leads them to wait longer to start saving. Another issue is misunderstanding the difference between advertised "average returns" of fluctuating investments, versus the actual returns the money earns.

Average returns do not equal actual returns, as we demonstrate on the Cash Flow calculator in our blog post, "Why Average ROR Doesn't Matter." (https://truthconcepts.com/why-average-ror-doesnt-matter) A 25% average return may actually equal a 0% actual return. How? Imagine a client, Jessica, invested $100,000 into an investment that had promised an average rate of return of 25% if she left the money alone for two years. In the first year, it earned 100%. So after the first year, the investment of $100,000 turned into $200,000.

Then, unfortunately, in the second year she experienced a rough patch and her account actually experienced a 50% loss. Now, her investment is right back where she started. So while her *average* return is 25%—and yes, that's mathematically correct—her actual yield is 0%.

Still in disbelief? An average is calculated by adding up all relevant sums and then dividing by the number of sums. In this case, our two rates are 100% and -50%. Divide that by two, and you get 25%.

How happy would you be with the broker who promised you an average of 25% only to receive an actual result of zero? You are probably not very happy, and yet the broker delivered on their promise. They're off the hook.

Are you starting to see why averages don't actually mean all that much when it comes to your finances? If you apply this logic to your investments supposedly averaging 12%, it's easy to see how that could mean almost anything. It could work out, or it could mean absolutely nothing. You could even end up with less. It's all smoke and mirrors.

The Importance of Mathematical Precision in Financial Strategy Work

As shown above, there is no doubt that math plays an essential role in financial strategy work. From calculating the compound interest on savings to determining the future value of investments, or a person's Human Life Value, financial decisions often rely on specific formulas and models that provide objective results. However, a financial strategist's ability to understand and apply these mathematical concepts is one of the primary reasons why clients seek out their expertise. If a strategist doesn't understand the difference between average and actual returns, for example, they won't be able to give the client the results they are seeking.

In another example, when setting retirement goals, a strategist will typically start by calculating the client's current savings, their expected rate of return, inflation rates, and the number of years until retirement. With this data, the strategist can use time value of money formulas to determine how much more the client needs to save in order to meet their retirement objectives. These calculations provide a clear, measurable path forward—if the client follows them, the math says they'll reach their goal.

But even here, a question arises: how accurate can these predictions truly be? Financial markets are inherently volatile. The future returns on investments are unknown, inflation rates fluctuate, and unexpected events can change the trajectory of even the most carefully constructed financial strategy. As much as we rely on mathematical precision, financial strategy work is not a perfect science.

The Illusion of Certainty in Financial Models

One of the biggest misconceptions in finance is that mathematical models can predict outcomes with perfect certainty. **The truth is that no model, no matter how sophisticated, can account for every variable in the real world.** In fact, the very act of predicting future financial outcomes is laden with assumptions about aspects like market returns, interest rates, and inflation—none of which are guaranteed to behave according to historical trends.

For example, a client may be working with a financial strategist who uses a 7% annual return assumption to project their future wealth. This is a common assumption based on historical stock market performance. But what happens if market returns fall short of this average, or if an economic recession occurs in the near future? Suddenly, the client's projections are no longer aligned with reality. Plus, any projected average return is not actual, as we proved a few pages back, and the **projections often do not take into account fees, taxes, and the drag of the bonds in the stock market portfolio.**

This does not mean that math is irrelevant in financial advising, but rather that strategists must acknowledge the limits of mathematical predictions. The "right" answer is rarely an absolute. Financial strategists must approach calculations with caution, ensuring they incorporate a range of possible outcomes and regularly adjust their strategies based on evolving circumstances.

Risk Management and the Math Principle

Risk is another area where the math principle can both help and hinder, depending on the situation. Many financial strategists use sophisticated risk models to determine the optimal asset allocation for clients, balancing risk and reward in ways that theoretically maximize returns while minimizing losses. However, the reality is that risk cannot always be quantified in a reliable way. Plus, there are insurance strategies that can be layered into the financial arena, yet are sometimes hard to quantify.

For example, a financial strategist might use statistical tools like the Sharpe ratio or value-at-risk (VaR) to evaluate the risk of a particular investment or portfolio. These models give clients a sense of how much risk they're taking on and how it compares to potential returns. But these tools rely heavily on past performance and market assumptions, which can change over time. What may have been considered a "low-risk" investment in the past could suddenly become more volatile due to changes in the economy, political instability, or even technological advances.

This is where the "right or wrong" dichotomy becomes problematic. Is a strategy "right" simply because it's mathematically sound based on historical data? Or is it "wrong" if it fails to account for the unpredictable nature of the future? While math can give financial strategists a useful framework, they must also be prepared to adapt and manage risk in ways that math alone cannot predict. Plus, what does one do when either an emergency or an opportunity arises? How do you calculate that?

The Role of Judgment and Experience in Financial Decisions

While math can provide us with answers based on objective data, financial decisions are rarely made in a vacuum. Clients bring their own hopes, fears, and circumstances into the equation, and these emotional factors can alter the outcome of a financial strategy. Financial strategists who rely solely on mathematical formulas may overlook the very real human elements at play.

For instance, consider a client who is deeply risk-averse after having lived through a market crash during a previous investment experience. Even if the math suggests a more aggressive investment strategy would be optimal for long-term growth, the client may not be comfortable with the potential for losses. **A skilled strategist must blend their mathematical understanding with empathy, adjusting their recommendations based on the client's emotional comfort level.** Or someone has heard Life Insurance is a bad investment. No matter what math they see, they may not be able to think open-mindedly.

This balance between math and human judgment is key. The "right" decision from a mathematical standpoint may not always be the "right" decision from a behavioral standpoint. Understanding how to bridge these two elements—math and behavior—is one of the most important skills a strategist can possess.

BRIDGING THE GAP BETWEEN MATH AND BEHAVIOR

When you make a decision out of fear,
it is almost always the wrong decision.

At the core of most financial decision-making lies a delicate balance between the mathematical precision of financial strategy and the messy, often unpredictable nature of human behavior. The best financial strategists understand that while math provides a roadmap, human behavior can significantly alter the course of that journey. Understanding the psychological factors that influence financial decisions is just as important as understanding the numbers.

The Behavioral Gap: Why Clients Often Deviate from the Strategy

One of the most significant challenges in financial advising is what experts refer to as the "behavioral gap"—the difference between the investment returns a client's portfolio is expected to generate and the actual returns they experience. This gap often occurs because clients, driven by emotions like fear, greed, or overconfidence, make decisions that deviate from their long-term financial strategy. Additionally, there may be products outside of the investment marketplace that could be beneficial, yet clients don't even know the questions to ask to access that option.

For example, during periods of market volatility, many clients panic and sell their investments in an attempt to avoid losses. This reaction is typically driven by a fear of losing money, which leads them to make decisions based on short-term emotions rather than long-term financial objectives. Unfortunately, these emotional decisions often lock in losses and prevent clients from benefiting from what can be an eventual market recovery.

According to a study by DALBAR[1], a leading research firm in the financial industry, individual investors consistently underperform the market due to poor behavior—buying and selling at the wrong times, failing to stick to their asset allocation, or becoming overly conservative after a market downturn. The difference between the expected and actual returns is a direct result of emotional decision-making, which, even though rooted in human psychology, can be mitigated with proper guidance. Furthermore, there are many other areas of a family's financial picture that can be optimized, yet many are only focusing on investing and investments.

Understanding the Psychology of Investing

The field of behavioral finance seeks to explain how psychological factors influence the way people make financial decisions. Many common cognitive biases affect people, including:

- **Loss Aversion**: People tend to fear losses more than they value gains, which can cause them to make overly conservative investment decisions.
- **Anchoring**: Investors may fixate on a specific piece of information, such as the price they paid for a stock, and allow that information to unduly influence their future decisions.
- **Overconfidence**: Some investors believe they can consistently beat the market, leading them to take excessive risks or ignore expert advice.
- **Herding Behavior**: Investors may follow the crowd, buying or selling based on what others are doing rather than their own analysis.

Each of these biases can lead to suboptimal financial decisions that deviate from a well-thought-out financial strategy. The role of the financial strategist is to help clients recognize these biases and understand how they can impact their financial behavior.

INTEGRATED STRATEGIES: SEEING THE BIG PICTURE

There is often a difference between peace of mind and financial efficiency.

Financial strategy is rarely just about choosing the best investment or making the right tax or insur-

[1] DALBAR, Inc. Quantitative Analysis of Investor Behavior (QAIB). Marlborough, MA: DALBAR, Inc., 2026.

ance decision; it's about integrating all aspects of a client's financial life into a cohesive strategy. Each financial decision has ripple effects across the entire arena, and a comprehensive approach ensures that the client's objectives are met without neglecting any key areas.

The Importance of a Holistic Approach to Personal Finance

A holistic approach involves looking at the entire financial picture: investment management, tax planning, retirement planning, insurance, estate planning, and more. An integrated strategy ensures that every decision made in one area of the client's life supports their broader financial objectives, reducing the chances of financial surprises. While typical financial planning began as recently as the 1960s, life insurance strategists have been doing holistic work for over 200 years. Most current-day financial planners and strategists never even look at, let alone take into account, the life insurance space.

For instance, when a holistic financial strategist creates a retirement plan for a client, they don't just focus on investments. They also consider factors like the client's tax situation, potential healthcare needs, life insurance, and estate planning goals. By integrating these factors into the overall approach, the strategist can help the client achieve a more secure and sustainable retirement.

In almost all cases, one area of personal finance will directly impact another. If the client is contributing heavily to a tax-deferred retirement account, for example, the strategist may recommend building assets outside of the retirement account box. In addition, they will look at a tax-efficient withdrawal strategy that minimizes tax liability in retirement.

Creating a Balanced, Dynamic Strategy

An effective integrated strategy is not a static document but a dynamic approach that evolves over time. Financial objectives change, life circumstances shift, and market conditions fluctuate. As a result, integrated strategies must be flexible and frequently reviewed. Regular meetings with clients allow the financial strategist to stay updated on changes in their clients' personal lives, as well as to monitor the progress of their investments, insurance, tax, debt paydown, and other financial objectives.

This kind of comprehensive, ongoing calibration also helps clients feel more certain. They can see the big picture, understanding how their current decisions fit into a larger, interconnected strategy. By addressing all aspects of their financial lives, the strategist builds trust and helps clients feel more confident about their future.

THE POWER OF FINANCIAL EDUCATION

What should the average person do? All they can.

One of the most significant factors in overcoming financial confusion is increasing financial literacy. A lack of understanding often leads to unnecessary fear and indecision, while a strong foundation of financial knowledge empowers clients to take control of their financial future. In fact, when clients feel more knowledgeable and confident about their finances, they tend to make smarter, less emotional decisions.

The Impact of Financial Education

Research shows that people who engage in financial education are more likely to make sound financial decisions, accumulate wealth, and retire comfortably. But despite the importance of financial literacy, many people still lack basic financial knowledge. A study by the National Financial Educators Council found that 60% of Americans failed a basic financial literacy test, with many struggling to understand concepts like interest rates, inflation, and compound growth.[2]

This lack of understanding leads to poor decision-making. For example, many individuals are putting extra money against a mortgage, while also having credit card balances with high interest rates. They think because of the larger size of the mortgage, it should be the focus, yet they fail to see the damage of the higher interest rate on the smaller debt. Additionally, families will lock up money in retirement plans before they have any emergency funds, forcing them into high-interest credit card debt if emergencies pop up or opportunities arise. Financial strategists have a unique opportunity to bridge this knowledge gap. By educating their clients about the math behind financial decisions, they can empower them to make informed choices and build long-term financial certainty.

Financial Education as Empowerment

Financial education goes beyond just understanding how to invest. It's about comprehending the full landscape of one's financial situation, including cash flow analysis, tax planning, insurance, and estate planning, to name a few. When strategists educate their clients, they don't just improve their financial outlook—they help them feel more certain and confident in their decisions.

For example, imagine a young professional named Alex who starts working with a financial strategist in his mid-twenties. Instead of merely helping Alex invest, the strategist educates him on the importance of the time value of money, cash flow control methods, the cash value of whole life insurance, and the risks of consumer debt. Over the next few years, Alex becomes financially literate, making smart decisions about cash flow, insurance, investing, and protecting his wealth. When it's time for Alex to buy his first home or start a family, he is equipped with the knowledge to make sound decisions based on his evolving financial situation.

---

[2] National Financial Educators Council. National Financial Literacy Test: Results, Data, Q & A. Accessed April 15, 2026. https://www.financialeducatorscouncil.org/national-financial-literacy-test/

EMOTIONAL INTELLIGENCE IN FINANCIAL ADVISING

People often know what they don't want, yet knowing what they want is imperative, so that we can match their money with their mortal lives.

While financial knowledge is important, emotional intelligence (EQ) is just as critical in the strategist-client relationship. **EQ involves the ability to understand and manage your own emotions, as well as the emotions of others.** In financial strategy, this skill is essential for creating a supportive and productive relationship.

The Role of Emotions in Financial Decision-Making

Money decisions are often not purely logical. Emotions like fear, greed, and anxiety play a significant role in how people make choices about their finances. For example, during periods of market volatility, investors may panic and sell their stocks in a fit of anxiety, only to regret the decision later when the market potentially recovers.

Financial strategists need to be attuned to their clients' emotional states, especially when clients are dealing with high-stakes financial situations. Whether it's the stress of approaching retirement or the grief of losing a spouse, strategists who exhibit high emotional intelligence can help clients navigate these emotional waters and make better decisions.

THE ROLE OF TECHNOLOGY IN MODERN FINANCIAL ADVICE

Computers can only tell us pure economics, not necessarily what is best for our family.

In today's rapidly evolving financial landscape, technology plays an increasingly important role in the personal finance process. Financial technology (FinTech) tools, from robo-strategists to various personal finance apps, can provide clients with more data and insights than ever before. However, with this technological advancement comes the challenge of ensuring that clients still receive personalized advice that takes their unique circumstances into account.

Financial Planning Tools and Apps

The rise of financial planning software and apps has also revolutionized the way clients engage with their finances. Tools like Credit Karma, YNAB (You Need a Budget), and Personal Capital *can* give clients a comprehensive view of their financial health, helping them track spending, savings, and investments in real-time. Yet they often don't show things like opportunity cost.

The Truth Concepts calculators and tools discussed at length in this book are examples of technology that help strategists and clients make informed decisions about their money and their future, while taking both the gains and the costs into consideration. Being able to plug numbers in and see in real-time how certain payments or investments would affect the big picture provides the advantage of projecting into the future and making faster, more accurate decisions.

Effective financial tools also allow strategists to monitor their clients' progress, making it easier to adjust strategies as needed. For example, if a strategist notices that a client is building up more cash for opportunities, they can revisit their Financial Doctrine and Objective list together to decide what the next step should be. Many Truth Concepts strategists utilize a cash flow control structure called Currence. If you are interested in an invitation for your own personal use, go here: https://livecurrence.com/individuals.

If you are a Financial Strategist and want to test drive the platform at no charge for ninety days, go here: https://livecurrence.com/strategist-affiliates-cia/?ref=akpfo2

Currence is the opposite of budgeting. Everybody knows we need to eat healthy, but diets still exist even though they are ineffective. Budgets are the same way. In some situations, especially short term, diets and budgeting produce positive results for a period of time. Yet getting a healthy body and healthy finances requires a long-term game.

Currence aims to turn unconscious spending into unconscious savings for the rest of one's life. Where most people default to spending, the Currence default is saving. The same way you unconsciously spend money, Currence will unconsciously / automatically help you save money. You don't have to actively do it because it's a structure in place that takes care of the discipline.

Budgeting is restricting, actually trying to predict the future, rarely effective for more than a month, and literally causes extreme family and marital stress and frustration. Currence is the opposite of all of that. It's freeing, present-focused, and proven over many years to be effective and enables a choice architecture that supports family fun, inspiration, and joy around money. Over Currence's history, the saving average is over 20% of income. If you ask someone to save that, they'll say no way! But Currence does it for you.

The Promise and Pitfalls of Technology

Robo-strategists are one technological advancement that has gained popularity in recent years due to their ability to automate portfolio management and lower costs for clients. These platforms use algorithms to build and manage investment portfolios based on the client's risk tolerance, financial goals, and time horizon. While they are cost-effective and easy to use, robo-strategists lack the human touch and personalized guidance that comes with working directly with a financial strategist.

We advocate for a combination of a human strategist and technology tools that will inform, streamline, and automate the decisions the client makes. This scenario allows for both efficiency and personalization, making it an appealing option for a broad range of clients.

While technology has the potential to streamline financial advising and provide valuable insights, it's important that both clients and strategists maintain a human connection. Technology should be seen as a complement to, not a replacement for, personalized financial advice. Financial strategists still need to listen to their clients, understand their unique situation, and offer tailored recommendations based on the client's objectives, rather than simply relying on algorithms or generic advice. **The calculators and tools I build should support the conversation, and nothing can replace the judgment and guidance of an experienced strategist.**

THE POWER OF CLARITY IN FINANCIAL DECISION-MAKING

Navigating the world of personal finance doesn't have to be overwhelming. By focusing on the key foundational philosophies—transparency, accountability, emotional intelligence, financial education, and clear communication—clients can make informed, empowered decisions about their money.

With the right calculators and tools, clients can move from confusion to clarity. It's not just about understanding the math behind financial decisions. It's also about building trusted relationships with their strategists so they feel heard, supported, and educated. Then they are more likely to take ownership of their financial future and stay committed to their long-term goals.

Financial strategists and clients can collaborate to build a solid financial strategy—one that is based on a clear understanding of objectives and outcomes. With the right calculators and tools, knowledge, and support, every client can and should feel confident that they are making the best decisions for their future.

Chapter 2: Five Fundamental Calculators

I have lived with the numbers for forty years.
I know when they're not right.

WHAT ARE THE FIVE FINANCIAL CALCULATORS?

The five financial calculators (see image next page) are reciprocal with one another and are based on the five major financial variables: present asset value, future asset value, interest rate, time period, and cash flow (i.e. payment into account or withdrawal from account). Each of the five calculators helps you determine one of those variables, while the remaining four variables are used to make the calculation. Sometimes a variable is $0, as in "no payment."

For example, if you want to find the interest rate of something (Rate), what information do you need? You would need to know:

- How much the account value is today (Present Value) and in the future (Future Value)
- How long you're measuring the growth—is the time period a year, 180 months, two quarters? (Time)
- Are there any withdrawals or payments to the account? (Payment)

When you type these numbers into the appropriate fields in the Rate calculator, then it will calculate the interest rate for you.

Or, if you want to know how long it would take to save $100,000 (Time) you would need to know:

- How much do you already have? (Present Value)
- How much will you be putting away, and how often? (Payment)
- What is your account earning in interest? (Rate)

- What is your target savings? (Future Value)

When you type the above data into the appropriate fields in the Time calculator, it will calculate the time it will take you to save $100,000.

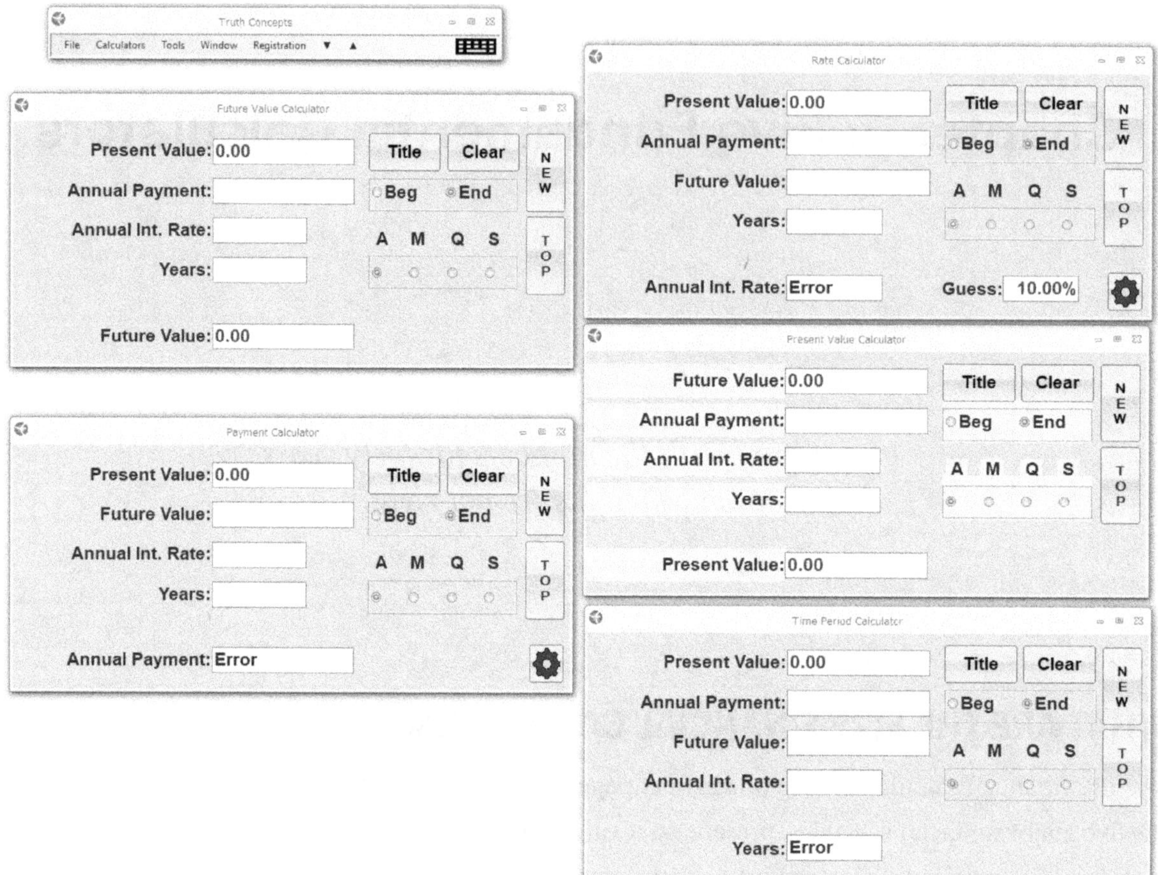

ORIGINS

What motivated me to create these five financial calculators? When I was just getting into personal finance fresh out of college, the HP12C was the only financial calculator that was available. The problem with a handheld calculator like the HP12C was that anytime you put a number in it, you only have one entry field and it disappears. So trying to teach someone how to calculate these five core financial numbers on a single handheld calculator was hard. That's why **I created the five financial calculators, so all five data points could be seen and adjusted at the same time.**

As you can see from the list above, all five financial variables are intrinsically connected. A wealth of knowledge awaits you in these small, but mighty calculators. To demonstrate just how potent they can be, let's discuss some examples of how you might use each of the individual financial calculators or two or three at once.

These small financial calculators let you see the impact of the time value of money, one of the harder concepts to get across to our linear brains. It is *the* differentiator between grade-school math and personal finance math, and why we cannot use *simple* handheld calculators when calculating many aspects of personal finance.

Let me demonstrate this in two ways. First, I will take one example through all five calculators.

Starting with Future Value, we know we have $100,000 in an account already (Present Value), and we are adding $10,000 a year (Payment) at the beginning of the year, with an Annual Interest Rate of 10.00% for ten years. We are trying to figure out what the value of the account will be in the Future (ten years). The answer is $434,686, as you can see below.

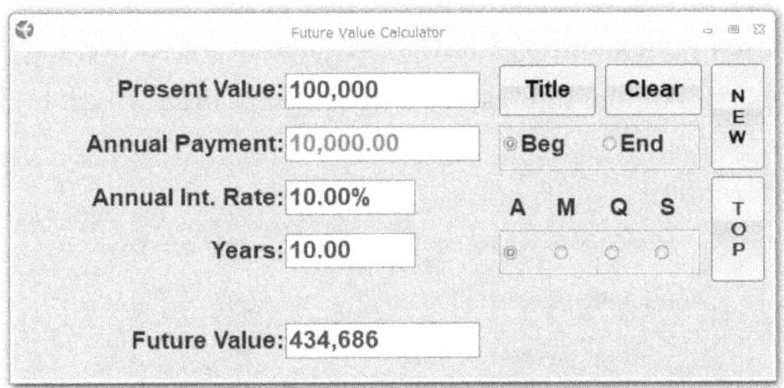

What if we knew that we wanted $434,686 in the future, and we knew that we are adding $10,000 a year (Payment) at the beginning of the year, with an Annual Interest Rate of 10.00% for ten years. We are trying to figure out what the initial deposit (Present Value) should be. We can use the Present Value Calculator to give us the answer of $100,000.

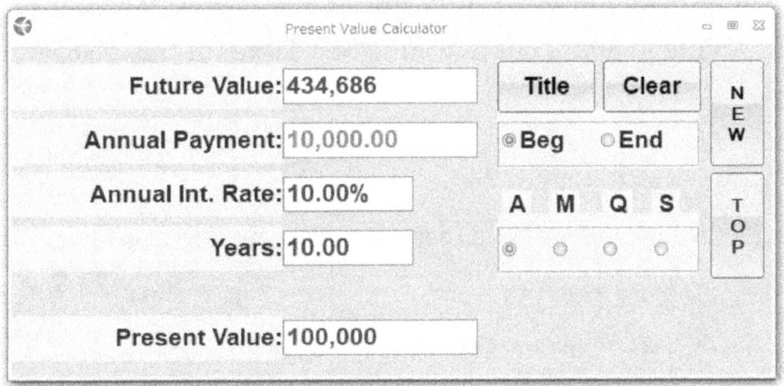

What if we knew that we had $100,000 now, wanted $434,686 in the future, and could earn an Annual Interest Rate of 10.00% for ten years. We are trying to figure out what the Payment, or contribution should be. We can use the Payment Calculator to give us the answer of $10,000 deposited into the account at the beginning of each year.

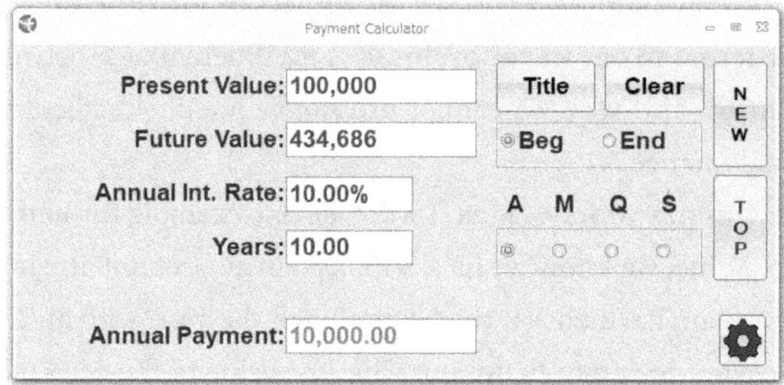

What if we knew that we had $100,000 now, we are adding $10,000 a year (Payment) at the beginning of the year (for ten years), and we wanted $434,686 in the future, ten years from now. We are trying to figure out what the Annual Interest Rate would be in order to get to our Future Value.

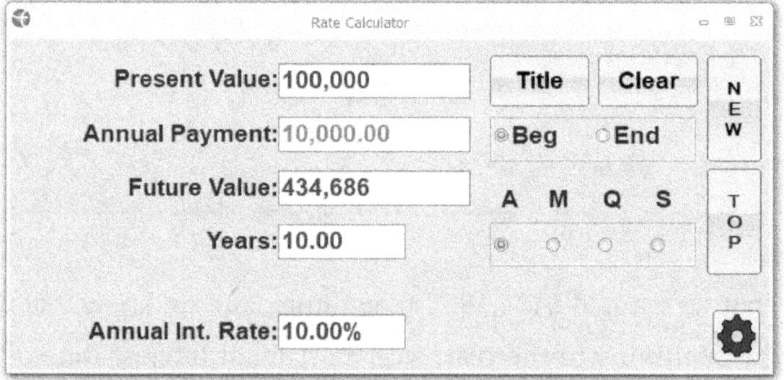

What if we knew that we had $100,000 now, were adding $10,000 a year (Payment) at the beginning of the year, wanted $434,686 in the future, and we knew that we could earn an Annual Interest Rate of 10.00%. We are trying to figure out how long of a Time (in this case, years) it would take us to get to the Future Value.

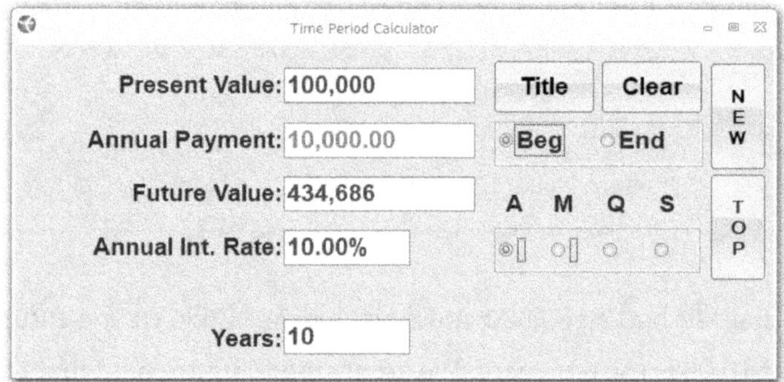

So we can see that all five of these calculators calculate a different aspect of the time value of money depending on what our unknown value is, as long as we know the other four assumptions.

The following is a second run through of the Five Financial Calculators with real world examples.

FUTURE VALUE CALCULATOR

The Future Value Calculator allows you to calculate what an account will be based on your current actions. We frequently use Future Value to show the time value of money—the potential of a sum over time when interest is applied.

This *time value of money calculation* can show you how much money you can accumulate and grow (assuming an Interest Rate) over time.

The Future Value Calculator can help individuals make decisions about extra money they may have. Say Joey, an eighteen-year-old fresh out of high school, decides to start a business. That generates an extra $100 a month for him to save, and he can safely earn 3% after taxes and fees. He wonders how much he would have in thirty years by making that $100 payment each month. By plugging the numbers into the Future Value Calculator, he learns he would have $58,274. With this information, he can decide whether that $100 payment to a savings account is worthwhile to him or not. Again, we are going slow and starting small here, literally and figuratively.

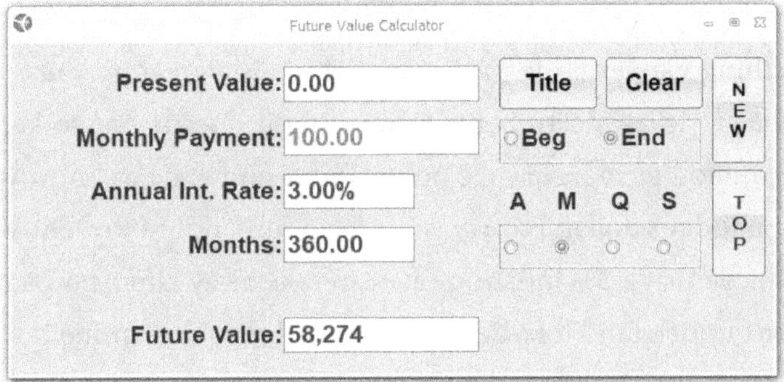

PRESENT VALUE CALCULATOR

The Present Value Calculator is a way to reverse engineer your objectives. Let's think about a high school freshman headed to college in four years who just got an inheritance. She wants to know how much of the inheritance to set aside to make sure she has $200,000 when she starts college and is confident she can earn 4% net of taxes and fees. She doesn't want to have to add anything to the account along the way.

If she put $200,000 in as Future Value (the amount she wants in the future), an Annual Payment of $0, an Annual Interest Rate of 4%, and a time frame of 4 Years:

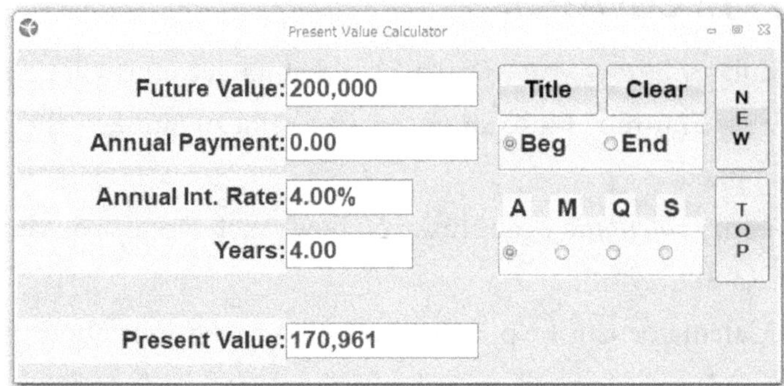

The calculator shows her she would have to deposit $170,961 now in order to have $200,000 at the end of the year four years from now.

Additionally, we use Present Value to help with inflation calculations.

Inflation affects everything, sometimes positively, sometimes negatively. Let's begin with a negative aspect, where inflation reduces the value of dollars in the future compared to what they are able to purchase today.

If we look at something like term life insurance (which is a great product when used in the right strategy), it typically has a "level" death benefit, meaning it doesn't rise to keep pace with inflation. When we look at a $1 million term insurance policy today and want to know what it will be worth in buying power (based on today's dollars) thirty years from now, only a Present Value calculator can tell us that. It is hard to believe that a 3% inflation rate can take away almost 60% of the value over thirty years. Most people don't understand this, and it is impossible to determine it without a Present Value calculator.

Let's say we have a client, Mary, who currently has a $1 million term policy because she wants to leave that amount of money to her family upon death. If she is fifty today, and dies young at age seventy-nine, and inflation is assumed at 3%, that $1 million will only be worth $411,987. So the check will say $1 million, but it will only buy $411,987 worth of today's goods and services.

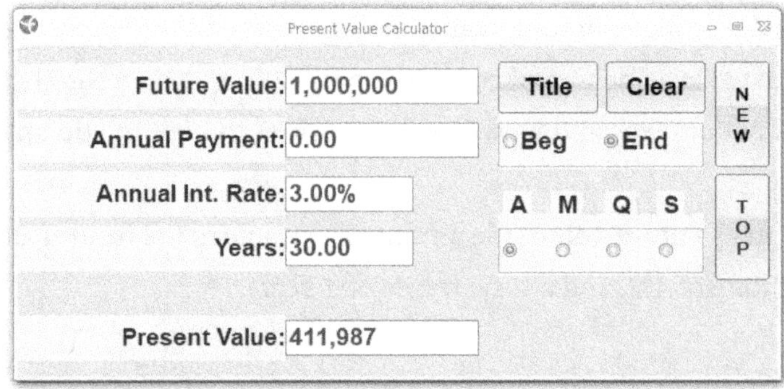

Other things it affects positively, such as your level mortgage payment and level life insurance premiums, due to a reduction of costs. Additionally, investment real estate rental income is affected positively because rental payments increase due to inflation. Let's look at how it benefits you as it relates to your mortgage payment. A payment of $2,000 today will still read $2,000 on your statement in thirty years, yet it will only feel like $603.59.

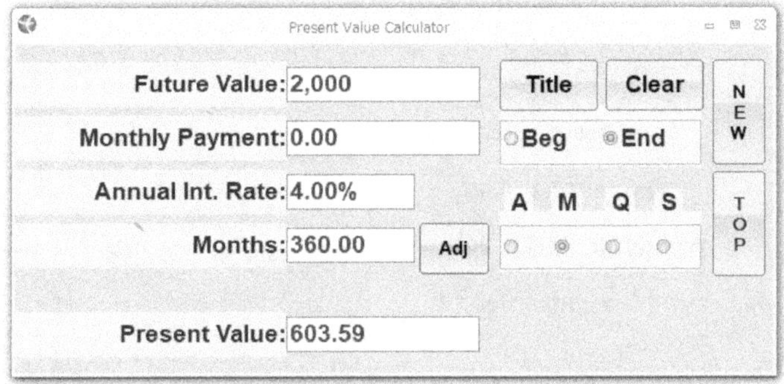

So just as inflation reduces the value of assets in the future, it also reduces the impact of costs in the future. This helps us see that inflation truly does benefit some things positively.

PAYMENT CALCULATOR

Payment calculators are used to determine periodic cash flows to reach a certain future value at a given interest rate. The Payment is a stream of money you are either putting in or taking out of an account along the way. You can make adjustments as you see fit, like making the time frame shorter, longer, or increasing/decreasing the interest rate.

For example, if you know you need $100,000 for a down payment in two years, and you could earn 4%, you could figure out how much to put in the account (your monthly payment) of $4,009.16.

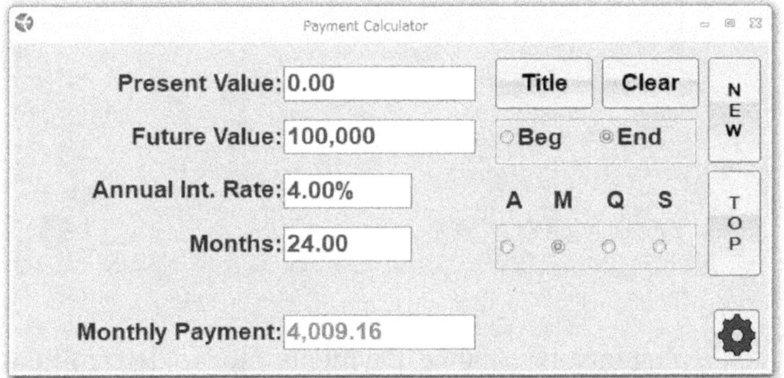

If all you had was a handheld simple calculator, you could divide $100,000 by twenty-four months to get $4,166.67, but it doesn't account for the interest you are earning along the way over the two years. This is why you have to use a financial calculator, in this case a Payment Calculator, so that you get the correct payment with the impact of interest earnings.

Another helpful example of the Payment Calculator is to figure out payments on a loan. Notice the

"Present Value" has switched to "Loan Balance" because the number was input as a negative since you owe money. Let's continue the above example and assume you will have a mortgage of $400,000 at 6% for 360 months. The Payment Calculator shows your monthly mortgage payment would be $2,398.20, made at the end of the month, not including taxes and insurance.

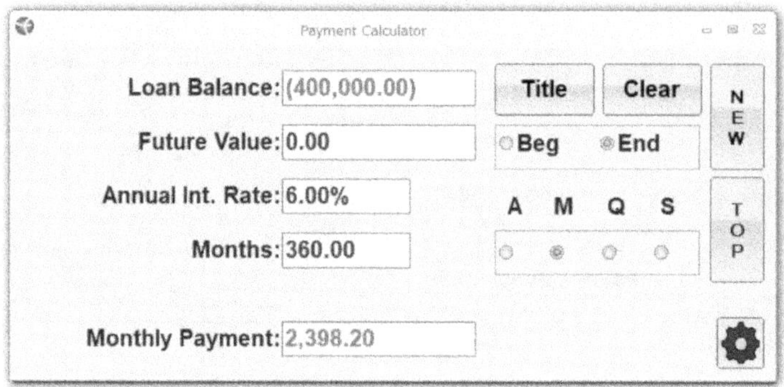

RATE CALCULATOR

The Rate Calculator is often misunderstood and has more applications than you might think. In addition to helping you determine what your interest rate is on an account, the Rate Calculator can help you figure out what Rate you are paying (like on a loan).

For example, say your friend said if you could lend him $10,000 now, he would pay you back $15,000 in ten years. You can see the Annual Interest Rate on your $10,000 would be 4.14%.

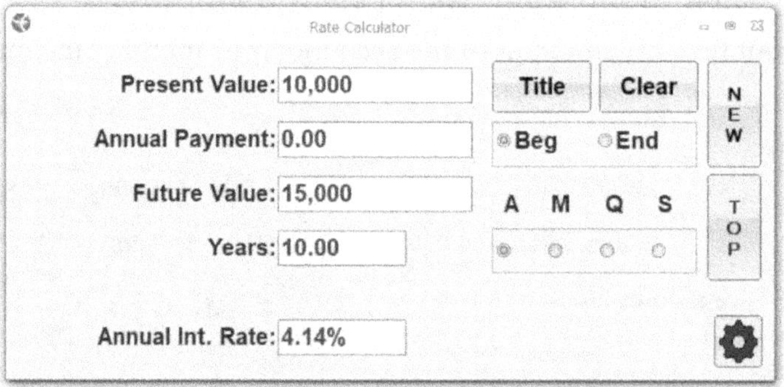

Alternatively, for a loan, plug in your balance, payments, etc., to determine what rate you're being charged. Here's what a car purchase would look like if you were solving for the interest rate. It is also a good example of where $0 is one of the inputs because, in the future, we show the car loan being paid off, with a $0 balance.

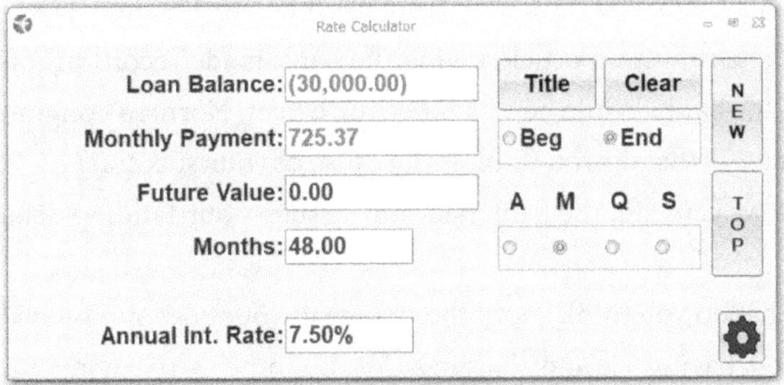

Here's another bank example to better understand Rate. In the 1980s, we saw bank savings rates crossing over into 10%, 11%, and even 12%. They were hovering around 9% for a long time, and everyone thought that would be the new standard. When we look at those numbers, **it's important to think about how banks make money—off the spread between what they're paying for people's money and what people are paying them to borrow money.**

The reason banks pay depositors is so they can loan depositors' money out to somebody else at a higher rate. If the bank pays me 9%, then sublets my money to you for 15%, they don't have any money in the transaction (outside of what they pay the depositors to rent their money); they just shuffle the papers. People say the bank is making 6% (15% in earnings and 9% in costs). That's how many people think about interest rates. **Yet to get to a real understanding, convert the interest rate to actual dollars.**

Let's say I deposit $100 in the bank. The bank pays me $9 to rent my money for the year. They turn around and loan $100 to you and charge you $15. That's a 66.7% markup. **Any retail business that can buy widgets for $9 and turn around and sell them for $15 is making a 66.7% gross profit.**

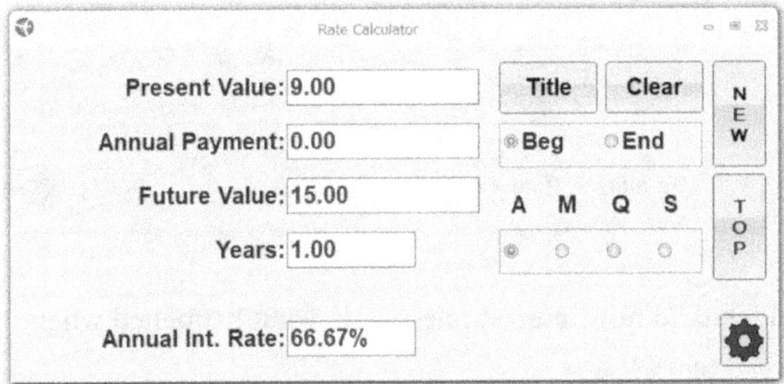

The $100 was never the bank's money. All they did was mark up money, just like marking up hammers or whatever a retail business would sell.

When I was a young adult, I learned that sometimes even the people at the banks don't understand how interest rates work. In our small town, I banked at one particular bank, and we went through a timeframe where the Federal Reserve dropped interest rates massively. This was a big change, a big stress on the monetary system. CD rates went from 9% down to 3% almost overnight.

After that change, there was an article saying the bank made record profits. Norman Baker, my mentor, and I visited the bank. While he was renewing a loan, Norman congratulated the bankers on the article, asking them, "What do you think is the cause of your success?"

They said, "When we came in, the bank had some issues—outstanding debt problems, bad loans, and people we didn't need."

Norman said, "What do you think about the change in your cost of money?"

They said, "We were paying 9% and charging 15%, but now we're paying 3% and charging 9%. It's the same 6% spread." But the truth was that the same 6% spread of 3% to 9% bumped the profit up to a 200% interest rate. Alan Greenspan was head of the Federal Reserve at the time, and when the banks got into trouble, he lowered interest rates under the guise of helping the public. Then all the banks started making record profits.

We need to put the interest rates in dollar amounts in order to understand the true profit margin for the banks. Before the massive drops in interest rates, their cost was 9%, or $9 for every $100 they loaned out. They rented the $100 from depositors by paying them a 9% rate to have their money in an account. Why? Because then they could loan that money out at 15%, or $15 for every $100 they loan.

If we look at it in a Rate Calculator, investing $9 to get $15 per year is not 6%, but actually 66.7%. The reason for this is because the $100 was not a cost to the bank; it only cost them $9 to rent the money from the depositor.

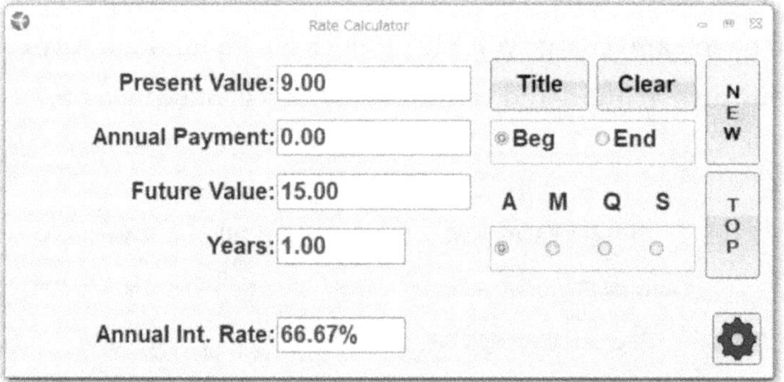

So now that we understand how interest rates work, what happened when they dropped the rates and kept the same spread of 6%?

As stated before, it's important to express interest rates in dollars so we can get to the whole truth of the matter. Under the new rates, now the bank only has to pay 3%, or $3 of rent on $100, in the form of interest to the depositor. They're going to take in less gross because now the borrowing rate for the consumer is 9%, or $9 per $100. But when we put that in the calculator, it shows the gross profit rate has gone up from 66.67% to 200%.

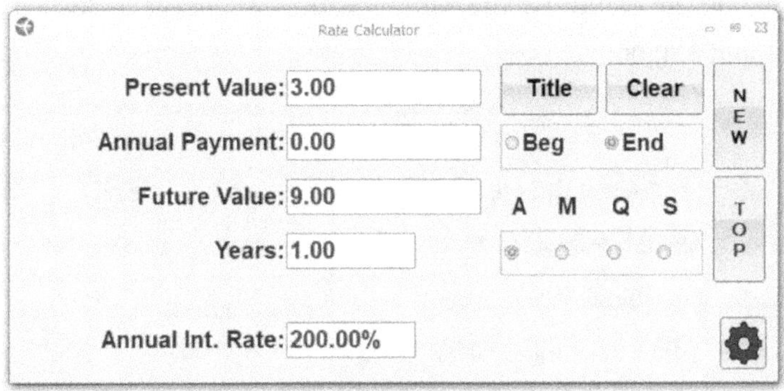

How is that possible? Let's say the bank has only $9 to invest. On each $100 transaction, they make $6. On the first transaction, the $9 cost for $15 of income yields $6. When the rates dropped, they had a $3 cost, so they received $9 of income, which is the same $6 per-transaction profit. However, with the same $9, they can do three of the latter transactions. In other words, they can take the same $9 and use it three times—3 x 66.67 = a 200% rate of return.

One unique thing about the rate calculator is that there is not a formula for Rate, like there is a numerical, mathematical formula for Future Value, Present Value, Payment, and Time. Rate calculations have to use iteration. The calculator makes a guess to see if it got to the right answer each time, and keeps guessing until it gets it right.

TIME PERIOD CALCULATOR

The Time Period Calculator is just what it sounds like—it can tell you how long it will take you to accomplish something. Common uses could be to figure out how long it will take you to accomplish your savings objective based on what you're doing now, or how much longer you have to pay down a loan.

Here's an example of what it would look like if you're trying to figure out how much longer you have to pay on your mortgage. You know your loan balance, your payment, and your interest rate.

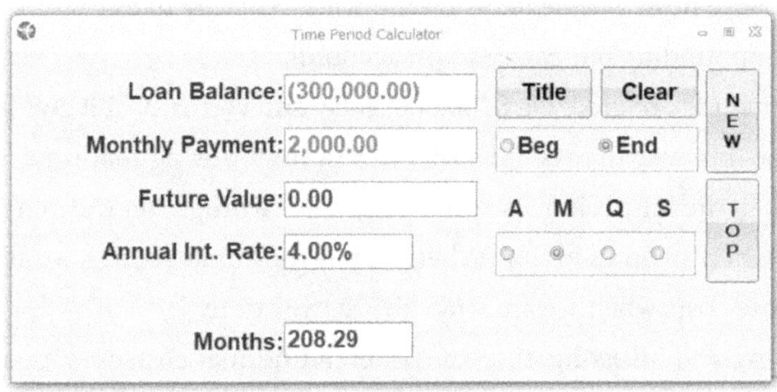

Or if we look back at Joey, who was saving $100 a month at 3%, and he wanted to know when he would accumulate $30,000, he could use the Time Period Calculator to show him it would take 224 months to reach his stated $30,000.

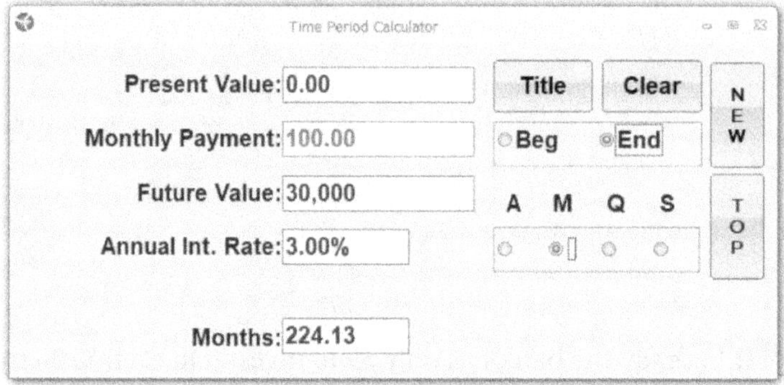

The time value of money can be a difficult personal financial concept to understand. Human beings don't exist in time; we exist in the present moment. It often takes people years to fully understand this concept, so be patient with yourself. The concept is really about what your money is going to be worth once the element of time is applied.

OPPORTUNITY: POSITIVE AND NEGATIVE

Thankfully, humans are wired to look for the positive. In most cases, and especially in personal finance, we seek what we can gain. This is what a positive opportunity looks like: you put small amounts of money in, you get a larger amount of money out. Humans think this is how investing works, yet financial strategists see people lose money all the time. Sometimes it is from investments, sometimes it is from costs to gain those investments. Costs are essentially a negative opportunity. We measure both positive and negative opportunities with interest rates. You'll even see the abbreviation COM, Cost Of Money, in various places, which represents the net earnings rate that is used to calculate the true loss.

Because of the impact of interest along with *time*, the interest is where opportunity comes from. **Another way to see opportunity cost is as a negative opportunity**. Most people understand "positive opportunity" because most people focus on the wins. Nobody likes to think about the losses. We prefer to focus on compounding our earnings on accounts.

For example, if somebody offered you $200,000 today and you said, "I'll give it back to you in twenty years," they'd say no, because they could earn interest on it during that time, so they would expect not only the $200,000 in the future, but also future interest earnings. Yet we aren't taught to include the time value of money when it comes to *cost*. When we pay for things (costs), we also have to include the loss of interest on those costs when we are strategizing over time.

When we are saving and investing, there are often additional costs to support that savings or investment strategy, such as taxes on the earnings and fees. Whatever you have to pay for to earn those earnings has a cost and a *loss of potential earnings into the future*. Because of the time value of money, you must incorporate additional payments, costs, and earnings into your calculations. All of those are either wearing down or boosting your opportunity.

THE TIME VALUE OF MONEY

With a Future Value calculator, you can also demonstrate *opportunity cost*, or how much money you could be missing out on. While it's functionally the same calculation, the context is critically different.

For example, let's say you spend $1,000 in cash on a spur-of-the-moment purchase. You might think there's no hidden cost there, yet there *is* an opportunity cost. If you chose not to make that purchase and instead put that money into an account earning 5%, in ten years you could have $1,629. In thirty years, you could have $4,322. **Obviously, these are not big dollar amounts, yet we are just beginning, and sometimes it is best to learn with smaller amounts, both literally and figuratively.**

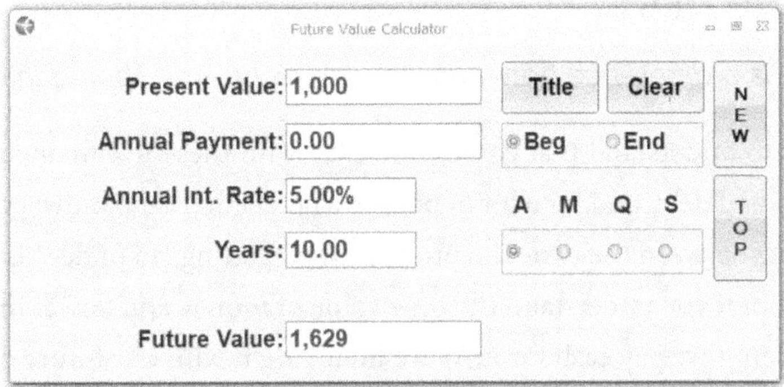

While you might not feel that loss, if you simply spend the money, you lose the opportunity to ever earn those same dollars again. Sure, you might get another $1,000 you can save later, but you'll never get that time back, or what that time would have done for you.

One way we can visualize time value of money is this: Let's say I have three oranges, and you give me two. I now have five oranges. But how many oranges do I have in twenty years?

There's a whole set of calculations you need to do to understand what time does to money (or the oranges). It could make more money (like planting orange seeds for future trees), or it could be affected by inflation over time (like a pest that decreases the yield of oranges) and decrease in value. Society, and even some financial strategists—when it's to their benefit—want to add money up like oranges. But they don't face the reality of the money (or the oranges) going bad or getting used up.

How can you have an inflated cost of phantom money? Actually, it's a very real number. The only way you can see inflated future costs as real numbers is when you start to incorporate multiple accounts.

Most people don't pay taxes on earnings they make from the asset that created the taxable earnings. Let's say you have money in a particular high-yield 4% savings account, and it looks like it's growing. But you don't realize you're paying money for taxes from another account or from your income.

When we take taxes out of the account that created the tax liability (netting), we can easily see the impact of opportunity cost because the account gets reduced by more than the sum of the taxes. When we pay taxes from another source (a different account), it is difficult to see the real impact of that tax cost. See the example covered in Calculator 17: Accumulation.

We can actually lose money (negative opportunity) solely due to the external costs (taxes, management fees, etc.) if we focus solely on the growth and don't realize the impact of cost. What could you have earned on that cash flow flowing to those costs?

While the Time Period calculator calculates time for us, all five of these calculators are time value of money calculators. Without factoring in the impact of time, most financial calculations are incorrect. The time value of money means that any amount of money has an interest cost or benefit for any time it exists beyond a single day. It's really about opportunity—positive or negative.

UNDERSTANDING DEBT

There is a difference between "having debt" and "being in debt."

Another key concept to understand that comes into play with these five financial calculators is debt. There's good debt and bad debt, and for a lot of people who get on that bandwagon of being debt-free, it's hard to differentiate between the two. The problem with getting rid of debt is that people think it's cheaper to pay it off. But if you understand the time value of money and how it impacts us, everything we buy we finance, even if we pay cash for it. We're financing it with our future dollars.

One example of good debt is this: If I can get a home mortgage at 4%, yet I am confident in an investment that pays 5%, then taking on the 4% debt is a good thing. It is "having debt," not "being in debt." If we borrow from the bank, we can see the interest we're paying—it's much more straightforward. When we pay cash, however, we're oblivious to the fact that we lost that opportunity over time.

When interest rates for borrowing are lower than what we can earn, we shouldn't pay that debt back any faster than we have to. **18% credit card debt is bad debt. For it to make sense, you'd have to earn 18% after tax to be at zero.** But on lower interest rates, it makes sense to keep the debt and funnel extra money to investments.

Everybody wants to earn a high rate of return, but they often don't understand what that actually means. If you were more efficient with your debt and other payments, you could actually make much more. **People often try to add and subtract rates, yet if they exchange the rate for dollars and use a financial calculator, they get the *whole* truth.**

A common use of the Payment Calculator is showing people how . Why not? In our article, "," we break it down. With interest rates on car loans at 7% in 2025, you may be tempted to take an offer of a 0% car loan without hesitation. However, it's important to take all the information into consideration before you make a decision. Not all 0% car loans are actually 0%, and you may find you could have made a better decision in the end when it is too late to do anything about it. Remember: the interest rate is only one piece of the puzzle. You must also consider how much you'll be paying each month and what a lower car payment could do to increase your ability to save for other things.

Car dealerships have different prices for cash deals than they do for financed deals. Let's say you are looking at purchasing a car with a $35,000 sticker price. When you talk to the salesperson, they quote you $30,000 to buy the car if you pay cash. This is because of rebates available from the manufacturer. They may also offer you 0% financing, yet it will be based on the full $35,000 price, and no rebate.

If you try to finance the car with payments at the cash price of $30,000, the dealership will back out. They won't say as much, but they want you to take the 0% financing precisely because it's not 0%. They know that people are more influenced by lower interest rates, even though they are paying more for the car.

Unfortunately, the reason they can offer you "discounted" interest rates is because they add the interest into the cost of the car. Stated again (since this is a major area of misunderstanding), when purchasing a car, the dealership may offer you either a $5,000 rebate *or* a 0% financing deal. You don't get both. And that $5,000 difference is actually the interest cost built into the price of the car.

Let's do the math so you can see clearly how the interest is baked into the 0% financing. In this instance, the dealership is offering a car for $35,000. They're offering either 0% financing over forty-eight months, or you can pay cash and get a $5,000 rebate.

Let's put the 0% financing scenario into a Payment Calculator. Notice the Loan Balance is $35,000. When you do that, the monthly payment comes out to $729.17.

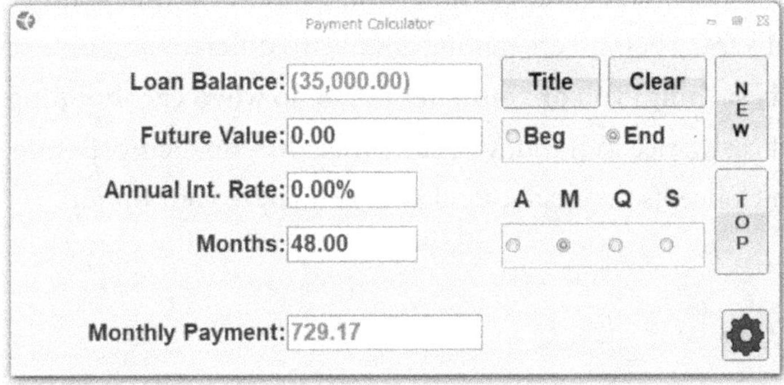

If instead you take the cash offer of $30,000 with the rebate of $5,000, you finance $30,000 with your own banker for the same forty-eight months. If your banker charged you the same monthly payment of $729.17, that would equate to a 7.77% rate, as shown on the Truth In Lending statement. The payment is exactly the same, so how can the dealership call it 0%, while your banker has to call it 7.77%?

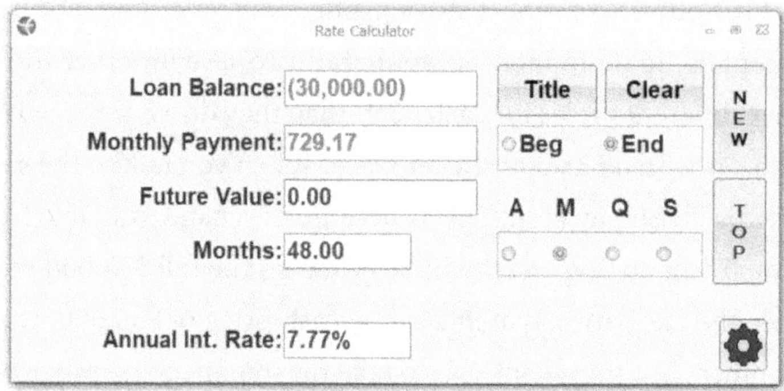

The reason is pretty simple: to offer the 0% interest rate, the car company added the interest cost to the price. This same "half-truth" is used for most of the abnormally low interest rates that car companies typically advertise. And there are almost always rebates. Some of them simply aren't published, you have to ask for them.

You may think that the best option would be to actually pay cash, and that might be true, but we have to consider all the variables. If we have cash sitting around that is not earning more than 7.77% net after costs, we may want to consider paying cash. This would work only if we invest the $729.17 per month that we are not having to pay to the car loan. On the other hand, if we have the opportunity to earn more than 7.77% net after costs, we may be better off taking the car loan with its payments and putting the cash toward the investment. See the Automobiles Calculator section for more on this issue.

The moral of the story here is that the car financing offered at a dealership is not what it seems. 0% financing is not actually 0% when we are talking about two different amounts of money ($35,000 and $30,000). **One of the best things you or your clients can do when car shopping is to ask for the cash price.** Then, with that cash price in mind, you seek your own financing. Before you make a decision, you can use the Truth Concepts financial calculators to analyze your option

WEIGHING RISK

The more difficult and important piece to consider and measure is the impact of risk. Let's look at a house, for example. The more money we put into something we don't technically own that could be taken away from us (like a house), the *more* risky it is, not less risky. Whenever the borrowing rate is less than the earning rate, we should borrow.

But we also have to consider what kind of risk we have when we lock our money up in a house. **There are times when a peace of mind decision overrides pure financial efficiency.** Someone may know mathematically that they shouldn't pay their house off, but they may be so stuck in fear and scarcity that they have to pay their house off or they can't sleep at night. So that person may decide to put all their money toward paying off the mortgage even though it's not only financially inefficient, it's also risky. But to them, their perceived peace of mind is worth the high-risk and negative opportunity.

Through this book, my five financial calculators, and continued financial education, I hope to combat the fear that causes people to make these kinds of costly decisions. They hear so much advice out there telling them all debt is bad. Debt is not inherently good or bad; it just is. What's important is to weigh how the rates make it either a wise choice or a poor choice. **There is a big difference between *being* in debt and *having* debt.**

Having debt is when our assets exceed our liabilities. The banks model this by renting money from us. They are going into debt to get money that's not theirs to sublet it out to somebody else. If it's good for the banks, it ought to be good for us from a financial standpoint. We can't do all the things they do (i.e., we don't have access to money from the Federal Government). However, we can do a lot if we don't believe debt to be an absolutely bad thing.

It's important to understand we are always financing things. Some people think as long as they're paying cash for something they're not financing it. Yet they are not calculating the fact that those dollars are no longer invested. It's not the financing that's the problem, it's having more things than you can afford that's the problem. If you're limited to cash, you can only buy what you can pay cash for. But if you go down to the bank and they're offering 2% financing and you are earning 5% net in an investment, it does not make any sense to take your 5% money to pay off 2% debt. You would be way better off leaving your 5% money growing and paying installments on the 2% debt. That is the least risky choice to make.

GET ACCESS TO THE FIVE FINANCIAL CALCULATORS

As you can see, there are many ways you can use the five financial calculators to explore Future Value, Present Value, Payment, Rate, and Time Period. They can help you work through conceptual stumbling blocks, fine-tune your financial strategies, and get the numbers you need to make educated financial decisions.

To get access to these calculators, of Truth Concepts. This will get you access to the entire software suite for your trial period, including our larger, more specialized calculators. Then, when your thirty-day license is up, instead of paying to renew, you can simply hit "Continue" on the Registration window to disable everything except for these five financial calculators, as well as the IRR Calculator (Internal Rate of Return), for your personal use. See the Appendix for more information.

Chapter 3: Why Simplify Software?

When I created the five financial calculators, I did so with the intention of helping people take responsibility for their own financial future. If we can all understand these core personal financial principles—Future Value, Present Value, Payment, Interest Rate, and Time Period—in a way that doesn't require a masters in finance, we'll be empowered to make conscious, clear financial decisions. Instead of being limited in knowledge and lacking the tools to do basic calculations, now both strategists and their clients can understand the numbers in a simplified way. With these calculators, strategists will be confident in the advice they're giving, and clients will know when the advice they're given is true or not.

NECESSITY OF SIMPLIFICATION

The only rule for this study group is to leave our egos at the door.

One of the more difficult things in the financial world is simplifying the information so it's digestible while still maintaining enough detail to make it valid. Unfortunately, one of the shadier tools of the financial industry is confusion. Financial strategists sometimes confuse their clients, so the clients will do whatever the strategist says because they don't understand the calculations. The client thinks, "I guess you know what you're talking about, and I'm not smart enough to do the calculations, so I'll just trust you." A lot of that confusion and complication is just cost and extra work that doesn't accomplish anything. The same can be true of a mortgage broker, car insurance salesperson, or the HR representative at work who says you should set up your 401(k) plan. They may be consciously confusing their clients, or they may be confused or mis-educated themselves and passing it on to their clients.

In many cases, simplification could look like just putting your money into a life insurance policy and leaving it there; you'd be better off than continually moving it the way some strategists recommend, which complicates things. Confusion happens frequently to people with higher-level income because they don't have time to look at their finances often. Their strategists buy off-shore trusts, complex real estate, etc., and make risky moves, often from the standpoint of a law change. If their financial decisions were simplified by using these five calculators, most people could understand the choices they and their strategists are making.

If we can simplify financial decisions for young adults early on in their teens and twenties, especially as they become young parents, we can make millions of dollars of difference over the course of their lives and their children's lives. Dave Mozeika, the creator of the app, Currence, started working with a group of physicians fresh out of school doing their residency when they were making less than $100,000 a year. They joined Currence, and because of the strategies it employs, they built significant wealth from simplifying finances and increasing savings so early in their careers. Now, those doctors are making close to $1 million dollars a year, and they're saving huge amounts of money because they have a simple tool to help them.

USER-FRIENDLY INTERFACES FACILITATE BETTER DECISION-MAKING

In creating the five financial calculators (and the rest of the calculators you'll read about in this book), I prioritized features that were user-friendly in order to quickly demystify what can be complex financial concepts. It's always a struggle to balance between including enough detail to get a correct answer and overwhelming the user to the point that they feel it's too much trouble to put the data in the calculator. That's the toughest battle I faced in the calculator creation process.

What I've tried to do with the calculators is allow for both—more detail and less detail—to be entered, and the calculator will provide clear answers either way, some more general, others more accurate and detailed. **The calculators are designed to be as simple or as thorough as you need.** The difference is in how you use them and the numbers you enter.

ACCURATE FORMULAS AND DATA

I didn't use HTML code (like is necessary for websites) when creating the calculators because HTML coding doesn't allow for packing in the amount of data that I use on a single screen. Yet every single calculator I've created can be shown graphically as well as numerically in screenshots. Certain software has tried to dumb calculations down to make them more accessible, but then the data shown is not entirely accurate because it doesn't have enough detail to be truly applicable. However, if I attempted to fit all the data I use in HTML coding, it would fill pages and pages, and the amount of scrolling that would require is extremely frustrating for the end-user. If you're trying to make a financial decision, but you can't see the inputs *and* the final numbers, it becomes difficult to process the decision because you can't see all the information. Our brain wants to see all the numbers at once.

The tool I use does spreadsheet calculations that are all computer-based. It's like using excel formulas to feed data to calculators. You'd have to write a crazy amount of code for every cell in HTML code to duplicate what I do with the formulas and data. In the end, I prefer my tools to be simple to use and as accurate and detailed as possible.

IS IT A WONDERFUL LIFE? SIMPLIFYING DECISIONS

The five financial calculators were developed to address a significant gap in personal financial software: most existing tools focus solely on isolated decisions, like analyzing a mortgage or a single investment. And while our calculators can do that, they offer a bigger picture view that takes into account how one financial decision may affect the others. Financial reality isn't micro—it's interconnected. Every financial decision impacts others, and strategists need tools that reflect this interconnectedness.

The Asset Flow™ calculator addresses this gap by providing a holistic financial picture. It allows users to conduct comprehensive "what-if" scenarios, enabling them to see clearly how decisions like funding college education, working with life insurance, or navigating the stock market interplay with each other. By moving beyond accumulation—merely piling money into accounts—to strategizing for income distribution during retirement, the Asset Flow™ calculator simplifies complex, holistic, financial strategy work.

Consider the classic scene from the movie *It's a Wonderful Life*, where the character George Bailey wishes on a cigar lighter (akin to a magic lamp) as a kid, "I wish I had a million dollars . . . hot dog!" Many of us can relate, as we often dream about having a million dollars without thinking about how that translates into actual income during retirement, or how that will affect our other finances.

If *It's a Wonderful Life* was made today, ninety-five years later, taking inflation into account, George Bailey would have to say, "I wish I had sixteen million dollars . . . hot dog!"

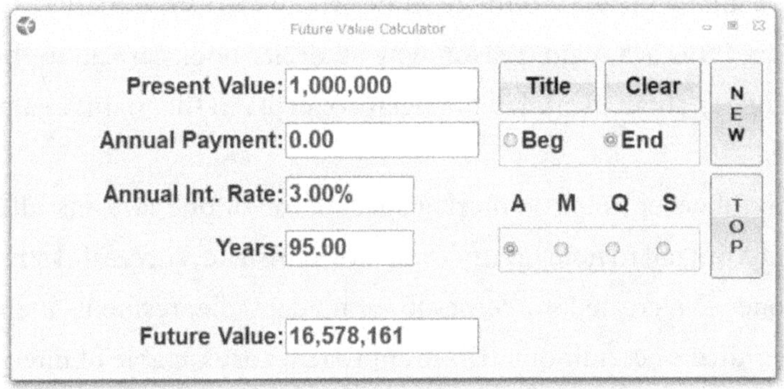

Yet people still think of $1 million as a lot of money. This is a great example of how collective mindsets can get stuck. $100 million is actually the next big space, but it's too big of a mental jump for people now, so most people are stuck at $1 million.

If we accumulate $1 million, we can use the calculators to see what it looks like from a distribution perspective. It takes a lot more strategy work and data to fully understand the impact $1 million could have. Everything else is just theory or guesswork. Plugging the numbers into the Asset Flow™ calculator can help clients understand how small actions with their money can yield big results.

Many financial clients today grapple with this mindset. The calculators simplify their understanding by demonstrating the practical implications of their financial choices. They help strategists and their clients transform abstract goals into tangible, actionable steps that will get them the results they seek.

ENCOURAGEMENT FOR STRATEGISTS: TRUST BUILT ON CLARITY AND ACCURACY

Adopting these simplified yet powerful calculators is essential for financial strategists who wish to establish genuine trust and clarity with their clients. Far too often, financial strategies are shared conceptually without the backing of accurate, verifiable math. This leads clients to make decisions based on trust alone, without understanding the true implications or accuracy of the advice they're given.

One of the reasons for developing these calculators was that it's difficult to do financial calculations with only a handheld calculator. When financial strategists use a handheld calculator to prove or disprove a concept, it's typically not taking into account all the elements involved, and therefore, it's not the correct math. Financial math can be complicated; our calculators simplify it *and* ensure it's accurate.

The five main calculators are specifically designed to empower strategists to answer this foundational question: "How do you know it's right?" With these calculators, strategists can show the math behind financial concepts to their clients. This mathematical transparency combats misinformation, eliminating guesswork and reliance on potentially misleading concepts.

You'd be surprised how many financial strategists hear something from a buddy in financial product sales that has no basis in math at all, then pass that information on to their clients. "Joe told me it's right." Well, our calculators take it to the level of proof—here's the math. My wife, Kim Butler, is a financial strategist, and this is a major reason why all of her books are about busting lies. There are an immense amount of lies about everyday financial concepts in the mainstream press and on all the social media channels.

Financial work should never hinge on market speculation or one-size-fits-all strategies that promise extraordinary results but fail to hold up under scrutiny. Instead, successful strategists use simplified calculators, like the ones I've created, to come up with adaptable, resilient financial approaches that perform reliably under diverse conditions. These approaches are capable of navigating life's inevitable uncertainties, whether market crashes, personal upheavals, or economic downturns.

For example, during real estate market crashes like we experienced in 2008, strategists who guided clients using adaptable cash-flow based properties weathered those crashes better than those who speculated on ever-increasing property values. Simplified, accurate calculators empower strategists not only to provide mathematically sound advice but also to confidently revise strategies when circumstances change or new insights arise.

Ultimately, the simplicity of these calculators facilitates trust between strategists and their

clients, empowering both to make informed, confident financial decisions that withstand the test of time and circumstance.

SIMPLE CALCULATORS LEAD TO THE TRUTH: INTEGRITY IN ACTION

Financial calculators don't just help us do math—they help us get to the truth. Strategists have a responsibility to use them with integrity, not just to validate what sounds good. I once reviewed another strategist's flashy concept at the request of a strategist. After I pointed out everything misleading or outright incorrect, the strategist told me, "Well, my clients really like it, so I'm going to sell it to them anyway." That's not strategy—that's salesmanship without substance. It wastes everyone's time and money.

I get that people need to earn a living. But it is possible to make a living while being mathematically honest and ethically grounded. Some strategists lean into what sounds impossible—because it's easier to sell the sensational. But the best financial approach isn't the flashiest one. As a good friend of mine says, "What's the perfect financial picture? It's the one that works in all situations."

Life doesn't follow a perfect thirty-year projection. Real financial leadership means helping clients build adaptable strategies that can withstand market crashes, life transitions, and economic surprises without forcing them into bad decisions. Can the finances adapt and evolve regardless of the circumstances? When comparing the numbers for two different approaches, will the one that's circumstance-proof ultimately end up with the same amount of money as the flashier one? Typically, a solid financial strategy has less exposure to market fluctuations and puts the client in a better cash position, so they can flex and adapt regardless of circumstances instead of succumbing to them.

As I mentioned, in 2008, people with cash and flexibility didn't just survive—they capitalized. Those overleveraged or stuck in rigid environments lost hard. The crashes we experienced in the real estate market were awful. But they didn't affect everyone. People who had the right strategy in place (and had cash) weren't forced to sell in a down market. Other people had no cash or wiggle room, so they were forced to sell. Yet we still have people who think real estate will be going up 20% every year over the next thirty years. Sure, that could happen, but I wouldn't bet my future on it. This is why it's important to be in a position to be able to move and not have to succumb to whatever the market throws at you.

Kim's story: *I've seen both sides of the financial strategy scene. Earlier in my career, I followed mainstream financial advice. I recommended mortgage prepayments and maxing out qualified plans—until I saw, year after year, that it didn't work. I was horrified at what my clients were losing. I had to go back, admit where I was wrong, and ask clients to change course. It wasn't easy, but once you see the whole truth, you can't unsee it. And if you have integrity, you can't ignore it either. You want to be able to look clients in the eye and tell them in full honesty that the financial decisions you recommend will benefit them and truly be in their best interest, now and in the long run.*

At the end of the day, we don't just want our clients to win on paper—we want to stand with them thirty or sixty years from now and say, “We did the best we could. We prepared for the unexpected. And we did it with honesty and clarity.” These financial calculators—when used with wisdom and truth—are some of the best tools we have to do just that.

Chapter 4: The Calculators—Part One

How can we have so much knowledge about money and yet still not understand it?

There are a total of seventeen calculators in the Truth Concepts' Suite of Calculators, in addition to the basic five mentioned in Chapter 2. In this chapter, I'll introduce and share best practices for the first eight of those seventeen additional calculators.

EVER-EVOLVING CALCULATORS

First I want to note that a calculator I created might get used differently today than it would have ten or twenty years ago when I first came up with it. This is why I continually review my calculators and make adjustments so they can evolve over time as the financial industry and client needs evolve. While math is objectively black and white, how we calculate *financial* math can change and improve. It can also be made simpler as we understand more about how people use the calculators.

For example, I am currently working on adding buttons to a calculator I created ten years ago. **I'm always asking, "What if we could do that better?"** We're always adding to and tweaking the calculators to make them better. The whole point is to make them simpler, not just for the strategist to use, but also for the client to understand. That's where most of the motivation for upgrading them comes from: *how can we make this calculation quicker and to the point?*

I'm currently working on getting the calculator to adjust interest rates, taxes, term insurance costs, and fees in order to quickly show someone how much money they can take out of their account each year and what will be left after they do. We keep testing all the numbers, but the most important component is what the client will actually get out of the process.

Time spent going back and forth between calculators complicates things for the client. With our Payment Calculator, for example, trying to shortcut that process by creating one button that will do a calculation quickly means the strategist talking with the client can focus on the big picture and the exact number on the calculator. The new button on our payment section of this calculator will calculate how much I can take out and what that action will do to the account over time.

A client might ask, "How much can I pull out of my account each year and keep it at $100,000 (or some other amount) all the way until my death?" We can use trial and error and keep guessing, but that takes much more time for the client (and the strategist). So essentially I'm creating a shortcut with the payment section that is less distracting and time-consuming for both the strategist and the client.

So much software gets set and forgotten without any intentional evolution, but I am committed to listening to what the strategists using my calculators are doing, and what clients are talking about. I listen carefully and then brainstorm solutions to challenges they pose or problems they want to solve more efficiently. Then I go into the calculator software and make the tweaks needed.

Listening to what strategists are thinking aloud, such as "How do I do X, Y, or Z?" helps me fine-tune the calculators over time to serve them and their clients better. Partnering with strategists and strategists is a huge benefit to me. We have people who owned the calculators three to four years ago who say, "Everything is so different now!" Yes, that's true, because we're continually improving them. Unlike Windows (they change it and you have to relearn it all), we try to keep what we have somewhat similar and incorporate these additions to be simply extra bonuses that make strategists' jobs easier.

WHAT SPARKS THE NEXT STEP OF EVOLUTION FOR A CALCULATOR?

Often I'll read something in an article that sparks my interest and gets me to consider updating a calculator. Or, in the process of using the software, I'll notice something clunky. The two main ways evolution is driven for our calculators are:

1. I am using a calculator and realize there are places it could be more seamless, or
2. I get input from strategists who are looking for a calculator to do something additional or different.

Since I know where the math came from for each calculator, and how the calculators were put together, someone can ask me a question in a seminar or over the phone, and I know how to pull a particular calculator and change it on the spot. That definitely happens from time to time.

Another form of evolution comes from the challenge I often pose for myself: "How can I make this calculator do *this*?" **I'm often modifying a calculator to take on more responsibility or capability.** I see that as a whole different type of evolution than making a small tweak. It involves a lot more trial and error and stems from a more creative, big-picture strategic perspective.

CREATIVE AND COLORFUL EVOLUTION

When I build a brand new calculator, I like the start of the process, but I don't like the drudgery involved in testing it. It requires days of monotonous work to ensure it runs smoothly and consistently. Since it is repeating a lot of what I've already done, it gets old fast. However, I see each iteration or evolution of a calculator in the creative stage as a brand new process every time, and that is the most exciting part.

One example of an update I did that made a big difference was when I redid all the color schemes of the various columns, and also added a dark background. Colors enable us to look quickly at the numbers and know what we are looking at without much thinking. Certain colors are associated with certain things, and using consistent colors for columns and fonts helps your brain quickly learn and recognize what you're doing in each calculator. (Since this book is not in color, if you want to see them, we recommend the Kindle version of this book or the 30-day free trial at TruthConcepts.com.)

I used macros in Excel to start the programming, and I got tired of changing colors and having different coding for cases where cells were protected or not, so I wrote a whole macro that will ask questions and build color for the column. The new program builds and makes columns for me in the colors I want. This is an example of creating in an efficient way that uses color to optimize our clients' experience with financial math.

You can now of your Truth Concepts calculator. It's important to be able to create an aesthetic you enjoy looking at, and one that you feel is visually pleasing to work with. In addition, it's helpful to be sure that you can read all of the charts and graphs you create when using the software. We also recognized the value in having the color scheme of the numbered charts stay the same across every calculator so you can build a visual language as you use Truth Concepts.

THE IMPORTANCE OF A VISUAL LANGUAGE

When we say visual language, what we mean is that we want you to be able to look at any Truth Concepts calculator and be able to identify what you're looking for easily. You build this visual language by making certain features look uniform across every calculator. Now, every time you use a calculator, you can be sure that when you use Cash Flow, the column colors will represent the same *concepts* as the columns from Diversification, and so on.

We've done this so that as you become familiar with the software and use it more and more, your brain is going to make those connections and you're going to get faster at interpreting what your calculators say. This also eliminates any room for error, because a yellow column in one calculator will mean the same thing as a yellow column in another. You don't have to learn what each column means individually, because each color represents the same idea in every calculator.

COLUMN COLORS: WHAT DO THEY MEAN?

Below, you'll see a Cash Flow calculator. We've left it blank so that you only have to consider the column colors, not the numbers. Let's go over what they are and what they represent.

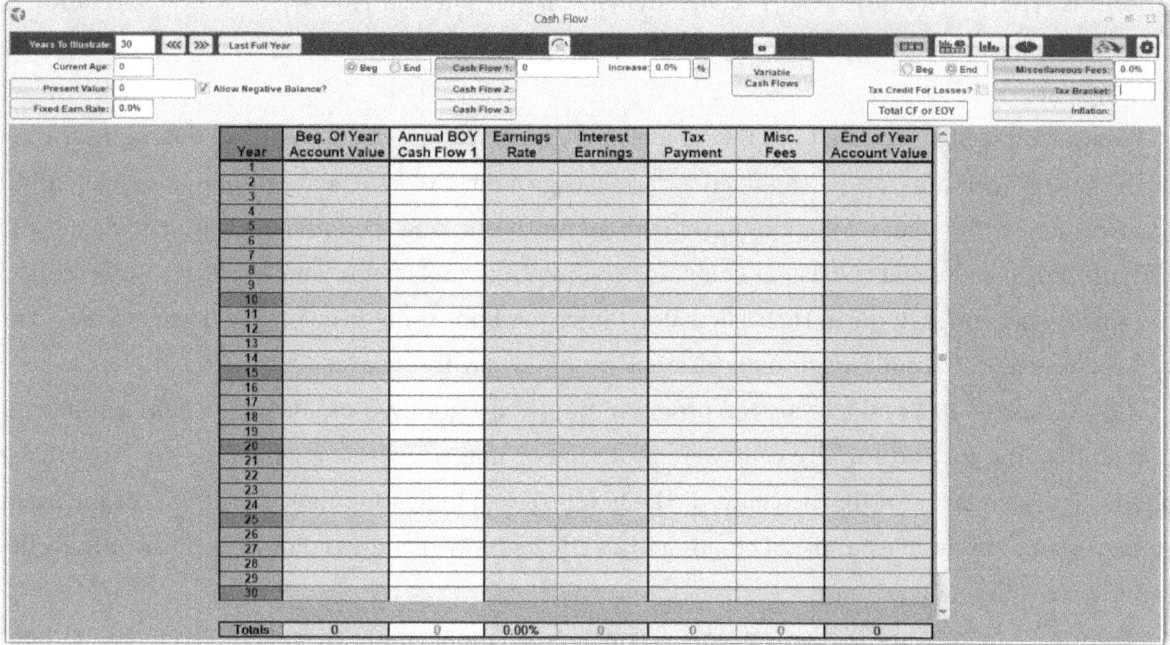

Blue Columns: Account Values

In every calculator, blue columns represent Account Values. These can be Beginning of Year Values or End of Year Values, and will usually be situated on the far left and far right of your Truth Concepts charts respectively. If you want to know how much is in your client's account in a particular year, keep your eye out for blue columns.

When life insurance is involved, Cash Value is represented in blue columns, since it's a liquid account your clients can access.

You'll also note that Deflated Account Values are included here if you add an inflation cost. While normally you would have to use a Financial Calculator from the Tools section to calculate the effect of inflation, several calculators now include it in the data and the charts.

If you open Loan Analysis, you'll see the columns are a bit different than you'd expect. Rather than blue being called "Account Value," blue represents "Loan Balance." This is strictly to represent that it's meant to be a declining balance, though conceptually it's still the same—it's the value of the account being represented.

Yellow Columns: Cash Flows

If you want to see the money that is moving, look for yellow columns that represent Cash Flows (shown above as the second column from the "Year" column). This can be money moving toward you, or money moving away from you (deposits or withdrawals).

In some calculators, "Cash Flows" may be represented by loan money that's moving through someone's personal economy.

Green Columns: Earnings

If you want to know what a particular account is earning, look for the green columns (shown above as the third and fourth columns from the "Year" column). It's important to note that earnings include the Earnings Rate, which is a percentage, and Interest Earnings, which is your dollar figure. Both represent a change to the account based on external earnings, not your personal cash flow.

Orange Columns: Fees and Taxes

If you're looking for money that is being siphoned from an account, look no further than the orange columns (shown above as the fifth and sixth columns from the "Year" column). Orange columns represent any taxes that reduce the Account Values, as well as fees like management fees.

In a calculator like Loan Analysis, you'll see that Interest Charged and Principal Payment are orange columns. Meanwhile, the full loan payment is in yellow. This is to represent the total Cash Flow of the loan payment (yellow), as well as the individual charges that make up that payment (orange).

You'll also see that in some calculators, term insurance is in orange. This represents that term insurance is strictly a cost, since there is no guarantee of a death benefit unless you die during that term of time.

Purple Columns: Legacy

Finally, there are purple columns. These columns represent legacy, in most cases, this means the Death Benefit from permanent life insurance, yet it can also more generally represent money designated for heirs. You'll see this in calculators like Funding, shown below (the rightmost column is purple).

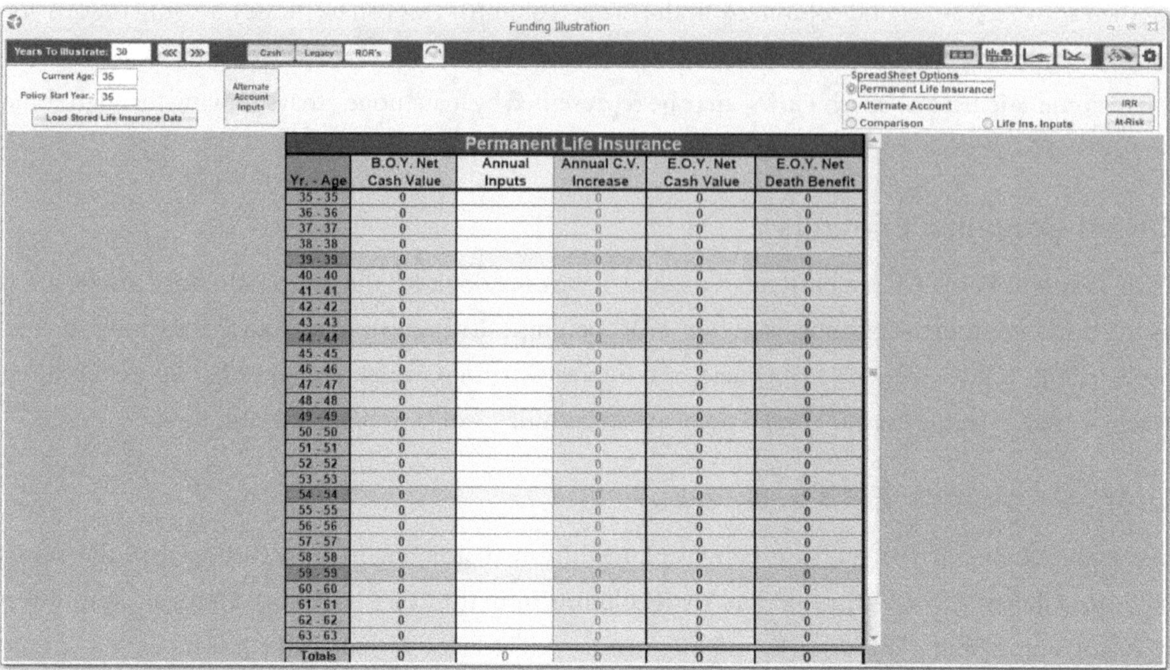

Permanent Life Insurance

Yr. - Age	B.O.Y. Net Cash Value	Annual Inputs	Annual C.V. Increase	E.O.Y. Net Cash Value	E.O.Y. Net Death Benefit
35 - 35	0		0	0	0
36 - 36	0		0	0	0
37 - 37	0		0	0	0
38 - 38	0		0	0	0
39 - 39	0		0	0	0
40 - 40	0		0	0	0
41 - 41	0		0	0	0
42 - 42	0		0	0	0
43 - 43	0		0	0	0
44 - 44	0		0	0	0
45 - 45	0		0	0	0
46 - 46	0		0	0	0
47 - 47	0		0	0	0
48 - 48	0		0	0	0
49 - 49	0		0	0	0
50 - 50	0		0	0	0
51 - 51	0		0	0	0
52 - 52	0		0	0	0
53 - 53	0		0	0	0
54 - 54	0		0	0	0
55 - 55	0		0	0	0
56 - 56	0		0	0	0
57 - 57	0		0	0	0
58 - 58	0		0	0	0
59 - 59	0		0	0	0
60 - 60	0		0	0	0
61 - 61	0		0	0	0
62 - 62	0		0	0	0
63 - 63	0		0	0	0
Totals	0	0	0	0	0

FONT COLORS: WHAT DO THEY MEAN?

Apart from the colors of the columns, you should also be aware of the font colors used in the calculator. Primarily, the font color indicates the *direction* of money.

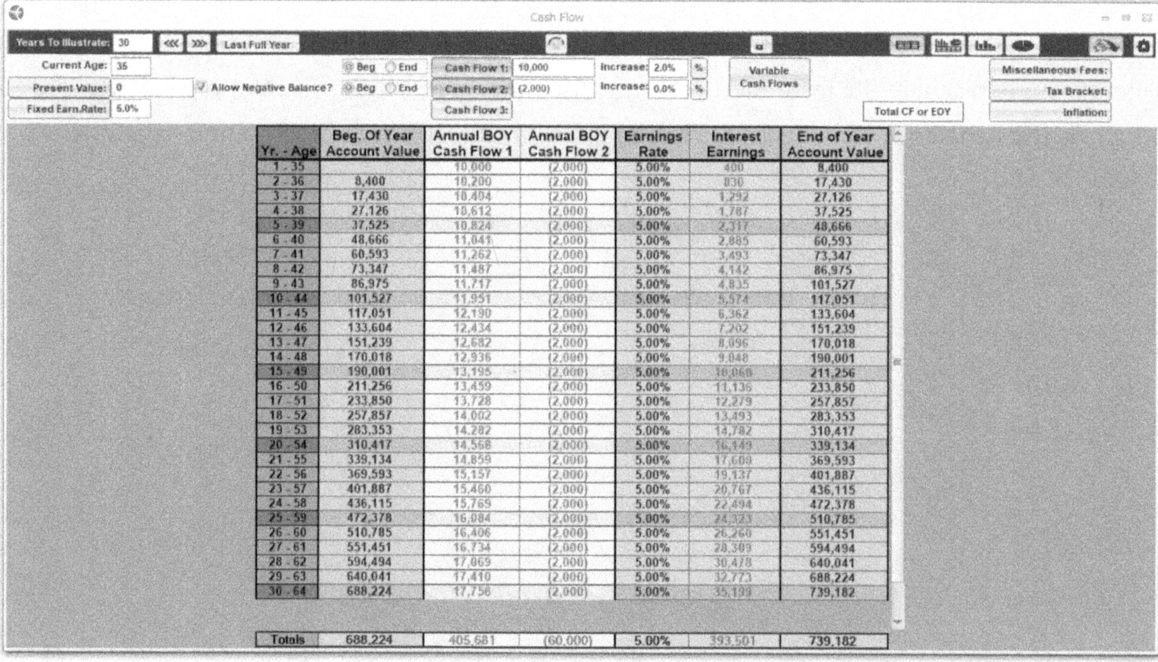

Yr. - Age	Beg. Of Year Account Value	Annual BOY Cash Flow 1	Annual BOY Cash Flow 2	Earnings Rate	Interest Earnings	End of Year Account Value
1 - 35		10,000	(2,000)	5.00%	400	8,400
2 - 36	8,400	10,200	(2,000)	5.00%	830	17,430
3 - 37	17,430	10,404	(2,000)	5.00%	1,292	27,126
4 - 38	27,126	10,612	(2,000)	5.00%	1,787	37,525
5 - 39	37,525	10,824	(2,000)	5.00%	2,317	48,666
6 - 40	48,666	11,041	(2,000)	5.00%	2,885	60,593
7 - 41	60,593	11,262	(2,000)	5.00%	3,493	73,347
8 - 42	73,347	11,487	(2,000)	5.00%	4,142	86,975
9 - 43	86,975	11,717	(2,000)	5.00%	4,835	101,527
10 - 44	101,527	11,951	(2,000)	5.00%	5,574	117,051
11 - 45	117,051	12,190	(2,000)	5.00%	6,362	133,604
12 - 46	133,604	12,434	(2,000)	5.00%	7,202	151,239
13 - 47	151,239	12,682	(2,000)	5.00%	8,096	170,018
14 - 48	170,018	12,936	(2,000)	5.00%	9,048	190,001
15 - 49	190,001	13,195	(2,000)	5.00%	10,060	211,256
16 - 50	211,256	13,459	(2,000)	5.00%	11,136	233,850
17 - 51	233,850	13,728	(2,000)	5.00%	12,279	257,857
18 - 52	257,857	14,002	(2,000)	5.00%	13,493	283,353
19 - 53	283,353	14,282	(2,000)	5.00%	14,782	310,417
20 - 54	310,417	14,568	(2,000)	5.00%	16,149	339,134
21 - 55	339,134	14,859	(2,000)	5.00%	17,600	369,593
22 - 56	369,593	15,157	(2,000)	5.00%	19,137	401,887
23 - 57	401,887	15,460	(2,000)	5.00%	20,767	436,115
24 - 58	436,115	15,769	(2,000)	5.00%	22,494	472,378
25 - 59	472,378	16,084	(2,000)	5.00%	24,323	510,785
26 - 60	510,785	16,406	(2,000)	5.00%	26,260	551,451
27 - 61	551,451	16,734	(2,000)	5.00%	28,309	594,494
28 - 62	594,494	17,069	(2,000)	5.00%	30,478	640,041
29 - 63	640,041	17,410	(2,000)	5.00%	32,773	688,224
30 - 64	688,224	17,758	(2,000)	5.00%	35,199	739,182
Totals	688,224	405,681	(60,000)	5.00%	393,501	739,182

Red Font

This is *very* important: red font does not necessarily indicate a loss, it indicates the direction in which money is flowing (shown above as the second column from the "Yr. - Age" column).

Money that is flowing away from you is represented by red font. For example, if you are paying a premium or making a contribution to an asset, that money is flowing away from your pocket and into your account, so it's red. This is true even if the asset belongs to the person funding it because it indicates the movement, *not* a loss/gain.

However, you may also notice that negative interest rates, taxes, and other figures are represented in red. While these *do* represent a loss, they also indicate money moving away from the account (and not into *your* pocket).

Green Font

Green font, on the other hand, is money moving toward you (shown above as the third and fifth columns from the "Yr. - Age" column). So money you withdraw from an account is going to be green because it's going from your account to your pocket.

Of course, it can also represent a gain, because it's money moving toward your account (and not *from* your pocket).

Based on the Cash Flow calculator above, you can give it a quick glance and note that $10,000 is moving from your pockets to your account each year, and $2,000 is flowing back into your pockets from your account.

This simple shift in perspective is going to make it that much easier to interpret your Truth Concepts charts and start thinking about money in terms of Cash Flow rather than profit and loss.

WHY THE CALCULATORS WERE CREATED AND THEIR BEST USES—PART 1

Calculator 6: Internal Rate of Return

If a simple calculator is all I need, I'm not going to overcomplicate it.

Purpose: The Internal Rate of Return (IRR) calculator is for calculating the internal rate of return on *varying* streams of payments and withdrawals.

Why It Was Created: Most people have no idea how to calculate interest with varying payment streams. We have the simple Interest Rate calculator in the first five calculators and if you have a level payment, the Interest Rate calculator and the IRR calculator will give you the same results.

However, when you have a different payment in a particular year (i.e., Joe invests $10,000 a year for five years, then $15,000 a year for ten more years to get $1 million at the end of the fifteenth year and doesn't know what interest rate that investment is earning over that fifteen year period of time, or how to calculate it), the IRR calculator can help. We can put the amount he invests in the IRR calculator, and we can see the annual internal rate or return, or interest rate, plainly stated at the top.

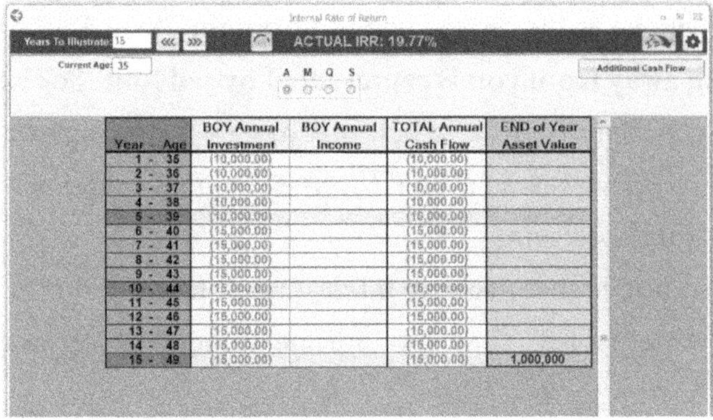

Year - Age	BOY Annual Investment	BOY Annual Income	TOTAL Annual Cash Flow	END of Year Asset Value
1 - 35	(10,000.00)		(10,000.00)	
2 - 36	(10,000.00)		(10,000.00)	
3 - 37	(10,000.00)		(10,000.00)	
4 - 38	(10,000.00)		(10,000.00)	
5 - 39	(10,000.00)		(10,000.00)	
6 - 40	(15,000.00)		(15,000.00)	
7 - 41	(15,000.00)		(15,000.00)	
8 - 42	(15,000.00)		(15,000.00)	
9 - 43	(15,000.00)		(15,000.00)	
10 - 44	(15,000.00)		(15,000.00)	
11 - 45	(15,000.00)		(15,000.00)	
12 - 46	(15,000.00)		(15,000.00)	
13 - 47	(15,000.00)		(15,000.00)	
14 - 48	(15,000.00)		(15,000.00)	
15 - 49	(15,000.00)		(15,000.00)	1,000,000

We do want to be aware that this does not take into consideration any fees or taxes.

The beauty of this calculator is that it doesn't matter what inputs are put into it. In the financial world, somebody may come in and propose something against a strategy a client already has. For example, Mary puts $10,000 into an account, and her financial strategist has shown her she will get $200,000 over time. Then a different strategist says, "I can double that." But they make that case by putting two times as much money in. Will that actually produce the rate of return promised? **This is where the IRR calculator helps with the objective numbers.** It gets rid of all the hype and shows the straight rate of return.

The IRR calculator helps people see the deal more objectively, and often they find out they will only get back as much money as they put in. They may get a stream of income and principal back, yet over time they come up even. Clients are often shocked by the results; it's not as high as they thought it would be.

Case Study: Your client wants to invest in an oil well and, ignoring the tax implications for a moment, is told $100,000 in now, $10,000 out annually for ten years. It should be obvious that it is a 0% IRR, yet sometimes it helps to have it in black and white. BOY means "Beginning of Year."

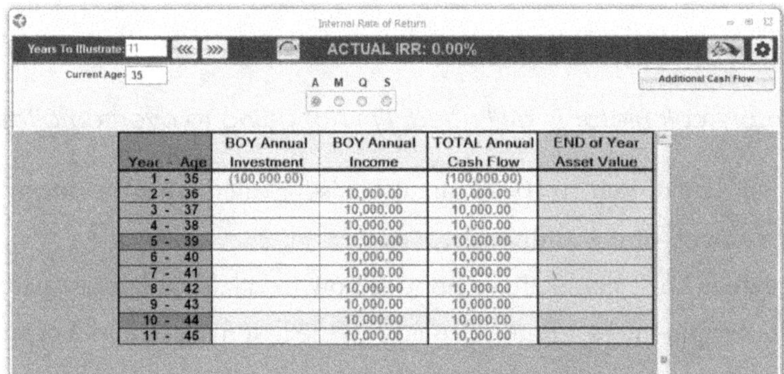

Year - Age	BOY Annual Investment	BOY Annual Income	TOTAL Annual Cash Flow	END of Year Asset Value
1 - 35	(100,000.00)		(100,000.00)	
2 - 36		10,000.00	10,000.00	
3 - 37		10,000.00	10,000.00	
4 - 38		10,000.00	10,000.00	
5 - 39		10,000.00	10,000.00	
6 - 40		10,000.00	10,000.00	
7 - 41		10,000.00	10,000.00	
8 - 42		10,000.00	10,000.00	
9 - 43		10,000.00	10,000.00	
10 - 44		10,000.00	10,000.00	
11 - 45		10,000.00	10,000.00	

What would it be if the income was $15,000 a year?

Internal Rate of Return

Years To Illustrate: 11 ACTUAL IRR: 8.14%

Current Age: 35 A M Q S Additional Cash Flow

Year - Age	BOY Annual Investment	BOY Annual Income	TOTAL Annual Cash Flow	END of Year Asset Value
1 - 35	(100,000.00)		(100,000.00)	
2 - 36		15,000.00	15,000.00	
3 - 37		15,000.00	15,000.00	
4 - 38		15,000.00	15,000.00	
5 - 39		15,000.00	15,000.00	
6 - 40		15,000.00	15,000.00	
7 - 41		15,000.00	15,000.00	
8 - 42		15,000.00	15,000.00	
9 - 43		15,000.00	15,000.00	
10 - 44		15,000.00	15,000.00	
11 - 45		15,000.00	15,000.00	

Best Uses: When it comes to varying streams of cash flow, whether due to amounts of money going into an investment or coming out, the IRR calculator gives us the number we need, which is the Rate of Return after everything is accounted for. It's the great equalizer, and one of my favorite financial measuring sticks. It serves as a great comparison tool.

To do an IRR calculation on an HP12C (my mentor, Norman, was a master at it) is a nightmare. It's extremely difficult to remember what you did in year two when you are in year three. With our IRR calculator, every year is on there, so you can see the numbers year by year and compare them.

From a pure efficiency standpoint, the IRR calculator is essential. Financial efficiency is really measured in rate of return. The fact that I put more money into an account or investment isn't actual efficiency. This calculator helps us answer the question: are we creating more perceived "efficiencies," or are we actually creating more money?

Calculator 7: Loan Analysis

There is no such thing as simple interest.

Purpose: The Loan Analysis calculator calculates amortization schedules, and the benefit of paying back loans under various scenarios (like comparing a fifteen-year and a thirty-year mortgage). It also allows you to compare paying the loan back at different rates, and compare two loan scenarios for deductible and non-deductible loans.

Why It Was Created: This calculator goes back to my story about being at the bank with Norman Baker and the confusion of raising his interest from 4-5% being a 25% increase, not a 1% increase. People in general don't understand how interest rates work on loans, so the Loan Analysis calculator shows them how a loan actually works, and gives them an amortization schedule so they can pay it off.

Case Study: Let's look at sixty months of a current loan balance. This was an equipment lease, but we're going to treat it like a loan. There's a balance of $50,000 at 23.5%. And there were sixty remaining monthly payments.

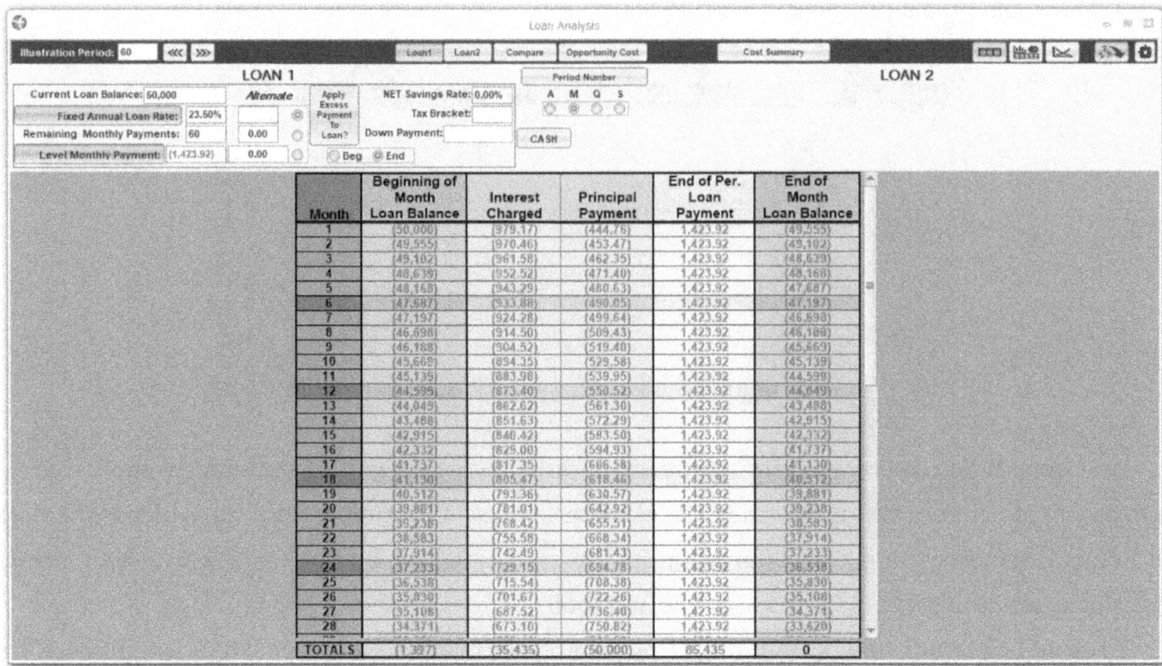

Month	Beginning of Month Loan Balance	Interest Charged	Principal Payment	End of Per. Loan Payment	End of Month Loan Balance
1	(50,000)	(979.17)	(444.76)	1,423.92	(49,555)
2	(49,555)	(970.46)	(453.47)	1,423.92	(49,102)
3	(49,102)	(961.58)	(462.35)	1,423.92	(48,639)
4	(48,639)	(952.52)	(471.40)	1,423.92	(48,168)
5	(48,168)	(943.29)	(480.63)	1,423.92	(47,687)
6	(47,687)	(933.88)	(490.05)	1,423.92	(47,197)
7	(47,197)	(924.28)	(499.64)	1,423.92	(46,698)
8	(46,698)	(914.50)	(509.43)	1,423.92	(46,188)
9	(46,188)	(904.52)	(519.40)	1,423.92	(45,669)
10	(45,669)	(894.35)	(529.58)	1,423.92	(45,139)
11	(45,139)	(883.98)	(539.95)	1,423.92	(44,599)
12	(44,599)	(873.40)	(550.52)	1,423.92	(44,049)
13	(44,049)	(862.62)	(561.30)	1,423.92	(43,488)
14	(43,488)	(851.63)	(572.29)	1,423.92	(42,915)
15	(42,915)	(840.42)	(583.50)	1,423.92	(42,332)
16	(42,332)	(829.00)	(594.93)	1,423.92	(41,737)
17	(41,737)	(817.35)	(606.58)	1,423.92	(41,130)
18	(41,130)	(805.47)	(618.46)	1,423.92	(40,512)
19	(40,512)	(793.36)	(630.57)	1,423.92	(39,881)
20	(39,881)	(781.01)	(642.92)	1,423.92	(39,238)
21	(39,238)	(768.42)	(655.51)	1,423.92	(38,583)
22	(38,583)	(755.58)	(668.34)	1,423.92	(37,914)
23	(37,914)	(742.49)	(681.43)	1,423.92	(37,233)
24	(37,233)	(729.15)	(694.78)	1,423.92	(36,538)
25	(36,538)	(715.54)	(708.38)	1,423.92	(35,830)
26	(35,830)	(701.67)	(722.26)	1,423.92	(35,108)
27	(35,108)	(687.52)	(736.40)	1,423.92	(34,371)
28	(34,371)	(673.10)	(750.82)	1,423.92	(33,620)
TOTALS	(1,397)	(35,435)	(50,000)	85,435	0

Right-clicking on the Remaining Monthly Payments box actually allows you to calculate the time from the payment. Say you don't know how much time is left and you want to determine that. You put in a payment of $2,000, and the calculator will tell you there are 34.677 months left.

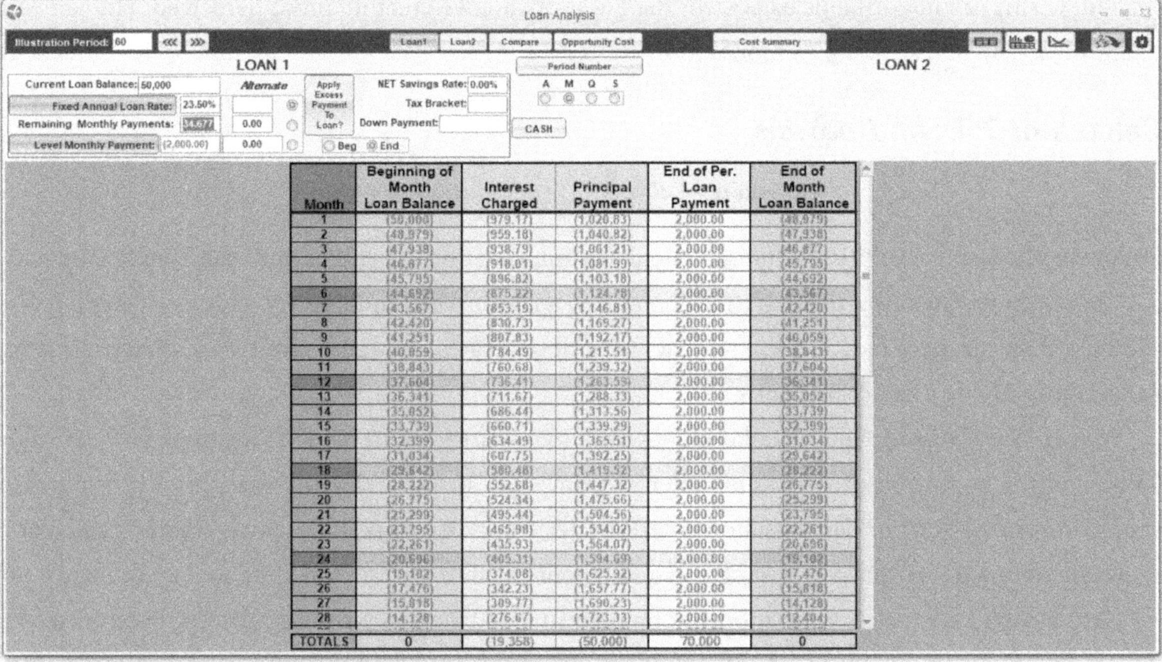

Month	Beginning of Month Loan Balance	Interest Charged	Principal Payment	End of Per. Loan Payment	End of Month Loan Balance
1	(50,000)	(979.17)	(1,020.83)	2,000.00	(48,979)
2	(48,979)	(959.18)	(1,040.82)	2,000.00	(47,938)
3	(47,938)	(938.79)	(1,061.21)	2,000.00	(46,877)
4	(46,877)	(918.01)	(1,081.99)	2,000.00	(45,795)
5	(45,795)	(896.82)	(1,103.18)	2,000.00	(44,692)
6	(44,692)	(875.22)	(1,124.78)	2,000.00	(43,567)
7	(43,567)	(853.19)	(1,146.81)	2,000.00	(42,420)
8	(42,420)	(830.73)	(1,169.27)	2,000.00	(41,251)
9	(41,251)	(807.83)	(1,192.17)	2,000.00	(40,059)
10	(40,059)	(784.49)	(1,215.51)	2,000.00	(38,843)
11	(38,843)	(760.68)	(1,239.32)	2,000.00	(37,604)
12	(37,604)	(736.41)	(1,263.59)	2,000.00	(36,341)
13	(36,341)	(711.67)	(1,288.33)	2,000.00	(35,052)
14	(35,052)	(686.44)	(1,313.56)	2,000.00	(33,739)
15	(33,739)	(660.71)	(1,339.29)	2,000.00	(32,399)
16	(32,399)	(634.49)	(1,365.51)	2,000.00	(31,034)
17	(31,034)	(607.75)	(1,392.25)	2,000.00	(29,642)
18	(29,642)	(580.48)	(1,419.52)	2,000.00	(28,222)
19	(28,222)	(552.68)	(1,447.32)	2,000.00	(26,775)
20	(26,775)	(524.34)	(1,475.66)	2,000.00	(25,299)
21	(25,299)	(495.44)	(1,504.56)	2,000.00	(23,795)
22	(23,795)	(465.98)	(1,534.02)	2,000.00	(22,261)
23	(22,261)	(435.93)	(1,564.07)	2,000.00	(20,696)
24	(20,696)	(405.31)	(1,594.69)	2,000.00	(19,102)
25	(19,102)	(374.08)	(1,625.92)	2,000.00	(17,476)
26	(17,476)	(342.23)	(1,657.77)	2,000.00	(15,818)
27	(15,818)	(309.77)	(1,690.23)	2,000.00	(14,128)
28	(14,128)	(276.67)	(1,723.33)	2,000.00	(12,404)
TOTALS	0	(19,358)	(50,000)	70,000	0

Alternatively, if you know what the time is, you can solve for the payment, even though the time is the default.

Best Uses: When we take out a loan, we aren't always given a schedule to pay it back. This calculator can do that, show amortization, and show the balance, principal, and interest pieces independently. If it's a tax-deductible loan, you can put tax brackets in the calculator to show you the true net costs.

Being able to put two different loan choices in one calculator so that you can compare one to another with all the facts is one of this calculator's best uses. With different rates and payback timeframes, the Loan Analysis calculator helps to explain the math portion of loans and can help a strategist and client decide the best option to questions like: do I take a thirty-year mortgage or fifteen-year mortgage? With this calculator, you can look at the options side by side.

Calculator 8: Borrowing Strategy

When the policy loan becomes a license to buy,
you're sending your clients down the wrong path.

Purpose: The Borrowing Strategy calculator illustrates the principles of banking (borrowing and paying back) with varying interest rates, strategies, and money sources.

Why It Was Created: This calculator could be used for any account we could put up as collateral. It's a way to combine saving and investing with the most efficient way of spending, whether that's cash or through loans. I have strategists who really like this one to get their points across regarding borrowing money, especially against life insurance.

What makes a life insurance policy powerful? Borrowing against it, or the cash value? Is it the loan or the cash value that makes a life insurance policy powerful?

A lot of people think that because of some of the language that is being used, somehow a loan makes a policy effective. Yet, it is the cash value that is the important piece.

Cash value should be used for emergencies first and opportunities second. Otherwise, it becomes a license to spend, and that's dangerous.

This calculator helps strategists and clients determine the best borrowing strategy for a given scenario.

Case Study: Let's say a client has a brand-new car and they've been in the habit of buying one every eight years or so. They know they could finance this car in a variety of ways, and they've learned borrowing against their Life Insurance Cash Value is one of them. They also understand that all loans must be paid back in order to be "honest bankers," even though there are YouTubers saying they don't have to pay the loan back.

While it is true that upon death, the life insurance company will utilize some of the death benefit to pay off the loan, you can't efficiently leave a loan on the policy books for decades without the total amount of interest becoming so large that the policy implodes (falls apart from the inside).

They have decided to put $10,000 a year into this brand-new policy in order to prepare for their next car purchase eight years in the future. Current interest rates are the following: 5% at the insurance company and 7% at their bank. They decide to pay back their loan to the insurance company (that is against their cash value) at 6%, so they'll contribute a little extra to their PUAs. PUAs are "paid-up additional insurance" that creates extra cash value and more death benefit.

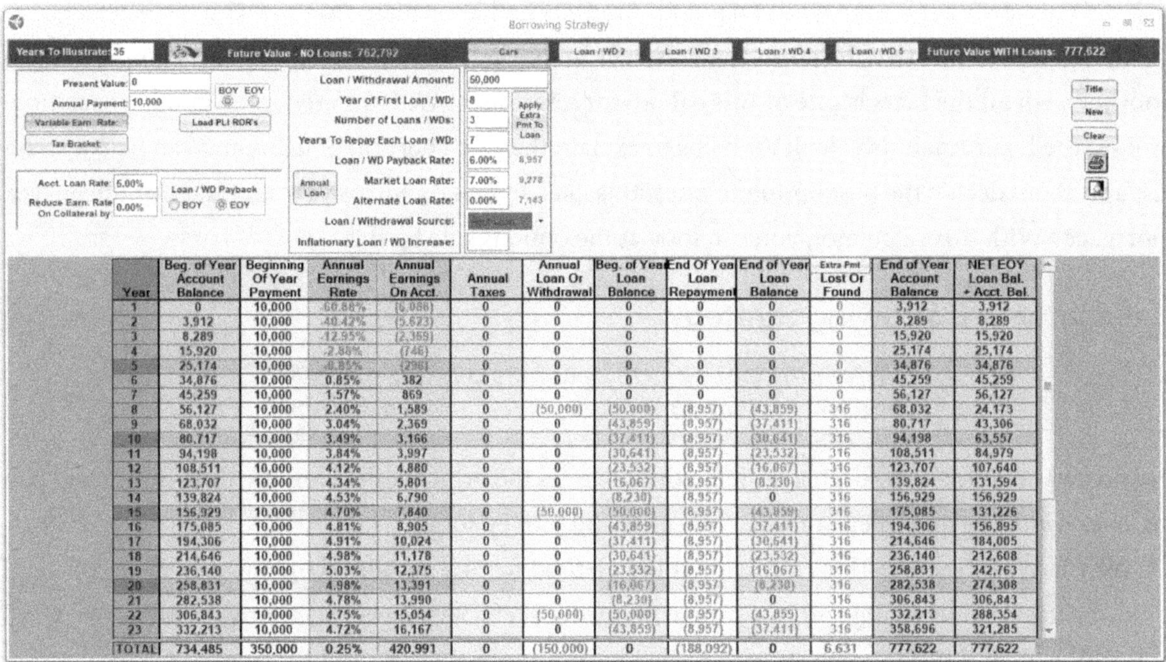

Year	Beg. of Year Account Balance	Beginning Of Year Payment	Annual Earnings Rate	Annual Earnings On Acct.	Annual Taxes	Annual Loan Or Withdrawal	Beg. of Year Loan Balance	End Of Year Loan Repayment	End of Year Loan Balance	Extra Pmt Lost Or Found	End of Year Account Balance	NET EOY Loan Bal. + Acct. Bal.
1	0	10,000	-60.88%	(6,088)	0	0	0	0	0	0	3,912	3,912
2	3,912	10,000	-40.42%	(5,623)	0	0	0	0	0	0	8,289	8,289
3	8,289	10,000	-12.95%	(2,369)	0	0	0	0	0	0	15,920	15,920
4	15,920	10,000	-2.88%	(746)	0	0	0	0	0	0	25,174	25,174
5	25,174	10,000	-0.85%	(296)	0	0	0	0	0	0	34,876	34,876
6	34,876	10,000	0.85%	382	0	0	0	0	0	0	45,259	45,259
7	45,259	10,000	1.57%	869	0	0	0	0	0	0	56,127	56,127
8	56,127	10,000	2.40%	1,589	0	(50,000)	(50,000)	(8,957)	(43,859)	316	68,032	24,173
9	68,032	10,000	3.04%	2,369	0	0	(43,859)	(8,957)	(37,411)	316	80,717	43,306
10	80,717	10,000	3.49%	3,166	0	0	(37,411)	(8,957)	(30,641)	316	94,198	63,557
11	94,198	10,000	3.84%	3,997	0	0	(30,641)	(8,957)	(23,532)	316	108,511	84,979
12	108,511	10,000	4.12%	4,880	0	0	(23,532)	(8,957)	(16,067)	316	123,707	107,640
13	123,707	10,000	4.34%	5,801	0	0	(16,067)	(8,957)	(8,230)	316	139,824	131,594
14	139,824	10,000	4.53%	6,790	0	0	(8,230)	(8,957)	0	316	156,929	156,929
15	156,929	10,000	4.70%	7,840	0	(50,000)	(50,000)	(8,957)	(43,859)	316	175,085	131,226
16	175,085	10,000	4.81%	8,905	0	0	(43,859)	(8,957)	(37,411)	316	194,306	156,895
17	194,306	10,000	4.91%	10,024	0	0	(37,411)	(8,957)	(30,641)	316	214,646	184,005
18	214,646	10,000	4.98%	11,178	0	0	(30,641)	(8,957)	(23,532)	316	236,140	212,608
19	236,140	10,000	5.03%	12,375	0	0	(23,532)	(8,957)	(16,067)	316	258,831	242,763
20	258,831	10,000	4.98%	13,391	0	0	(16,067)	(8,957)	(8,230)	316	282,538	274,308
21	282,538	10,000	4.78%	13,990	0	0	(8,230)	(8,957)	0	316	306,843	306,843
22	306,843	10,000	4.75%	15,054	0	(50,000)	(50,000)	(8,957)	(43,859)	316	332,213	288,354
23	332,213	10,000	4.72%	16,167	0	0	(43,859)	(8,957)	(37,411)	316	358,696	321,285
TOTAL	734,485	350,000	0.25%	420,991	0	(150,000)	0	(188,092)	0	6,631	777,622	777,622

Above you can see that the account with no loans would have grown to $762,792, while the account with loans and a 6% payback would grow to $777,622. This is assuming there were three cars purchased, all at $50,000, and each paid back over seven years at 6%. There was enough value left over on car one to make a down payment on car two, etc.

Best Uses: This calculator is good for determining what source to borrow from, like a bank, or against, like cash value, and how to pay the money back using a strategy that works for an individual client and their sources.

Calculator 9: Revolving Credit

There's no more magic in borrowing money from a life insurance company than anywhere else.

Purpose: The Revolving Credit calculator enables you to prove which is the most economical way to pay down or pay off consumer debt. Snowball, avalanche, or cash-flow-based methods are all demonstrable.

Why It Was Created: Credit is so easy to get nowadays, especially when talking about consumer debt and credit cards. Many people are trying to understand: how do I get out of debt and apply my money in the best way to do so? There are different strategies. **One you may have heard of is Dave Ramsey's debt snowball; they talk about it like it's more efficient, but in actuality it's not; it simply provides a psychological benefit.**

The Revolving Credit calculator allows us to play with different approaches based on interest rates. It will always come down to which option will pay off debt the fastest. While you can pay off the highest interest rate (regardless of the size of the loan), it may only be slightly more efficient. The psychology of getting debt paid down early on and paying off smaller loans or debt may be more beneficial. We can use this calculator to estimate the numbers for whichever option a client chooses.

The other thing this calculator shows us is how big of a part revolving credit plays in our credit score. The amount of available credit to the amount used is a critical ratio; the smaller that ratio, the better. On a credit report, each credit card or debt is a single unit. Having a greater total number of those actually carries more weight.

Case Study: Tony has a $100,000 credit limit, has borrowed $50,000, and could have a few other $10,000 credit cards that are empty. Each one of those will weigh equally. Tony might actually want to keep the unused credit cards because it helps boost his overall credit score. This calculator shows the best ways for Tony to pay off his debt and keep his credit score high.

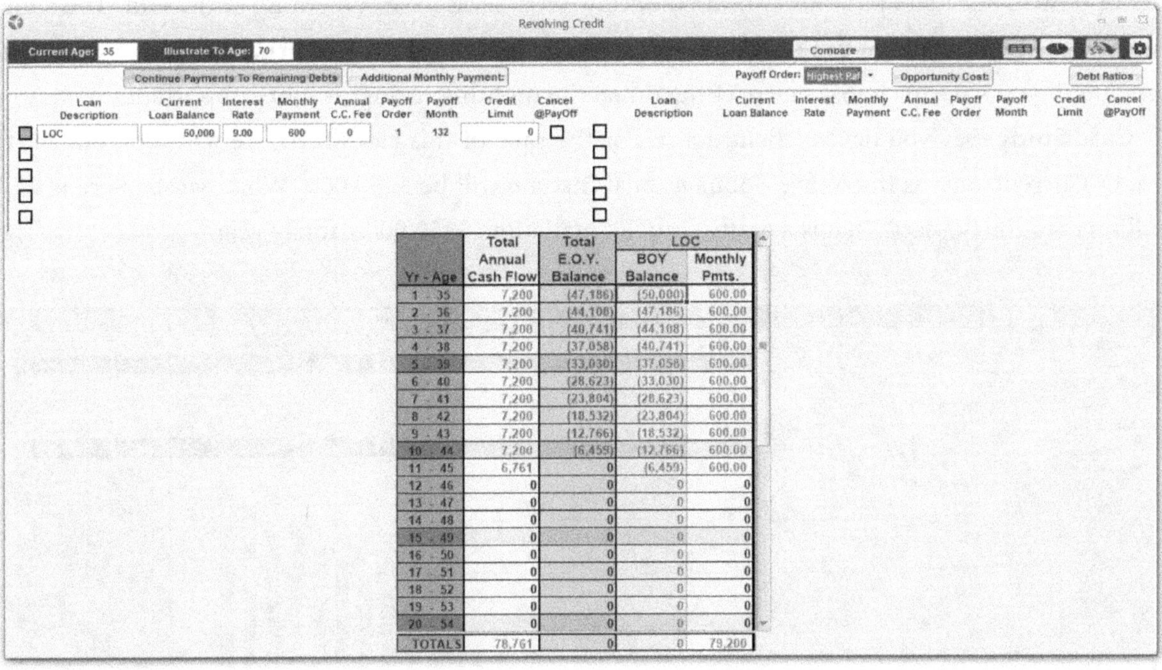

Yr - Age	Total Annual Cash Flow	Total E.O.Y. Balance	LOC BOY Balance	LOC Monthly Pmts.
1 - 35	7,200	(47,186)	(50,000)	600.00
2 - 36	7,200	(44,108)	(47,186)	600.00
3 - 37	7,200	(40,741)	(44,108)	600.00
4 - 38	7,200	(37,058)	(40,741)	600.00
5 - 39	7,200	(33,030)	(37,058)	600.00
6 - 40	7,200	(28,623)	(33,030)	600.00
7 - 41	7,200	(23,804)	(28,623)	600.00
8 - 42	7,200	(18,532)	(23,804)	600.00
9 - 43	7,200	(12,766)	(18,532)	600.00
10 - 44	7,200	(6,459)	(12,766)	600.00
11 - 45	6,761	0	(6,459)	600.00
12 - 46	0	0	0	0
13 - 47	0	0	0	0
14 - 48	0	0	0	0
15 - 49	0	0	0	0
16 - 50	0	0	0	0
17 - 51	0	0	0	0
18 - 52	0	0	0	0
19 - 53	0	0	0	0
20 - 54	0	0	0	0
TOTALS	78,761	0	0	79,200

Best Uses: The Revolving Credit calculator is great for showing the percentage of overall revolving credit a client has, as well as the weighted percentage. It can help a financial strategist determine the best way for a client to pay off debt, as well as examine how to improve their credit score.

Calculator 10: Maximum Potential

Our ability to work and earn a living is the greatest asset we have.

Purpose: The Maximum Potential calculator shows where a person's focus should be financially to reach their maximum potential. The emphasis is on saving money rather than seeking a higher rate of return as it identifies full capability, then reduces it by taxes, debt service, lifestyle, and inflation.

Why It Was Created: This one is a serious "Norman Baker" calculator; it is really a comprehensive way to show how over time small tweaks in reducing spending, and putting more money into savings, can make a big impact. This is assuming there is a structure in place to enable the reduction in spending goes directly to savings. The calculations from this one show how small changes can have a massive impact over time. Sometimes that's extremely motivational for clients.

Most people are hesitant to talk to a financial strategist because they're afraid they'll have to spend money on a financial product somewhere instead of buying a boat or eating out more often. That's a concern that Maximum Potential can ease by showing them the straightforward numbers that will result from their decisions.

If we could earn a 100% rate of return, but we put zero dollars in, how much return do we get? Zero. If you don't put any money in, you cannot reach your maximum potential. Let's say I earn zero rate of return, but I still put money aside monthly. I'll at least have something at the end. **The short takeaway is that what you put in is more important than the rate of return.** They do work in tandem, but if you have to choose one over the other, the monthly savings is more important.

Case Study: Say you have a client, John. For the sake of this case study, we will look out thirty years. "Current Age" is thirty-five. John's annual income will be $250,000. What we see here is $7.5 million over thirty years. That is a pretty simple calculation: $250,000 x thirty years.

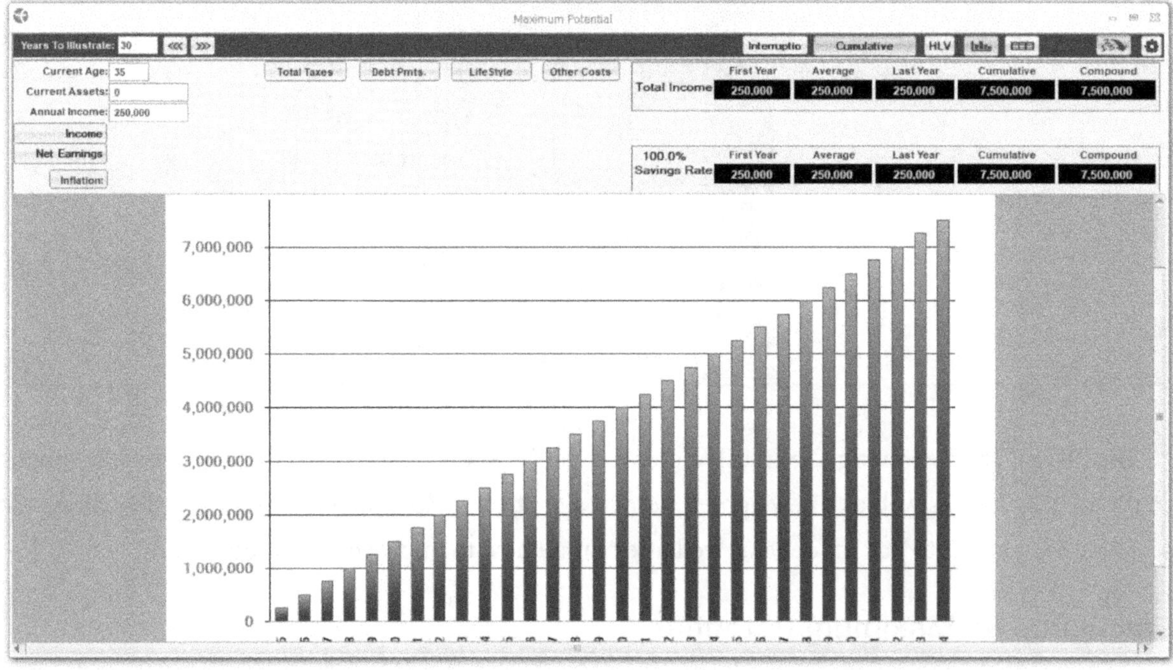

That is a shocking number for most people. Based on John's $250,000 income, $7.5 million is going to pass through his hands over the next thirty years. We need to understand that our ability to work and earn a living is probably the greatest asset we have.

Is John going to be happy if he stays at $250,000 a year across this timeframe while the cost of living is increasing? No. So let's use a 4% increase. So what we see now is not $7.5 million, but just over $14 million, is actually going to pass through John's hands over the next thirty years.

If the ability to earn is your greatest asset, does it make sense to protect some of that? That answer opens up a discussion of disability income protection and death benefits equal to Human Life Value.

What if John didn't have any expenses? Could he save and invest all of his income? What if he could do that at 4.5%? This shows just over $26 million maximum potential. Obviously, this is an unrealistic example with no expenses, however, it can wake us up and create a desire to keep some of that money.

John making $250,000 at the top tax bracket is probably paying 20% of his income in federal taxes, but we're talking about total taxes: state tax, sales tax, hotel tax, breathing tax, etc. This is at least 35% of his income gone. If we calculate that, what we see here is he paid out around $5 million in taxes, yet it took $9 million away from his future. The total went from $26 million to $17 million for a difference of $9 million.

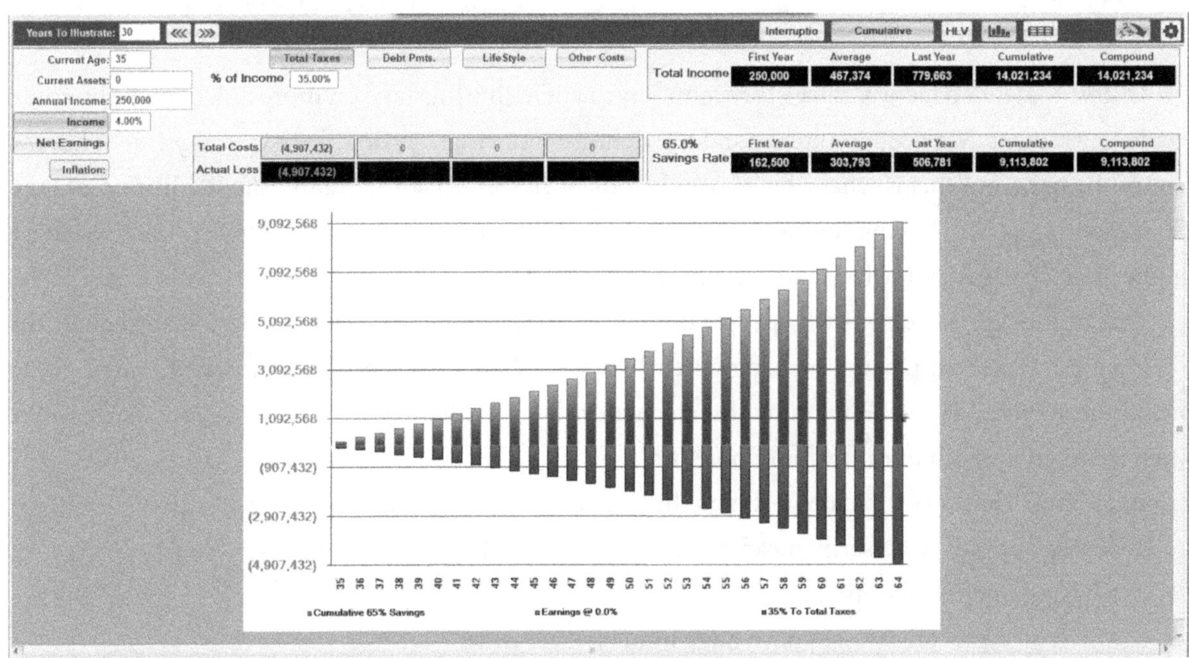

So why did $5 million paid in tax take $9 million from John's future away? Time value of money.

What about debt service? We put 30% on that (which is a minimum since our house is going to be around 30% of our income) and 32% for Lifestyle.

What we see at the end of the chart is that John had a maximum potential of $26 million, but he ended up with a whopping $828,000.

He's saving 3%, which is probably more than the average American, and his last year's income was $779,000, so he just barely has more than one year's income.

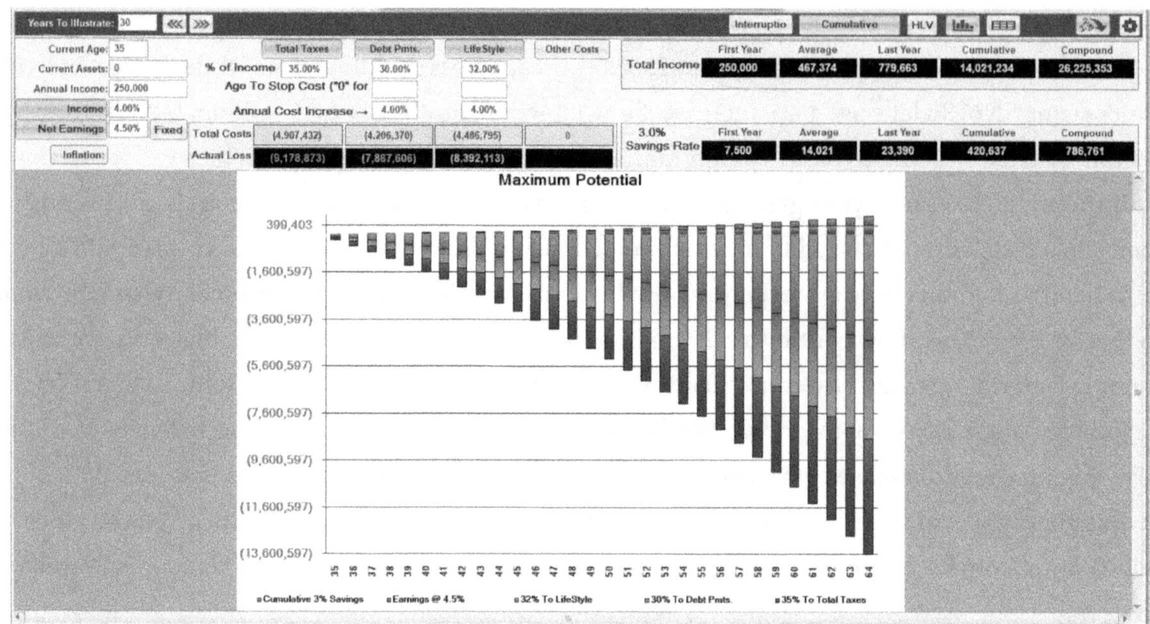

Unfortunately, so many strategists recommend a client like this take on more risk because he could get larger returns. We need to understand the definition of risk. It is not likely you're going to hit one out of the park, but that is what a lot of people look at risk as. **Risk is actually the likelihood of loss.** So literally what we're being told is to increase our likelihood of losing everything so that we have a higher rate of return. On what planet does that make sense?

One of the biggest reasons why people don't want to save is because they automatically equate the saving aspect to them having to change their lifestyle. What we've been taught is that you've got to make cuts in your lifestyle. But I think this calculator shows brilliantly that that's not necessarily where we have to go to reach our maximum potential.

Best Uses: There are three main things this calculator was designed to demonstrate:

1. Savings doesn't necessarily mean a reduction in lifestyle,
2. Chasing interest rates isn't the answer, and
3. Small incremental changes have huge impacts over time.

Calculator 11: Automobile Purchases

There is a big difference between interest payment and interest cost. We cannot get rid of the interest cost.

Purpose: The Automobile Purchases calculator shows the "true cost of paying cash" for automobiles or any other large purchase.

Why It Was Created: An automobile is such a big expense for most people, so we created this calculator specifically for that large expense. However, this calculator could be used for any major expense. I simply chose automobiles because almost everybody has one, they can be quite expensive, and it's just part of life, so we best understand the financial potential and pitfalls around vehicles.

The cost of an automobile in the early 1900s was a full year's salary. Many cars now still are that expensive. But most people don't think twice about buying a car every four years. This calculator is about figuring out how we pay for a major expense like that and seeing the impact of it on the rest of our finances.

The calculator addresses the thought that if we pay cash, we've gotten rid of an interest cost. **We always have an interest cost when we buy things, even with cash; we just don't know how to calculate it.** When we finance with a lending institution, we can see the cost of interest clearly. But when we pay with cash, though we're not financing it through a bank, we're financing it with our *future assets.* You may be debt-free, but you're also money-free when you pay for such a large expense with cash.

This calculator plays into the idea of opportunity cost. It's such a huge thing to consider, and it's very real. That's one of the problems I see with Dave Ramsey's approach. He advocates for just liquidating your cash and paying off all your debt, but then you don't have anything, financially speaking.

Case Study: Let's look at what this really means and the true cost of paying cash for an automobile (or other large expense). Say we look forward to thirty-five years out. This individual, Aisha, has $250,000, and she is adding $30,000 a year to this account.

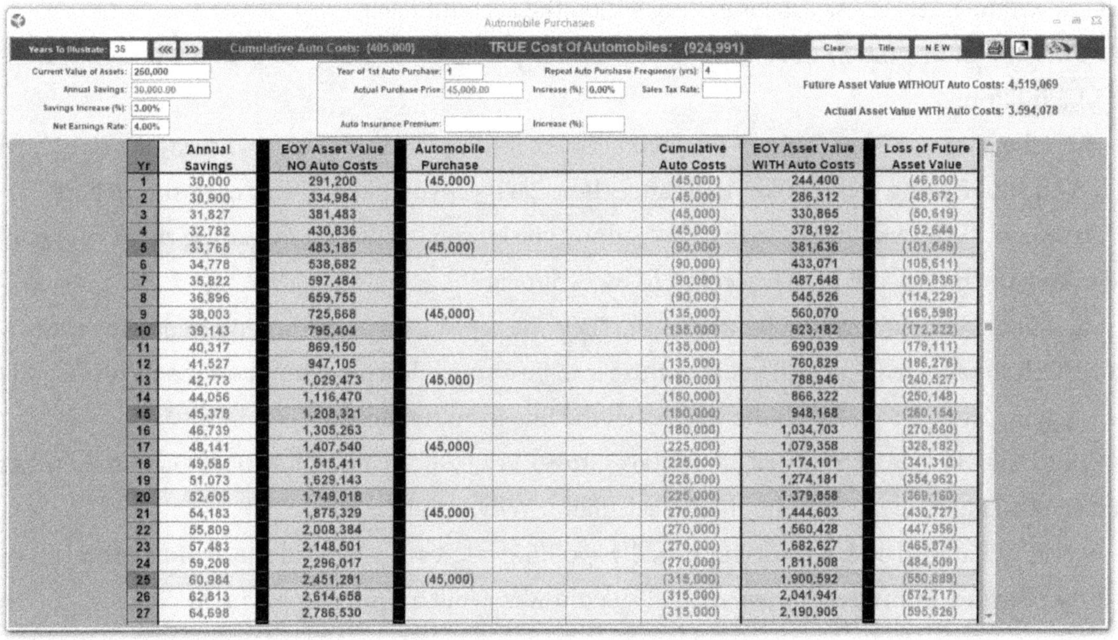

Automobile Purchases

Years To Illustrate: 35 | Cumulative Auto Costs: (405,000) | TRUE Cost Of Automobiles: (924,991) | Clear | Title | NEW

Current Value of Assets: 250,000
Annual Savings: 30,000.00
Savings Increase (%): 3.00%
Net Earnings Rate: 4.00%

Year of 1st Auto Purchase: 1
Repeat Auto Purchase Frequency (yrs): 4
Actual Purchase Price: 45,000.00
Increase (%): 0.00%
Sales Tax Rate:
Auto Insurance Premium:
Increase (%):

Future Asset Value WITHOUT Auto Costs: 4,519,069
Actual Asset Value WITH Auto Costs: 3,594,078

Yr	Annual Savings	EOY Asset Value NO Auto Costs	Automobile Purchase	Cumulative Auto Costs	EOY Asset Value WITH Auto Costs	Loss of Future Asset Value
1	30,000	291,200	(45,000)	(45,000)	244,400	(46,800)
2	30,900	334,984		(45,000)	286,312	(48,672)
3	31,827	381,483		(45,000)	330,865	(50,619)
4	32,782	430,836		(45,000)	378,192	(52,644)
5	33,765	483,185	(45,000)	(90,000)	381,636	(101,549)
6	34,778	538,682		(90,000)	433,071	(105,611)
7	35,822	597,484		(90,000)	487,648	(109,836)
8	36,896	659,755		(90,000)	545,526	(114,229)
9	38,003	725,668	(45,000)	(135,000)	560,070	(165,598)
10	39,143	795,404		(135,000)	623,182	(172,222)
11	40,317	869,150		(135,000)	690,039	(179,111)
12	41,527	947,105		(135,000)	760,829	(186,276)
13	42,773	1,029,473	(45,000)	(180,000)	788,946	(240,527)
14	44,056	1,116,470		(180,000)	866,322	(250,148)
15	45,378	1,208,321		(180,000)	948,168	(260,154)
16	46,739	1,305,263		(180,000)	1,034,703	(270,560)
17	48,141	1,407,540	(45,000)	(225,000)	1,079,358	(328,182)
18	49,585	1,515,411		(225,000)	1,174,101	(341,310)
19	51,073	1,629,143		(225,000)	1,274,181	(354,962)
20	52,605	1,749,018		(225,000)	1,379,858	(369,160)
21	54,183	1,875,329	(45,000)	(270,000)	1,444,603	(430,727)
22	55,809	2,008,384		(270,000)	1,560,428	(447,956)
23	57,483	2,148,501		(270,000)	1,682,627	(465,874)
24	59,208	2,296,017		(270,000)	1,811,508	(484,509)
25	60,984	2,451,281	(45,000)	(315,000)	1,900,592	(550,689)
26	62,813	2,614,658		(315,000)	2,041,941	(572,717)
27	64,698	2,786,530		(315,000)	2,190,905	(595,626)

She was told that if she increased her savings each year with inflation, that would inflation-proof her assets.

Is that true? *No.*

Inflation impacts the big pile of existing money. So while you're inflation-proofing your contributions, inflation is going to impact the existing dollars a lot worse. And there's just no way to counteract that.

The cure for inflation is: more money, more work, and more savings. Focus on what you can control, and work more, earn more, save more. There are all kinds of financial potential if you do those three things.

Inflation is going to impact everything the same: all your savings, all your investments, all your assets. So, the conversation should not be about what an inflation rate might be, as there isn't much we can do about it. The conversation should be about certainty and uncertainty; we have to have certainty assets in our life in order to fend off the uncertainty risk on the uncertain assets.

So what is your choice for "certainty" assets? Cash? High-yield savings accounts? Cash value of whole life insurance? How does cash compare to cash value for a certainty asset?

Life insurance belongs in the category of a savings vehicle, not an investment vehicle. What can beat it that isn't going to get hurt by inflation as much? All kinds of things, but that's the wrong comparison to make.

Sure, my real estate, my stocks, etc., all have the potential to outpace inflation, but they are "uncertain" assets. However, because I have that piece of certainty in my life insurance, I can pursue the uncertainty assets.

The certain assets protect my uncertain assets.

Let's return to Aisha. She is increasing her savings by 3%: $30,000 this year, $30,900 next year, and so on down the line. Let's say she is getting 4% on the account itself.

At the end of this timeframe, if she stayed on this path and nothing fluctuated all the way out, we see $4.5 million.

Then she goes to a Dave Ramsey Financial Peace seminar. And Dave says, "I see that you're buying cars. And you're using your banker to finance these cars, yet you have all this cash sitting here."

Dave says, "Why would you do that? Why don't you eliminate interest by getting rid of your banker and taking the money out of this account to buy your car?"

So Aisha buys a car for $45,000 with cash. Then she repeats this auto-buying frequency every four years. Each time there is enough value in the car to be a small down payment on the next car, and she keeps paying cash of $45,000 all the way down the line from her account.

With Dave's help, Aisha turned $4,519,069 into $3,594,078. She bought $405,000 worth of the cars, yet it took $924,991 away from her in the calculator. Why is that?

How is it that with cash she was supposedly avoiding interest costs? **Did she avoid an interest cost, or did she avoid an interest *payment*?** All she did was avoid an interest payment. She did not avoid the interest costs.

This calculator helps us wrap our heads around the idea that *cash has value*. Just because Aisha isn't financing her cars doesn't mean she's not paying interest. She still is paying interest, just from a place that is hard to see. This is even more dangerous for this reason, you won't know about the problem until it may be too late to do anything to fix it.

How many people are buying a car every four years, especially with a couple of kids involved?

***

Now let's look at it the other way around: Aisha never met Dave Ramsey. She has found the money to make her payment on her car, and she has continued her savings. So while it might not have been as efficient, she would end up with $4.5 million instead of $3.6 million.

It's hard for people to look at opportunity cost in the form of "let's take this cost called 'opportunity cost' and use a competitive interest rate to measure the long-term impact of it." It seems like phantom money, but it's not.

This Automobile Purchase calculator is one of the calculators I came up with so that just about everybody gets past that struggle of believing that "cash has no value."

You can go through this calculator very simply, just putting in the savings and a few cars, and it will prove the point. And sometimes, for strategists, keeping it super simple with as little detail as possible gets the client to see the picture more quickly.

Best Uses: This calculator is best used to calculate and compare the difference between paying for a large expense with cash (and the opportunity cost) versus financing it, taking into account the interest rate.

Calculator 12: Education Cost

We must understand the real world vs. pure economics.

Purpose: The Education Cost calculator demonstrates the major impact on parents' assets and cash flow that paying for private high school and/or college has; it can also calculate education "need."

Why It Was Created: Many people nowadays have no idea how much education actually costs. It is crazy expensive. We're not saying don't educate your kids. We're simply saying with as big of a cost as it is, make sure your education decision makes sense. To spend four years at a $50,000/year university to do basket-weaving (or some other subject you don't know how you will apply to your career) is ridiculous.

Students often make decisions on where to go based on what the campus looks like. That is a hard no for me! The parents don't realize that rather than education being perceived as a special gift or privilege, so many kids take it for granted and aren't ready for it. For kids to go to school and make C's, D's, or F's, it's not worth it for a parent to be paying such a large sum of money.

Sending two kids to a $40,000/year university will cost a couple during their retirement phase $100,000/year. How? That's what this calculator shows us. Understand what you're biting off with an education decision, and ensure it makes sense *financially*. A lot of kids who are more entrepreneurial struggle in the classroom and get labeled with ADD or ADHD. They might've been much better off being given money to start their own business instead of going to school.

Case Study: With this calculator, we have the option to look at it from the student standpoint and the parents' standpoint by toggling back and forth using a button up top.

For this example, we'll put three kids in the calculator, and I'm going to check three students' information on the check boxes.

We put in the age of seven, eight, and nine. When are they going to start school? Typically, at eighteen years old. We enter: "Years of School" (four), "Tuition" ($25,000), and "Tuition Increase" (7%).

You can see for the youngest child, it's going to cost $257,000 to pay for school between the ages of eighteen and twenty-two. We put sixty-five for distribution age. We set the mortality age to ninety. This decision lost the youngest child $83,000 a year of retirement income.

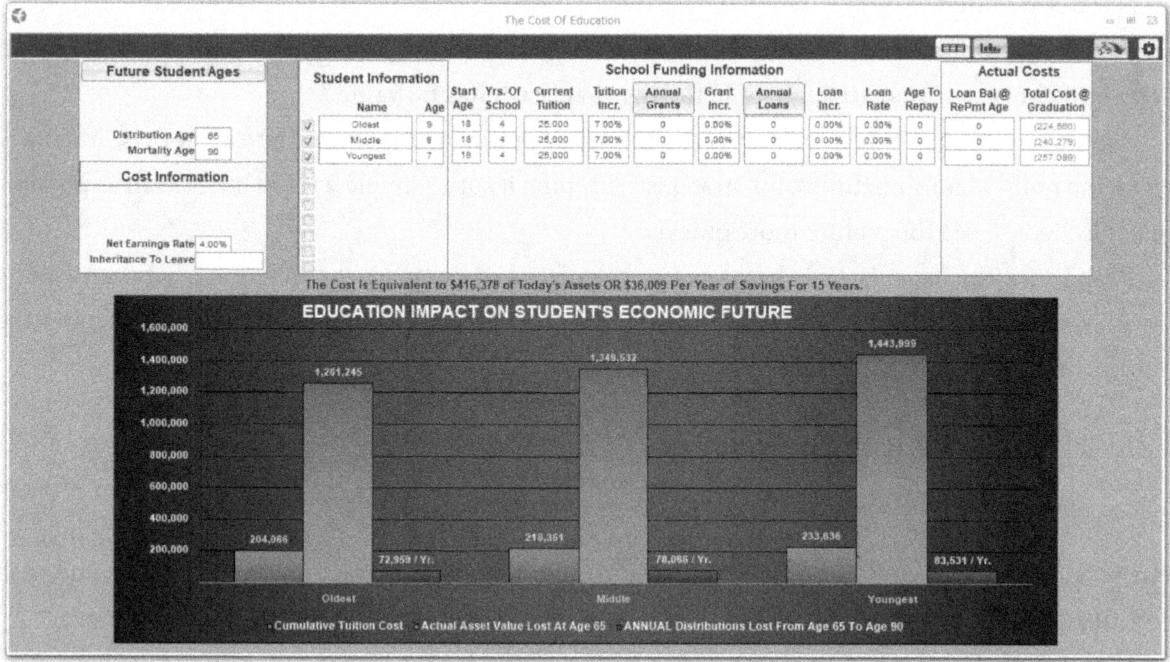

That was from the standpoint of the child paying for college. Now let's flip it over to the parents paying. We can see tuition costs of $656,000, and we can see $1.15 million in assets lost, which equates to a loss of $66,778 of an annual distribution from age sixty-five to ninety for the parent.

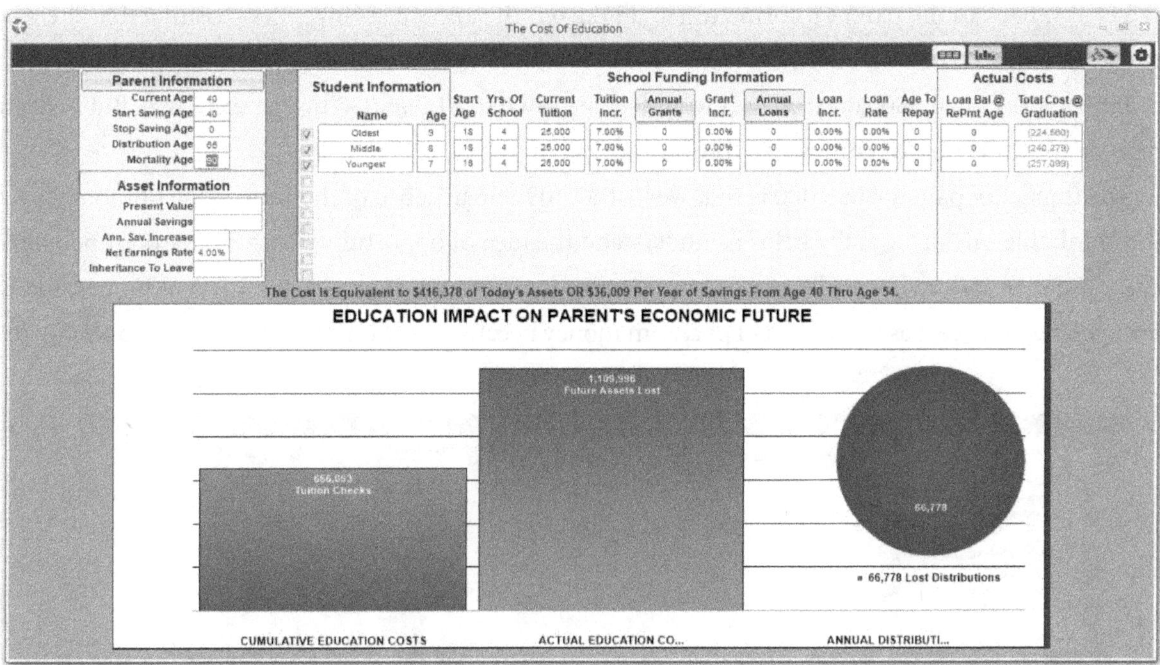

In the light blue, it says this cost is equivalent to $416,378 of today's assets or $36,009 per year of savings from age forty through age fifty-four.

If the family can't handle $36,000 a year, then what if they agreed to increase their savings by 3% a year to help? Put 3% in the "Ann. Sav. Increase" box. It will show us how you can start saving at $29,675 and grow that over time. Still a very large number for most.

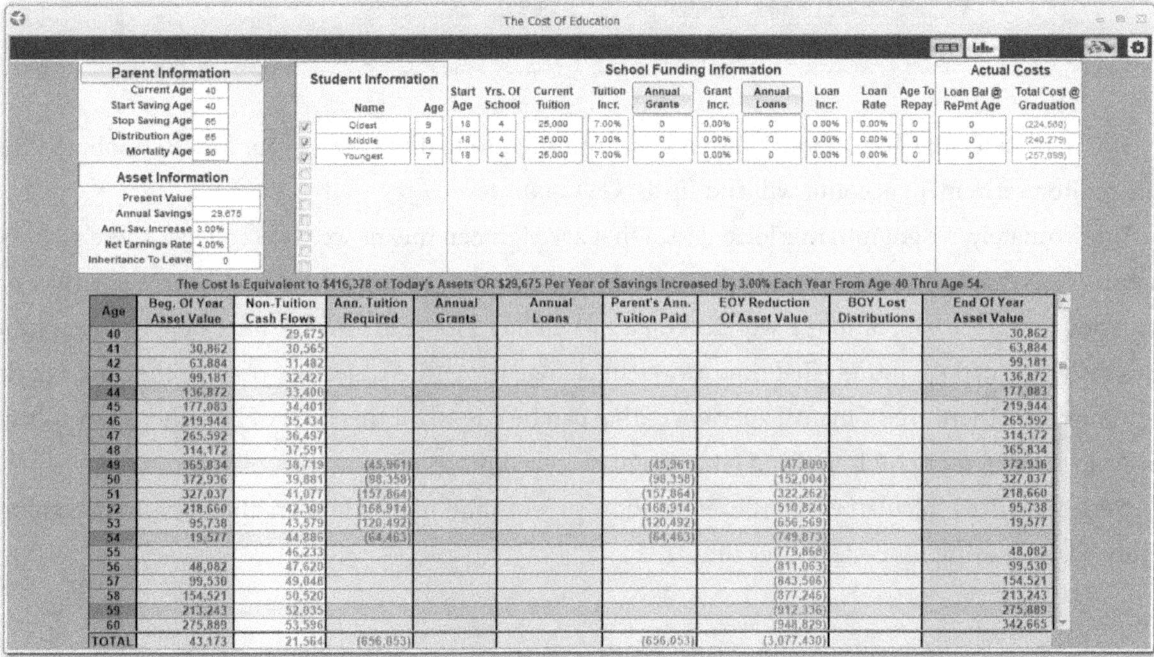

The Cost Is Equivalent to $416,378 of Today's Assets OR $29,675 Per Year of Savings Increased by 3.00% Each Year From Age 40 Thru Age 54.

Age	Beg. Of Year Asset Value	Non-Tuition Cash Flows	Ann. Tuition Required	Annual Grants	Annual Loans	Parent's Ann. Tuition Paid	EOY Reduction Of Asset Value	BOY Lost Distributions	End Of Year Asset Value
40		29,675							30,862
41	30,862	30,565							63,884
42	63,884	31,482							99,181
43	99,181	32,427							136,872
44	136,872	33,400							177,083
45	177,083	34,401							219,944
46	219,944	35,434							265,592
47	265,592	36,497							314,172
48	314,172	37,591							365,834
49	365,834	38,719	(45,961)			(45,961)	(47,800)		372,936
50	372,936	39,881	(98,358)			(98,358)	(152,004)		327,037
51	327,037	41,077	(157,864)			(157,864)	(322,262)		218,660
52	218,660	42,309	(168,914)			(168,914)	(510,824)		95,738
53	95,738	43,579	(120,492)			(120,492)	(656,569)		19,577
54	19,577	44,886	(64,463)			(64,463)	(749,873)		
55		46,233					(779,868)		48,082
56	48,082	47,620					(811,063)		99,530
57	99,530	49,048					(843,506)		154,521
58	154,521	50,520					(877,246)		213,243
59	213,243	52,035					(912,336)		275,889
60	275,889	53,596					(948,829)		342,665
TOTAL	43,173	21,564	(656,053)			(656,053)	(3,077,430)		

Let's go back to the parent information and take out the annual savings. Let's assume that the parents have $500,000 of assets today.

If the parents had $500,000 today, it would have grown to $1,396,000 by age sixty-five. But instead, we took $656,000 out for cumulative tuition checks.

The impact of paying $656,000 is that we lost $1,109,996 because of the time value of money.

I think this calculator really helps us understand the idea of opportunity cost. It's hard for people to take a number and say, let's add an opportunity cost by compounding its rate. It is real money, but to most people they see it as some kind of phantom money because you don't have the money to work with.

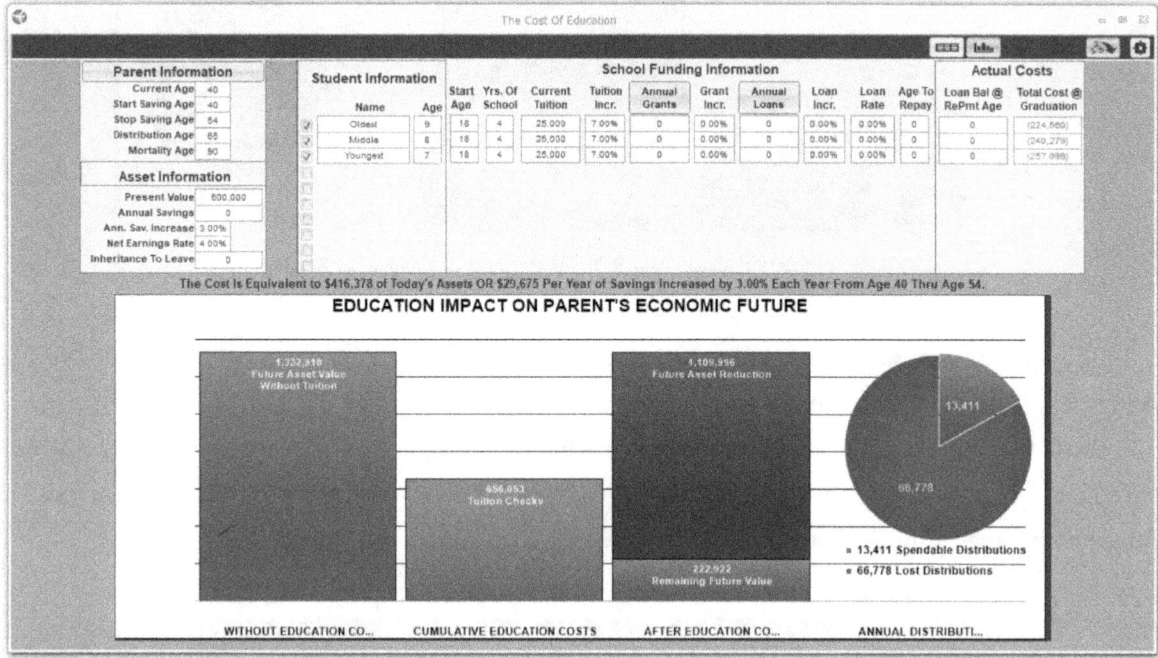

You may be feeling good about how you're committed to taking care of your kids' schooling. That $1.5 million retirement account will end up as $231,000.

Unfortunately, we got into this locked idea that age eighteen means we go to college. There's a huge maturity gap that happens from eighteen to twenty, and if you can send them somewhere else (like on a mission, a service trip, or to the workforce), they will be more ready for the next step. Not everyone lives the way you do at home. That time away can change the entire trajectory of what they want to do with their life. There are so many experiences that can be chosen at this time of life other than college that may benefit your children—and your finances—even more.

Best Uses: This calculator is best used to show parents and high schoolers the impact and opportunity cost of paying for college over time.

Calculator 13: Funding Illustration

There are no deals in the insurance industry, everything is a trade-off. Less risk to them = more risk to client and vice versa.

Purpose: The Funding Illustration calculator allows the user to compare life insurance illustrations (with or without loans) to an alternate savings account with identical cash flows.

Why It Was Created: This is the calculator we use to measure the efficiency of whole life insurance. This calculator shows the whole truth around the growth of cash value after taking into account taxes, fees, and the cost of the death benefit, to show the effective rate of return.

When we made this calculator, instead of the typical approach of "buy term and invest the difference compared to whole life," we chose to acknowledge that both term life insurance (the kind that is protection only) and whole life insurance (the kind that builds an asset) have a place in most family's finances. We recommend utilizing Human Life Value, which is the maximum amount of any type of life insurance a company would approve on a person.

Traditional rules of thumb for Human Life Value are:

- Fifteen to thirty times income for individuals who are working,
- 50% of that for spouses who are not working,
- 25% of that for children, and
- One times gross worth (or one x assets) for wealthier families.

Identifying Human Life Value is more helpful than many "needs analysis" approaches often found in the life insurance industry because it treats each person as a value creator in the family's life and replaces that value upon death. This is truly what "insurance" of any type should do, replace the value of what got lost.

This calculator provides a view of the asset known as Whole Life and compares it to similar assets like checking and savings accounts, money markets, and CDs. It demonstrates the equivalent yield that needs to be earned on another liquid asset after taxes and fees are paid.

So often, personal finance decisions are done in a vacuum, and strategists don't look at the ripples from each decision. We live in a finite economy; every decision made will impact every other decision. For example, when you become aware that whole life insurance cash value currently grows at about 4%, you think you could earn that on your high-yield savings account. Yet you forget the ripple effect of taxes and term insurance costs on your savings account. This calculator enables you to take all of that into consideration.

Case Study:

We will start with a thirty-five-year-old and look out thirty-five years into the future.

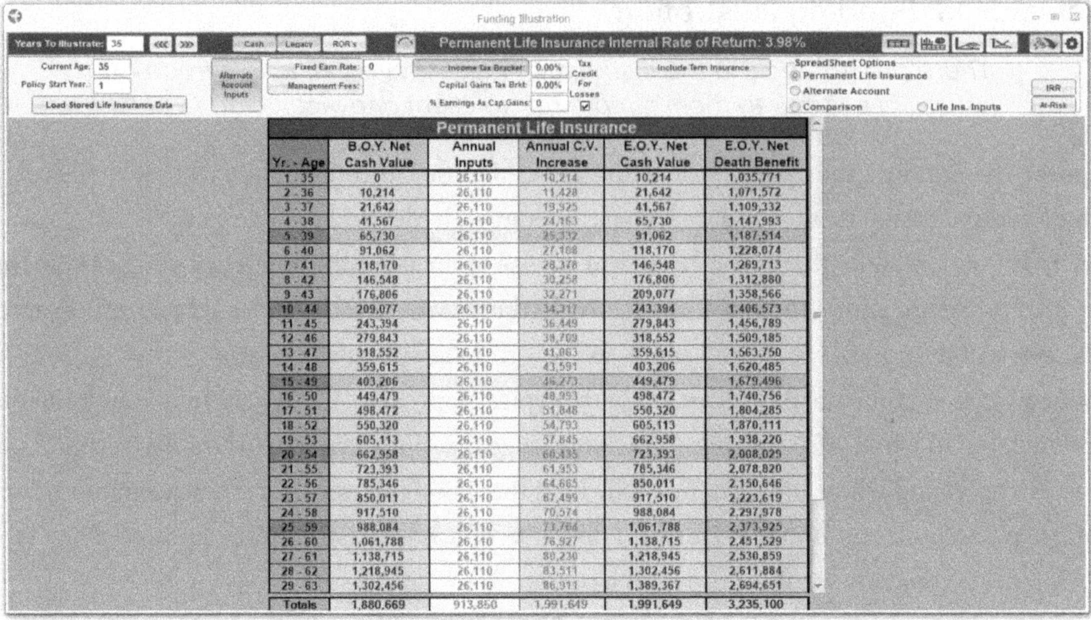

Permanent Life Insurance Internal Rate of Return: 3.98%

Permanent Life Insurance

Yr. - Age	B.O.Y. Net Cash Value	Annual Inputs	Annual C.V. Increase	E.O.Y. Net Cash Value	E.O.Y. Net Death Benefit
1 - 35	0	26,110	10,214	10,214	1,035,771
2 - 36	10,214	26,110	11,428	21,642	1,071,572
3 - 37	21,642	26,110	19,925	41,567	1,109,332
4 - 38	41,567	26,110	24,163	65,730	1,147,993
5 - 39	65,730	26,110	25,332	91,062	1,187,514
6 - 40	91,062	26,110	27,108	118,170	1,228,074
7 - 41	118,170	26,110	28,378	146,548	1,269,713
8 - 42	146,548	26,110	30,258	176,806	1,312,880
9 - 43	176,806	26,110	32,271	209,077	1,358,566
10 - 44	209,077	26,110	34,317	243,394	1,406,573
11 - 45	243,394	26,110	36,449	279,843	1,456,789
12 - 46	279,843	26,110	38,709	318,552	1,509,185
13 - 47	318,552	26,110	41,063	359,615	1,563,750
14 - 48	359,615	26,110	43,591	403,206	1,620,485
15 - 49	403,206	26,110	46,273	449,479	1,679,496
16 - 50	449,479	26,110	48,993	498,472	1,740,756
17 - 51	498,472	26,110	51,848	550,320	1,804,285
18 - 52	550,320	26,110	54,793	605,113	1,870,111
19 - 53	605,113	26,110	57,845	662,958	1,938,220
20 - 54	662,958	26,110	60,435	723,393	2,008,029
21 - 55	723,393	26,110	61,953	785,346	2,078,820
22 - 56	785,346	26,110	64,665	850,011	2,150,646
23 - 57	850,011	26,110	67,499	917,510	2,223,619
24 - 58	917,510	26,110	70,574	988,084	2,297,978
25 - 59	988,084	26,110	73,704	1,061,788	2,373,925
26 - 60	1,061,788	26,110	76,927	1,138,715	2,451,529
27 - 61	1,138,715	26,110	80,230	1,218,945	2,530,859
28 - 62	1,218,945	26,110	83,511	1,302,456	2,611,884
29 - 63	1,302,456	26,110	86,911	1,389,367	2,694,651
Totals	1,880,669	913,850	1,991,649	1,991,649	3,235,100

As you can see above, the Funding Illustration has had a life insurance illustration pasted into the Inputs, Cash Value, and Death Benefit columns. These came from the Life Insurance Values tool. (See Chapter 6.)

You'll notice the top line that states Permanent Life Insurance Internal Rate of Return is 3.98% (which will exactly match the thirty-fifth year of the IRR column on the life insurance values tool).

Now, because of the way people have been conditioned by the media and other places, 3.98% is not going to be exciting. **This is where the difference between the numbers by themselves and the numbers put into context is very important.**

It is important to understand that 3.98% is a phenomenal rate for a safe, liquid asset. What kind of assets are safe and liquid? Basically, checking accounts, cash, money markets, and savings. Are any of those anywhere close to earning 3.98% after taxes and any fees? *No*!

Now what's interesting is the way life insurance companies present their numbers on their websites: all as gross dividends. The Funding calculator presents the net, net, net. This 3.98% is net of taxes, fees, and the cost of the death benefit.

What does that mean? Well, we want to compare this against one of those assets above, like a savings account or checking account, money market, etc. When we have to pay tax annually on the growth of savings accounts, it makes a big difference. We hear the annual gross return, that's before tax on those other accounts.

So, to compare it to a savings account, we'll put in a 24% tax bracket.

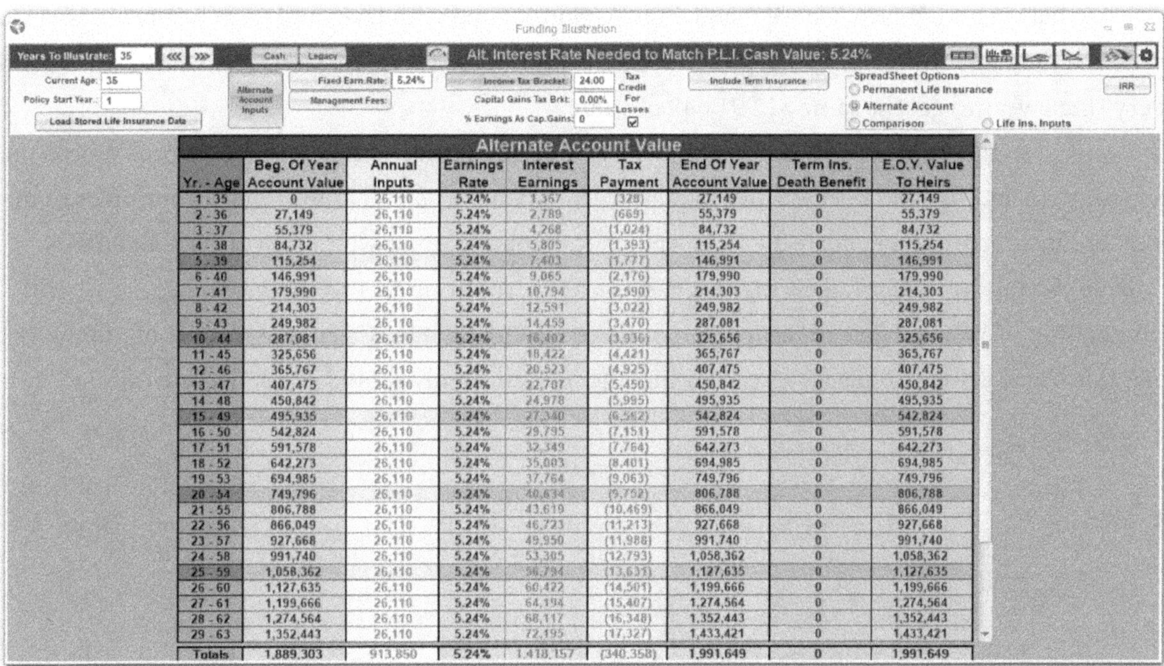

Alt. Interest Rate Needed to Match P.L.I. Cash Value: 5.24%

Years To Illustrate: 35 · Current Age: 35 · Policy Start Year: 1 · Fixed Earn Rate: 5.24% · Income Tax Bracket: 24.00 · Capital Gains Tax Brkt: 0.00% · % Earnings As Cap.Gains: 0

Alternate Account Value

Yr. - Age	Beg. Of Year Account Value	Annual Inputs	Earnings Rate	Interest Earnings	Tax Payment	End Of Year Account Value	Term Ins. Death Benefit	E.O.Y. Value To Heirs
1 - 35	0	26,110	5.24%	1,367	(328)	27,149	0	27,149
2 - 36	27,149	26,110	5.24%	2,789	(669)	55,379	0	55,379
3 - 37	55,379	26,110	5.24%	4,268	(1,024)	84,732	0	84,732
4 - 38	84,732	26,110	5.24%	5,805	(1,393)	115,254	0	115,254
5 - 39	115,254	26,110	5.24%	7,403	(1,777)	146,991	0	146,991
6 - 40	146,991	26,110	5.24%	9,065	(2,176)	179,990	0	179,990
7 - 41	179,990	26,110	5.24%	10,794	(2,590)	214,303	0	214,303
8 - 42	214,303	26,110	5.24%	12,591	(3,022)	249,982	0	249,982
9 - 43	249,982	26,110	5.24%	14,459	(3,470)	287,081	0	287,081
10 - 44	287,081	26,110	5.24%	16,402	(3,936)	325,656	0	325,656
11 - 45	325,656	26,110	5.24%	18,422	(4,421)	365,767	0	365,767
12 - 46	365,767	26,110	5.24%	20,523	(4,925)	407,475	0	407,475
13 - 47	407,475	26,110	5.24%	22,707	(5,450)	450,842	0	450,842
14 - 48	450,842	26,110	5.24%	24,978	(5,995)	495,935	0	495,935
15 - 49	495,935	26,110	5.24%	27,340	(6,562)	542,824	0	542,824
16 - 50	542,824	26,110	5.24%	29,795	(7,151)	591,578	0	591,578
17 - 51	591,578	26,110	5.24%	32,349	(7,764)	642,273	0	642,273
18 - 52	642,273	26,110	5.24%	35,003	(8,401)	694,985	0	694,985
19 - 53	694,985	26,110	5.24%	37,764	(9,063)	749,796	0	749,796
20 - 54	749,796	26,110	5.24%	40,634	(9,752)	806,788	0	806,788
21 - 55	806,788	26,110	5.24%	43,619	(10,469)	866,049	0	866,049
22 - 56	866,049	26,110	5.24%	46,723	(11,213)	927,668	0	927,668
23 - 57	927,668	26,110	5.24%	49,950	(11,988)	991,740	0	991,740
24 - 58	991,740	26,110	5.24%	53,305	(12,793)	1,058,362	0	1,058,362
25 - 59	1,058,362	26,110	5.24%	56,794	(13,631)	1,127,635	0	1,127,635
26 - 60	1,127,635	26,110	5.24%	60,422	(14,501)	1,199,666	0	1,199,666
27 - 61	1,199,666	26,110	5.24%	64,194	(15,407)	1,274,564	0	1,274,564
28 - 62	1,274,564	26,110	5.24%	68,117	(16,348)	1,352,443	0	1,352,443
29 - 63	1,352,443	26,110	5.24%	72,195	(17,327)	1,433,421	0	1,433,421
Totals	1,889,303	913,850	5.24%	1,418,157	(340,358)	1,991,649	0	1,991,649

Now look at what that did to the rate of return. It would have to earn 5.24% every single year and be able to pay the tax annually, and end up with $1,991,649, the same amount of cash shown before.

If I want to provide the same protection for my family in the event of an unlikely early demise, how would I do that with my CD, checking account, or money market? I would buy term insurance, so let's include that.

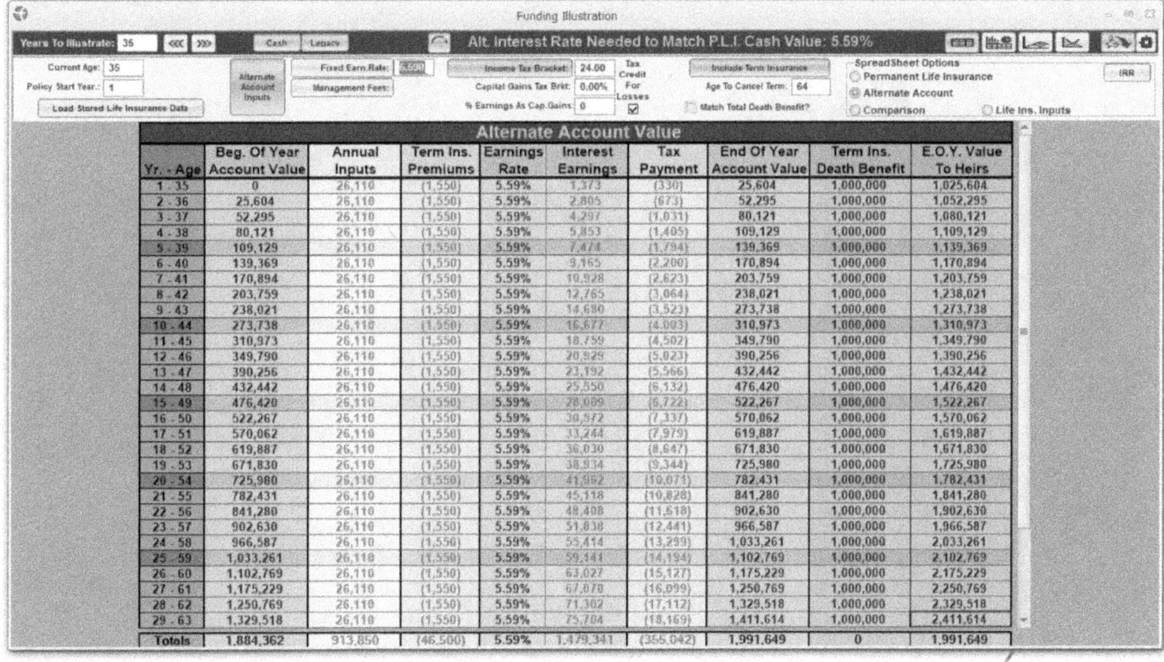

Alt. Interest Rate Needed to Match P.L.I. Cash Value: 5.59%

Years To Illustrate: 35 · Current Age: 35 · Policy Start Year: 1 · Fixed Earn Rate: 5.59% · Income Tax Bracket: 24.00 · Capital Gains Tax Brkt: 0.00% · % Earnings As Cap.Gains: 0 · Include Term Insurance · Age To Cancel Term: 64

Alternate Account Value

Yr. - Age	Beg. Of Year Account Value	Annual Inputs	Term Ins. Premiums	Earnings Rate	Interest Earnings	Tax Payment	End Of Year Account Value	Term Ins. Death Benefit	E.O.Y. Value To Heirs
1 - 35	0	26,110	(1,550)	5.59%	1,373	(330)	25,604	1,000,000	1,025,604
2 - 36	25,604	26,110	(1,550)	5.59%	2,805	(673)	52,295	1,000,000	1,052,295
3 - 37	52,295	26,110	(1,550)	5.59%	4,297	(1,031)	80,121	1,000,000	1,080,121
4 - 38	80,121	26,110	(1,550)	5.59%	5,853	(1,405)	109,129	1,000,000	1,109,129
5 - 39	109,129	26,110	(1,550)	5.59%	7,474	(1,794)	139,369	1,000,000	1,139,369
6 - 40	139,369	26,110	(1,550)	5.59%	9,165	(2,200)	170,894	1,000,000	1,170,894
7 - 41	170,894	26,110	(1,550)	5.59%	10,928	(2,623)	203,759	1,000,000	1,203,759
8 - 42	203,759	26,110	(1,550)	5.59%	12,765	(3,064)	238,021	1,000,000	1,238,021
9 - 43	238,021	26,110	(1,550)	5.59%	14,680	(3,523)	273,738	1,000,000	1,273,738
10 - 44	273,738	26,110	(1,550)	5.59%	16,677	(4,003)	310,973	1,000,000	1,310,973
11 - 45	310,973	26,110	(1,550)	5.59%	18,759	(4,502)	349,790	1,000,000	1,349,790
12 - 46	349,790	26,110	(1,550)	5.59%	20,929	(5,023)	390,256	1,000,000	1,390,256
13 - 47	390,256	26,110	(1,550)	5.59%	23,192	(5,566)	432,442	1,000,000	1,432,442
14 - 48	432,442	26,110	(1,550)	5.59%	25,550	(6,132)	476,420	1,000,000	1,476,420
15 - 49	476,420	26,110	(1,550)	5.59%	28,009	(6,722)	522,267	1,000,000	1,522,267
16 - 50	522,267	26,110	(1,550)	5.59%	30,572	(7,337)	570,062	1,000,000	1,570,062
17 - 51	570,062	26,110	(1,550)	5.59%	33,244	(7,979)	619,887	1,000,000	1,619,887
18 - 52	619,887	26,110	(1,550)	5.59%	36,030	(8,647)	671,830	1,000,000	1,671,830
19 - 53	671,830	26,110	(1,550)	5.59%	38,934	(9,344)	725,980	1,000,000	1,725,980
20 - 54	725,980	26,110	(1,550)	5.59%	41,962	(10,071)	782,431	1,000,000	1,782,431
21 - 55	782,431	26,110	(1,550)	5.59%	45,118	(10,828)	841,280	1,000,000	1,841,280
22 - 56	841,280	26,110	(1,550)	5.59%	48,408	(11,618)	902,630	1,000,000	1,902,630
23 - 57	902,630	26,110	(1,550)	5.59%	51,838	(12,441)	966,587	1,000,000	1,966,587
24 - 58	966,587	26,110	(1,550)	5.59%	55,414	(13,299)	1,033,261	1,000,000	2,033,261
25 - 59	1,033,261	26,110	(1,550)	5.59%	59,141	(14,194)	1,102,769	1,000,000	2,102,769
26 - 60	1,102,769	26,110	(1,550)	5.59%	63,027	(15,127)	1,175,229	1,000,000	2,175,229
27 - 61	1,175,229	26,110	(1,550)	5.59%	67,078	(16,099)	1,250,769	1,000,000	2,250,769
28 - 62	1,250,769	26,110	(1,550)	5.59%	71,302	(17,112)	1,329,518	1,000,000	2,329,518
29 - 63	1,329,518	26,110	(1,550)	5.59%	75,704	(18,169)	1,411,614	1,000,000	2,411,614
Totals	1,884,362	913,850	(46,500)	5.59%	1,479,341	(355,042)	1,991,649	0	1,991,649

Now that we have this in, we see the savings account paired with taxes and term insurance because that is the only way to truly get an apples to apples comparison. It proves we would have to earn 5.59% every single year to get the same $1,991,649 of value.

Best Uses: This calculator is best used to look at all the pieces of the decision to buy Whole Life Insurance, including both the cash value and the death benefit, as well as the long-term ripples of that decision. It compares them correctly in an apples-to-apples manner when considering all factors.

Note: We always recommend income earners are insured up to their Human Life Value with a combination of Whole Life and term insurance. See Calculator #16, Cash Flow, for proof of how Human Life Value actually replaces a person's income to their family should death occur early.

Chapter 5: The Calculators—Part Two

Eliminate "government" from our vocabulary and replace it with "taxpayers."

In this chapter, we'll continue exploring each of the calculators I've created—why I created them, case studies that demonstrate how they work, and the best uses for each. But first, I thought I'd share a bit about my process of developing a new calculator.

DEVELOPING NEW CALCULATORS

The beauty of being the creator of these calculators is that I can see the gaps when something is missing. I listen closely to strategists and clients, and I do my own research and calculations daily. In this process, I occasionally come across an idea for a new calculator that goes beyond evolving a current one.

As of the writing of this book, I'm working on a new calculator on debt that involves debunking myths and getting to the truth (just as all my calculators do). As you may have read in the previous chapter under the calculator for Automobile Purchases, I am passionate about clients understanding the numbers around debt so they know when debt can help them and when it can hurt them. This new calculator will help them do just that. I'm excited to share it once it's fully released. You can stay up-to-date on our latest calculators at TruthConcepts.com.

Developing new calculators is both exciting and grueling for me. I can see their potential for helping more clients and strategists, and to fulfill that potential I go through a rigorous process of testing and tweaking them to make sure they do the calculations correctly. I also put them through third-party testing to ensure they are easy to use. Each of the remaining eight calculators below were developed and tested by me this same way, and they stand the test of time.

WHY THE CALCULATORS WERE CREATED AND THEIR BEST USES—PART 2

The best question in the world is, "Compared to what?"
Thanks go to Daniel Pink.

Calculator 14: Real Estate Analysis

Purpose: The Real Estate Analysis calculator does in-depth real estate calculations and analysis for any real estate investment, allowing you to show the actual rate of return a property is earning.

Why It Was Created: Just before this version of my financial software was created, back in 2008, I was working directly with clients along with my wife, Kim Butler, and colleague, John Baker. A majority of those clients were entrepreneurs in Arizona, where there was a hot real estate market at the time. Yet they had no way of knowing if they were actually making money on their real estate investments. They would say things like, "I don't know . . . we've had this property for a while, but we can't tell if we're making money on it or not." I created a calculator specifically for this client group so they could see their positive or negative rate of return.

Case Study: One of our clients called in at one point and said, "I'm in the middle of buying a new piece of real estate, but I don't know exactly what that rate of return will be. And secondly, will it make sense for me to borrow money at 8% from the life insurance company?" At that point, I modified the calculator and went through the exercise; it was an eye-opener how much it improved his rate of return by borrowing against his life insurance for the down payment. It increased his rate of return from 25% to close to 100%! This was because he didn't directly have any money in the deal; it was the insurance company's money. He basically had the real estate for free (or the closest thing to free).

Since then, the Real Estate Analysis calculator has helped a lot of real estate investors make decisions. It's all about the differential between the rates. You have to see what each property is doing on an Annual IRR (Internal Rate of Return) basis in order to compare them to any other investment you could have your money invested in.

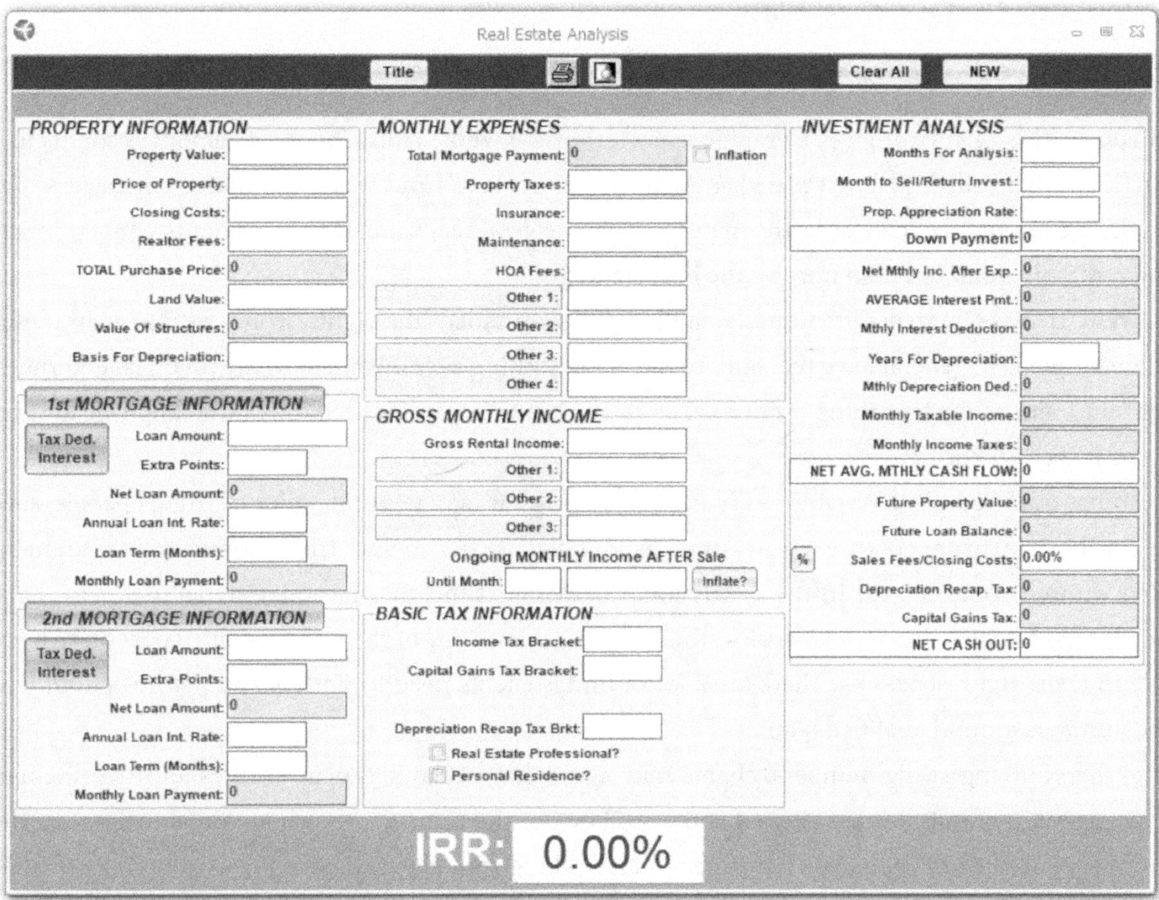

Robert Kiyosaki says your home is a liability. In my Truth Concepts class, which we call Truth Training, I talk people through why that is. We have the option in the calculator to analyze our home as a personal residence. Kiyosaki leaves out a key calculation: when it's your personal residence, you get an investment *and* a place to live. If you don't buy the house, then you have to pay rent. The rent you would pay for that same house would typically cost you more than the monthly mortgage payment if you were to buy that piece of property. When you put that in the equation, you can see a decent rate of return on the home. When you enter a home purchase without those details, Kiyosaki is right—it doesn't have a great rate of return.

Most people like the idea of real estate investing. With all things considered: costs, tax advantages, etc., this calculator gives you the facts. Is this a good deal or not? We encourage clients to plug their numbers in there to ensure their real estate deal makes sense. The other advantage to this calculator is that it causes people to ask questions they should be asking and maybe haven't yet when investing in real estate, such as: What are the taxes on this piece of property and the cost of maintenance?

Best Uses: This calculator is best used when determining if a real estate investment (and all the math surrounding it) will have a positive or negative rate of return.

Calculator 15: Qualified Plan

Federal Income tax deferral is actually a tax lien at an unknown rate.

Purpose: This calculator gives a graphic overview of the whole truth about retirement accounts like 401(k)s (often called qualified plans). It includes the costs to fund them, the management fees that erode them, and how ineffective the match and tax deferral really are. **It shows clients why *not* maxing out their qualified plan may be the best strategy.**

Why It Was Created: Oftentimes, qualified plans are called "the eighth wonder of the world." Retirement plans in general have that aura of the greatest thing ever invented. Many financial entertainers tout them as the best thing ever because it's all about "tax savings." Some of the language around it, however, is incorrect.

What qualified plans provide really isn't tax savings; it's tax deferral. A lot of things people have heard about them are not true. I warn strategists: *do not* use this to undermine somebody's retirement plan without some context in the discussion. That context includes facts like: Qualified plans have terrible usage due to the liquidity rules around them, and it's one of the worst assets to pass on to heirs due to taxes and restrictions. There are a lot of things clients need to understand before getting into the numbers around qualified plans.

When looking at the numbers, clients may agree that a qualified plan violates all the principles we've agreed on, but they get excited and say, "Look at the return!" Yet when you actually plug the numbers into the calculator, you may find yourself asking your client, "Is it really worth tying up money you don't have access to when the return is 4-6%?" That's actually not a great return for having to lock money up for a long period of time.

It's all about the net return with this calculator. Everybody always looks at the gross return (like "I'm making 8% in the marketplace!"). But no, they're actually not making that after fees and taxes paid when exiting the retirement plan.

Case Study: I would recommend that you wait to be invited into this conversation with a client. If you say, "I'm showing you why your qualified plan is an awful thing to do," that person likely heard, "You're an awful person for choosing this." Or even worse, "Your spouse is awful for choosing it." **However, if someone says, "I really don't think my qualified plan is doing what I thought it was supposed to," then you can say, "Oh, would you like to see how that works?"** That's a different conversation.

For example, let's take a thirty-five-year-old now with a projected age of sixty-five. The Present Value is $100,000 with an earnings rate of 8%.

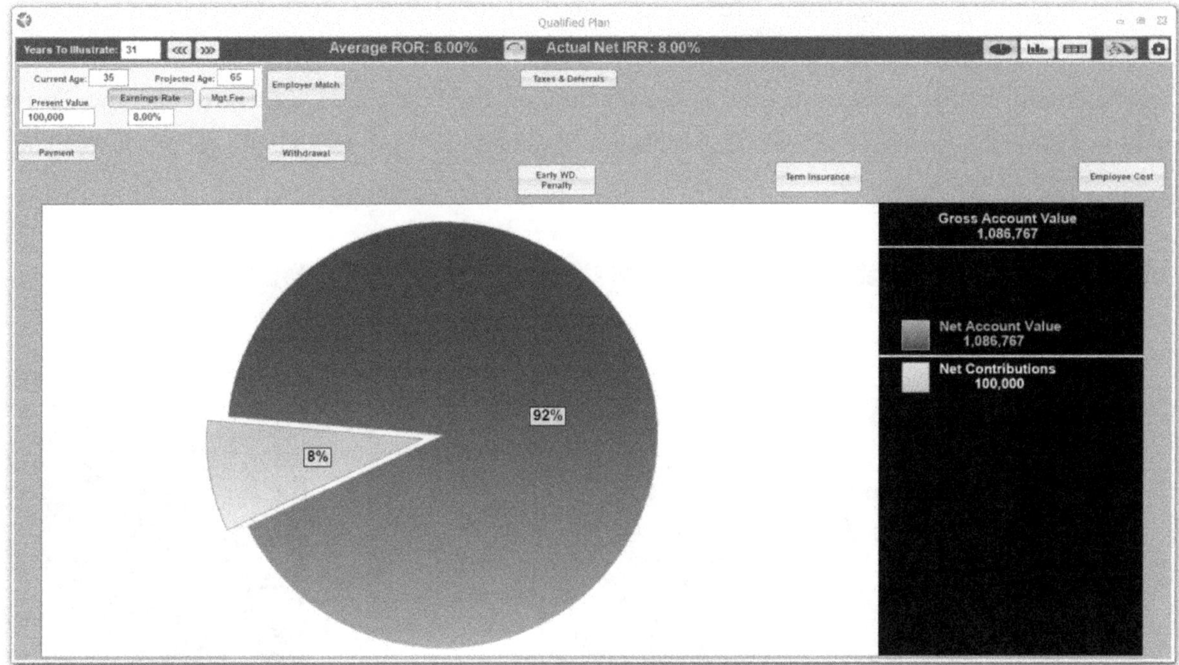

The 8% I'm including here is the gross rate in the marketplace before management fees. That's looking pretty good at a net account value of $1,086,767. And let's say the client is also putting in $19,500 a year.

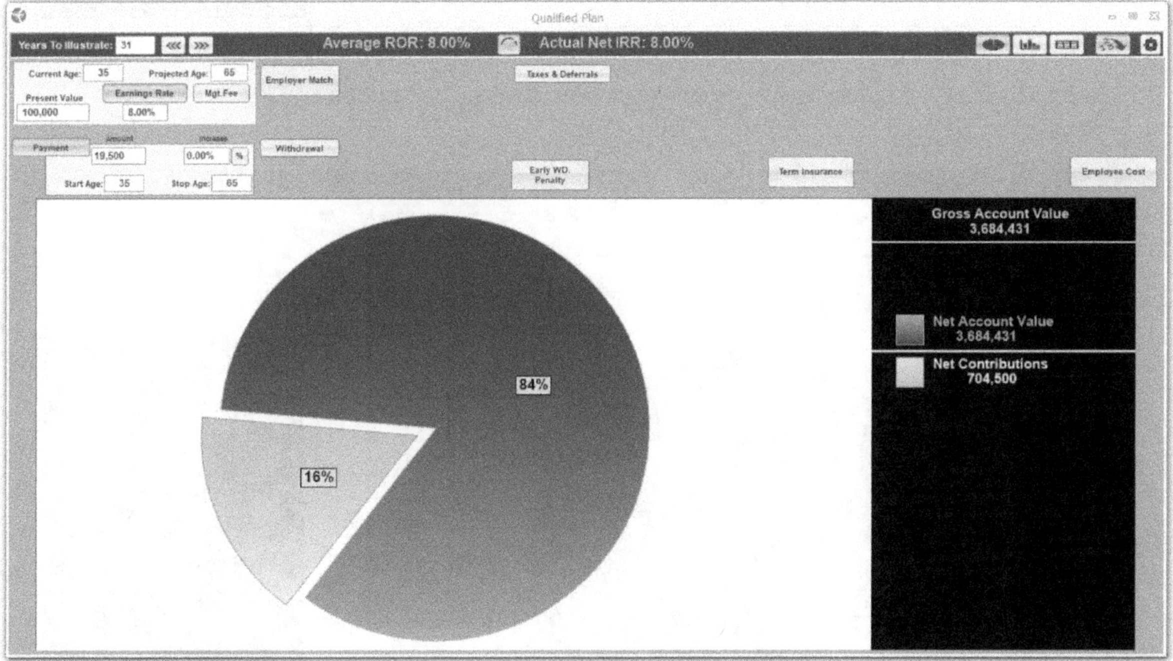

That bumps the Gross Account Value up to $3,684,431 over this time frame. Are there any other reasons why you like this qualified money besides this phenomenal return?

They might say, "I can get some free money from the federal government, and my employer gives me a 50% match."

The employer match, let's say, is 50%, but it's 50% on the first 2% of your gross income. You're making $150,000 a year. In the Max. Contribution Matched box I put in $3,000 (2% of the $150,000 income).

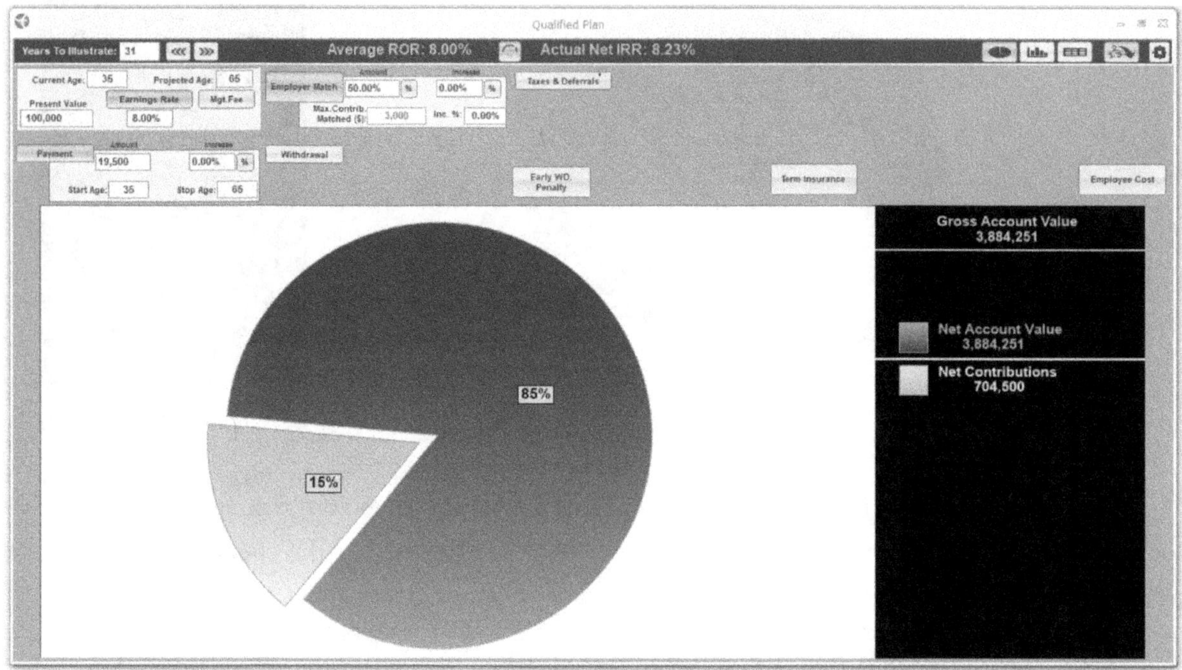

Now let's look at the federal government's portion. Let's go to tax deferral.

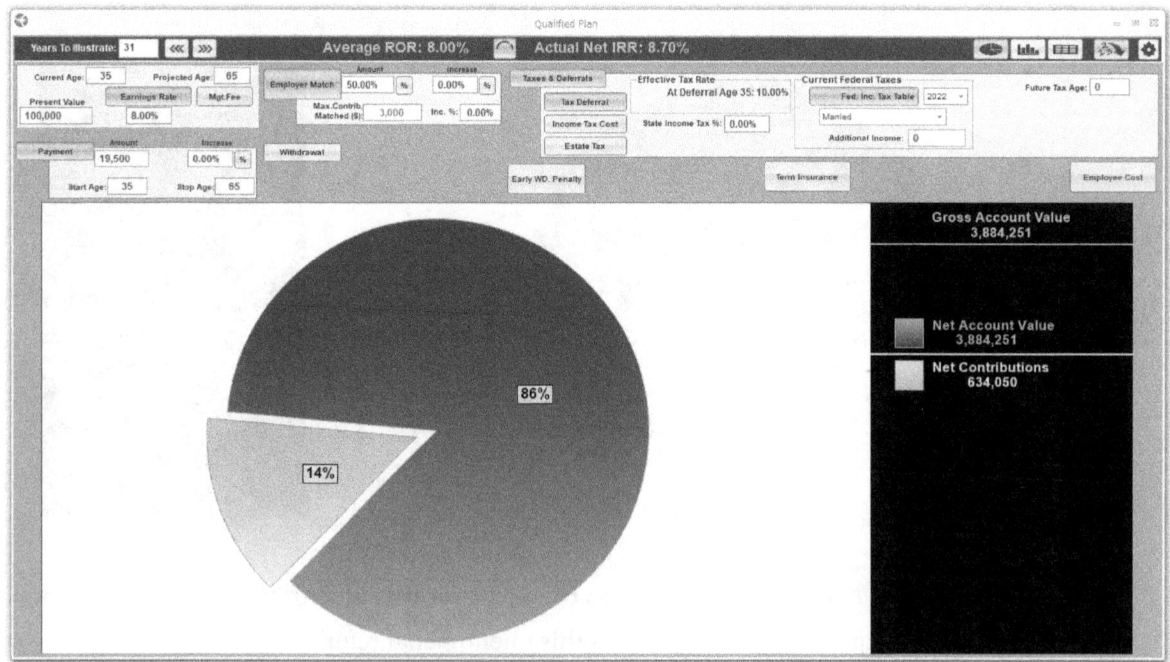

We'll use the federal income tax table now. As you'll see in the next chapter, we can only impact tax rates on the highest marginal rate for that family. Tax rates are all on last dollars earned, but the only way we can impact somebody's income is by increasing their taxable income or increasing their deductions. We can't take these deductions out in the middle or the bottom of the tax bracket; the deferral happens at the maximum marginal rate, where the last dollars are earned.

Let's say they have $30,000 worth of taxable deductions, not counting the deduction for the qualified plan, then their other taxable income is $120,000 (for a total of $150,000). So we're going to put $120,000 in the Addl. Income box. The calculator will tell us that it is at the 22% tax rate. That's where the deduction is.

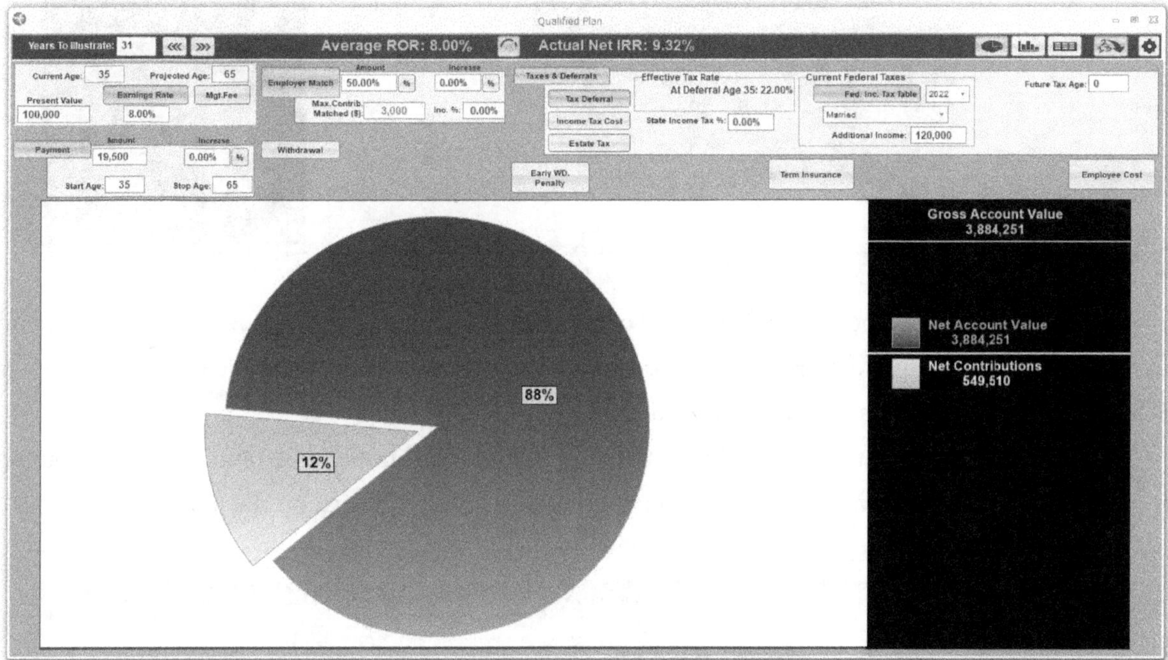

All we did was put that information in there, then we turned on the tax deferral, and looked at the difference it makes in gross account value.

We didn't have as much cost due to some of the money coming from the deduction and some from the match, so the rate of return went up to 9.32%, but the amount of money we have didn't change. We still only put $19,500 in there, and we still only have $3,884,251. **This is a huge surprise for most people, especially if they heard about a 50% match.**

Sometimes people say, "Well, I want to keep it in there because it's growing really well right now and the match is free money." You can empathise with that while still helping them consider the new money they are adding every year so they make the best decision for their family with the whole truth around this qualified plan.

Then let's add a management fee of 2%, which covers plan costs as well.

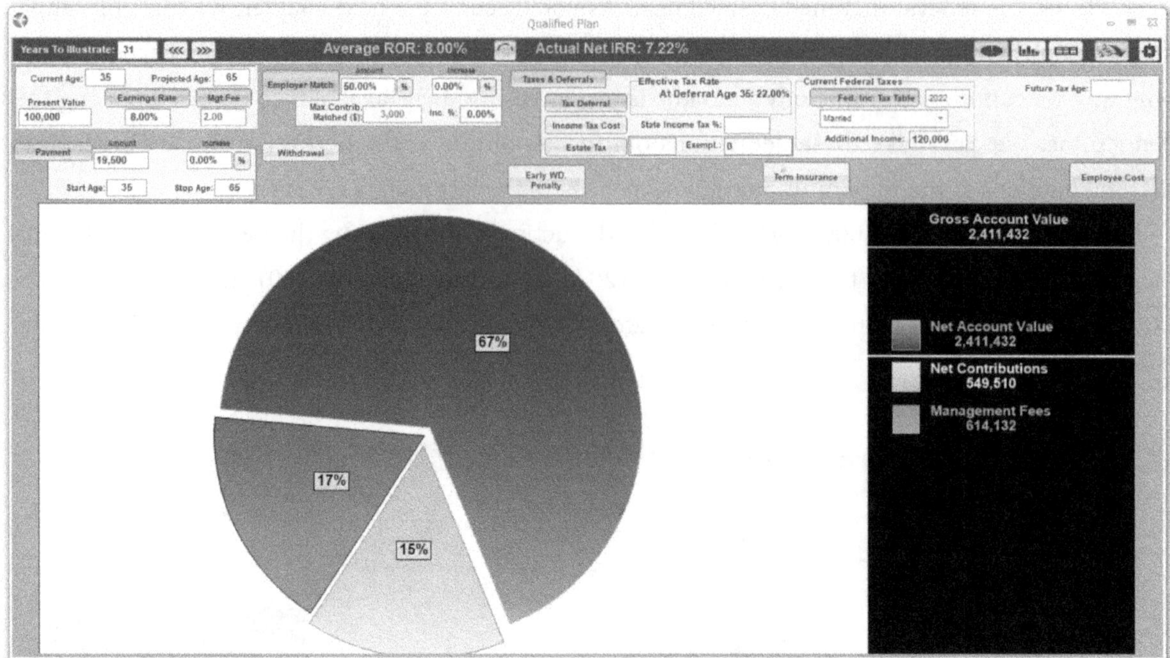

The fee alone, just two points, took away all of the benefits we got from the federal government and our employer. How do I know that? Because our rate of return is now 7.22%; it's below the 8% that we were getting from the gross earnings on the account.

And what about taxes at the end? I know that your CPA would not let you take this money out all in one lump sum. But we want to look at it on that basis first, so we'll turn on the tax cost.

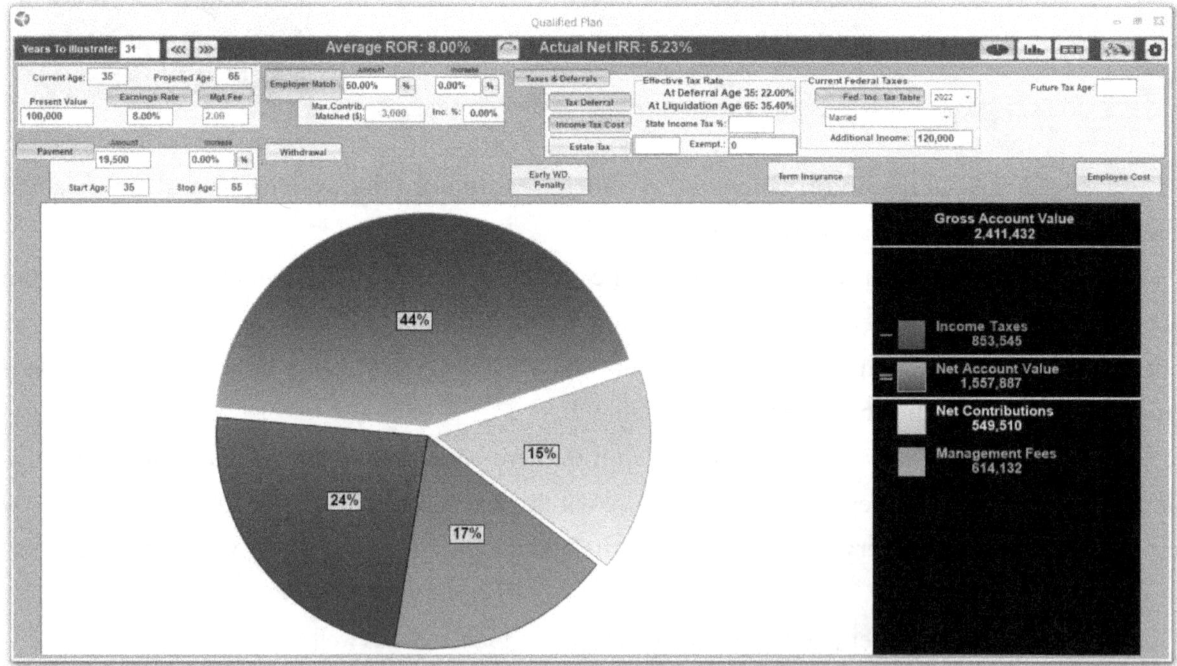

And when we turn on the tax cost, we see that there is $853,545 in tax if we were to liquidate at that point in time, which brings us to a 5.23% rate of return.

Now, to understand how that works, I need a basic calculator. Let's see what the federal government's investment was because, really, if you think about it, the federal government did without tax on this account for thirty-one years. Age thirty-five to sixty-five is thirty-one years in total.

Thirty-one years to get $853,000. Did they give up money? Or did they invest that stream to get $853,000?

What we're told is, we get to earn money on the federal government's money. Right?

Basically, the federal government gave up a cumulative $154,990 in tax revenue over thirty-one years in order to get $853,000 in tax revenue. **Looks to me like the federal government earned money on the "free" money they gave to the client.**

This is exactly the opposite of what we think or what we're often told about qualified plans and the federal government's rate of return. If the present value is $22,000, and payment is $19,500 x .22 (the tax bracket), it took $4,290 for thirty-one years, plus $22,000 previously deferred on the existing $100,000 in the account (what was a total of $154,990), to get $853,000.

The federal government made 8.23%! And that's net, because the federal government doesn't have to pay taxes on the earnings!

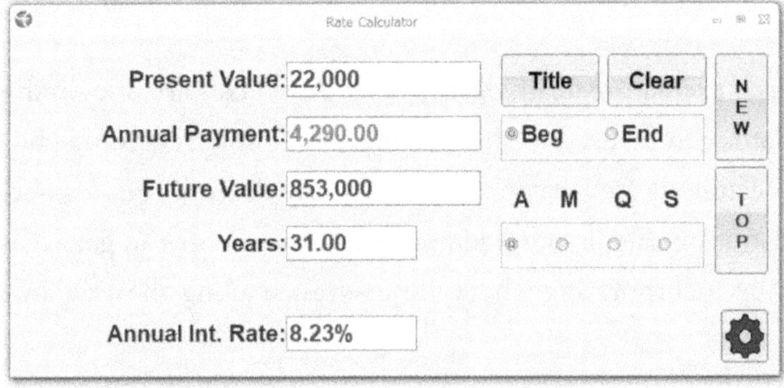

It is illegal for the federal government to invest in the stock market, but through 401(k)s and 403(b)s, that is exactly what they're doing.

To take it a bit further, above is an 8% gross example. And at one point your client says they'd be thrilled if they got 6%.

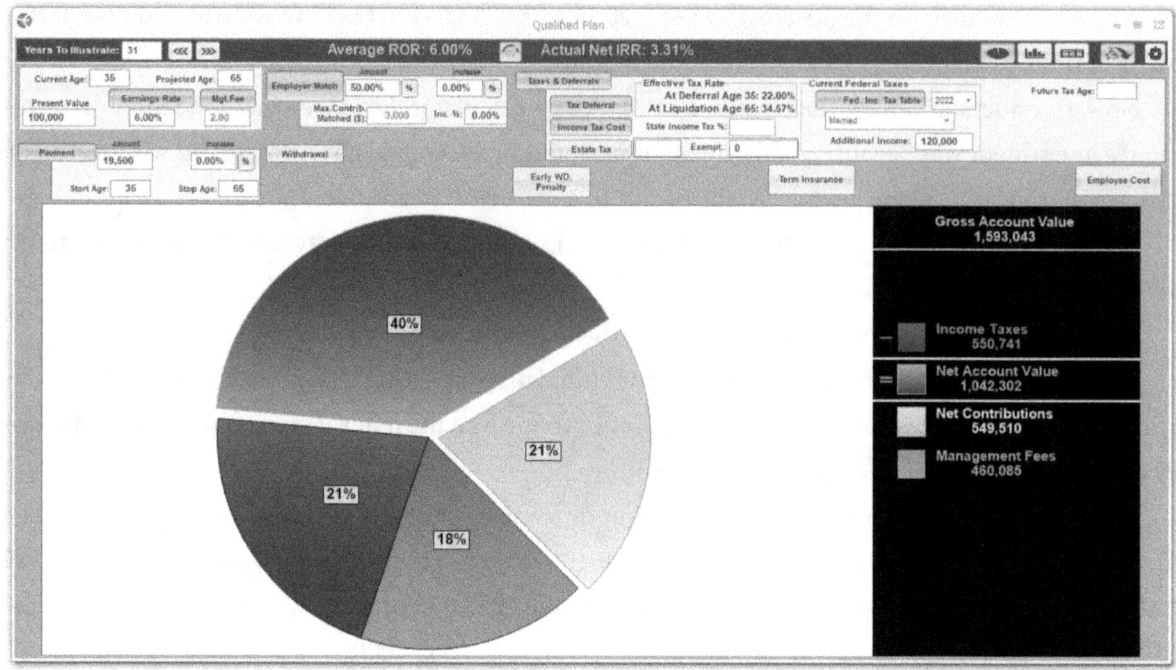

At 6% gross, after all facts fully considered as above, that's actually a 3.31% rate of return.

With a qualified plan, you're going to lock up money for thirty years minimum to get a whopping 3.31% rate of return?

And what happens if premature death occurs here? And taxes are due on this qualified plan? The Qualified Plan calculator can be used to show clients even more regarding choices around term life insurance, often the default choice for concerns of an early death. It can also be used in conjunction with the Funding Illustration calculator to demonstrate how clients can get access to cash and reduce exposure to taxation by incorporating whole life insurance along the way, in addition to the term insurance.

Best Uses: This calculator provides a way to show clients that taking the money they are putting in a qualified plan that is not matched, paying the tax on it, and putting it in a life insurance policy will give them more liquidity, a death benefit, and a return that is better than a qualified plan, as long as the conversation has context around it that includes economic principles so they can see the big picture. This is an example of a "Wealth Shift" from the list in the Appendix.

Calculator 16: Cash Flow

We all want to be right. If you're really seeking Truth,
you have to be willing to be wrong.

Purpose: The Cash Flow calculator provides for up to three different and varying payment and withdrawal streams with varying annual earnings rates. It can show an "average" versus "actual" rate of return (ROR), Human Life Value, Education Costs, and many other things.

Why It Was Created: This was an early calculator that shows what happens in an account with the ability to vary the inputs and outputs. In any year, you can change how much is going in, how much is coming out, and taxes. The Cash Flow calculator started fairly simple and now can show in-depth numbers in tandem with Currence, a cash flow control structure. For example, **it can prove that with Currence, you could capture money that is otherwise being spent unconsciously.**

It helps clients explore: What happens if we put some money in this account? Pull some money out there? In a year, you can show what the returns are, vary them, and add taxes, so you can project your cash flow.

I use this calculator a lot. While it doesn't have everything possible (like the Accumulation calculator does), it's simpler and often covers what needs to be covered, without confusing things with extra detail. We've used it for calculating education costs as well, before we had a dedicated calculator for that. It's like a full financial calculator with all of the elements displayed.

In a way, it's also like a Future Value calculator because it can vary all rates, inputs, outputs, and show the results. However, over time we've learned that sometimes it's better to cover something simply without a whole bunch of extraneous inputs. This is the same reason I might go back and use one of the five basic calculators (which you'll see demonstrated below in the Case Study).

Case Study:

If you are a consumer, or client, you want to know what your Human Life Value is. There are rules of thumb in the life insurance industry, and this calculator enables us to prove out those rules of thumb numerically.

As a strategist, do you offer to insure your clients for Human Life Value? If so, you probably help people buy term insurance in addition to Whole Life, so that the death benefit is close to the client's Human Life Value. If you are not, I see it creating a problem of liability for the life insurance agent, because whether you do a certain strategy or not, or are just focused on creating money on the side, in your client's mind, you are their life insurance professional.

Is term insurance good or bad?

Term insurance is what it is. Like anything, it can be used in the wrong strategy, and then that's bad. It's not the term insurance that's bad though, it's the strategy. And short term, term insurance is a great tool when used the right way.

So, where does this number on Human Life Value come from? That's a very difficult thing for people to wrap their head around. We're used to rules from the insurance companies of thirty times income for younger people or ten times income for older people. Or one times gross worth for wealthy people.

There are actuarial numbers used to determine those generalizations above. We can use them to calculate how much somebody could have in death benefit. **What I will tell you is the insurance companies are not going to insure you for more than you're worth**. So what the insurance company thinks you're worth is your economic human life value, but it's difficult for somebody who makes

$150,000 to see a need for $3 million in death benefit at twenty times earnings.

They might say, "I don't want to leave him or her rich when I'm gone."

You cannot leave anybody rich with life insurance; the best you can hope to do is replace the income of the deceased, and only if they don't expect any substantial raises along the way.

What if we are able to see what the numbers look like, and put that in perspective for clients so they understand how human life value works?

This is where the Cash Flow calculator comes in. Let's start by taking a thirty-five-year-old out thirty years to age sixty-four. I want to find out their net cash flow because I want to see what would happen if we took a lump sum and put it into an account, what it would take to pay out their income.

If they're making $150,000 gross income, the insurance company will typically allow them $3 million of death benefit. But let's see *what we actually have to replace in after-tax income.*

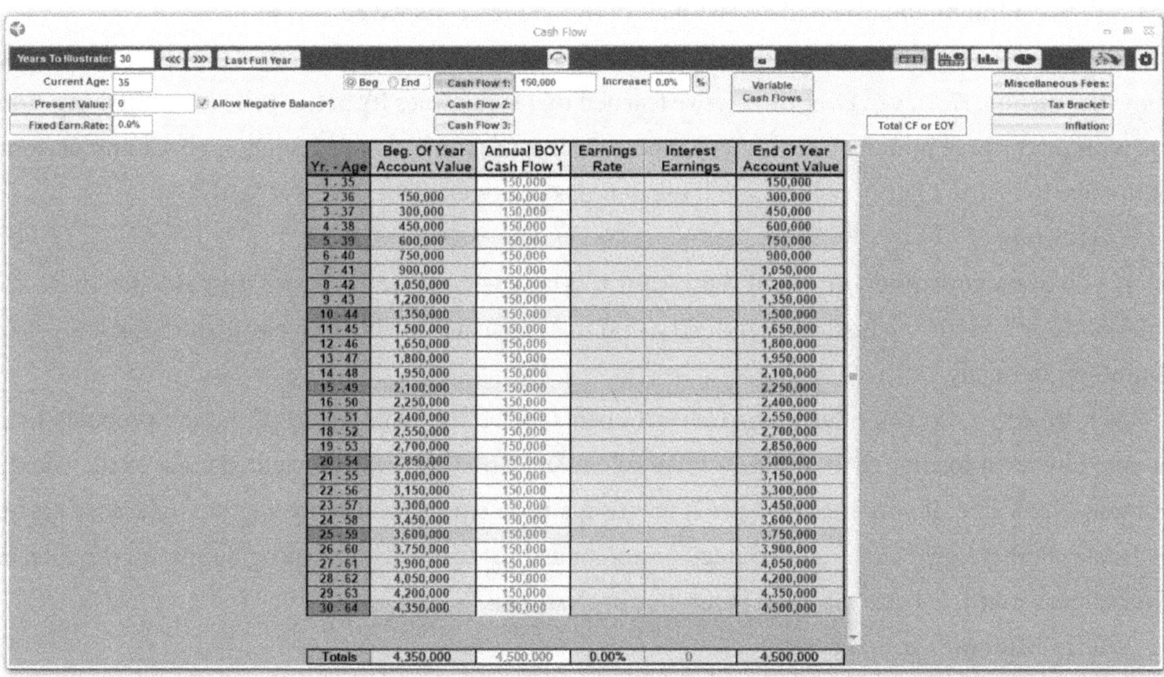

Yr. - Age	Beg. Of Year Account Value	Annual BOY Cash Flow 1	Earnings Rate	Interest Earnings	End of Year Account Value
1 - 35		150,000			150,000
2 - 36	150,000	150,000			300,000
3 - 37	300,000	150,000			450,000
4 - 38	450,000	150,000			600,000
5 - 39	600,000	150,000			750,000
6 - 40	750,000	150,000			900,000
7 - 41	900,000	150,000			1,050,000
8 - 42	1,050,000	150,000			1,200,000
9 - 43	1,200,000	150,000			1,350,000
10 - 44	1,350,000	150,000			1,500,000
11 - 45	1,500,000	150,000			1,650,000
12 - 46	1,650,000	150,000			1,800,000
13 - 47	1,800,000	150,000			1,950,000
14 - 48	1,950,000	150,000			2,100,000
15 - 49	2,100,000	150,000			2,250,000
16 - 50	2,250,000	150,000			2,400,000
17 - 51	2,400,000	150,000			2,550,000
18 - 52	2,550,000	150,000			2,700,000
19 - 53	2,700,000	150,000			2,850,000
20 - 54	2,850,000	150,000			3,000,000
21 - 55	3,000,000	150,000			3,150,000
22 - 56	3,150,000	150,000			3,300,000
23 - 57	3,300,000	150,000			3,450,000
24 - 58	3,450,000	150,000			3,600,000
25 - 59	3,600,000	150,000			3,750,000
26 - 60	3,750,000	150,000			3,900,000
27 - 61	3,900,000	150,000			4,050,000
28 - 62	4,050,000	150,000			4,200,000
29 - 63	4,200,000	150,000			4,350,000
30 - 64	4,350,000	150,000			4,500,000
Totals	4,350,000	4,500,000	0.00%	0	4,500,000

We will estimate it at $133,000 every year. Now, are they going to be happy with a level of $133,000 from now on? No, we expect at least a 3% or 4% raise. So we'll put 4% on the increase.

What we see is increasing income in the yellow column that we actually want to replace, starting at $133,000 and growing.

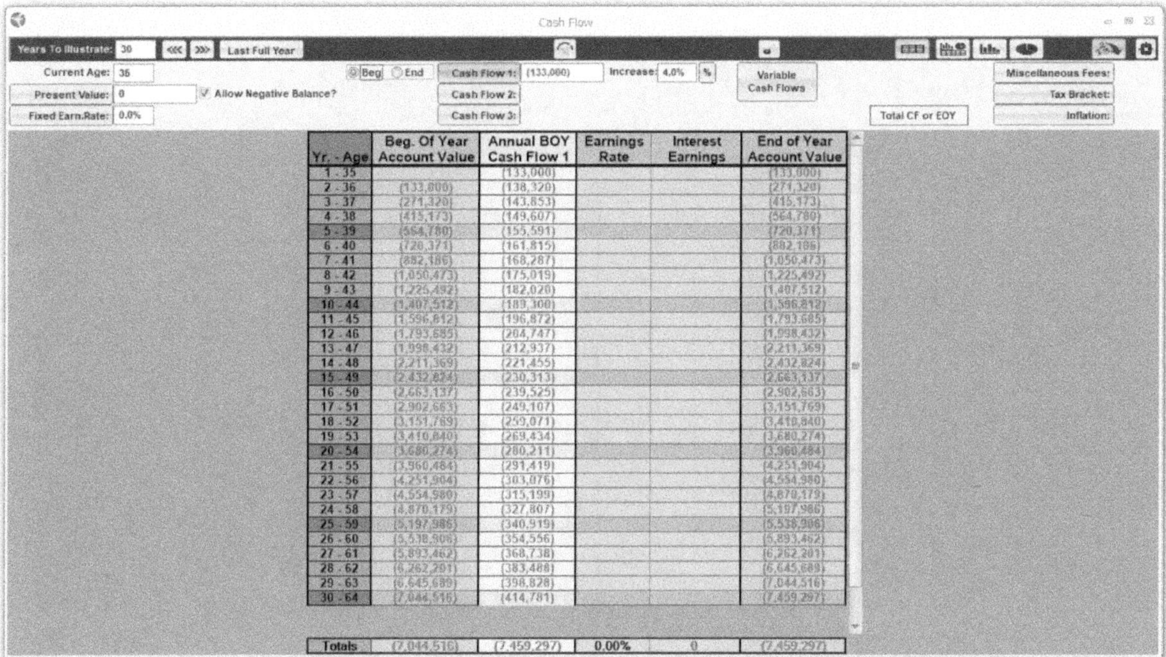

Yr. - Age	Beg. Of Year Account Value	Annual BOY Cash Flow 1	Earnings Rate	Interest Earnings	End of Year Account Value
1 - 35		(133,000)			(133,000)
2 - 36	(133,000)	(138,320)			(271,320)
3 - 37	(271,320)	(143,853)			(415,173)
4 - 38	(415,173)	(149,607)			(564,780)
5 - 39	(564,780)	(155,591)			(720,371)
6 - 40	(720,371)	(161,815)			(882,186)
7 - 41	(882,186)	(168,287)			(1,050,473)
8 - 42	(1,050,473)	(175,019)			(1,225,492)
9 - 43	(1,225,492)	(182,020)			(1,407,512)
10 - 44	(1,407,512)	(189,300)			(1,596,812)
11 - 45	(1,596,812)	(196,872)			(1,793,685)
12 - 46	(1,793,685)	(204,747)			(1,998,432)
13 - 47	(1,998,432)	(212,937)			(2,211,369)
14 - 48	(2,211,369)	(221,455)			(2,432,824)
15 - 49	(2,432,824)	(230,313)			(2,663,137)
16 - 50	(2,663,137)	(239,525)			(2,902,663)
17 - 51	(2,902,663)	(249,107)			(3,151,769)
18 - 52	(3,151,769)	(259,071)			(3,410,840)
19 - 53	(3,410,840)	(269,434)			(3,680,274)
20 - 54	(3,680,274)	(280,211)			(3,960,484)
21 - 55	(3,960,484)	(291,419)			(4,251,904)
22 - 56	(4,251,904)	(303,076)			(4,554,980)
23 - 57	(4,554,980)	(315,199)			(4,870,179)
24 - 58	(4,870,179)	(327,807)			(5,197,986)
25 - 59	(5,197,986)	(340,919)			(5,538,906)
26 - 60	(5,538,906)	(354,556)			(5,893,462)
27 - 61	(5,893,462)	(368,738)			(6,262,201)
28 - 62	(6,262,201)	(383,488)			(6,645,689)
29 - 63	(6,645,689)	(398,828)			(7,044,516)
30 - 64	(7,044,516)	(414,781)			(7,459,297)
Totals	(7,044,516)	(7,459,297)	0.00%	0	(7,459,297)

Now, one line up from the bottom, where you see $414,781 in the thirtieth year, it is the same as the $133,000 impacted by inflation. That may be hard to manage mentally. Yet is $414,781 going to buy any more than $133,000 does today? *I would argue it's going to buy less.* Why? Because more of that income is going to be exposed to those higher tax brackets. So even from a growth standpoint, it's the same dollars due to inflation, and we're increasing by four percent after tax, yet we're going to pay more taxes on those higher incomes. So it's actually going to spend like less, but we'll go with that for now.

We have a button up top, Present Value, which will calculate a number. $7.5 million is *what it is going to take today* to pay that income out.

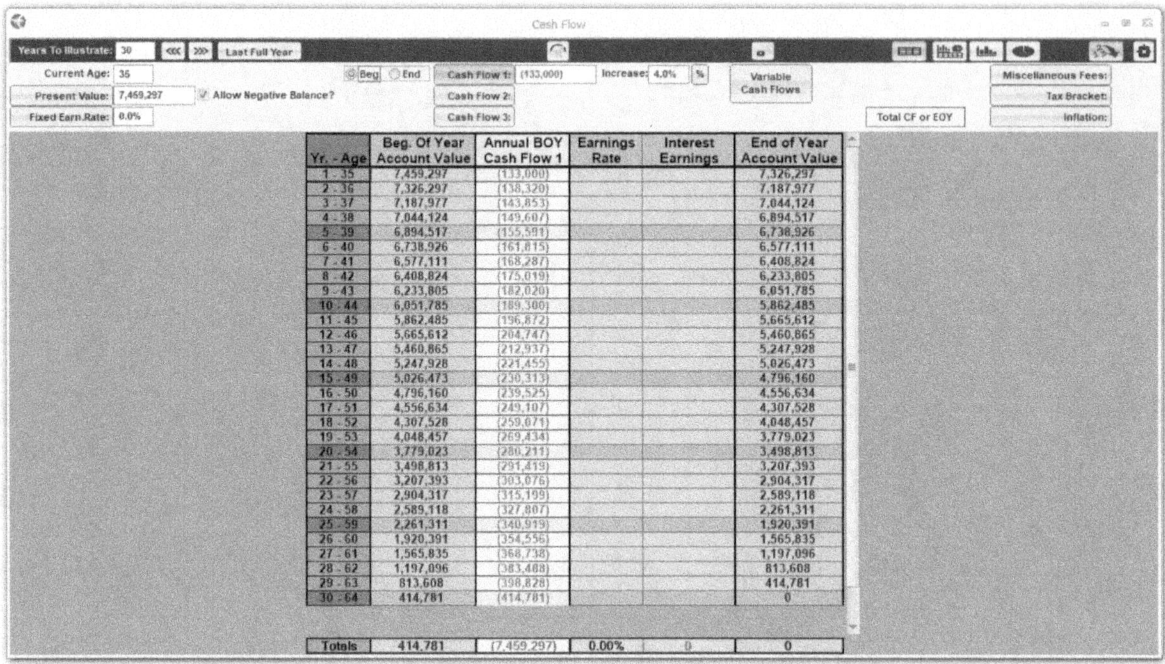

Yr. - Age	Beg. Of Year Account Value	Annual BOY Cash Flow 1	Earnings Rate	Interest Earnings	End of Year Account Value
1 - 35	7,459,297	(133,000)			7,326,297
2 - 36	7,326,297	(138,320)			7,187,977
3 - 37	7,187,977	(143,853)			7,044,124
4 - 38	7,044,124	(149,607)			6,894,517
5 - 39	6,894,517	(155,591)			6,738,926
6 - 40	6,738,926	(161,815)			6,577,111
7 - 41	6,577,111	(168,287)			6,408,824
8 - 42	6,408,824	(175,019)			6,233,805
9 - 43	6,233,805	(182,020)			6,051,785
10 - 44	6,051,785	(189,300)			5,862,485
11 - 45	5,862,485	(196,872)			5,665,612
12 - 46	5,665,612	(204,747)			5,460,865
13 - 47	5,460,865	(212,937)			5,247,928
14 - 48	5,247,928	(221,455)			5,026,473
15 - 49	5,026,473	(230,313)			4,796,160
16 - 50	4,796,160	(239,525)			4,556,634
17 - 51	4,556,634	(249,107)			4,307,528
18 - 52	4,307,528	(259,071)			4,048,457
19 - 53	4,048,457	(269,434)			3,779,023
20 - 54	3,779,023	(280,211)			3,498,813
21 - 55	3,498,813	(291,419)			3,207,393
22 - 56	3,207,393	(303,076)			2,904,317
23 - 57	2,904,317	(315,199)			2,589,118
24 - 58	2,589,118	(327,807)			2,261,311
25 - 59	2,261,311	(340,919)			1,920,391
26 - 60	1,920,391	(354,556)			1,565,835
27 - 61	1,565,835	(368,738)			1,197,096
28 - 62	1,197,096	(383,488)			813,608
29 - 63	813,608	(398,828)			414,781
30 - 64	414,781	(414,781)			0
Totals	414,781	(7,459,297)	0.00%	0	0

And we can see that we ended up with zero at the end. Yet if we could earn money on that side fund at 4%, then it's going to take $3,990,000, so that we can pull out $133,000 and up, going on down the line, and end up zeroing out at age sixty-five.

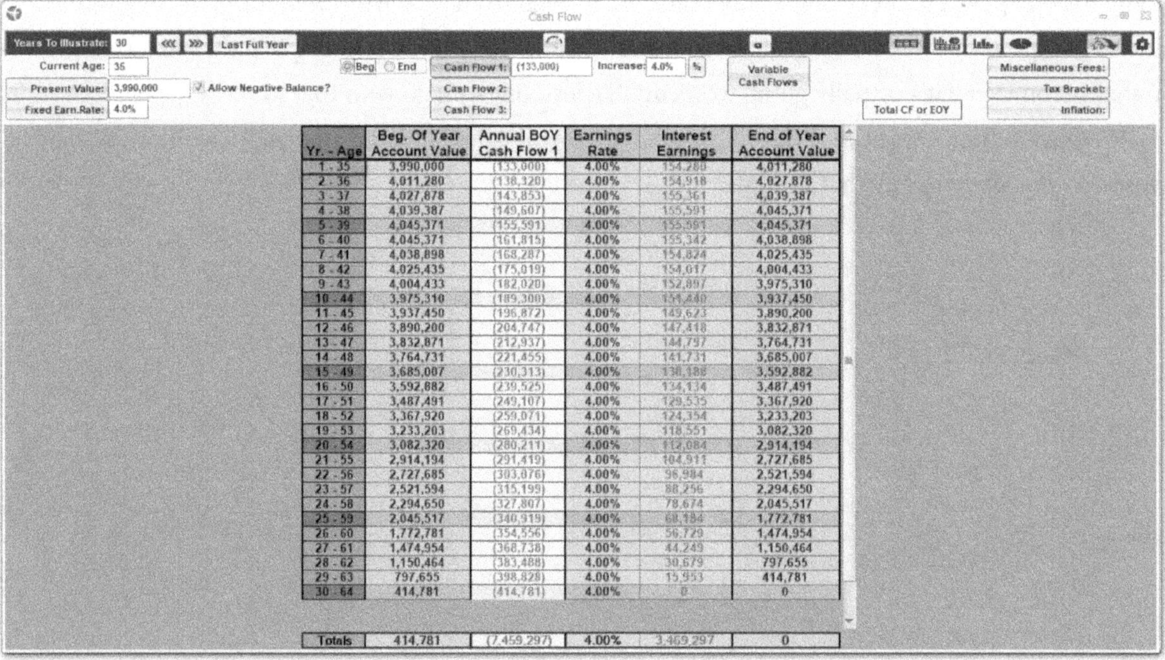

Yr. - Age	Beg. Of Year Account Value	Annual BOY Cash Flow 1	Earnings Rate	Interest Earnings	End of Year Account Value
1 - 35	3,990,000	(133,000)	4.00%	154,280	4,011,280
2 - 36	4,011,280	(138,320)	4.00%	154,918	4,027,878
3 - 37	4,027,878	(143,853)	4.00%	155,361	4,039,387
4 - 38	4,039,387	(149,607)	4.00%	155,591	4,045,371
5 - 39	4,045,371	(155,591)	4.00%	155,591	4,045,371
6 - 40	4,045,371	(161,815)	4.00%	155,342	4,038,898
7 - 41	4,038,898	(168,287)	4.00%	154,824	4,025,435
8 - 42	4,025,435	(175,019)	4.00%	154,017	4,004,433
9 - 43	4,004,433	(182,020)	4.00%	152,897	3,975,310
10 - 44	3,975,310	(189,300)	4.00%	151,440	3,937,450
11 - 45	3,937,450	(196,872)	4.00%	149,623	3,890,200
12 - 46	3,890,200	(204,747)	4.00%	147,418	3,832,871
13 - 47	3,832,871	(212,937)	4.00%	144,797	3,764,731
14 - 48	3,764,731	(221,455)	4.00%	141,731	3,685,007
15 - 49	3,685,007	(230,313)	4.00%	138,188	3,592,882
16 - 50	3,592,882	(239,525)	4.00%	134,134	3,487,491
17 - 51	3,487,491	(249,107)	4.00%	129,535	3,367,920
18 - 52	3,367,920	(259,071)	4.00%	124,354	3,233,203
19 - 53	3,233,203	(269,434)	4.00%	118,551	3,082,320
20 - 54	3,082,320	(280,211)	4.00%	112,084	2,914,194
21 - 55	2,914,194	(291,419)	4.00%	104,911	2,727,685
22 - 56	2,727,685	(303,076)	4.00%	96,984	2,521,594
23 - 57	2,521,594	(315,199)	4.00%	88,256	2,294,650
24 - 58	2,294,650	(327,807)	4.00%	78,674	2,045,517
25 - 59	2,045,517	(340,919)	4.00%	68,184	1,772,781
26 - 60	1,772,781	(354,556)	4.00%	56,729	1,474,954
27 - 61	1,474,954	(368,738)	4.00%	44,249	1,150,464
28 - 62	1,150,464	(383,488)	4.00%	30,679	797,655
29 - 63	797,655	(398,828)	4.00%	15,953	414,781
30 - 64	414,781	(414,781)	4.00%	0	0
Totals	414,781	(7,459,297)	4.00%	3,469,297	0

There is another piece of danger that we have to be careful of with those that are left behind financially. This $3.9 million seems like all the money in the world to them. If a premature death occurs and that money gets blown, then they're out of money.

They're also out of money at age sixty-five, so that means they should have been saving all along the way, just like they would have been if that individual was living and earning that income. **We're replacing human economic value. It's not a license to spend.**

How many of you have heard of A.L. Williams or Prime America? What's interesting about them is if you look at the pre-authorized check charges on their structure of "buy term insurance and invest the difference," at one time they were charging 38% to pay monthly rather than annually on their term insurance.

So what happens to a $1 million term policy over time? Is it less valuable because of inflation?

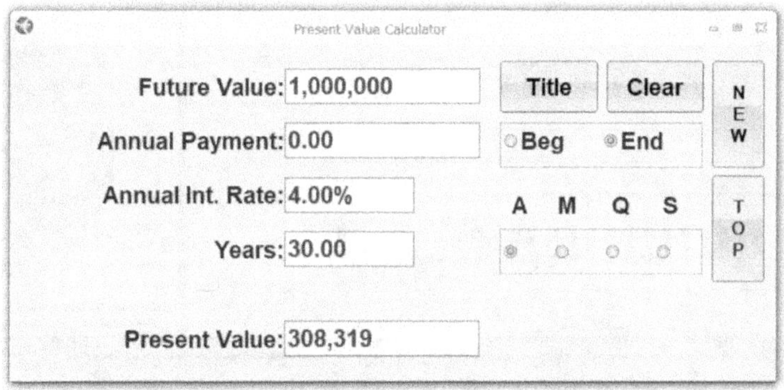

The Present Value calculator proves that the $1 million will only buy $308,319 worth of goods and services 30 years in the future. In effect, Prime America is actually proposing a declining death benefit with the theory that the closer you are to retirement age, the less "lost income" you need to fill. But look at what happens in the Cash Flow calculator.

We started at $3.9 million and we actually see this account has to grow for a period of time before it actually starts dropping as to what the need is to finish that time frame. That's in order to compensate for that increased cost of living on the other side.

I have had success sending this to the insurance company and getting them to issue more than what they were willing to initially because of the proof of the value of that income stream, hence the name: Human Life Value. What I primarily use this for, though, is just for the client to understand the amount of insurance that we're talking about, to see it's going to be less than what is actually needed in the account to replace the deceased's income. It's not a crazy amount of money. *It's also important, I think, that the family understands how this works, so that they don't go on a spending spree.* It would be easy to do when you have that much money dumped into the family's account after a death.

When you zero out the increase and zero out the earnings, you get the same results. So, is there a point showing that, or is it better shown if there's a difference in those two? I think people expect an increase in income, so I think it's helpful to have that up there.

I think we also need to highlight with the client that this is just cost of living increases, this does not take into account what happens if you get a major shift in your position, or you move up to a higher paying position, not from a cost of living standpoint, but from a job payout standpoint.

It's a lot easier for people to look back than it is to look forward. When this person sees $414,781 in the future, that's a lot harder to look at than it is for them to hear, "Hey, you had a job for the last ten years, here's what you were making then, and here is what you are making now."

It may be easier to think about our human life value on the Cash Flow calculator, Graphs section below.

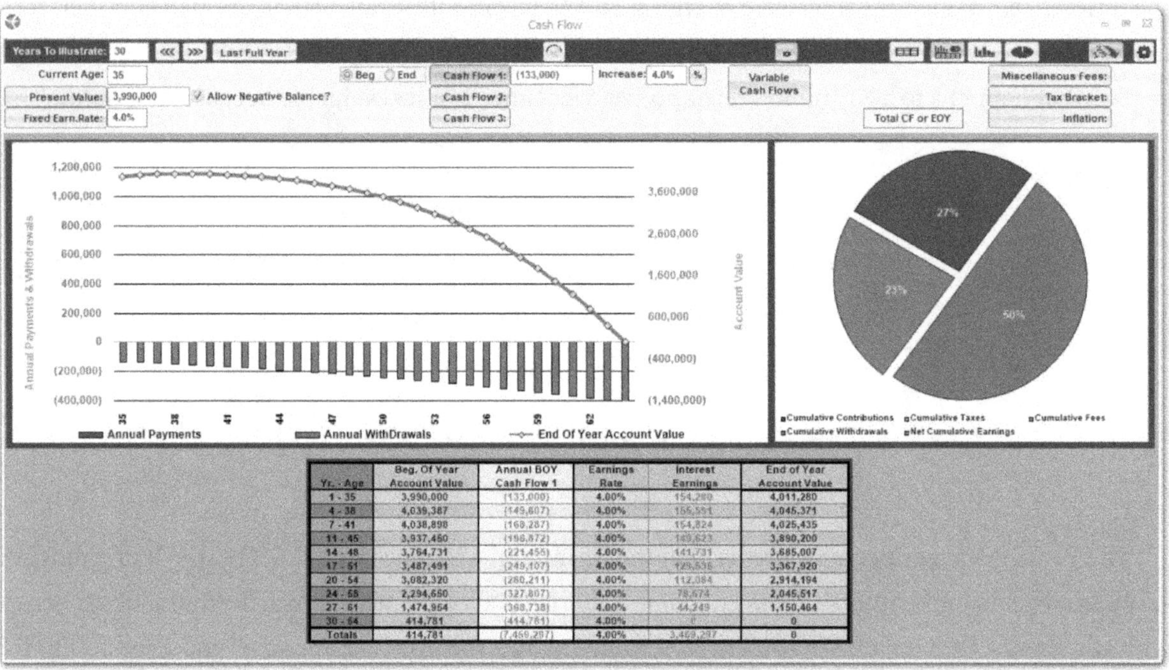

Yr. - Age	Beg. Of Year Account Value	Annual BOY Cash Flow 1	Earnings Rate	Interest Earnings	End of Year Account Value
1 - 35	3,990,000	(133,000)	4.00%	154,280	4,011,280
4 - 38	4,039,387	(149,607)	4.00%	155,591	4,045,371
7 - 41	4,038,898	(168,287)	4.00%	154,824	4,025,435
11 - 45	3,937,460	(196,872)	4.00%	149,623	3,890,200
14 - 48	3,764,731	(221,455)	4.00%	141,731	3,685,007
17 - 51	3,487,491	(249,107)	4.00%	129,536	3,367,920
20 - 54	3,082,320	(280,211)	4.00%	112,084	2,914,194
24 - 58	2,294,650	(327,807)	4.00%	78,674	2,045,517
27 - 61	1,474,964	(368,738)	4.00%	44,249	1,150,464
30 - 64	414,781	(414,781)	4.00%	0	0
Totals	414,781	(7,469,297)	4.00%	3,469,297	0

It's a lot easier for people to see and understand the picture than it is to just see the numbers.

Best Uses: The Cash Flow calculator is best used to show clients human life value, death benefits, and graphs demonstrating these numbers over time. It can also estimate various inputs and outputs in accounts to help clients with decision-making regarding big expenses, or simple analogies like Average does not equal Actual. (See Chapter 3.)

Calculator 17: Accumulation

The software should be a confidence builder for you before you meet with clients, and then something to back you up.

Purpose: The Accumulation calculator shows the effectiveness of money growing (taxable, tax deferred, tax deductible, and/or tax free) and it has multiple variable payment and withdrawal columns. It also has the ability to vary the earnings rate, and the ability to add term insurance and other costs.

Why It Was Created: This is a bigger Cash Flow calculator with more capability. The reason it's called the Accumulation calculator is because it's about the accumulation phase of wealth building. In contrast to the Distribution calculator (#18), the Accumulation calculator can actually do both calculations: show money going up (accumulating) and money coming out (distribution). It has more input and output columns in it than Distribution does. It also has the ability to introduce management fees at a higher level, term insurance costs, taxes, and a detailed tax breakdown of tax deferred, tax free, tax deductible, capital gains vs. income tax amounts, and Monte Carlo calculations.

Dr. Wade Pfau brought the idea of sequencing of returns into the mainstream. He's used super-computers to do billions of calculations to show impact. When we look at the S&P 500 Index, it may have averaged 12%, but because of sequencing of returns, the ups and downs change that actual number. **The sequencing of returns reduces from the average what the actual return is.** When we take it a step further, we find that where those returns happen (in what order) can create a whole different outcome from the average return. Hence my statement: average is not actual, as proven in Chapter 3.

What a Monte Carlo calculation does (say we have a whole stream of rates), is it takes those same rates of return and randomly rearranges them, putting them in a different order, to see the results. This changes what you actually end up with and helps you determine what percentage of the time does this account survive with this particular withdrawal strategy (i.e., how much money can you reasonably take out of an account until the account goes to zero or some pre-determined minimum amount of money).

To have a 95% chance of the account lasting forty years, the maximum you can take out is 3.5% level. But that's only true if it averages 12%! If you take out a 3.5% income, increasing (to overcome inflation), you may have only a 35% chance of the account lasting forty years. There's a possibility you might end up with a large amount leftover, but this strategy attempts to ultimately keep you from ending up with nothing. You could have a range of having $10 million left versus $0. Monte Carlo calculations show all those variations in the middle.

Why is it called Monte Carlo? Because gambling in Monte Carlo involves high-end rolling of the dice. If you're in the financial services industry and people use Monte Carlo as a verb, they're using a computer to calculate a stream of payments. Instead of a linear average year to year, they're scrambling and mixing it every time. The Accumulation calculator hasn't always had a Monte Carlo calculation, it just evolved into that over time based on the need for strategists to demonstrate it.

The initial thinking on designing the Accumulation calculator was about detail capability. The problem we found ourselves in was that with such a comprehensive calculator, if the client doesn't have all the numbers to enter, it gets confusing and frustrating. So we created the Accumulation calculator so strategists and clients could add columns that they need. It comes with three columns initially, but you can add the ones you need.

Case Study: I designed this calculator so I can add the things that I might want to add as I'm going through calculations.

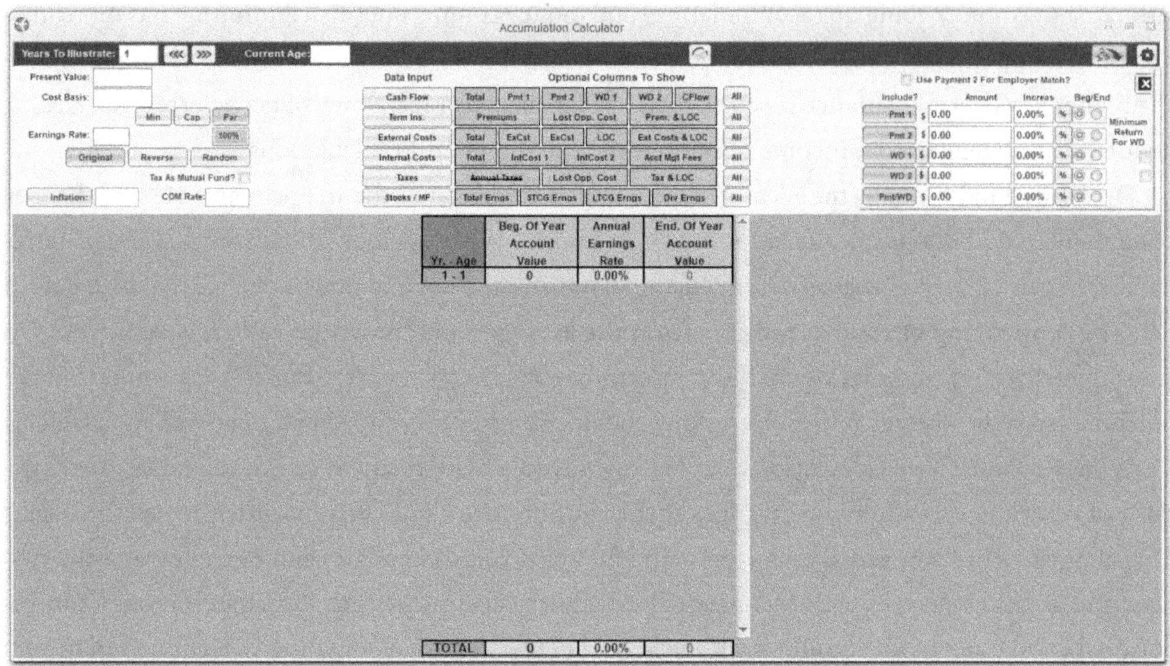

Let's put in thirty-five years, with $250,000 of Present Value. We won't have any cost basis on; this is going to be just a regular taxable account earning 5%.

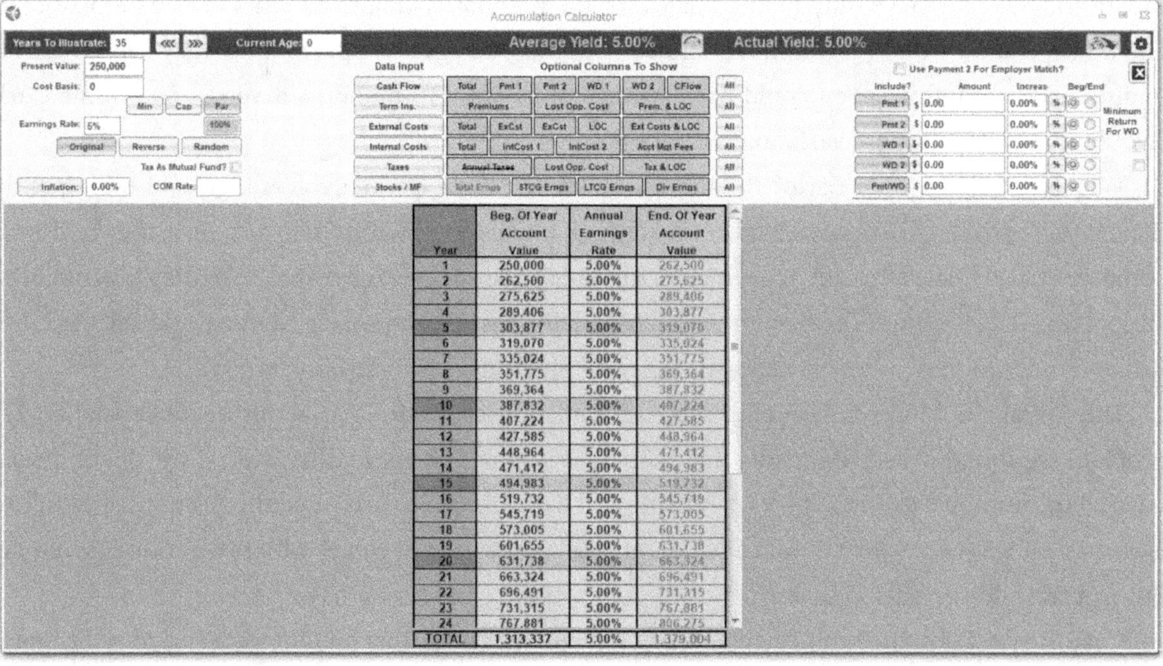

Year	Beg. Of Year Account Value	Annual Earnings Rate	End. Of Year Account Value
1	250,000	5.00%	262,500
2	262,500	5.00%	275,625
3	275,625	5.00%	289,406
4	289,406	5.00%	303,877
5	303,877	5.00%	319,070
6	319,070	5.00%	335,024
7	335,024	5.00%	351,775
8	351,775	5.00%	369,364
9	369,364	5.00%	387,832
10	387,832	5.00%	407,224
11	407,224	5.00%	427,585
12	427,585	5.00%	448,964
13	448,964	5.00%	471,412
14	471,412	5.00%	494,983
15	494,983	5.00%	519,732
16	519,732	5.00%	545,719
17	545,719	5.00%	573,005
18	573,005	5.00%	601,655
19	601,655	5.00%	631,738
20	631,738	5.00%	663,324
21	663,324	5.00%	696,491
22	696,491	5.00%	731,315
23	731,315	5.00%	767,881
24	767,881	5.00%	806,275
TOTAL	1,313,337	5.00%	1,379,004

What we see is that this would grow to $1,379,004, and we can see that both Average and Actual Yields are at 5%.

When we include taxes, we're going to see that the account dropped to $833,398.

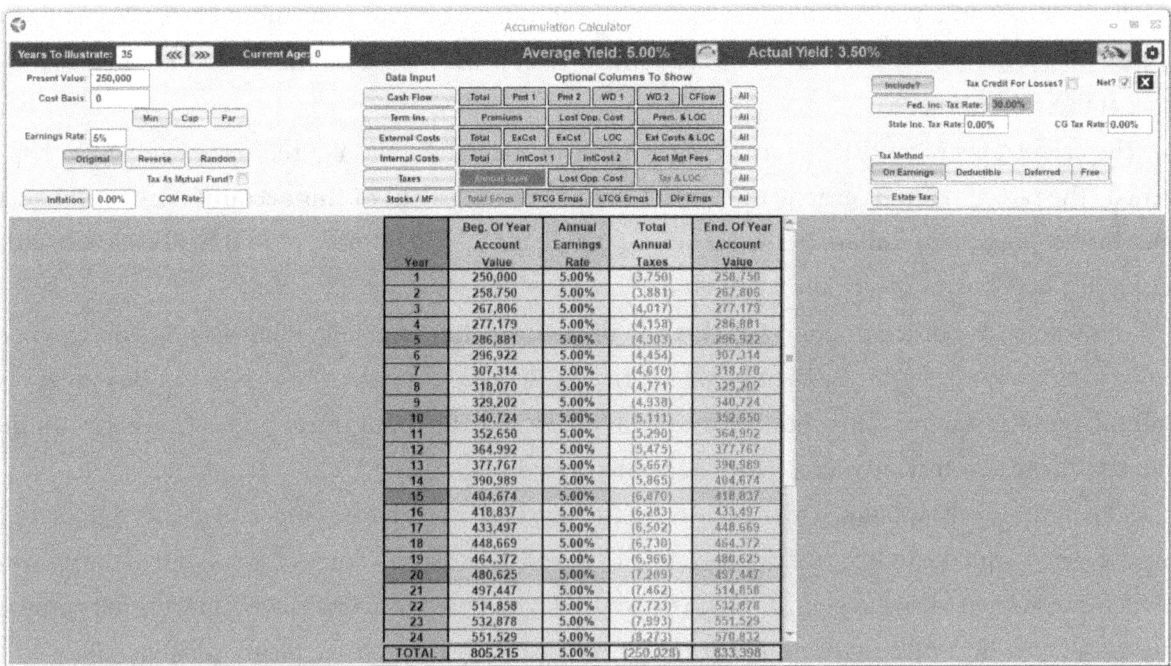

Year	Beg. Of Year Account Value	Annual Earnings Rate	Total Annual Taxes	End. Of Year Account Value
1	250,000	5.00%	(3,750)	258,750
2	258,750	5.00%	(3,881)	267,806
3	267,806	5.00%	(4,017)	277,179
4	277,179	5.00%	(4,158)	286,881
5	286,881	5.00%	(4,303)	296,922
6	296,922	5.00%	(4,454)	307,314
7	307,314	5.00%	(4,610)	318,070
8	318,070	5.00%	(4,771)	329,202
9	329,202	5.00%	(4,938)	340,724
10	340,724	5.00%	(5,111)	352,650
11	352,650	5.00%	(5,290)	364,992
12	364,992	5.00%	(5,475)	377,767
13	377,767	5.00%	(5,667)	390,989
14	390,989	5.00%	(5,865)	404,674
15	404,674	5.00%	(6,070)	418,837
16	418,837	5.00%	(6,283)	433,497
17	433,497	5.00%	(6,502)	448,669
18	448,669	5.00%	(6,730)	464,372
19	464,372	5.00%	(6,966)	480,625
20	480,625	5.00%	(7,209)	497,447
21	497,447	5.00%	(7,462)	514,858
22	514,858	5.00%	(7,723)	532,878
23	532,878	5.00%	(7,993)	551,529
24	551,529	5.00%	(8,273)	570,832
TOTAL	805,215	5.00%	(250,028)	833,398

So we see 3.5% is the Actual Yield. This is due to paying taxes on the growth of this account. The total taxes paid over this time are $250,028, "netted" (or taken out of) the account itself.

What if I pay the taxes out of another account? On the calculator below we see the account grew to $1,379,004.

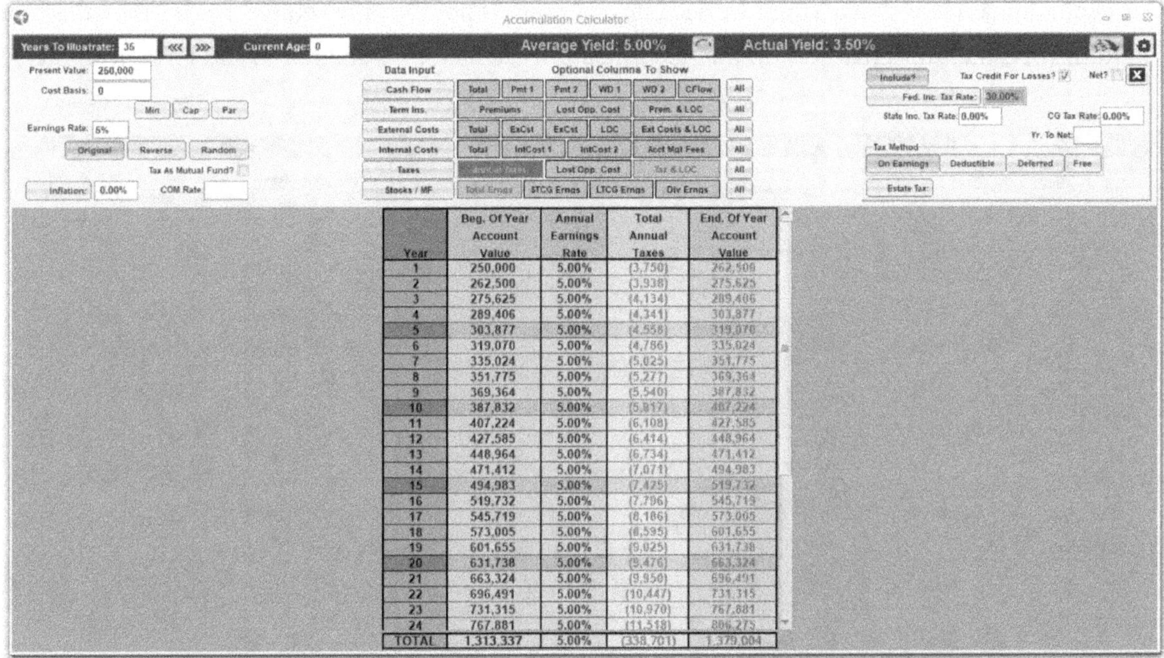

Year	Beg. Of Year Account Value	Annual Earnings Rate	Total Annual Taxes	End. Of Year Account Value
1	250,000	5.00%	(3,750)	262,500
2	262,500	5.00%	(3,938)	275,625
3	275,625	5.00%	(4,134)	289,406
4	289,406	5.00%	(4,341)	303,877
5	303,877	5.00%	(4,558)	319,070
6	319,070	5.00%	(4,786)	335,024
7	335,024	5.00%	(5,025)	351,775
8	351,775	5.00%	(5,277)	369,364
9	369,364	5.00%	(5,540)	387,832
10	387,832	5.00%	(5,817)	407,224
11	407,224	5.00%	(6,108)	427,585
12	427,585	5.00%	(6,414)	448,964
13	448,964	5.00%	(6,734)	471,412
14	471,412	5.00%	(7,071)	494,983
15	494,983	5.00%	(7,425)	519,732
16	519,732	5.00%	(7,796)	545,719
17	545,719	5.00%	(8,186)	573,005
18	573,005	5.00%	(8,595)	601,655
19	601,655	5.00%	(9,025)	631,738
20	631,738	5.00%	(9,476)	663,324
21	663,324	5.00%	(9,950)	696,491
22	696,491	5.00%	(10,447)	731,315
23	731,315	5.00%	(10,970)	767,881
24	767,881	5.00%	(11,518)	806,275
TOTAL	1,313,337	5.00%	(338,701)	1,379,004

And we can also see the taxes went up to a total of $338,701. Yet the rate of return did not go up.

Why? Because while you had more money in the account, you also paid more taxes. People don't realize this because their tax focus is usually once a year, while their account focus is as often as they look at their accounts.

The calculator did an IRR (internal rate of return) calculation and figured out exactly what happened. The rate of return is exactly the same. **I didn't take taxes out of this account, but I still had a cost for keeping those dollars in the account.** I didn't add a "cost of money" to the calculator manually, it just happens automatically when viewed holistically.

The whole idea of "compounding" that the financial institutions talk about has to stop at some point in time. Why? In this case study, we see that as the account grew, the annual tax due grew, it's painful, but it's bearable. This shows the annual taxes that extend out thirty years. At what point do you say, "I can't do that anymore? That's added to my existing tax bill."

Sometimes clients will say, "I'm making more money; I just don't have as much to spend." I think this is partly because of the strategy they've been told to use on their assets. If they're successful in the growth of their assets, their tax bill is going through the roof. Not because the tax rates are going up, but because their asset growth is causing their taxes to go up because they're not netting, *they're compounding.*

We can tax this account as a regular "on earnings." Or we can treat it as a "tax deductible" account. What does tax deductible mean? An example would be a 401(k), where the dollars that go in are deductible, and it grows tax deferred. Then 100% of everything coming out will be taxable.

"Tax deferred" refers to after-tax dollars with tax-deferred-growth, like an annuity. If you do select tax deferred, there's also an option for FIFO (First In, First Out) or LIFO (Last In, First Out) tax structure, depending on how that account works. Life insurance is not the only vehicle that is FIFO; there are also Roth IRAs that work that way. In the Accumulation calculator we could also add term insurance.

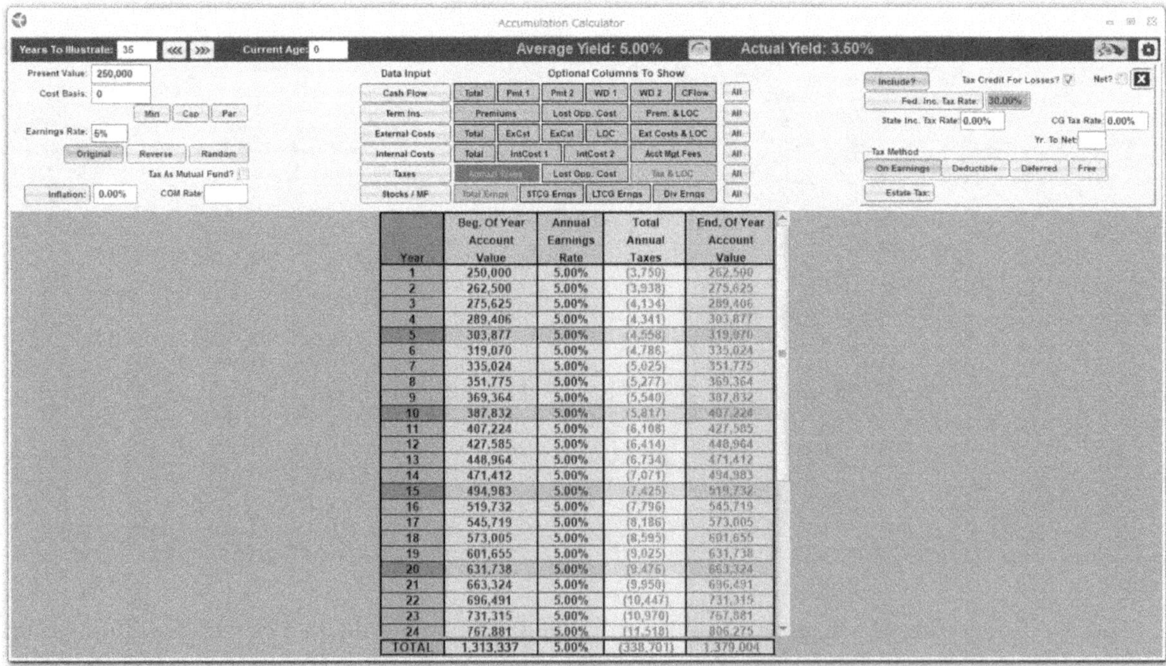

Year	Beg. Of Year Account Value	Annual Earnings Rate	Total Annual Taxes	End. Of Year Account Value
1	250,000	5.00%	(3,750)	262,500
2	262,500	5.00%	(3,938)	275,625
3	275,625	5.00%	(4,134)	289,406
4	289,406	5.00%	(4,341)	303,877
5	303,877	5.00%	(4,558)	319,070
6	319,070	5.00%	(4,786)	335,024
7	335,024	5.00%	(5,025)	351,775
8	351,775	5.00%	(5,277)	369,364
9	369,364	5.00%	(5,540)	387,832
10	387,832	5.00%	(5,817)	407,224
11	407,224	5.00%	(6,108)	427,585
12	427,585	5.00%	(6,414)	448,964
13	448,964	5.00%	(6,734)	471,412
14	471,412	5.00%	(7,071)	494,983
15	494,983	5.00%	(7,425)	519,732
16	519,732	5.00%	(7,796)	545,719
17	545,719	5.00%	(8,186)	573,005
18	573,005	5.00%	(8,595)	601,655
19	601,655	5.00%	(9,025)	631,738
20	631,738	5.00%	(9,476)	663,324
21	663,324	5.00%	(9,950)	696,491
22	696,491	5.00%	(10,447)	731,315
23	731,315	5.00%	(10,970)	767,881
24	767,881	5.00%	(11,518)	806,275
TOTAL	1,313,337	5.00%	(338,701)	1,379,004

We can enter the premium, taxes, cost of money (or opportunity cost), cash flow (five possible columns), withdrawals, external costs, internal costs, and more. Anything we put in the two withdrawal columns, positive or negative, is money coming out.

External costs are costs that you have because you chose a specific path, and there are some extra costs. For example, financial planning fees, term insurance costs, etc. *Internal costs* are (often) deductible costs that are coming out of the asset. An example could be a loan. We took a loan to make an investment. Therefore we get to write off that internal cost against investment gain. Please check with your CPA about this.

Unrealized long-term capital gains are like a stock that's held all the way to the end (typically that a stock manager forgot was there). I'll usually use a pretty low percentage there. It's amazing how many people think their stock portfolio is all tax-deferred. Not a lot of it is, especially the mutual funds. Maybe we'll put 10% there to show 10% of this asset is actually held all the way to the end.

The last one is *realized short-term capital gains*: these are turned over regularly and get income tax treatment. Remember, if you use mutual funds, you have to put in a cost basis. Otherwise it's going to assume that $250,000 is the basis and the rest is all unrealized capital gain.

You can put just about anything in this calculator and figure out a way to solve it or get a good picture of it.

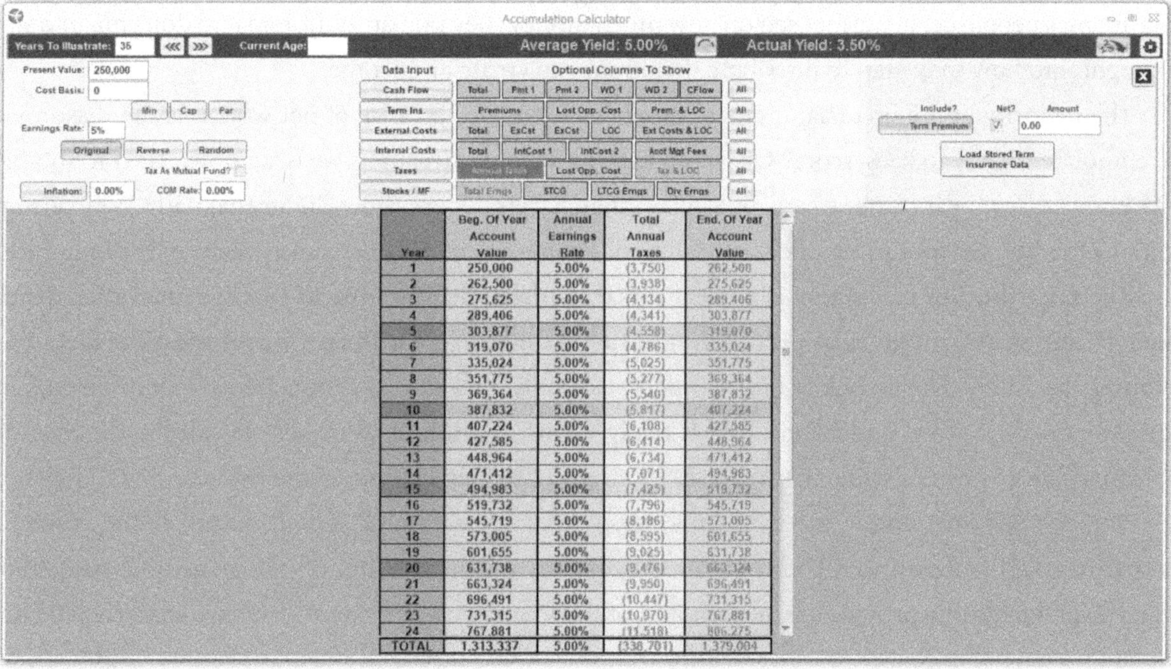

Year	Beg. Of Year Account Value	Annual Earnings Rate	Total Annual Taxes	End. Of Year Account Value
1	250,000	5.00%	(3,750)	262,500
2	262,500	5.00%	(3,938)	275,625
3	275,625	5.00%	(4,134)	289,406
4	289,406	5.00%	(4,341)	303,877
5	303,877	5.00%	(4,558)	319,070
6	319,070	5.00%	(4,786)	335,024
7	335,024	5.00%	(5,025)	351,775
8	351,775	5.00%	(5,277)	369,364
9	369,364	5.00%	(5,540)	387,832
10	387,832	5.00%	(5,817)	407,224
11	407,224	5.00%	(6,108)	427,585
12	427,585	5.00%	(6,414)	448,964
13	448,964	5.00%	(6,734)	471,412
14	471,412	5.00%	(7,071)	494,983
15	494,983	5.00%	(7,425)	519,732
16	519,732	5.00%	(7,796)	545,719
17	545,719	5.00%	(8,186)	573,005
18	573,005	5.00%	(8,595)	601,655
19	601,655	5.00%	(9,025)	631,738
20	631,738	5.00%	(9,476)	663,324
21	663,324	5.00%	(9,950)	696,491
22	696,491	5.00%	(10,447)	731,315
23	731,315	5.00%	(10,970)	767,881
24	767,881	5.00%	(11,518)	806,275
TOTAL	1,313,337	5.00%	(338,701)	1,379,004

Using the Reverse and Random buttons, you can try various income streams with various return orders and sequences (the Monte Carlo calculation). Everybody thinks they're doing 12% in the S&P 500 Index, but if you take 5% out per year for income, you only succeed with money left over 26% of the time. And understand that "succeeded" means you're out of money in thirty years. That should be scary and cause a person to look for an even better way. This is a great calculator to play around with and demonstrate Monte Carlo income simulations.

Best Uses: The Accumulation calculator might be best used to help clients see the fact that what their typical financial planner is telling them may not necessarily be true once all the numbers are entered. Its most valuable use is the Monte Carlo simulation. Imagine getting on a plane and the captain comes on the loudspeaker and says, "Welcome, thank you for flying with S&P Dividends today. We've got a 26% chance of landing safely. So buckle up and enjoy your flight." Would you fly with them? Is it worth the risk?

Calculator 18: Distribution

A mountain hike is successful only if you make it both up and down.

Purpose: The Distribution calculator shows money coming out of an account with varying interest rates. It allows for taxable, tax-deferred, tax-deductible, and/or tax-free accounts. It compares two different strategies for distribution, A and B.

Why It Was Created: I created this calculator to show what happens during the distribution phase, most often with and without Whole Life, though it could be used to compare a variety of distribution methods. Let's say we've accumulated $1 million, then we can look at how it will be distributed. Sometimes people get hyperfocused on how much money they pile up at the end and don't put enough thought into how they plan to distribute that money to create an income.

The majority of the financial industry emphasizes the importance of net worth. Is the reason we accumulate money to keep score? Or is it to have an income stream as we head down the mountain? *We* know it's for the income stream, but so few financial strategists show clients that path. Why pile up money (and do without in the short run) if it's not going to create an income stream in the long run?

The Distribution calculator is a great place to highlight the idea of the life insurance death benefit and the way it gives us permission to spend dollars in a different way during the distribution phase. Many people look at life insurance as simply a way to give money to someone else when they're gone. But if we understand how it really works, it unlocks strategies we can use for income streams—for the owner while they're alive. It's all about having choices in the future.

A good friend of mine, Vince D'Addona, says, "Smaller assets act like bigger assets in the presence of permanent life insurance." You could literally have a smaller amount of money in your assets that can be spendable *and* provide a larger amount of income to yourself if you also have a guaranteed life insurance payout at death.

The root reason for creating the Distribution calculator initially was to show what happens for the person who followed the "buy term, invest the difference" strategy. They get to retirement age, can't afford the term insurance anymore, and think it doesn't have any use anyway. It covered their income loss during their working years, and now they're past that and into the distribution phase. There's no guarantee the term insurance will last until they die, so it's no longer a useful product. It served its purpose as pure insurance against death and not leaving the family without a breadwinner. Now it's done its one job.

Let's look at scenario A (assets + no life insurance), and think about what happened with the money that piled up. Since we don't know how long we're going to live, the golden rule here is that you can't take more than the interest earned. We don't know what will happen as life expectancy grows and grows.

Alternatively, what if we ended up in the same place with the same, or even slightly less assets *and* a whole life insurance policy? Scenario B. Then we can treat the money a little differently.

This analogy may help: Let's say you knew you were going to win the lottery in your future. If you'd been guaranteed that was going to happen, it would change the way you'd treat money today. You can take greater risks. You can spend more principal. **Whole Life insurance provides that same type of permission slip or benefit.** We've got the guarantee that whole life insurance will pay out when we die *and* a guarantee of death. Those two, leveraged against each other, mean that your lottery win *is* going to happen in the future. Scenario B means you can do other things with your money that might be more efficient than being locked into Scenario A that is interest only.

Case Study: This calculator can be used to show the difference between two people's choices for distribution and see how those choices affect their access to cash flow.

Let's say Client A bought into the "buy term and invest the difference strategy." Client B bought whole life insurance and was disciplined, so that when increases in income occurred, they pushed that difference to other assets because the life insurance premiums were level. Client B bought other assets because they were accumulating cash inside the life insurance, to purchase assets outside the life insurance.

Is it possible that Client B with the whole life insurance could accumulate as much in assets outside or in addition to the life insurance as Client A? Yes!

Client B can buy whole life insurance, invest over time, and have as much in assets plus the life insurance policy as Client A had, who bought term life insurance.

For this case study, we will calculate for twenty years and use a present value of $2 million, indicating each client had that amount of investments (not in life insurance cash value).

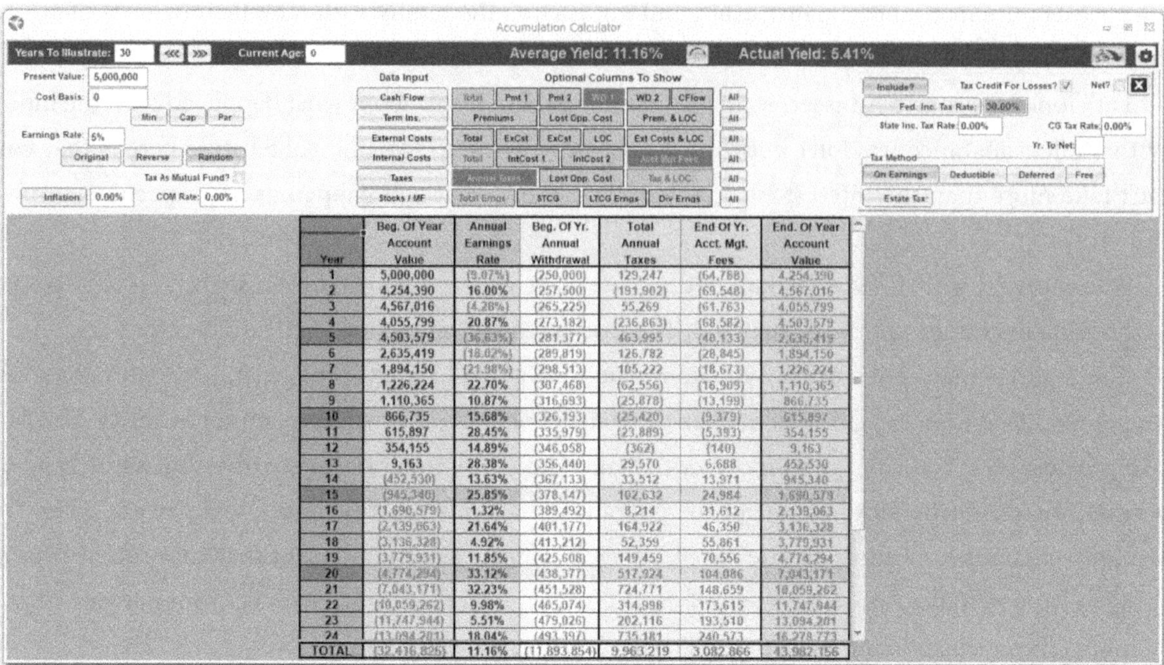

Year	Beg. Of Year Account Value	Annual Earnings Rate	Beg. Of Yr. Annual Withdrawal	Total Annual Taxes	End Of Yr. Acct. Mgt. Fees	End. Of Year Account Value
1	5,000,000	(9.07%)	(250,000)	129,247	(64,788)	4,254,390
2	4,254,390	16.00%	(257,500)	(191,902)	(69,548)	4,567,016
3	4,567,016	(4.28%)	(265,225)	55,269	(61,763)	4,055,799
4	4,055,799	20.87%	(273,182)	(236,863)	(68,582)	4,503,579
5	4,503,579	(36.63%)	(281,377)	463,995	(48,133)	2,635,419
6	2,635,419	(18.02%)	(289,819)	126,782	(28,845)	1,894,150
7	1,894,150	(21.98%)	(298,513)	105,222	(18,673)	1,226,224
8	1,226,224	22.70%	(307,468)	(62,556)	(16,909)	1,110,365
9	1,110,365	10.87%	(316,693)	(25,878)	(13,199)	866,735
10	866,735	15.68%	(326,193)	(25,420)	(9,379)	615,897
11	615,897	28.45%	(335,979)	(23,889)	(5,393)	354,155
12	354,155	14.89%	(346,058)	(362)	(140)	9,163
13	9,163	28.38%	(356,440)	29,570	6,688	452,530
14	(452,530)	13.63%	(367,133)	33,512	13,971	945,340
15	(945,340)	25.85%	(378,147)	102,632	24,984	1,690,579
16	(1,690,579)	1.32%	(389,492)	8,214	31,612	2,139,063
17	(2,139,863)	21.64%	(401,177)	164,922	46,350	3,136,328
18	(3,136,328)	4.92%	(413,212)	52,359	55,861	3,779,931
19	(3,779,931)	11.85%	(425,608)	149,459	70,556	4,774,294
20	(4,774,294)	33.12%	(438,377)	517,924	104,086	7,043,171
21	(7,043,171)	32.23%	(451,528)	724,771	148,659	10,059,262
22	(10,059,262)	9.98%	(465,074)	314,998	173,615	11,747,944
23	(11,747,944)	5.51%	(479,026)	202,116	193,510	13,094,201
24	(13,094,201)	18.04%	(493,397)	735,181	240,573	16,278,773
TOTAL	(32,416,826)	11.16%	(11,893,854)	9,963,219	3,082,866	43,982,156

We've arrived at seventy. Client A on the left bought into the "buy term and invest the difference" strategy. They have now cancelled the term insurance because the price was rising beyond their ability.

And now that we're in the retirement phase, probably more conservative with our investments, so we will assume 5%. How do you derive an income off of that $2 million? Do you take principal or interest only? You don't know how long you're going to live. What are your options?

The general rule is to never touch the principal. So we'll pull out Interest Only.

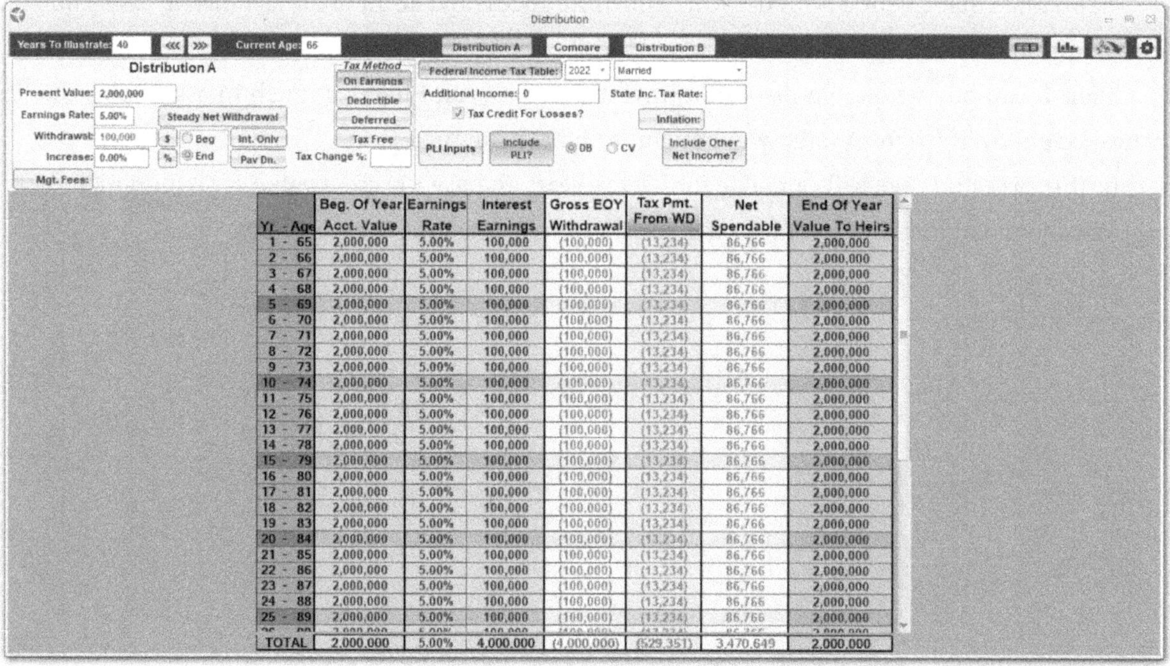

Yr - Age	Beg. Of Year Acct. Value	Earnings Rate	Interest Earnings	Gross EOY Withdrawal	Tax Pmt. From WD	Net Spendable	End Of Year Value To Heirs
1 - 65	2,000,000	5.00%	100,000	(100,000)	(13,234)	86,766	2,000,000
2 - 66	2,000,000	5.00%	100,000	(100,000)	(13,234)	86,766	2,000,000
3 - 67	2,000,000	5.00%	100,000	(100,000)	(13,234)	86,766	2,000,000
4 - 68	2,000,000	5.00%	100,000	(100,000)	(13,234)	86,766	2,000,000
5 - 69	2,000,000	5.00%	100,000	(100,000)	(13,234)	86,766	2,000,000
6 - 70	2,000,000	5.00%	100,000	(100,000)	(13,234)	86,766	2,000,000
7 - 71	2,000,000	5.00%	100,000	(100,000)	(13,234)	86,766	2,000,000
8 - 72	2,000,000	5.00%	100,000	(100,000)	(13,234)	86,766	2,000,000
9 - 73	2,000,000	5.00%	100,000	(100,000)	(13,234)	86,766	2,000,000
10 - 74	2,000,000	5.00%	100,000	(100,000)	(13,234)	86,766	2,000,000
11 - 75	2,000,000	5.00%	100,000	(100,000)	(13,234)	86,766	2,000,000
12 - 76	2,000,000	5.00%	100,000	(100,000)	(13,234)	86,766	2,000,000
13 - 77	2,000,000	5.00%	100,000	(100,000)	(13,234)	86,766	2,000,000
14 - 78	2,000,000	5.00%	100,000	(100,000)	(13,234)	86,766	2,000,000
15 - 79	2,000,000	5.00%	100,000	(100,000)	(13,234)	86,766	2,000,000
16 - 80	2,000,000	5.00%	100,000	(100,000)	(13,234)	86,766	2,000,000
17 - 81	2,000,000	5.00%	100,000	(100,000)	(13,234)	86,766	2,000,000
18 - 82	2,000,000	5.00%	100,000	(100,000)	(13,234)	86,766	2,000,000
19 - 83	2,000,000	5.00%	100,000	(100,000)	(13,234)	86,766	2,000,000
20 - 84	2,000,000	5.00%	100,000	(100,000)	(13,234)	86,766	2,000,000
21 - 85	2,000,000	5.00%	100,000	(100,000)	(13,234)	86,766	2,000,000
22 - 86	2,000,000	5.00%	100,000	(100,000)	(13,234)	86,766	2,000,000
23 - 87	2,000,000	5.00%	100,000	(100,000)	(13,234)	86,766	2,000,000
24 - 88	2,000,000	5.00%	100,000	(100,000)	(13,234)	86,766	2,000,000
25 - 89	2,000,000	5.00%	100,000	(100,000)	(13,234)	86,766	2,000,000
TOTAL	2,000,000	5.00%	4,000,000	(4,000,000)	(529,351)	3,470,649	2,000,000

We have $100,000 per year of income that we pay taxes on. Let's assume Client A has some Social Security and maybe a small pension, so we put $50,000 in the Additional Income box so that their investment income is taxed at the higher marginal bracket.

Side note: Most people are shocked when they see $2 million for retirement only creating $81,355 of income. How long has $1 million been the goal for retirement? And it often still is. People don't think about adjusting that number over time. Is it possible that we won't be earning 5% when we get there? What if it's only 3%? Then it's $50,155 a year after taxes. That's a pretty drastic difference.

When we look at this from the standpoint of the financial institution, how did they fare? Is the "buy term and invest the difference" strategy good for them? When we (the client) are putting our money into assets, who's using that money? Not the client. The financial institution is.

The real brilliance in that strategy for the financial institution is that when you get to the point when you think you will actually get to use your money, all you get is the small interest payment, while they get the bulk of the asset. And they're moving that money, and making money with your money, all the time.

So, if you're living on 5%, who's living on the 95%? Basically, all you get is the interest off the investment because you can't afford to risk living too long.

When you're stuck in a position where all you can take out is "interest only" and the bank is still using the full $2 million, they've got you trapped in the retirement phase where they still get to take advantage of you. So this calculator shows us that maybe that's not the best option.

Let's think about Client B on the right.

Client B bought permanent life insurance, and along the way they still invested in stocks, real estate, and other things. They created as much in assets outside the life insurance as the $2 million Client A did on the left. To demonstrate this, we put in $2 million for Client B at 5%.

And instead of taking interest only, we're going to do a "Pay Down," taking principal and interest over these twenty years because this individual knows the life insurance is there to back them up. Where did that money come from? Did it come out of life insurance? No, it came out of the assets. So Client B has life insurance now, that when he dies, is going to replace this asset.

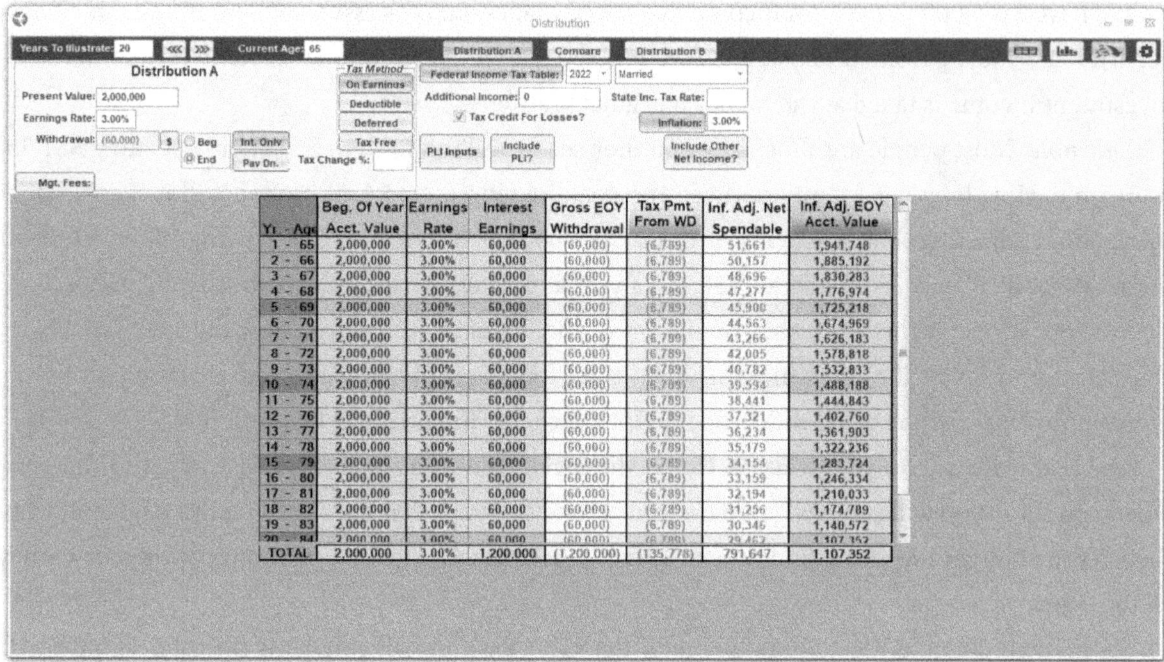

Yr - Age	Beg. Of Year Acct. Value	Earnings Rate	Interest Earnings	Gross EOY Withdrawal	Tax Pmt. From WD	Inf. Adj. Net Spendable	Inf. Adj. EOY Acct. Value
1 - 65	2,000,000	3.00%	60,000	(60,000)	(6,789)	51,661	1,941,748
2 - 66	2,000,000	3.00%	60,000	(60,000)	(6,789)	50,157	1,885,192
3 - 67	2,000,000	3.00%	60,000	(60,000)	(6,789)	48,696	1,830,283
4 - 68	2,000,000	3.00%	60,000	(60,000)	(6,789)	47,277	1,776,974
5 - 69	2,000,000	3.00%	60,000	(60,000)	(6,789)	45,900	1,725,218
6 - 70	2,000,000	3.00%	60,000	(60,000)	(6,789)	44,563	1,674,969
7 - 71	2,000,000	3.00%	60,000	(60,000)	(6,789)	43,266	1,626,183
8 - 72	2,000,000	3.00%	60,000	(60,000)	(6,789)	42,005	1,578,818
9 - 73	2,000,000	3.00%	60,000	(60,000)	(6,789)	40,782	1,532,833
10 - 74	2,000,000	3.00%	60,000	(60,000)	(6,789)	39,594	1,488,188
11 - 75	2,000,000	3.00%	60,000	(60,000)	(6,789)	38,441	1,444,843
12 - 76	2,000,000	3.00%	60,000	(60,000)	(6,789)	37,321	1,402,760
13 - 77	2,000,000	3.00%	60,000	(60,000)	(6,789)	36,234	1,361,903
14 - 78	2,000,000	3.00%	60,000	(60,000)	(6,789)	35,179	1,322,236
15 - 79	2,000,000	3.00%	60,000	(60,000)	(6,789)	34,154	1,283,724
16 - 80	2,000,000	3.00%	60,000	(60,000)	(6,789)	33,159	1,246,334
17 - 81	2,000,000	3.00%	60,000	(60,000)	(6,789)	32,194	1,210,033
18 - 82	2,000,000	3.00%	60,000	(60,000)	(6,789)	31,256	1,174,789
19 - 83	2,000,000	3.00%	60,000	(60,000)	(6,789)	30,346	1,140,572
20 - 84	2,000,000	3.00%	60,000	(60,000)	(6,789)	29,462	1,107,352
TOTAL	2,000,000	3.00%	1,200,000	(1,200,000)	(135,778)	791,647	1,107,352

Permanent whole life insurance opened up options on how to better spend an existing asset. Client B started at $141,840 of annual income, and it grew into $159,568. What's the one way we can counter inflation? More money.

Not only did we start at a higher income level, that income grew to help counter inflation. Plus people who hate to pay taxes really like to see this feature: look at the tax payment. What causes taxes to drop from $18,645 the first year to $917 out in the future? Less interest earned.

To reiterate: what if Client B sold all the assets they created and ended up with $2 million in cash to invest at 5%, and then took both principal and interest out over twenty years? It was the presence of life insurance that unlocked other strategies for them to use to create an income stream after the 20 year period.

If you think about it, we have *reduced the accumulation risk and the distribution risk because of the person's life insurance.* Even if Client B ends up with about half of what we thought they were going to asset wise, they still can pull out more income than what Client A is limited to.

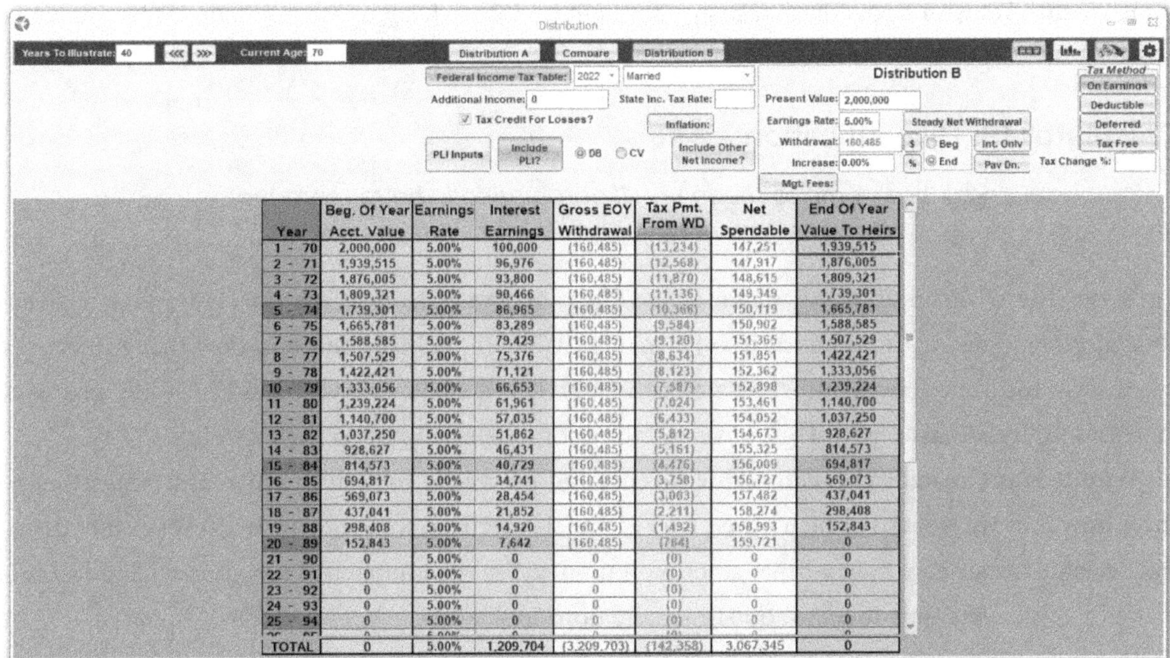

Year	Beg. Of Year Acct. Value	Earnings Rate	Interest Earnings	Gross EOY Withdrawal	Tax Pmt. From WD	Net Spendable	End Of Year Value To Heirs
1 - 70	2,000,000	5.00%	100,000	(160,485)	(13,234)	147,251	1,939,515
2 - 71	1,939,515	5.00%	96,976	(160,485)	(12,568)	147,917	1,876,005
3 - 72	1,876,005	5.00%	93,800	(160,485)	(11,870)	148,615	1,809,321
4 - 73	1,809,321	5.00%	90,466	(160,485)	(11,136)	149,349	1,739,301
5 - 74	1,739,301	5.00%	86,965	(160,485)	(10,366)	150,119	1,665,781
6 - 75	1,665,781	5.00%	83,289	(160,485)	(9,584)	150,902	1,588,585
7 - 76	1,588,585	5.00%	79,429	(160,485)	(9,120)	151,365	1,507,529
8 - 77	1,507,529	5.00%	75,376	(160,485)	(8,634)	151,851	1,422,421
9 - 78	1,422,421	5.00%	71,121	(160,485)	(8,123)	152,362	1,333,056
10 - 79	1,333,056	5.00%	66,653	(160,485)	(7,587)	152,898	1,239,224
11 - 80	1,239,224	5.00%	61,961	(160,485)	(7,024)	153,461	1,140,700
12 - 81	1,140,700	5.00%	57,035	(160,485)	(6,433)	154,052	1,037,250
13 - 82	1,037,250	5.00%	51,862	(160,485)	(5,812)	154,673	928,627
14 - 83	928,627	5.00%	46,431	(160,485)	(5,161)	155,325	814,573
15 - 84	814,573	5.00%	40,729	(160,485)	(4,476)	156,009	694,817
16 - 85	694,817	5.00%	34,741	(160,485)	(3,758)	156,727	569,073
17 - 86	569,073	5.00%	28,454	(160,485)	(3,003)	157,482	437,041
18 - 87	437,041	5.00%	21,852	(160,485)	(2,211)	158,274	298,408
19 - 88	298,408	5.00%	14,920	(160,485)	(1,492)	158,993	152,843
20 - 89	152,843	5.00%	7,642	(160,485)	(764)	159,721	0
21 - 90	0	5.00%	0	0	(0)	0	0
22 - 91	0	5.00%	0	0	(0)	0	0
23 - 92	0	5.00%	0	0	(0)	0	0
24 - 93	0	5.00%	0	0	(0)	0	0
25 - 94	0	5.00%	0	0	(0)	0	0
TOTAL	0	5.00%	1,209,704	(3,209,703)	(142,358)	3,067,345	0

Client A spent years building up this nest egg that they're afraid to touch, and it doesn't even serve them in retirement. The income for Client B has reduced the $2,000,000 asset to zero on purpose.

And notice below the Client on the right (Distribution B) now has the same amount of income from age ninety on. This was an income stream pulled from the life insurance policy and you will notice how small the income tax is. This is because the cash value of the life insurance is generating tax-efficient income.

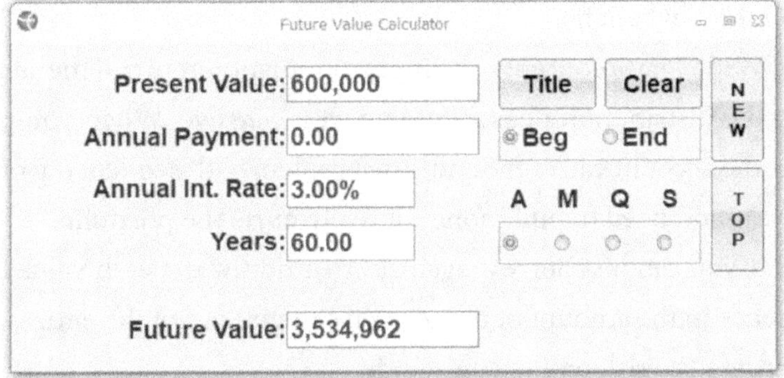

Best Uses: This calculator is really for taking any asset and talking about the different ways it can be distributed. It shows the difference between an "Interest Only" strategy and a "Pay Down" strategy. And it can demonstrate what happens with inflation. This is so valuable for retired people. At first everything's great. Then all of a sudden, they're not buying clothes, don't go out anymore, inflation comes on hard, and when people see it, it's tough. They took all the interest initially and then every following year, their money isn't going as far, and they're stuck with what feels like a decreasing income stream. Yet with a paydown strategy, we might be able to keep up with inflation; this calculator shows us how.

Calculator 19: Diversification

Risk has come to mean you'll automatically have more money whereas it actually means the likelihood of loss!

Purpose: The Diversification calculator shows the outcome of transferring assets from savings accounts, money markets, and bonds into Permanent Whole Life Insurance and how that reduces the taxes, term insurance costs, and risks along the way. It helps clients understand how life insurance increases both their asset base while alive and the net to their heirs upon their death.

Why It Was Created: This calculator was created primarily to combine two assets together to show how they interact with each other. Every financial decision we make impacts every other financial decision because we have a finite amount of money. Yet what happens in the financial industry is that strategists often only focus on one thing and don't look at the other accounts or impacts.

Diversification moves us in that direction, looking at multiple accounts together. It also allows us to pull in life insurance values and see what they can do. Most money managers have to follow modern portfolio theory, having some of the money in safe assets, typically bonds. You may have a portfolio split between equity and bonds. People often focus on one side only, yet your decision to put money in equities caused your decision to put money in bonds. There's a dramatic difference when we start shifting portfolios and examine both sides through this calculator.

I like to encourage clients to look at something more efficient and certain: let's make the "certainty asset" life insurance instead of bonds. Life insurance cash value growth will typically outperform bonds and provide additional benefits.

Going back to Dr. Wade Pfau's concepts, during accumulation returns, the sequencing impacts the numbers, but during the distribution phase, the impact is *massive.* When you pull money out of an account in a loss year, the account can't rebound. The problem with sequencing of returns is that when you have a negative year and need to pull money, it really hurts the portfolio.

With life insurance, you can just borrow against or withdraw the cash value until the market corrects itself. The difference in the amount of money you can pull out of the entire equation is quite a bit larger, and it also manages the risk on the equity side.

Case Study: Using this calculator to show diversification of existing money is a simple way to start and get points across very fast. We're going to do it one way with old existing money and one way with new additional money. While we could combine them, separating them out helps you see all the parts.

We are going to look at the Diversification Calculator and prove a simple Wealth Shift.

Looking at an existing account with $250,000 in it that is earning 2% and doesn't have any management fees associated with it. We'll put an Income Tax Rate of 24% for simplicity.

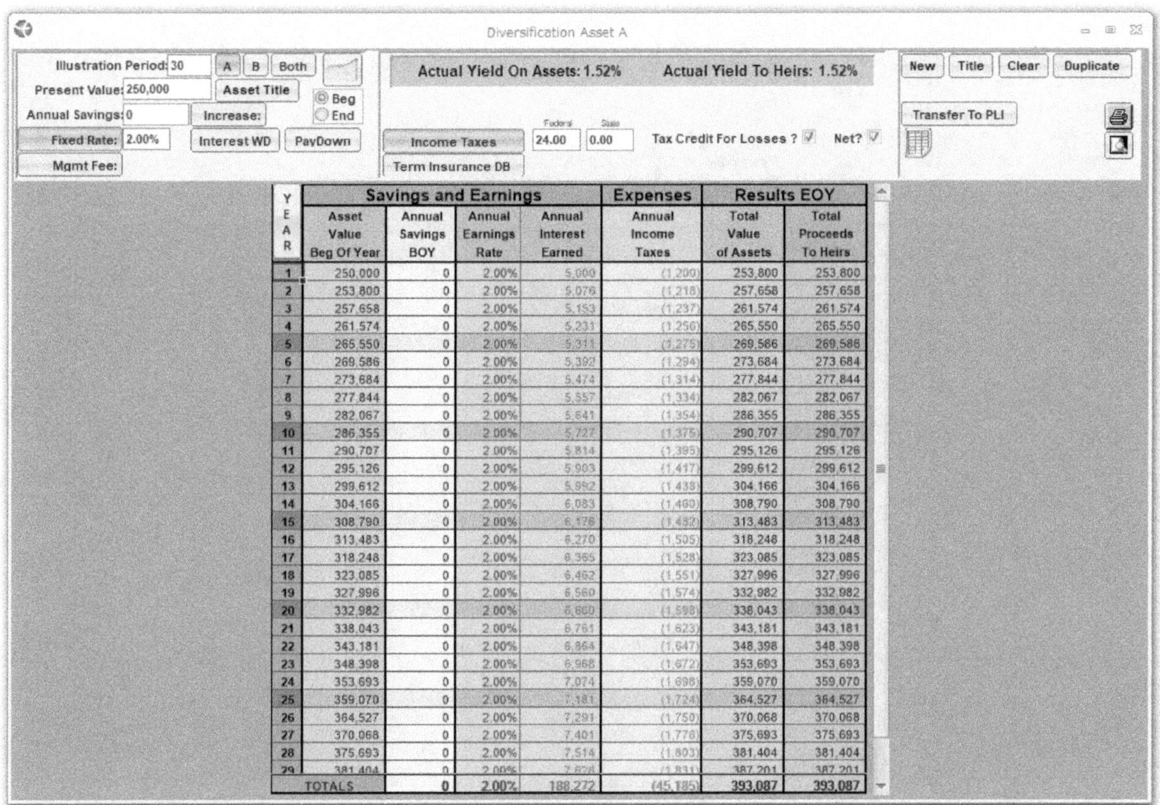

YEAR	Savings and Earnings				Expenses	Results EOY	
	Asset Value Beg Of Year	Annual Savings BOY	Annual Earnings Rate	Annual Interest Earned	Annual Income Taxes	Total Value of Assets	Total Proceeds To Heirs
1	250,000	0	2.00%	5,000	(1,200)	253,800	253,800
2	253,800	0	2.00%	5,076	(1,218)	257,658	257,658
3	257,658	0	2.00%	5,153	(1,237)	261,574	261,574
4	261,574	0	2.00%	5,231	(1,256)	265,550	265,550
5	265,550	0	2.00%	5,311	(1,275)	269,586	269,586
6	269,586	0	2.00%	5,392	(1,294)	273,684	273,684
7	273,684	0	2.00%	5,474	(1,314)	277,844	277,844
8	277,844	0	2.00%	5,557	(1,334)	282,067	282,067
9	282,067	0	2.00%	5,641	(1,354)	286,355	286,355
10	286,355	0	2.00%	5,727	(1,375)	290,707	290,707
11	290,707	0	2.00%	5,814	(1,395)	295,126	295,126
12	295,126	0	2.00%	5,903	(1,417)	299,612	299,612
13	299,612	0	2.00%	5,992	(1,438)	304,166	304,166
14	304,166	0	2.00%	6,083	(1,460)	308,790	308,790
15	308,790	0	2.00%	6,176	(1,482)	313,483	313,483
16	313,483	0	2.00%	6,270	(1,505)	318,248	318,248
17	318,248	0	2.00%	6,365	(1,528)	323,085	323,085
18	323,085	0	2.00%	6,462	(1,551)	327,996	327,996
19	327,996	0	2.00%	6,560	(1,574)	332,982	332,982
20	332,982	0	2.00%	6,660	(1,598)	338,043	338,043
21	338,043	0	2.00%	6,761	(1,623)	343,181	343,181
22	343,181	0	2.00%	6,864	(1,647)	348,398	348,398
23	348,398	0	2.00%	6,968	(1,672)	353,693	353,693
24	353,693	0	2.00%	7,074	(1,698)	359,070	359,070
25	359,070	0	2.00%	7,181	(1,724)	364,527	364,527
26	364,527	0	2.00%	7,291	(1,750)	370,068	370,068
27	370,068	0	2.00%	7,401	(1,776)	375,693	375,693
28	375,693	0	2.00%	7,514	(1,803)	381,404	381,404
29	381,404	0	2.00%	7,628	(1,831)	387,201	387,201
TOTALS		0	2.00%	188,272	(45,185)	393,087	393,087

Okay. So the first account is A, the second account is B, and then we have a, BOTH where you can see the combination of all of it, but we're just going to be using A, for this simpler exercise, then you can see use of B and BOTH in Cash Flow Bridge below.

What we see is this account of $250,000 grows to $393,087 by this timeframe net of taxes.

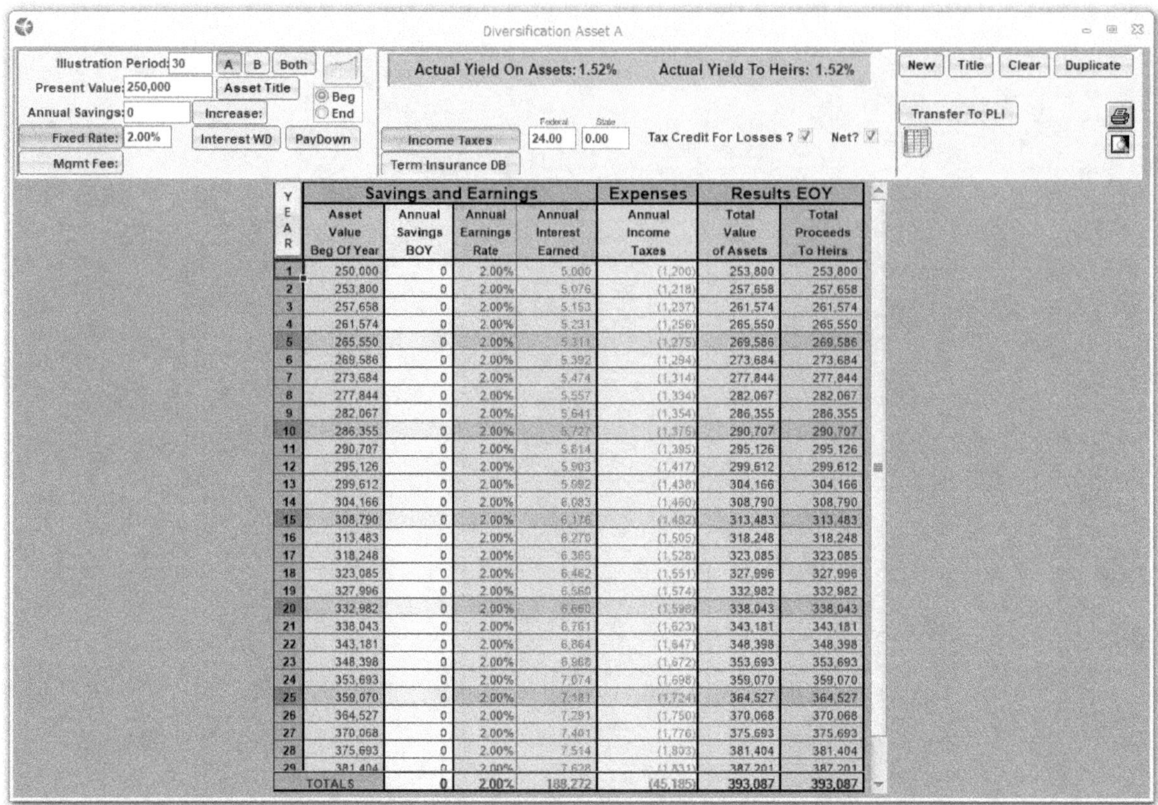

YEAR	Savings and Earnings				Expenses	Results EOY	
	Asset Value Beg Of Year	Annual Savings BOY	Annual Earnings Rate	Annual Interest Earned	Annual Income Taxes	Total Value of Assets	Total Proceeds To Heirs
1	250,000	0	2.00%	5,000	(1,200)	253,800	253,800
2	253,800	0	2.00%	5,076	(1,218)	257,658	257,658
3	257,658	0	2.00%	5,153	(1,237)	261,574	261,574
4	261,574	0	2.00%	5,231	(1,256)	265,550	265,550
5	265,550	0	2.00%	5,311	(1,275)	269,586	269,586
6	269,586	0	2.00%	5,392	(1,294)	273,684	273,684
7	273,684	0	2.00%	5,474	(1,314)	277,844	277,844
8	277,844	0	2.00%	5,557	(1,334)	282,067	282,067
9	282,067	0	2.00%	5,641	(1,354)	286,355	286,355
10	286,355	0	2.00%	5,727	(1,376)	290,707	290,707
11	290,707	0	2.00%	5,814	(1,395)	295,126	295,126
12	295,126	0	2.00%	5,903	(1,417)	299,612	299,612
13	299,612	0	2.00%	5,992	(1,438)	304,166	304,166
14	304,166	0	2.00%	6,083	(1,460)	308,790	308,790
15	308,790	0	2.00%	6,176	(1,482)	313,483	313,483
16	313,483	0	2.00%	6,270	(1,505)	318,248	318,248
17	318,248	0	2.00%	6,365	(1,528)	323,085	323,085
18	323,085	0	2.00%	6,462	(1,551)	327,996	327,996
19	327,996	0	2.00%	6,560	(1,574)	332,982	332,982
20	332,982	0	2.00%	6,660	(1,598)	338,043	338,043
21	338,043	0	2.00%	6,761	(1,623)	343,181	343,181
22	343,181	0	2.00%	6,864	(1,647)	348,398	348,398
23	348,398	0	2.00%	6,968	(1,672)	353,693	353,693
24	353,693	0	2.00%	7,074	(1,698)	359,070	359,070
25	359,070	0	2.00%	7,181	(1,724)	364,527	364,527
26	364,527	0	2.00%	7,291	(1,750)	370,068	370,068
27	370,068	0	2.00%	7,401	(1,776)	375,693	375,693
28	375,693	0	2.00%	7,514	(1,803)	381,404	381,404
29	381,404	0	2.00%	7,628	(1,831)	387,201	387,201
TOTALS		0	2.00%	188,272	(45,185)	393,087	393,087

This is what happens if it's "net", if the taxes come out of the account. If it's not "net", we're paying them from another source. And the account grows to $452,840 as shown below.

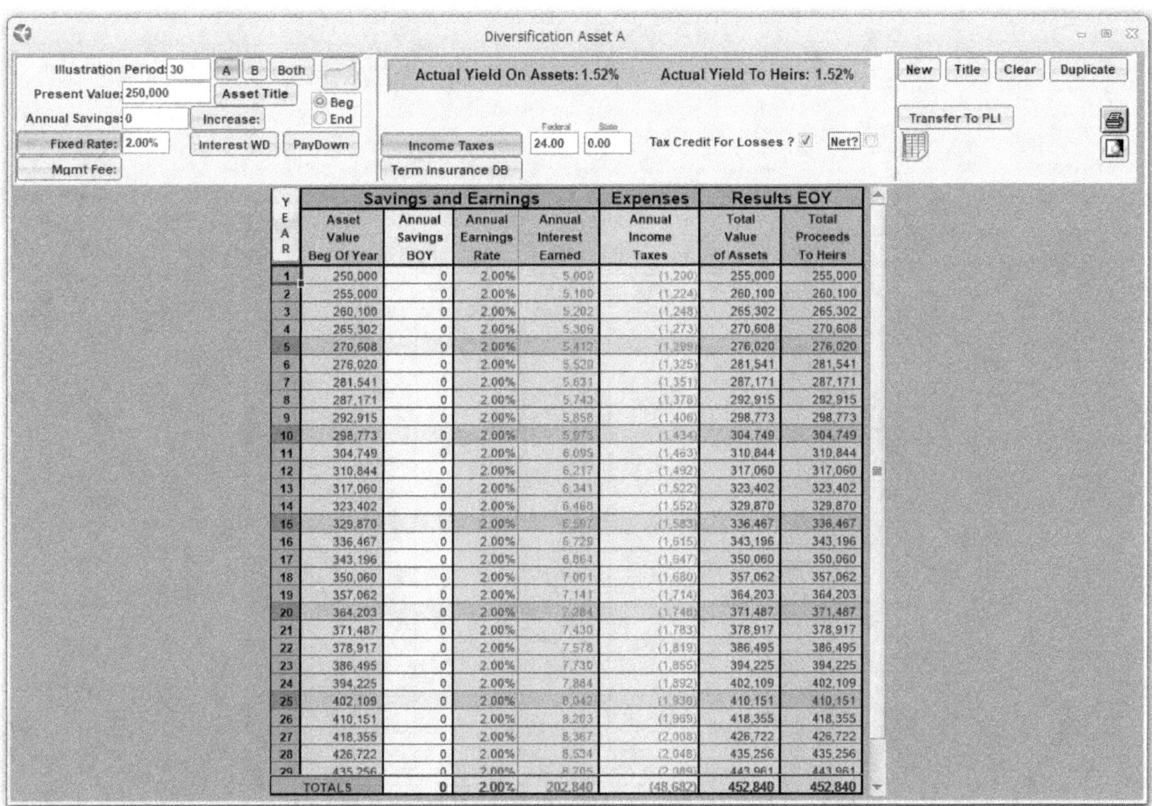

YEAR	Savings and Earnings				Expenses	Results EOY	
	Asset Value Beg Of Year	Annual Savings BOY	Annual Earnings Rate	Annual Interest Earned	Annual Income Taxes	Total Value of Assets	Total Proceeds To Heirs
1	250,000	0	2.00%	5,000	(1,200)	255,000	255,000
2	255,000	0	2.00%	5,100	(1,224)	260,100	260,100
3	260,100	0	2.00%	5,202	(1,248)	265,302	265,302
4	265,302	0	2.00%	5,306	(1,273)	270,608	270,608
5	270,608	0	2.00%	5,412	(1,299)	276,020	276,020
6	276,020	0	2.00%	5,520	(1,325)	281,541	281,541
7	281,541	0	2.00%	5,631	(1,351)	287,171	287,171
8	287,171	0	2.00%	5,743	(1,378)	292,915	292,915
9	292,915	0	2.00%	5,858	(1,406)	298,773	298,773
10	298,773	0	2.00%	5,975	(1,434)	304,749	304,749
11	304,749	0	2.00%	6,095	(1,463)	310,844	310,844
12	310,844	0	2.00%	6,217	(1,492)	317,060	317,060
13	317,060	0	2.00%	6,341	(1,522)	323,402	323,402
14	323,402	0	2.00%	6,468	(1,552)	329,870	329,870
15	329,870	0	2.00%	6,597	(1,583)	336,467	336,467
16	336,467	0	2.00%	6,729	(1,615)	343,196	343,196
17	343,196	0	2.00%	6,864	(1,647)	350,060	350,060
18	350,060	0	2.00%	7,001	(1,680)	357,062	357,062
19	357,062	0	2.00%	7,141	(1,714)	364,203	364,203
20	364,203	0	2.00%	7,284	(1,748)	371,487	371,487
21	371,487	0	2.00%	7,430	(1,783)	378,917	378,917
22	378,917	0	2.00%	7,578	(1,819)	386,495	386,495
23	386,495	0	2.00%	7,730	(1,855)	394,225	394,225
24	394,225	0	2.00%	7,884	(1,892)	402,109	402,109
25	402,109	0	2.00%	8,042	(1,930)	410,151	410,151
26	410,151	0	2.00%	8,203	(1,969)	418,355	418,355
27	418,355	0	2.00%	8,367	(2,008)	426,722	426,722
28	426,722	0	2.00%	8,534	(2,048)	435,256	435,256
29	435,256	0	2.00%	8,705	(2,089)	443,961	443,961
TOTALS		0	2.00%	202,840	(48,682)	452,840	452,840

This is an interesting thing, too. Going back to the whole idea of opportunity cost and opportunity gain. Financial institutions will encourage you to NOT pay taxes out of the account, because the account will grow faster.

Is that a true statement? Yes. If I don't take tax money out to pay taxes, it will grow faster. The problem is I just depleted another account to make that happen. So it didn't help me any. By doing that, it just helps them because there's more money in there. What happens is everything is always "net". *When we compound one account we're still negative in another account to pay the taxes. Norman used to say you were compounding your pockets and netting your pair of pants.*

We have a finite amount of money in our world. If we don't take the taxes out of this account to pay the taxes on this account, then they come from another account somewhere else. The beauty of that, if you're the financial institution, is that people don't keep track of it.

We can do the same thing with the term insurance. If I turn on the term insurance, I can also net that out of this account or be paying the premium as an additional cost from somewhere else.

And let's say they're taking the premiums out of the account. And they have $250,000 of term life insurance.

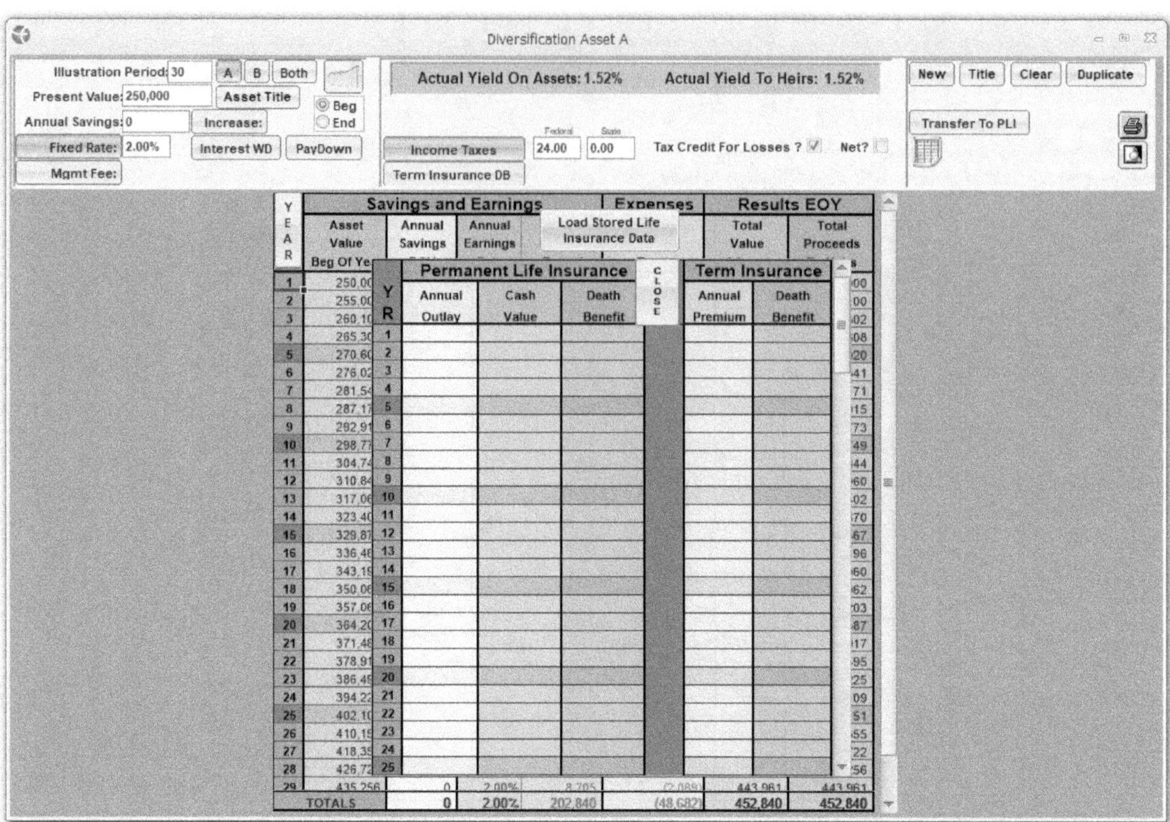

What we see is $250,000 of 30 year level term insurance for $388 a year for 30 years and then it gets cancelled as you can see in the 31st year below.

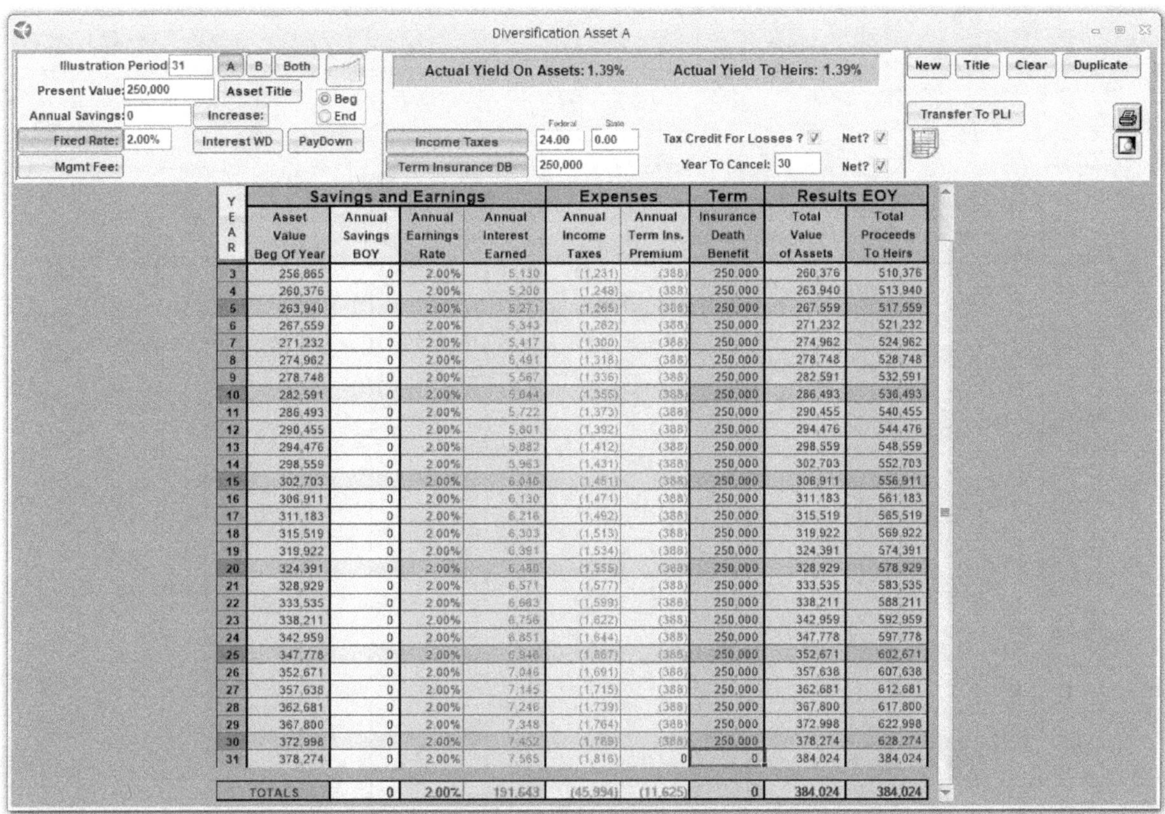

YEAR	Savings and Earnings				Expenses		Term	Results EOY	
	Asset Value Beg Of Year	Annual Savings BOY	Annual Earnings Rate	Annual Interest Earned	Annual Income Taxes	Annual Term Ins. Premium	Insurance Death Benefit	Total Value of Assets	Total Proceeds To Heirs
3	256,865	0	2.00%	5,130	(1,231)	(388)	250,000	260,376	510,376
4	260,376	0	2.00%	5,200	(1,248)	(388)	250,000	263,940	513,940
5	263,940	0	2.00%	5,271	(1,265)	(388)	250,000	267,559	517,559
6	267,559	0	2.00%	5,343	(1,282)	(388)	250,000	271,232	521,232
7	271,232	0	2.00%	5,417	(1,300)	(388)	250,000	274,962	524,962
8	274,962	0	2.00%	5,491	(1,318)	(388)	250,000	278,748	528,748
9	278,748	0	2.00%	5,567	(1,336)	(388)	250,000	282,591	532,591
10	282,591	0	2.00%	5,644	(1,355)	(388)	250,000	286,493	536,493
11	286,493	0	2.00%	5,722	(1,373)	(388)	250,000	290,455	540,455
12	290,455	0	2.00%	5,801	(1,392)	(388)	250,000	294,476	544,476
13	294,476	0	2.00%	5,882	(1,412)	(388)	250,000	298,559	548,559
14	298,559	0	2.00%	5,963	(1,431)	(388)	250,000	302,703	552,703
15	302,703	0	2.00%	6,046	(1,451)	(388)	250,000	306,911	556,911
16	306,911	0	2.00%	6,130	(1,471)	(388)	250,000	311,183	561,183
17	311,183	0	2.00%	6,216	(1,492)	(388)	250,000	315,519	565,519
18	315,519	0	2.00%	6,303	(1,513)	(388)	250,000	319,922	569,922
19	319,922	0	2.00%	6,391	(1,534)	(388)	250,000	324,391	574,391
20	324,391	0	2.00%	6,480	(1,555)	(388)	250,000	328,929	578,929
21	328,929	0	2.00%	6,571	(1,577)	(388)	250,000	333,535	583,535
22	333,535	0	2.00%	6,663	(1,599)	(388)	250,000	338,211	588,211
23	338,211	0	2.00%	6,756	(1,622)	(388)	250,000	342,959	592,959
24	342,959	0	2.00%	6,851	(1,644)	(388)	250,000	347,778	597,778
25	347,778	0	2.00%	6,946	(1,667)	(388)	250,000	352,671	602,671
26	352,671	0	2.00%	7,046	(1,691)	(388)	250,000	357,638	607,638
27	357,638	0	2.00%	7,145	(1,715)	(388)	250,000	362,681	612,681
28	362,681	0	2.00%	7,246	(1,739)	(388)	250,000	367,800	617,800
29	367,800	0	2.00%	7,348	(1,764)	(388)	250,000	372,998	622,998
30	372,998	0	2.00%	7,452	(1,789)	(388)	250,000	378,274	628,274
31	378,274	0	2.00%	7,565	(1,816)	0	0	384,024	384,024
TOTALS		0	2.00%	191,643	(45,994)	(11,625)	0	384,024	384,024

Since they canceled their term insurance, they just disinherited the kids.

So what if we had this account at $250,000 and pulled off the earnings and did something else with those dollars. Think of it like skimming the cream off the crop.

Go to "Transfer to PLI" on the right. We know we are earning $5000 a year ($250,000 x 2%). Yet we have to pay taxes so let's shift or transfer $4000 to Permanent Life Insurance (whole life) and see if we have improved things.

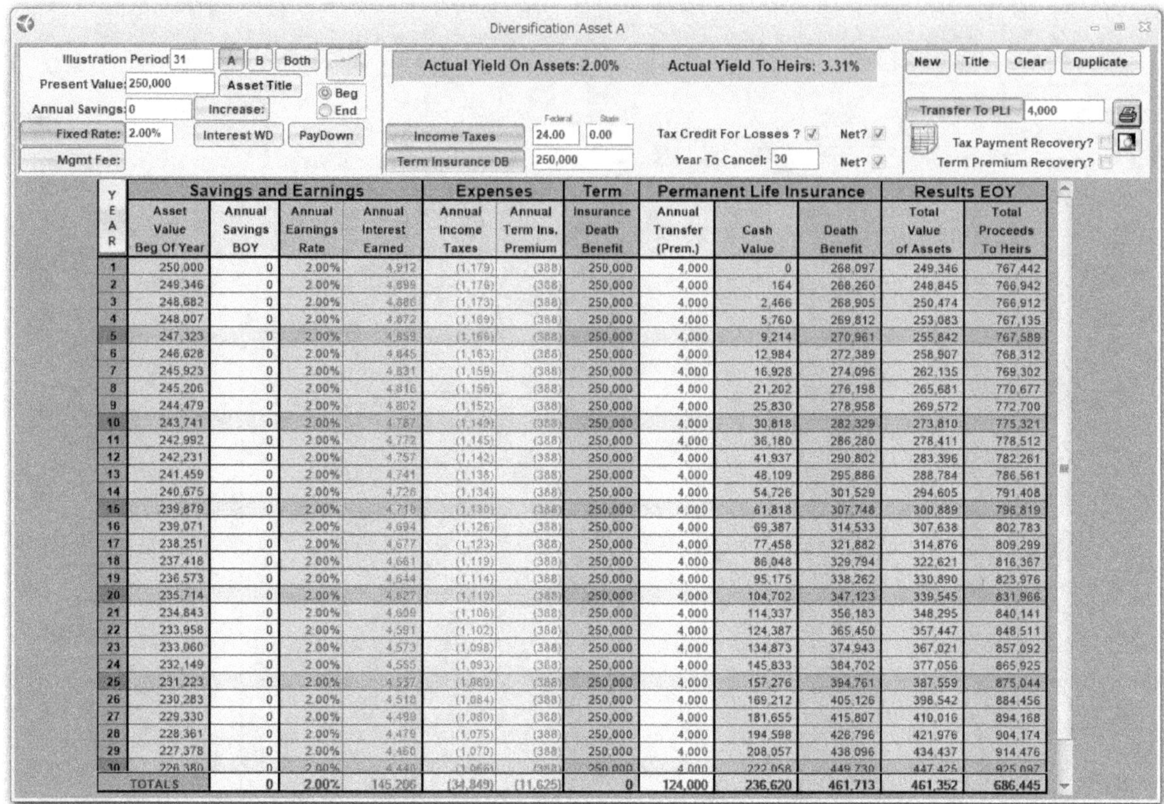

YEAR	Savings and Earnings				Expenses		Term	Permanent Life Insurance			Results EOY	
	Asset Value Beg Of Year	Annual Savings BOY	Annual Earnings Rate	Annual Interest Earned	Annual Income Taxes	Annual Term Ins. Premium	Insurance Death Benefit	Annual Transfer (Prem.)	Cash Value	Death Benefit	Total Value of Assets	Total Proceeds To Heirs
1	250,000	0	2.00%	4,912	(1,179)	(388)	250,000	4,000	0	268,097	249,346	767,442
2	249,346	0	2.00%	4,899	(1,176)	(388)	250,000	4,000	164	268,260	248,845	766,942
3	248,682	0	2.00%	4,886	(1,173)	(388)	250,000	4,000	2,466	268,905	250,474	766,912
4	248,007	0	2.00%	4,872	(1,169)	(388)	250,000	4,000	5,760	269,812	253,083	767,135
5	247,323	0	2.00%	4,859	(1,166)	(388)	250,000	4,000	9,214	270,961	255,842	767,589
6	246,628	0	2.00%	4,845	(1,163)	(388)	250,000	4,000	12,984	272,389	258,907	768,312
7	245,923	0	2.00%	4,831	(1,159)	(388)	250,000	4,000	16,928	274,096	262,135	769,302
8	245,206	0	2.00%	4,816	(1,156)	(388)	250,000	4,000	21,202	276,198	265,681	770,677
9	244,479	0	2.00%	4,802	(1,152)	(388)	250,000	4,000	25,830	278,958	269,572	772,700
10	243,741	0	2.00%	4,787	(1,149)	(388)	250,000	4,000	30,818	282,329	273,810	775,321
11	242,992	0	2.00%	4,772	(1,145)	(388)	250,000	4,000	36,180	286,280	278,411	778,512
12	242,231	0	2.00%	4,757	(1,142)	(388)	250,000	4,000	41,937	290,802	283,396	782,261
13	241,459	0	2.00%	4,741	(1,138)	(388)	250,000	4,000	48,109	295,886	288,784	786,561
14	240,675	0	2.00%	4,726	(1,134)	(388)	250,000	4,000	54,726	301,529	294,605	791,408
15	239,879	0	2.00%	4,710	(1,130)	(388)	250,000	4,000	61,818	307,748	300,889	796,819
16	239,071	0	2.00%	4,694	(1,126)	(388)	250,000	4,000	69,387	314,533	307,638	802,783
17	238,251	0	2.00%	4,677	(1,123)	(388)	250,000	4,000	77,458	321,882	314,876	809,299
18	237,418	0	2.00%	4,661	(1,119)	(388)	250,000	4,000	86,048	329,794	322,621	816,367
19	236,573	0	2.00%	4,644	(1,114)	(388)	250,000	4,000	95,175	338,262	330,890	823,976
20	235,714	0	2.00%	4,627	(1,110)	(388)	250,000	4,000	104,702	347,123	339,545	831,966
21	234,843	0	2.00%	4,609	(1,106)	(388)	250,000	4,000	114,337	356,183	348,295	840,141
22	233,958	0	2.00%	4,591	(1,102)	(388)	250,000	4,000	124,387	365,450	357,447	848,511
23	233,060	0	2.00%	4,573	(1,098)	(388)	250,000	4,000	134,873	374,943	367,021	857,092
24	232,149	0	2.00%	4,555	(1,093)	(388)	250,000	4,000	145,833	384,702	377,056	865,925
25	231,223	0	2.00%	4,537	(1,089)	(388)	250,000	4,000	157,276	394,761	387,559	875,044
26	230,283	0	2.00%	4,518	(1,084)	(388)	250,000	4,000	169,212	405,126	398,542	884,456
27	229,330	0	2.00%	4,499	(1,080)	(388)	250,000	4,000	181,655	415,807	410,016	894,168
28	228,361	0	2.00%	4,479	(1,075)	(388)	250,000	4,000	194,598	426,796	421,976	904,174
29	227,378	0	2.00%	4,460	(1,070)	(388)	250,000	4,000	208,057	438,096	434,437	914,476
30	226,380	0	2.00%	4,440	(1,066)	(388)	250,000	4,000	222,058	449,730	447,425	925,097
TOTALS		0	2.00%	145,206	(34,849)	(11,625)	0	124,000	236,620	461,713	461,352	686,445

Seeking to keep this account at about $250,000, make that $3,400 in the Transfer To PLI box.

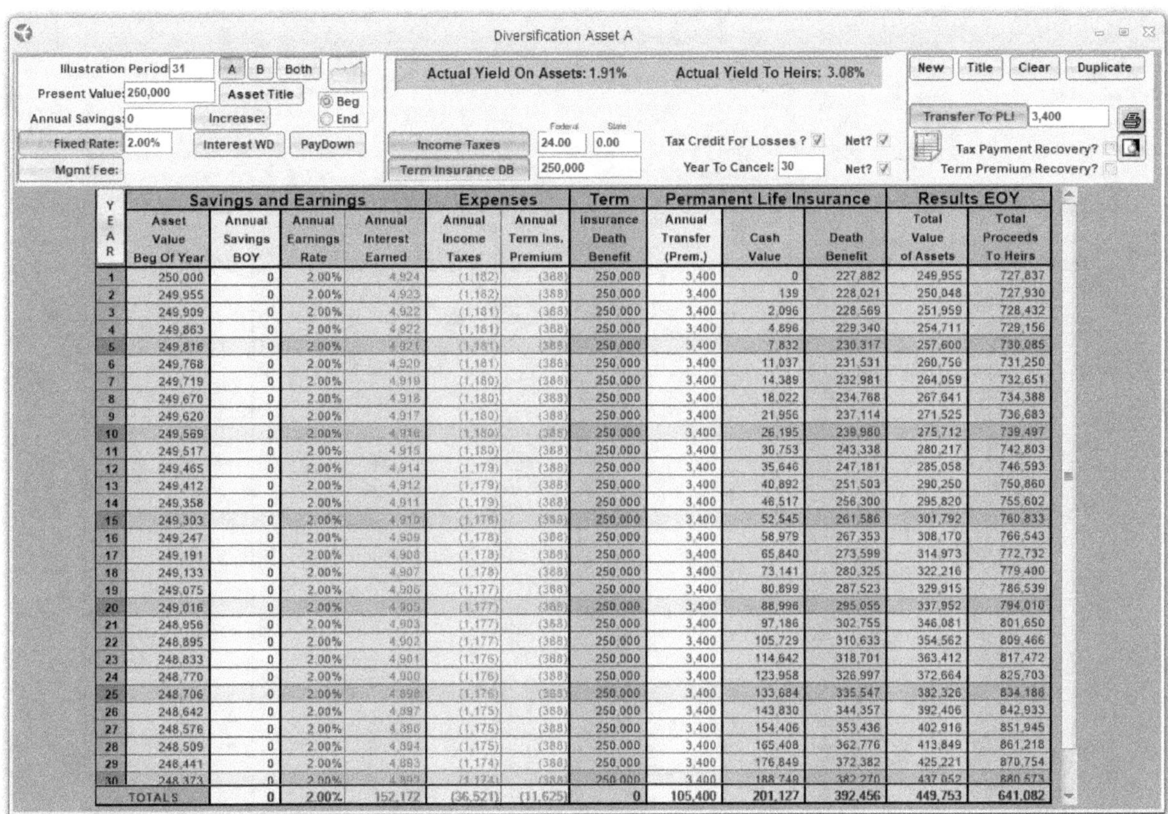

YEAR	Savings and Earnings				Expenses		Term	Permanent Life Insurance			Results EOY	
	Asset Value Beg Of Year	Annual Savings BOY	Annual Earnings Rate	Annual Interest Earned	Annual Income Taxes	Annual Term Ins. Premium	Insurance Death Benefit	Annual Transfer (Prem.)	Cash Value	Death Benefit	Total Value of Assets	Total Proceeds To Heirs
1	250,000	0	2.00%	4,924	(1,182)	(388)	250,000	3,400	0	227,882	249,955	727,837
2	249,955	0	2.00%	4,923	(1,182)	(388)	250,000	3,400	139	228,021	250,048	727,930
3	249,909	0	2.00%	4,922	(1,181)	(388)	250,000	3,400	2,096	228,569	251,959	728,432
4	249,863	0	2.00%	4,922	(1,181)	(388)	250,000	3,400	4,896	229,340	254,711	729,156
5	249,816	0	2.00%	4,921	(1,181)	(388)	250,000	3,400	7,832	230,317	257,600	730,085
6	249,768	0	2.00%	4,920	(1,181)	(388)	250,000	3,400	11,037	231,531	260,756	731,250
7	249,719	0	2.00%	4,919	(1,180)	(388)	250,000	3,400	14,389	232,981	264,059	732,651
8	249,670	0	2.00%	4,918	(1,180)	(388)	250,000	3,400	18,022	234,768	267,641	734,388
9	249,620	0	2.00%	4,917	(1,180)	(388)	250,000	3,400	21,956	237,114	271,525	736,683
10	249,569	0	2.00%	4,916	(1,180)	(388)	250,000	3,400	26,195	239,980	275,712	739,497
11	249,517	0	2.00%	4,915	(1,180)	(388)	250,000	3,400	30,753	243,338	280,217	742,803
12	249,465	0	2.00%	4,914	(1,179)	(388)	250,000	3,400	35,646	247,181	285,058	746,593
13	249,412	0	2.00%	4,912	(1,179)	(388)	250,000	3,400	40,892	251,503	290,250	750,860
14	249,358	0	2.00%	4,911	(1,179)	(388)	250,000	3,400	46,517	256,300	295,820	755,602
15	249,303	0	2.00%	4,910	(1,178)	(388)	250,000	3,400	52,545	261,586	301,792	760,833
16	249,247	0	2.00%	4,909	(1,178)	(388)	250,000	3,400	58,979	267,353	308,170	766,543
17	249,191	0	2.00%	4,908	(1,178)	(388)	250,000	3,400	65,840	273,599	314,973	772,732
18	249,133	0	2.00%	4,907	(1,178)	(388)	250,000	3,400	73,141	280,325	322,216	779,400
19	249,075	0	2.00%	4,906	(1,177)	(388)	250,000	3,400	80,899	287,523	329,915	786,539
20	249,016	0	2.00%	4,905	(1,177)	(388)	250,000	3,400	88,996	295,055	337,952	794,010
21	248,956	0	2.00%	4,903	(1,177)	(388)	250,000	3,400	97,186	302,755	346,081	801,650
22	248,895	0	2.00%	4,902	(1,177)	(388)	250,000	3,400	105,729	310,633	354,562	809,466
23	248,833	0	2.00%	4,901	(1,176)	(388)	250,000	3,400	114,642	318,701	363,412	817,472
24	248,770	0	2.00%	4,900	(1,176)	(388)	250,000	3,400	123,958	326,997	372,664	825,703
25	248,706	0	2.00%	4,898	(1,176)	(388)	250,000	3,400	133,684	335,547	382,326	834,186
26	248,642	0	2.00%	4,897	(1,175)	(388)	250,000	3,400	143,830	344,357	392,406	842,933
27	248,576	0	2.00%	4,896	(1,175)	(388)	250,000	3,400	154,406	353,436	402,916	851,945
28	248,509	0	2.00%	4,894	(1,175)	(388)	250,000	3,400	165,408	362,776	413,849	861,218
29	248,441	0	2.00%	4,893	(1,174)	(388)	250,000	3,400	176,849	372,382	425,221	870,754
30	248,373	0	2.00%	4,892	(1,174)	(388)	250,000	3,400	188,749	382,270	437,052	880,573
TOTALS		0	2.00%	152,172	(36,521)	(11,625)	0	105,400	201,127	392,456	449,753	641,082

So now we have taken out too much, yet you get the idea of what we're trying to do. We've shifted the interest (or taken the cream off the crop) and the software automatically shows us the combination of both columns. So now we have this cash value and this death benefit that we've picked up. Could we get rid of the term insurance now?

Yes. And what we're going to see is at this point is the software is going to adjust the overall picture to keep it even and so we still have some term premiums. Why? Because we didn't have $250,000 of total coverage until we crossed over about the 13th year.

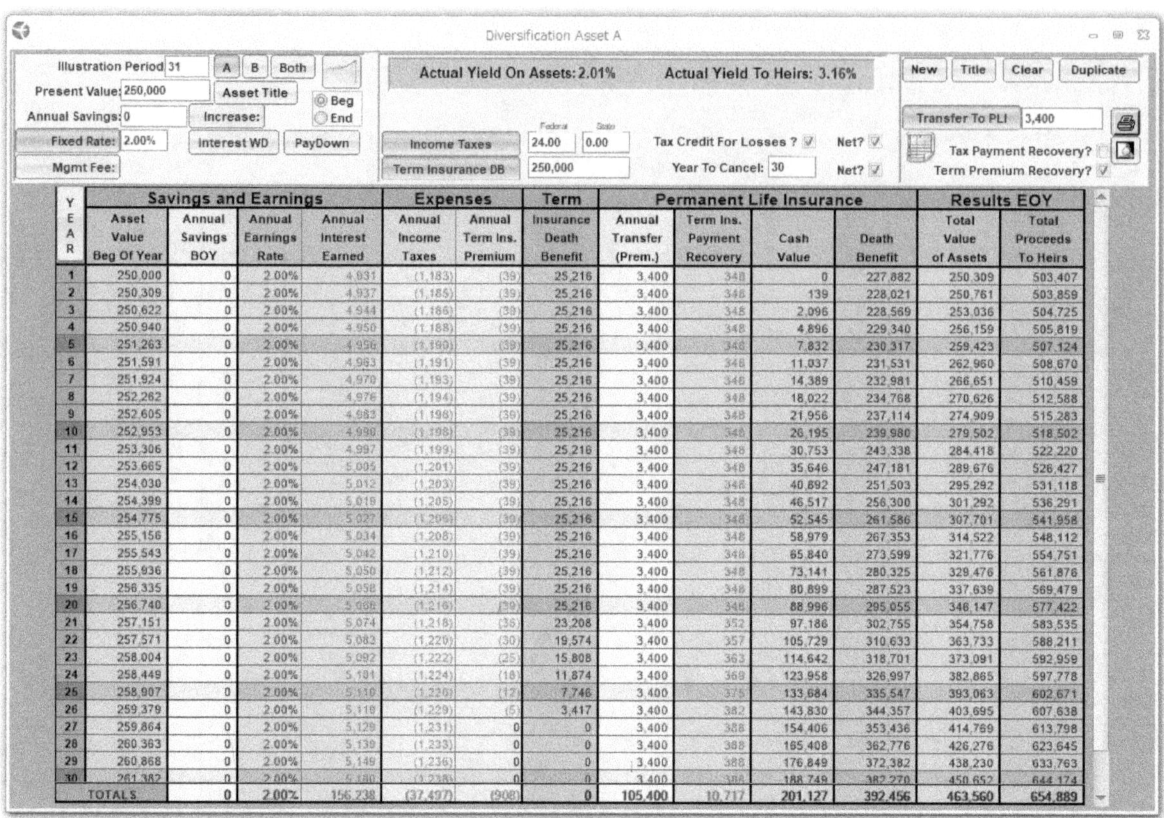
Diversification Asset A

Illustration Period 31 | A | B | Both
Present Value: 250,000 | Asset Title | Beg / End
Annual Savings: 0 | Increase:
Fixed Rate: 2.00% | Interest WD | PayDown
Mgmt Fee:

Actual Yield On Assets: 2.01% | Actual Yield To Heirs: 3.16%

Income Taxes | Federal 24.00 | State 0.00 | Tax Credit For Losses ? ✓ | Net? ✓
Term Insurance DB | 250,000 | Year To Cancel: 30 | Net? ✓

New | Title | Clear | Duplicate
Transfer To PLI 3,400
Tax Payment Recovery?
Term Premium Recovery? ✓

YEAR	Savings and Earnings				Expenses		Term	Permanent Life Insurance				Results EOY	
	Asset Value Beg Of Year	Annual Savings BOY	Annual Earnings Rate	Annual Interest Earned	Annual Income Taxes	Annual Term Ins. Premium	Insurance Death Benefit	Annual Transfer (Prem.)	Term Ins. Payment Recovery	Cash Value	Death Benefit	Total Value of Assets	Total Proceeds To Heirs
1	250,000	0	2.00%	4,931	(1,183)	(39)	25,216	3,400	348	0	227,882	250,309	503,407
2	250,309	0	2.00%	4,937	(1,185)	(39)	25,216	3,400	348	139	228,021	250,761	503,859
3	250,622	0	2.00%	4,944	(1,186)	(39)	25,216	3,400	348	2,096	228,569	253,036	504,725
4	250,940	0	2.00%	4,950	(1,188)	(39)	25,216	3,400	348	4,896	229,340	256,159	505,819
5	251,263	0	2.00%	4,956	(1,190)	(39)	25,216	3,400	348	7,832	230,317	259,423	507,124
6	251,591	0	2.00%	4,963	(1,191)	(39)	25,216	3,400	348	11,037	231,531	262,960	508,670
7	251,924	0	2.00%	4,970	(1,193)	(39)	25,216	3,400	348	14,389	232,981	266,651	510,459
8	252,262	0	2.00%	4,976	(1,194)	(39)	25,216	3,400	348	18,022	234,768	270,626	512,588
9	252,605	0	2.00%	4,983	(1,196)	(39)	25,216	3,400	348	21,956	237,114	274,909	515,283
10	252,953	0	2.00%	4,990	(1,198)	(39)	25,216	3,400	348	26,195	239,980	279,502	518,502
11	253,306	0	2.00%	4,997	(1,199)	(39)	25,216	3,400	348	30,753	243,338	284,418	522,220
12	253,665	0	2.00%	5,005	(1,201)	(39)	25,216	3,400	348	35,646	247,181	289,676	526,427
13	254,030	0	2.00%	5,012	(1,203)	(39)	25,216	3,400	348	40,892	251,503	295,292	531,118
14	254,399	0	2.00%	5,019	(1,205)	(39)	25,216	3,400	348	46,517	256,300	301,292	536,291
15	254,775	0	2.00%	5,027	(1,206)	(39)	25,216	3,400	348	52,545	261,586	307,701	541,958
16	255,156	0	2.00%	5,034	(1,208)	(39)	25,216	3,400	348	58,979	267,353	314,522	548,112
17	255,543	0	2.00%	5,042	(1,210)	(39)	25,216	3,400	348	65,840	273,599	321,776	554,751
18	255,936	0	2.00%	5,050	(1,212)	(39)	25,216	3,400	348	73,141	280,325	329,476	561,876
19	256,335	0	2.00%	5,058	(1,214)	(39)	25,216	3,400	348	80,899	287,523	337,639	569,479
20	256,740	0	2.00%	5,066	(1,216)	(39)	25,216	3,400	348	88,996	295,055	346,147	577,422
21	257,151	0	2.00%	5,074	(1,218)	(36)	23,208	3,400	352	97,186	302,755	354,758	583,535
22	257,571	0	2.00%	5,083	(1,220)	(30)	19,574	3,400	357	105,729	310,633	363,733	588,211
23	258,004	0	2.00%	5,092	(1,222)	(25)	15,808	3,400	363	114,642	318,701	373,091	592,959
24	258,449	0	2.00%	5,101	(1,224)	(18)	11,874	3,400	369	123,958	326,997	382,865	597,778
25	258,907	0	2.00%	5,110	(1,226)	(12)	7,746	3,400	375	133,684	335,547	393,063	602,671
26	259,379	0	2.00%	5,118	(1,229)	(5)	3,417	3,400	382	143,830	344,357	403,695	607,638
27	259,864	0	2.00%	5,129	(1,231)	0	0	3,400	388	154,406	353,436	414,769	613,798
28	260,363	0	2.00%	5,139	(1,233)	0	0	3,400	388	165,408	362,776	426,276	623,645
29	260,868	0	2.00%	5,149	(1,236)	0	0	3,400	388	176,849	372,382	438,230	633,763
30	261,382	0	2.00%	5,160	(1,238)	0	0	3,400	388	188,749	382,270	450,652	644,174
TOTALS		0	2.00%	156,238	(37,497)	(908)	0	105,400	10,717	201,127	392,456	463,560	654,889

So now we pushed the efficiency up to 2.01% from 1.39% and graphically it looks like these two charts below: Assets and Estate Value to Heirs. Small differences short term, large differences long term.

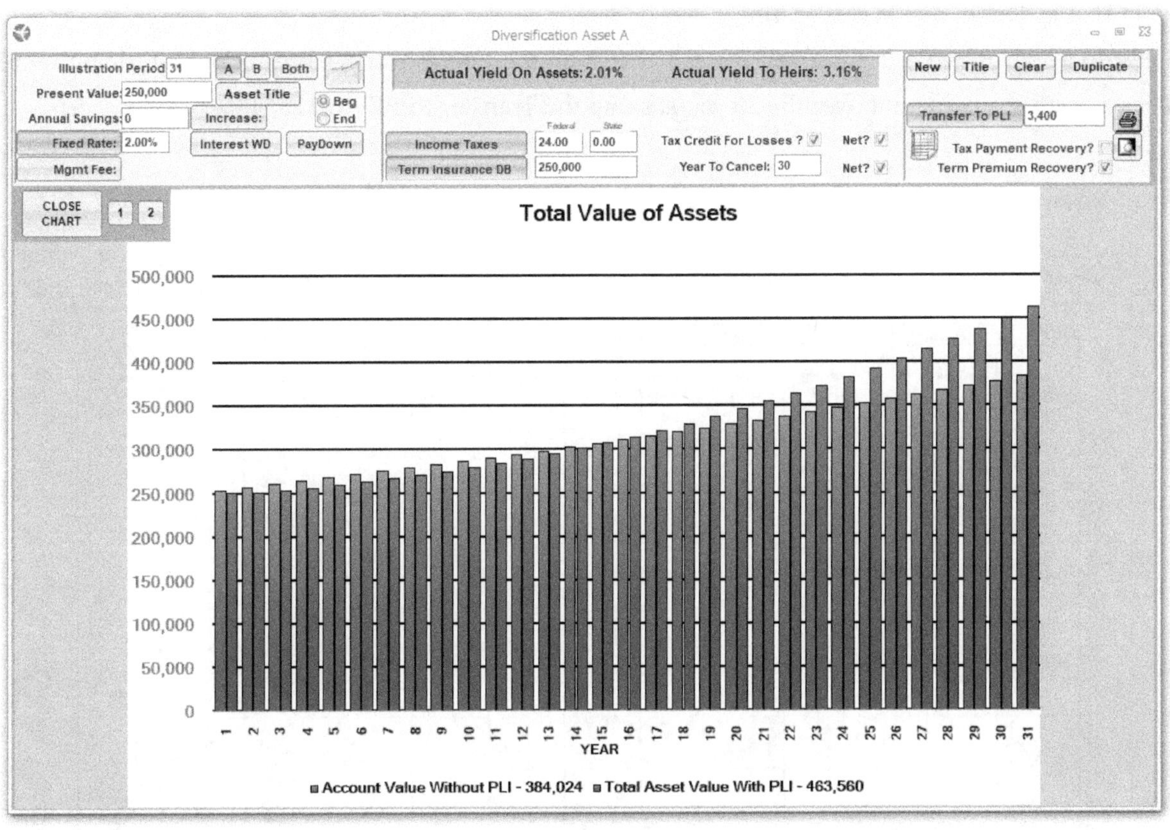
Diversification Asset A
Illustration Period 31
Present Value: 250,000
Annual Savings: 0
Fixed Rate: 2.00%
Mgmt Fee:
Asset Title
Increase:
Interest WD
PayDown
Beg
End
Actual Yield On Assets: 2.01%
Actual Yield To Heirs: 3.16%
Income Taxes 24.00 0.00
Term Insurance DB 250,000
Tax Credit For Losses ?
Net?
Year To Cancel: 30
New
Title
Clear
Duplicate
Transfer To PLI 3,400
Tax Payment Recovery?
Term Premium Recovery?
CLOSE CHART
Total Value of Assets
YEAR
Account Value Without PLI - 384,024
Total Asset Value With PLI - 463,560

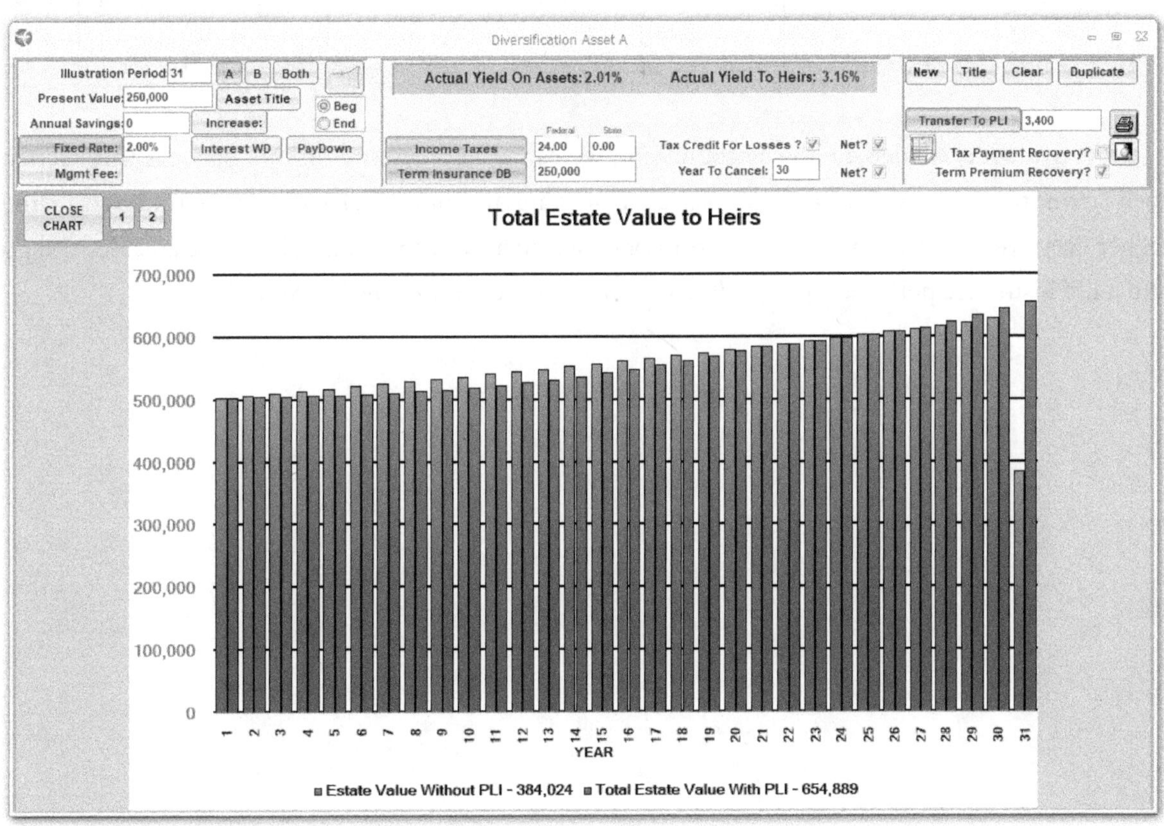
Diversification Asset A
Illustration Period 31
Present Value: 250,000
Annual Savings: 0
Fixed Rate: 2.00%
Mgmt Fee:
Actual Yield On Assets: 2.01%
Actual Yield To Heirs: 3.16%
Income Taxes 24.00 0.00
Term Insurance DB 250,000
Year To Cancel: 30
Transfer To PLI 3,400
CLOSE CHART
Total Estate Value to Heirs
YEAR
Estate Value Without PLI - 384,024
Total Estate Value With PLI - 654,889

Part II, Pay Down as a Wealth Shift

Let's do a "pay down" on this asset. Instead of just taking interest only, let's pull out a little bit more. Let's zero this account out over the 30 years, so up the Transfer to PLI to $10,500.

Diversification Asset A

Illustration Period 31 | A | B | Both
Present Value: 250,000 | Asset Title | Beg | End
Annual Savings: 0 | Increase:
Fixed Rate: 2.00% | Interest WD | PayDown
Mgmt Fee:

Actual Yield On Assets: 2.88% Actual Yield To Heirs: 5.17%

Income Taxes — Federal 24.00 State 0.00 — Tax Credit For Losses ? Net?
Term Insurance DB 250,000 — Year To Cancel: 30 Net?

New | Title | Clear | Duplicate
Transfer To PLI 10,500
Tax Payment Recovery?
Term Premium Recovery?

YEAR	Savings and Earnings				Expenses		Term	Permanent Life Insurance				Results EOY	
	Asset Value Beg Of Year	Annual Savings BOY	Annual Earnings Rate	Annual Interest Earned	Annual Income Taxes	Annual Term Ins. Premium	Insurance Death Benefit	Annual Transfer (Prem.)	Term Ins. Payment Recovery	Cash Value	Death Benefit	Total Value of Assets	Total Proceeds To Heirs
1	250,000	0	2.00%	4,790	(1,150)	0	0	10,500	388	0	703,753	243,140	946,894
2	243,140	0	2.00%	4,653	(1,117)	0	0	10,500	388	429	704,183	236,606	940,359
3	236,177	0	2.00%	4,514	(1,083)	0	0	10,500	388	6,474	705,875	235,581	934,982
4	229,107	0	2.00%	4,372	(1,049)	0	0	10,500	388	15,119	708,257	237,049	930,187
5	221,930	0	2.00%	4,229	(1,015)	0	0	10,500	386	24,187	711,273	238,830	925,916
6	214,643	0	2.00%	4,083	(980)	0	0	10,500	388	34,083	715,021	241,330	922,267
7	207,246	0	2.00%	3,935	(944)	0	0	10,500	388	44,437	719,501	244,174	919,238
8	199,737	0	2.00%	3,785	(908)	0	0	10,500	388	55,655	725,019	247,768	917,132
9	192,113	0	2.00%	3,632	(872)	0	0	10,500	388	67,805	732,265	252,178	916,639
10	184,374	0	2.00%	3,477	(835)	0	0	10,500	386	80,897	741,114	257,414	917,630
11	176,517	0	2.00%	3,320	(797)	0	0	10,500	388	94,972	751,486	263,512	920,026
12	168,540	0	2.00%	3,181	(759)	0	0	10,500	388	110,084	763,354	270,526	923,797
13	160,442	0	2.00%	2,999	(720)	0	0	10,500	383	126,285	776,700	278,507	928,922
14	152,221	0	2.00%	2,834	(680)	0	0	10,500	388	143,656	791,514	287,532	935,389
15	143,876	0	2.00%	2,668	(840)	0	0	10,500	388	162,271	807,839	297,674	943,242
16	135,403	0	2.00%	2,498	(600)	0	0	10,500	388	182,142	825,648	308,943	952,450
17	126,801	0	2.00%	2,326	(558)	0	0	10,500	388	203,328	844,939	321,398	963,008
18	118,069	0	2.00%	2,151	(516)	0	0	10,500	388	225,877	865,710	335,081	974,914
19	109,204	0	2.00%	1,974	(474)	0	0	10,500	388	249,835	887,938	350,040	988,143
20	100,205	0	2.00%	1,794	(431)	0	0	10,500	388	274,842	911,198	365,910	1,002,266
21	91,068	0	2.00%	1,611	(387)	0	0	10,500	388	300,134	934,980	381,927	1,016,773
22	81,793	0	2.00%	1,426	(342)	0	0	10,500	388	326,515	959,307	398,891	1,031,684
23	72,376	0	2.00%	1,238	(297)	0	0	10,500	388	354,041	984,225	416,858	1,047,042
24	62,817	0	2.00%	1,046	(251)	0	0	10,500	388	382,812	1,009,843	435,924	1,062,955
25	53,112	0	2.00%	852	(205)	0	0	10,500	388	412,848	1,036,247	456,108	1,079,507
26	43,260	0	2.00%	655	(157)	0	0	10,500	388	444,182	1,063,456	477,439	1,096,714
27	33,258	0	2.00%	455	(109)	0	0	10,500	388	476,844	1,091,493	499,947	1,114,597
28	23,104	0	2.00%	252	(60)	0	0	10,500	388	510,819	1,120,339	523,614	1,133,134
29	12,795	0	2.00%	46	(11)	0	0	10,500	380	546,150	1,150,002	548,480	1,152,332
30	2,330	0	2.00%	(163)	39	0	0	10,500	388	582,902	1,180,541	574,608	1,172,247
TOTALS		0	2.00%	74,237	(17,817)	0	0	325,500	11,625	621,128	1,211,997	602,048	1,192,917

Now overtime, we deplete this account, and we can see everything on one page: as this account goes down, the cash value of the life insurance goes up and our Total Value is continuing to climb higher every year. So we're just shifting from one asset to another. It's difficult to take an asset and put it in a life insurance policy lump sum. It needs to go in over time. This is a Wealth Shift.

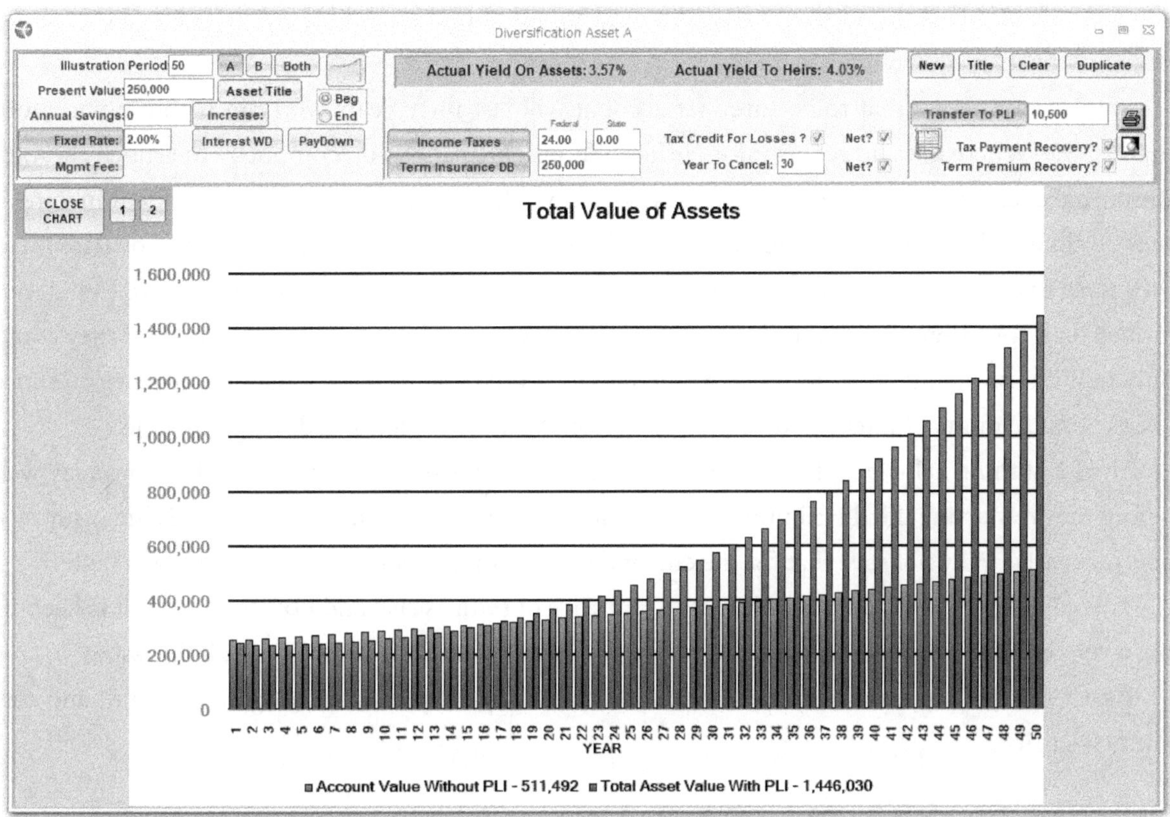

The money is actually just *shifting*, from the investment to the life insurance cash value, like skimming the cream off the crop.

We don't talk about this as much as we should: the idea of making $1 do the job of more than one thing. We have a life insurance policy that is our cash reserve to solve emergencies, take advantage of opportunities, and it has a tax free death benefit, and possibly some disability or long term care protection. If we can get $1 doing four things, we can eliminate four other costs.

There is a whole article with this concept at Cash Flow Bridge (https://bit.ly/4u2QtJE or the QR code below). **That article demonstrates the Diversification Cash Flow Bridge, which shows a financial strategy designed to optimize retirement income by integrating whole life insurance with traditional investment portfolios.**

We know that averages aren't the same as actuals, but that sequence of returns is a killer in the retirement phase. Dr. Wade Pfau challenged the old Trinity study that stated that if you have an asset, you can pull off 5% of the account value and not run out of money. And then they moved it to about 4%, and now they are saying it is 3.5%.

Pfau's paper shows that to be sure that account will last forty years, you can withdraw no more than 2.36%. Where does he get his info? He has billions of iterations on computers to crunch this out. People have said, as fund managers, that they could greatly increase somebody's retirement income if they could decide when to take money out. Yet here's the problem: when people get into retirement, they have to eat every day, and they can't wait a year or so to pull money out. They have to pull out money on a consistent basis. And that blows up the other end of the sequence. Whereas if they could only pull it out when the market was up, it would be more beneficial.They had to pay taxes on those losses because mutual funds end up storing old capital gains that get sold during this time.

The ideal thing is for people to know all of this when they're younger and put this into play well before they're starting the distribution. Why would you want to take money out of this life insurance contract early? Why not save that for the end and make it make everything else this much better?

This calculator is brilliant at showing the sequence of returns risk and how to solve it. It is becoming a very common discussion point for people, but they often don't understand all the issues.

Best Uses: To split a portfolio and use the bonds to buy life insurance for greater wealth and certainty over time.

Calculator 20: Future Requirements

Uncertainty is what gives the certainty of life flavor.
People like getting on the rollercoaster, but they still put their seatbelt on.

Purpose: Future Requirements is a retirement projections calculator used to show ROR (rate of return), necessary to have sufficient retirement income with or without consuming assets.

Why It Was Created: This calculator is just a quick way to show how for most people, the idea of retiring at fifty-five, sixty, or sixty-five, is not going to work. It's a quick way to show how stopping work that early, and living another forty or fifty years with your current lifestyle, won't work out financially.

Because of the information relayed, this calculator can be brutal. My mentor, Norman, told me a story long ago. When he was young, eight or nine, he'd gone to stay with his grandparents during the summer for a month. He was always underfoot while his grandmother was in the kitchen. She gave him a bag of walnuts and a hammer, and he took it out onto the sidewalk. He turned the first few walnuts into big greasy spots. It took a while for him to get the hang of cracking a nut carefully to get to the meat inside.

This calculator is kind of a greasy spot maker, so it's important to be careful how you use it. It's short, brutal, and gets to the point. You can put in whatever numbers you want, and it shows what it would take to do what you want to do, which is often to earn a higher rate of return than reasonably possible.

Say a person comes in and says, "My parents worked all the way to age sixty-five, and there's no way I'm doing that!" This calculator will show them that due to increases in longevity, living longer will require them to work many *more* years.

It's a quick and easy way to look into the future of what it's going to take, return-wise and time-wise, to maintain a lifestyle in terms of retirement dollars.

Essentially, it's the accumulation and the distribution calculators combined.

Case Study: For this case study, we will look at a thirty-five-year-old currently earning $150,000, with no existing assets. Their federal income taxes plus Social Security and medicare taxes are 21%. They have Fixed Lifestyle Expenses taking 35% of their income and Discretionary Lifestyle Expenses taking 30% of their income.

To maintain their current lifestyle in retirement, we will use their Last Working Year of Fixed and Discretionary Expenses. So we can see it would take $97,500 of Future Income per year in today's dollars to maintain their current lifestyle in the future. This reflects no longer paying earned income taxes because we are no longer working. And it reflects not saving any more.

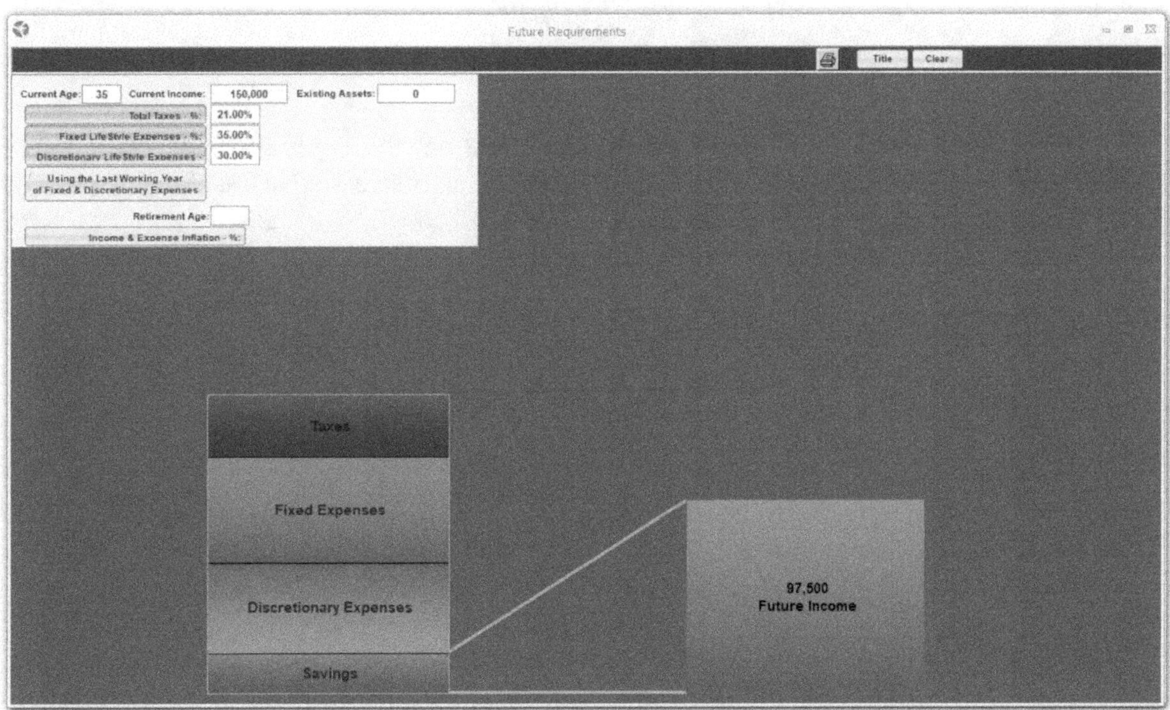

However, this does not reflect the impact of inflation. If we look at a Retirement Age of sixty-five and an Income and Expense Inflation of 3%, it would actually take $236,658 per year in the future to be the same as $97,500 is today.

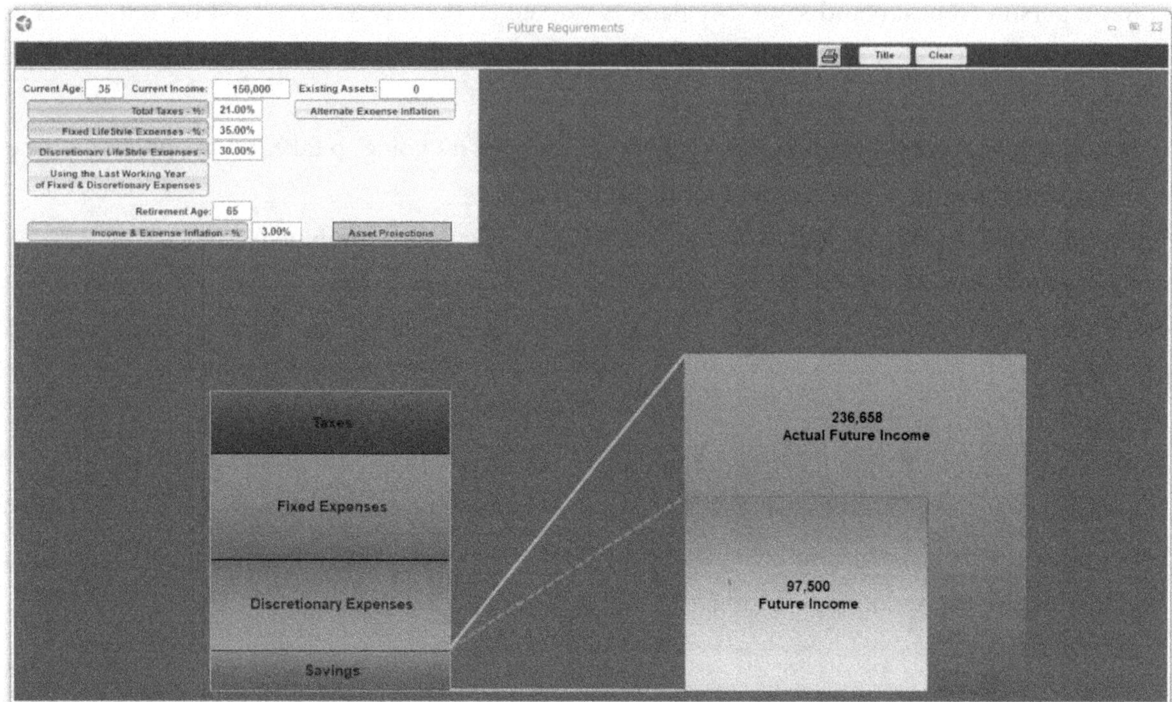

If we want to follow the 4% rule, meaning we only take 4% of our Future Asset Value per year to live on, then it would take an Asset worth $5,916,452 at Age sixty-five, so that 4% of that Asset is the needed $236,658 per year.

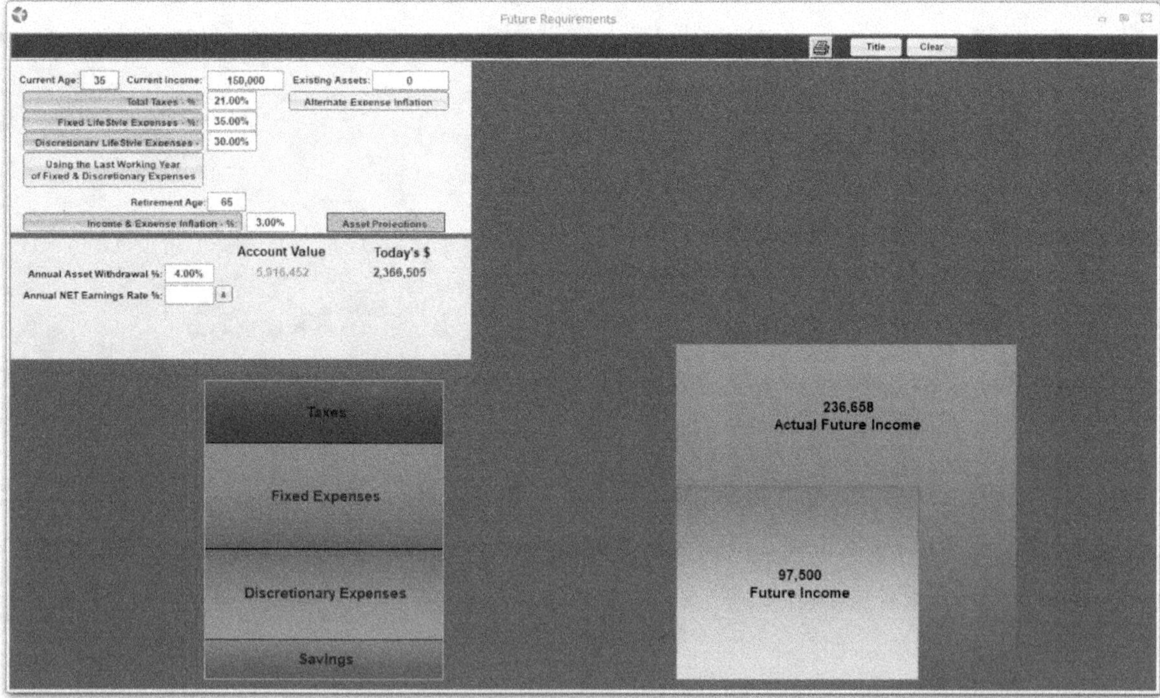

So what are we going to have to earn on our 14% to Savings (100% - 21% Taxes - 65% Expenses = 14% to Savings)?

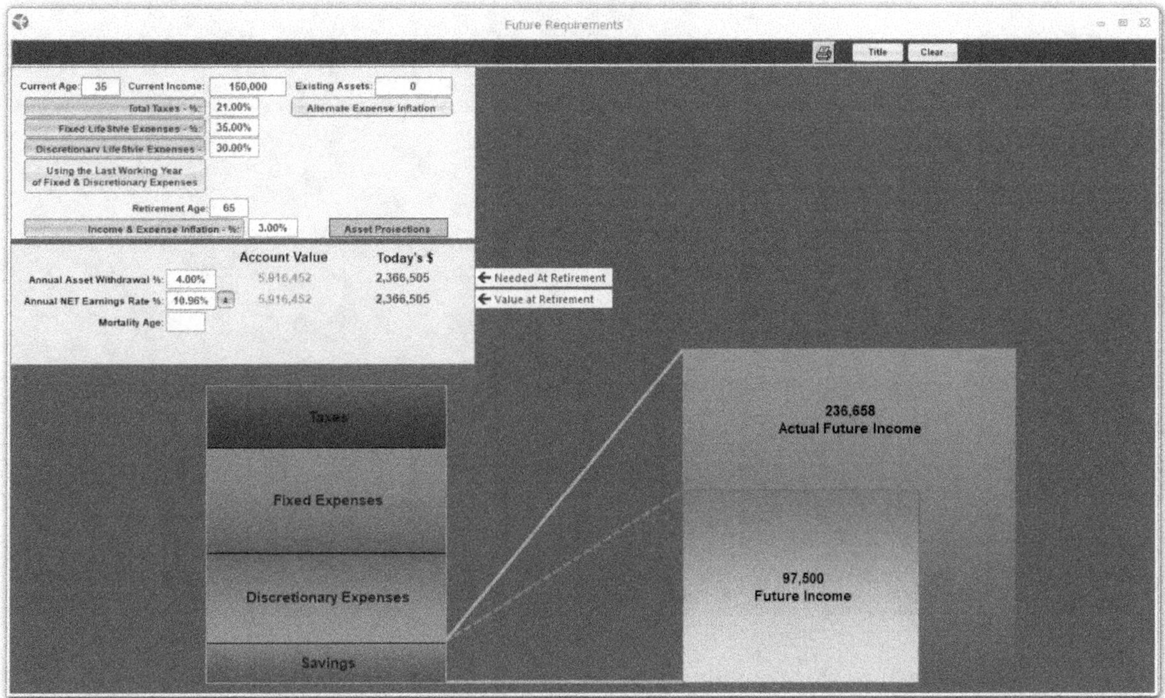

The answer is 10.96% every single year with no down years. And this means 10.96% after all fees and taxes!

If we wish to pass the equivalent of this Asset in today's dollars to our heirs, assuming death at age ninety-five, we would have to earn 7.24%, after taxes and fees, with no down years, all during our retirement.

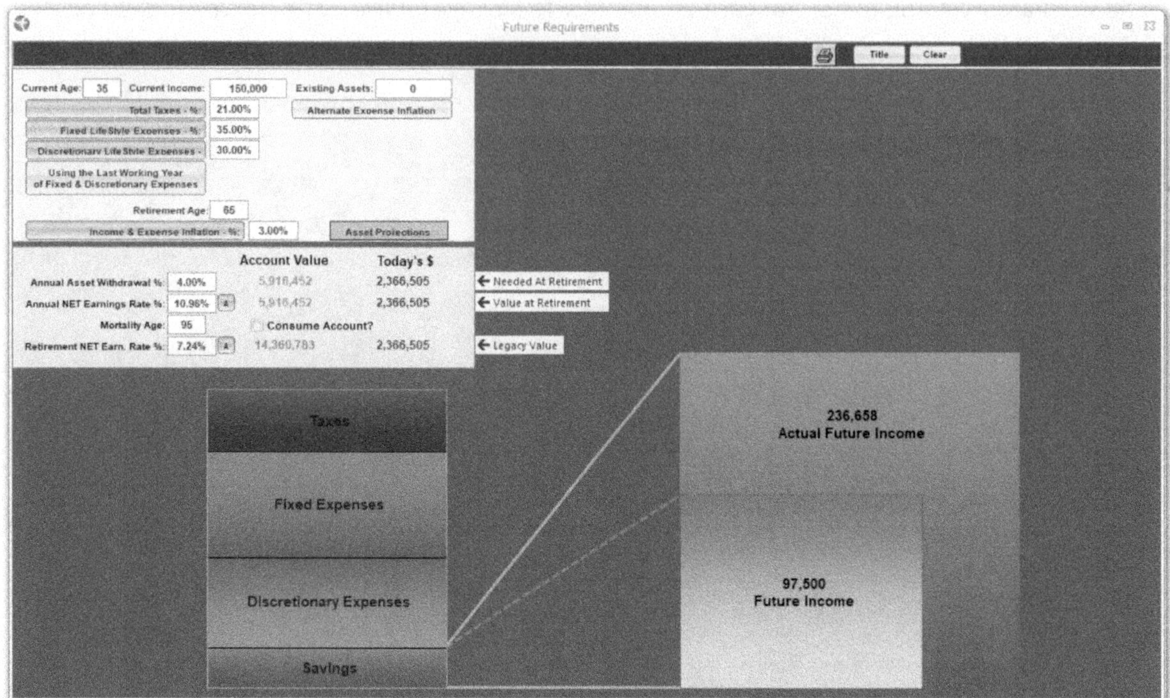

If we choose to Consume the Account and leave nothing to our heirs, we would have to earn 4.55% after taxes and fees, with no down years, and we would have nothing left over.

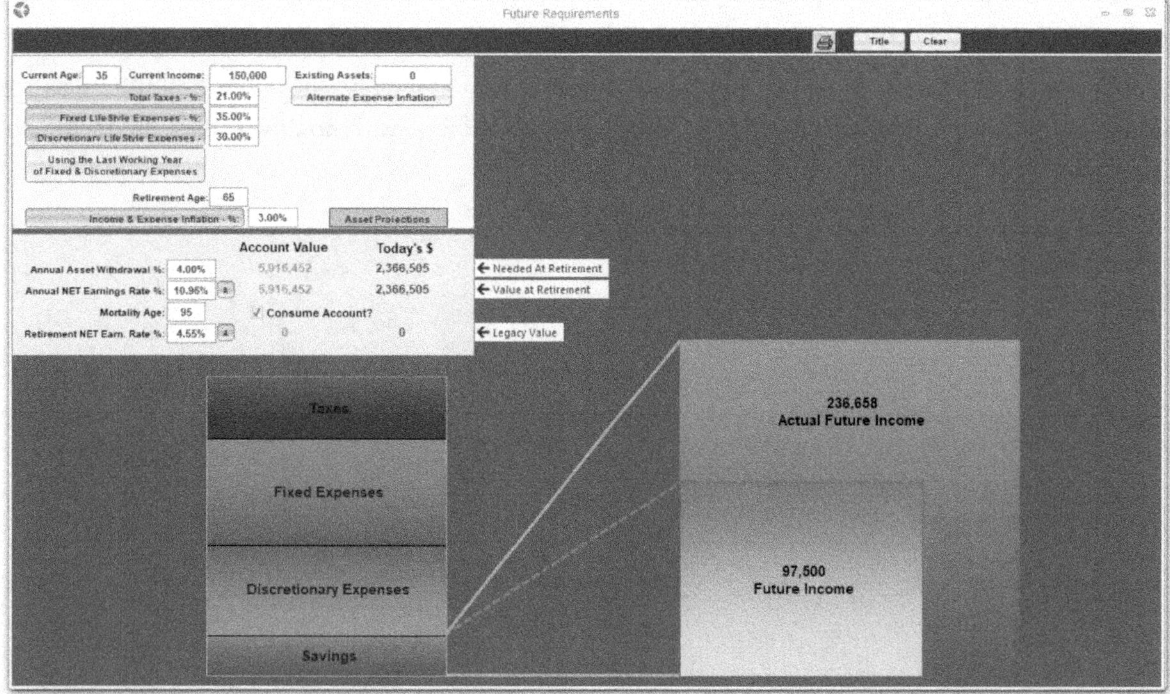

This is difficult, if not impossible, to do with any level of certainty, so let's look at a more reasonable solution. First, let's extend the Retirement Age to age seventy. Second, let's slow the *rate of increase* on our Discretionary Lifestyle Expenses to 1.5%. This will require the Net Earnings Rate on our Assets during our working years to be 6.58%. Again, this is after fees and taxes and could still be a challenge. Additionally, the Earnings Rate during Retirement has been dropped to 2.9% after fees and taxes, and there would be no money left at age ninety-five.

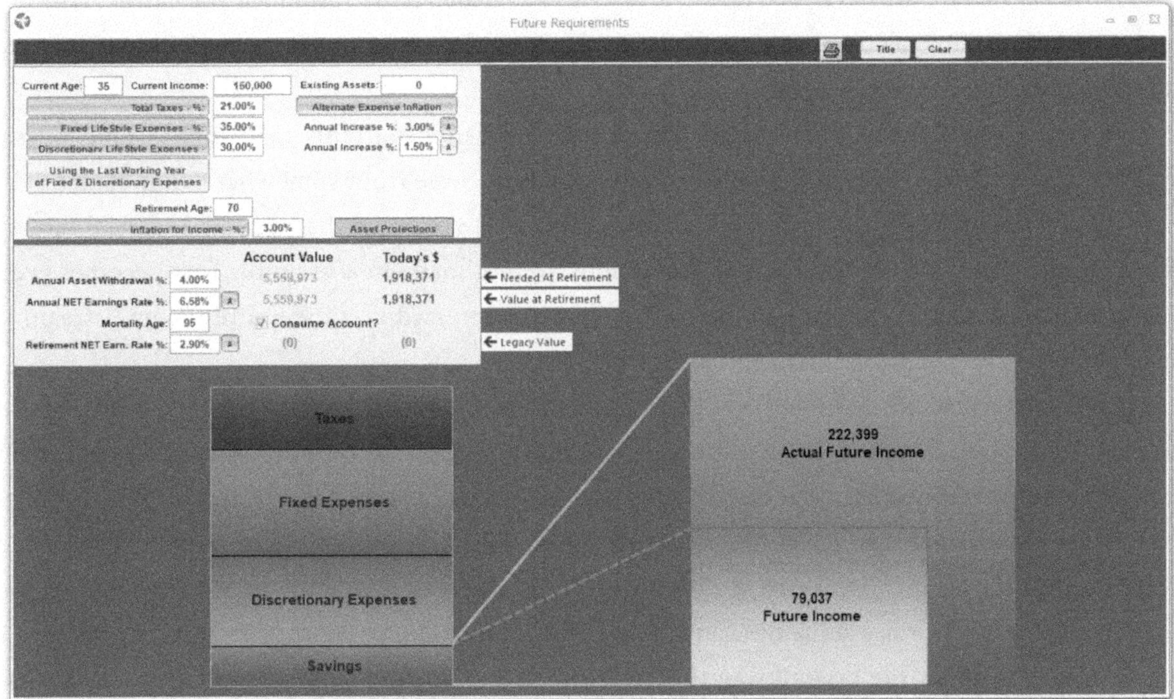

Best Uses: This calculator, above all, can serve as a wake-up call for clients who say, "I have no money, but I want you to tell me how I can retire in the next twenty years, because that's as long as I'm going to work." Or, it can be used for clients who want to plan over the years to come so they are prepared for retirement.

Since financial strategists have difficulty showing income for retirement, there is a lot of commentary about being able to live on a very low percentage of our current income. Most people spend more money on the weekend than they do during the week when they are working. **And now in retirement, basically every day is a Saturday.**

Calculator 21: Asset Flow™

People think of protection and accumulation as separate, but with the right tool, you can have both in one asset.

Purpose: Asset Flow™ is the "all-in" calculator that demonstrates any person's entire financial life. It can be used simply with just a few assets, combined with life insurance, or in a complex fashion like a Retirement Plan or a Financial Plan. **Its goal is to show you how to take Assets and create Cash Flow.**

Why It Was Created: In the financial industry, a lot of people talk about climbing the mountain, what it takes to get to the peak, with a lot of discussion about net worth and highest rate of return. Yet everything they are calculating is based on average returns, which are often overpromissory. Furthermore, there is very little discussion about getting down the mountain.

The whole point of piling up money is so you can spend it during the distribution phase of your life. Whatever dollars you have piled up, their value to you depends on how much you can actually use and spend them. This calculator allows you to see that, as well as the fact that every decision we make affects every other decision we make.

For example, if I'm going to put a particular amount of money in this particular taxable investment, now I've created an additional tax cost that's got to come from somewhere. Someone might say, "Look how great this account did," but they might not be seeing that they had to steal money from another spot in their life. Financial decisions are not made in a vacuum. This becomes even more obvious when tax-deferred retirement dollars are accessed and the entire income stream is taxable.

Many people just pile up money and then they lock themselves into areas they can't change (such as qualified money: IRAs and 401(k)s—these are subject to tax laws *at the time*—and the government has total control). Has the government changed tax laws over history? Yes, rarely, but most tax laws have been grandfathered in. Qualified retirement money is an exception. They make changes, and their justification is "because you're getting tax deferral, we get to decide the rules in the future." We end up stuck with the rules at the time and are usually not grandfathered in.

People tend to let the tax tail wag the investment dog. We get too hung up on the fact that we're paying tax on investment income. It's short-sighted if we don't look to the future. We may have avoided tax at a lower bracket, but then we may pay a price at a higher bracket. How do you estimate this if you don't have all the parts: Social Security, etc., in your analysis? This is what the Asset Flow™ calculator does for us.

Furthermore, it enables us to ask what happens if we do this strategy with this product and pick up additional benefits. Can you reduce cost in other areas that actually *increases* income over time and sets you up for success in the distribution phase?

That's one of the key pieces that's left out when we look at whole life insurance—it doesn't have a great rate of return or beat stocks over ten years, yet it adds in additional benefits so that when you get to the distribution phase, the fact that you have life insurance in place opens up the door to spend those other assets and completely change the distribution phase.

What assets we have available for that distribution phase will dictate what strategies we can take advantage of. Thirty years from now, the financial landscape will not look anything like what it looks like today. We can make all the guesses we want, but they're all assumptions based on the financial environment today. If we are locking ourselves in based on a calculation thirty years from now, that's unrealistic. A plan or strategy needs to work in all scenarios. Most people would rather have a 100% chance of getting to only 95% of their target wealth in the future than a 50/50 chance of getting to 100%.

Asset Flow™ is designed to take assets and create cash flow. That's the number one job of wealth (contrary to popular belief that the number one job is to pile up assets to create wealth). Taking assets and creating cash flow is the hardest thing to do in personal finance with any semblance of certainty.

Being able to look at our finances and say, "What happens if this gray swan or black swan event occurs along the way? What is the highest amount of certainty we can build into our assets?" It may be that the cost of protection is too much, depending on the way somebody's trying to protect assets, yet without the data, you can't even make that decision. Most likely, strategically placing assets, like whole life insurance, that garner a decent rate of return while also creating the pay-down ability shown in Calculator 18, makes the spendability of all those other assets so much greater.

It's difficult when you put software together like these calculators, because in order to have enough detail to be valid, you need *a lot* of detail. Humans aren't designed to look at spreadsheets most of the time. It's a difficult balance to get enough detail to make it accurate *and* understandable to the layperson. That was one of our motivations with Asset Flow, and I have erred on the side of needing more detail. The accuracy has to rule out above and beyond the aesthetic for me.

Ideally the strategist, who should understand the numbers, is the person tasked with dealing with all the intricacies of the numbers, and can put them in the form of a graph. This is the chart that shows what this will look like in the future, here's the distribution and income, cost of living, expenses, and how they will rise, how far your money will last in the future, combined with what you get from Social Security. When will you run out and how much do you leave to heirs?

We would be remiss without mentioning inflation one more time, especially when it comes to Asset Flow™. The only way to beat inflation is to have more money, plain and simple. However, on the flip side, people make decisions today based on today's expenses, not taking into account what something will cost at least thirty years out. They often have no idea what it takes. From everything I've seen, expenses will triple over a thirty-year time frame!

There's an inflation component to each section of the Asset Flow™ calculator, so you can inflate each section to see how it will all be affected over time. There is also the "Paste Special" capability, so each Wealth Shift is immediately impacted each year with actual taxes (not an average tax rate). It iterates the cash flow stream to adjust for the taxes and fees impacted by the results of the cash flow that year so the net result is zero (after expenses) every year.

Case Study:

Review the notes and charts below, visit https://truthconcepts.com/assetflow, or scan the QR code on the next page to learn more.

The above QR code will give you the ability to watch over 30 minutes of video created by David Osmond, a Financial Strategist, that demonstrates how the Asset Flow™ calculator enables him to help clients see their Assets in a new light. Instead of focusing on Net Worth accumulation, they see their Assets as vital for Cash Flow creation.

The starting point was a money market account, a 15-year mortgage and term life insurance. Typical advice would say that getting to $1,000,000 at retirement is the goal. Yet which is best, typical or truthful?

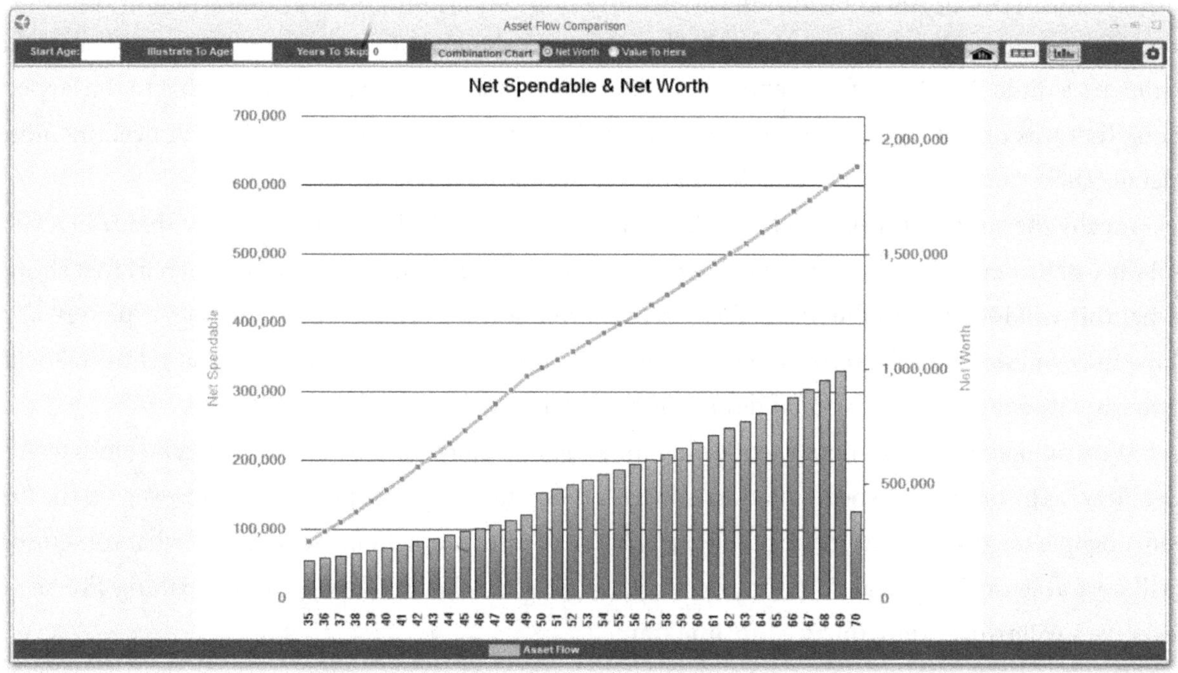

The first Wealth Shift was selecting the surplus from their money market account and purchasing whole life policies on each of them. Being able to Compare both situations via Asset Flow Base and Alternate Trailway 1 helps the clients see that they have an improved net worth and exactly the same cash flow.

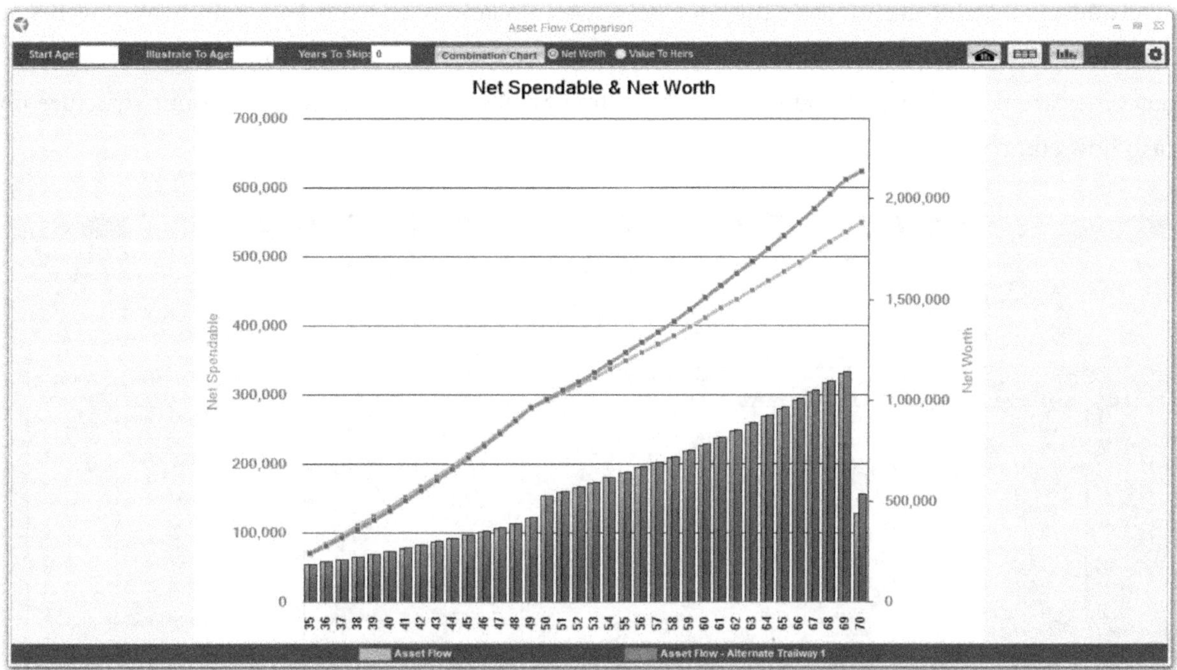

We can pull together all the assets for both accumulation and distribution phases of wealth to view both numerically and graphically.

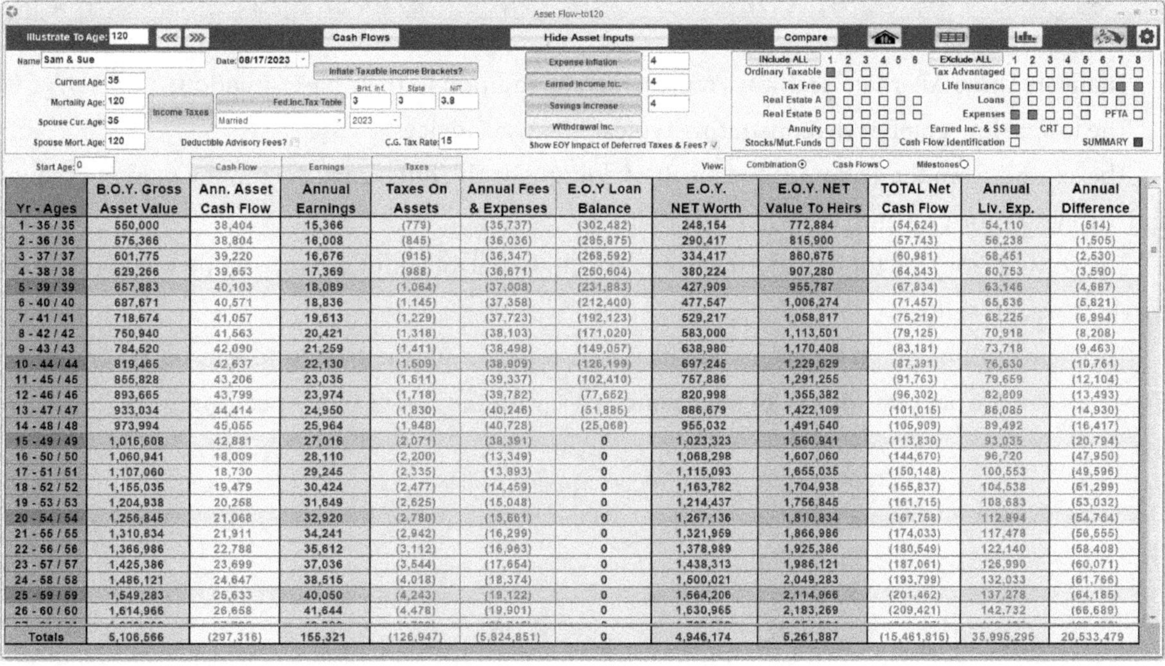

Yr - Ages	B.O.Y. Gross Asset Value	Ann. Asset Cash Flow	Annual Earnings	Taxes On Assets	Annual Fees & Expenses	E.O.Y Loan Balance	E.O.Y. NET Worth	E.O.Y. NET Value To Heirs	TOTAL Net Cash Flow	Annual Liv. Exp.	Annual Difference
1 - 35 / 35	550,000	38,404	15,366	(779)	(35,737)	(302,482)	248,154	772,884	(54,624)	54,110	(514)
2 - 36 / 36	576,366	38,804	16,008	(845)	(36,036)	(285,875)	290,417	815,900	(57,743)	56,238	(1,505)
3 - 37 / 37	601,775	39,220	16,676	(915)	(36,347)	(268,592)	334,417	860,675	(60,981)	58,451	(2,530)
4 - 38 / 38	629,266	39,653	17,369	(988)	(36,671)	(250,604)	380,224	907,280	(64,343)	60,753	(3,590)
5 - 39 / 39	657,883	40,103	18,089	(1,064)	(37,008)	(231,883)	427,909	955,787	(67,834)	63,146	(4,687)
6 - 40 / 40	687,671	40,571	18,836	(1,145)	(37,358)	(212,400)	477,547	1,006,274	(71,457)	65,636	(5,821)
7 - 41 / 41	718,674	41,057	19,613	(1,229)	(37,723)	(192,123)	529,217	1,058,817	(75,219)	68,225	(6,994)
8 - 42 / 42	750,940	41,563	20,421	(1,318)	(38,103)	(171,020)	583,000	1,113,501	(79,125)	70,918	(8,208)
9 - 43 / 43	784,520	42,090	21,259	(1,411)	(38,498)	(149,057)	638,980	1,170,408	(83,181)	73,718	(9,463)
10 - 44 / 44	819,465	42,637	22,130	(1,509)	(38,909)	(126,199)	697,245	1,229,629	(87,391)	76,630	(10,761)
11 - 45 / 45	855,828	43,206	23,035	(1,611)	(39,337)	(102,410)	757,886	1,291,255	(91,763)	79,659	(12,104)
12 - 46 / 46	893,665	43,799	23,974	(1,718)	(39,782)	(77,652)	820,998	1,355,382	(96,302)	82,809	(13,493)
13 - 47 / 47	933,034	44,414	24,950	(1,830)	(40,246)	(51,885)	886,679	1,422,109	(101,015)	86,085	(14,930)
14 - 48 / 48	973,994	45,055	25,964	(1,948)	(40,728)	(25,068)	955,032	1,491,540	(105,909)	89,492	(16,417)
15 - 49 / 49	1,016,608	42,881	27,016	(2,071)	(38,391)	0	1,023,323	1,560,941	(113,830)	93,035	(20,794)
16 - 50 / 50	1,060,941	18,009	28,110	(2,200)	(13,349)	0	1,068,298	1,607,060	(144,670)	96,720	(47,950)
17 - 51 / 51	1,107,060	18,730	29,245	(2,335)	(13,893)	0	1,115,093	1,655,035	(150,148)	100,553	(49,596)
18 - 52 / 52	1,155,035	19,479	30,424	(2,477)	(14,459)	0	1,163,782	1,704,938	(155,837)	104,538	(51,299)
19 - 53 / 53	1,204,938	20,268	31,649	(2,625)	(15,048)	0	1,214,437	1,756,845	(161,715)	108,683	(53,032)
20 - 54 / 54	1,256,845	21,068	32,920	(2,780)	(15,661)	0	1,267,136	1,810,834	(167,758)	112,994	(54,764)
21 - 55 / 55	1,310,834	21,911	34,241	(2,942)	(16,299)	0	1,321,969	1,866,986	(174,033)	117,478	(56,555)
22 - 56 / 56	1,366,986	22,788	35,612	(3,112)	(16,963)	0	1,378,989	1,925,386	(180,549)	122,140	(58,408)
23 - 57 / 57	1,425,386	23,699	37,036	(3,544)	(17,654)	0	1,438,313	1,986,121	(187,061)	126,990	(60,071)
24 - 58 / 58	1,486,121	24,647	38,515	(4,018)	(18,374)	0	1,500,021	2,049,283	(193,799)	132,033	(61,766)
25 - 59 / 59	1,549,283	25,633	40,050	(4,243)	(19,122)	0	1,564,206	2,114,966	(201,462)	137,278	(64,185)
26 - 60 / 60	1,614,966	26,658	41,644	(4,478)	(19,901)	0	1,630,965	2,183,269	(209,421)	142,732	(66,689)
Totals	5,106,566	(297,316)	155,321	(126,947)	(5,824,851)	0	4,946,174	5,261,887	(15,461,815)	35,995,295	20,533,479

Optimizing wealth means getting all of the dollars to be as efficient as possible. In this case, implementing a Wealth Shift by using a 30 year mortgage instead of a 15 year mortgage frees up cash flow on a monthly basis while also reducing the overall cost of the mortgage. (See Calculator 7, Loan Analysis)

Additionally, shifting some of the money market dollars away from banks and into life insurance companies increases guarantees and improves tax efficiency. Asset Flow™ demonstrates what outcomes are possible when you structure cash flow with Currence, an app + account structure for cash flow control.

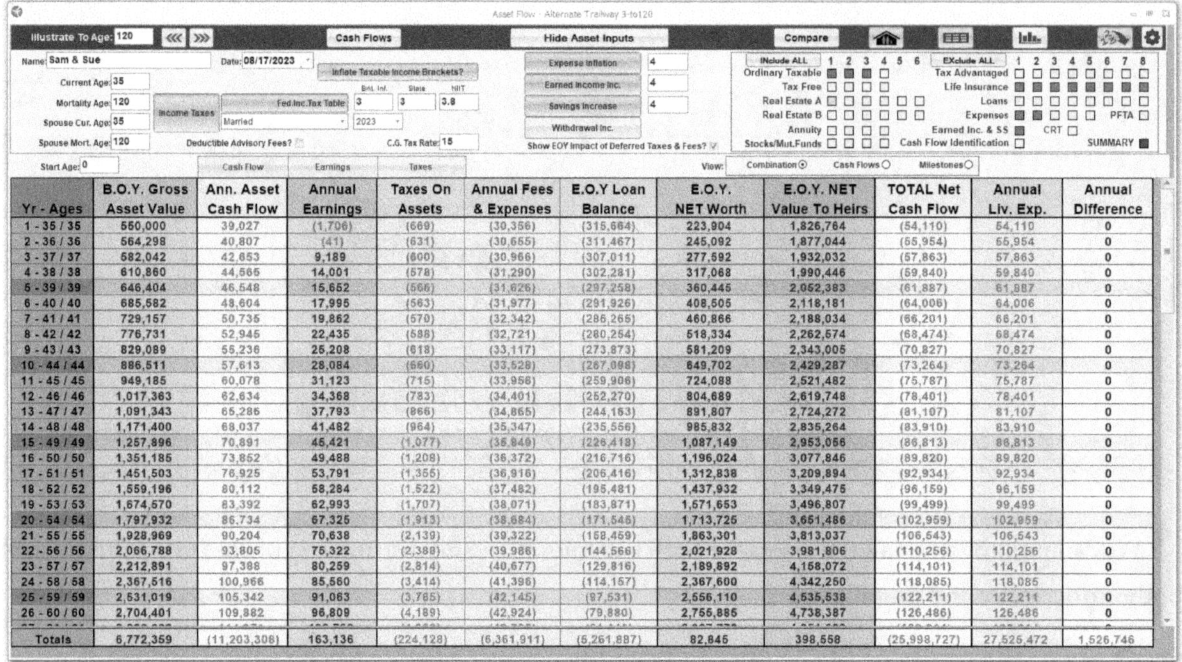

Yr - Ages	B.O.Y. Gross Asset Value	Ann. Asset Cash Flow	Annual Earnings	Taxes On Assets	Annual Fees & Expenses	E.O.Y Loan Balance	E.O.Y. NET Worth	E.O.Y. NET Value To Heirs	TOTAL Net Cash Flow	Annual Liv. Exp.	Annual Difference
1 - 35 / 35	550,000	39,027	(1,706)	(669)	(30,356)	(315,664)	223,904	1,826,764	(54,110)	54,110	0
2 - 36 / 36	564,298	40,807	(41)	(631)	(30,655)	(311,467)	245,092	1,877,044	(55,954)	55,954	0
3 - 37 / 37	582,042	42,653	9,189	(600)	(30,966)	(307,011)	277,592	1,932,032	(57,863)	57,863	0
4 - 38 / 38	610,860	44,565	14,001	(578)	(31,290)	(302,281)	317,068	1,990,446	(59,840)	59,840	0
5 - 39 / 39	646,404	46,548	15,652	(566)	(31,626)	(297,258)	360,445	2,052,383	(61,887)	61,887	0
6 - 40 / 40	685,582	48,604	17,995	(563)	(31,977)	(291,926)	408,505	2,118,181	(64,006)	64,006	0
7 - 41 / 41	729,157	50,735	19,862	(570)	(32,342)	(286,265)	460,866	2,188,034	(66,201)	66,201	0
8 - 42 / 42	776,731	52,945	22,435	(588)	(32,721)	(280,254)	518,334	2,262,574	(68,474)	68,474	0
9 - 43 / 43	829,089	55,236	25,208	(618)	(33,117)	(273,873)	581,209	2,343,005	(70,827)	70,827	0
10 - 44 / 44	886,511	57,613	28,084	(660)	(33,528)	(267,098)	649,702	2,429,287	(73,264)	73,264	0
11 - 45 / 45	949,185	60,078	31,123	(715)	(33,958)	(259,906)	724,088	2,521,482	(75,787)	75,787	0
12 - 46 / 46	1,017,363	62,634	34,368	(783)	(34,401)	(252,270)	804,689	2,619,748	(78,401)	78,401	0
13 - 47 / 47	1,091,343	65,286	37,793	(866)	(34,865)	(244,163)	891,807	2,724,272	(81,107)	81,107	0
14 - 48 / 48	1,171,400	68,037	41,482	(964)	(35,347)	(235,556)	985,832	2,835,264	(83,910)	83,910	0
15 - 49 / 49	1,257,896	70,891	45,421	(1,077)	(35,849)	(226,418)	1,087,149	2,953,056	(86,813)	86,813	0
16 - 50 / 50	1,351,185	73,852	49,488	(1,208)	(36,372)	(216,716)	1,196,024	3,077,846	(89,820)	89,820	0
17 - 51 / 51	1,451,503	76,925	53,791	(1,355)	(36,916)	(206,416)	1,312,838	3,209,894	(92,934)	92,934	0
18 - 52 / 52	1,559,196	80,112	58,284	(1,522)	(37,482)	(195,481)	1,437,932	3,349,475	(96,159)	96,159	0
19 - 53 / 53	1,674,570	83,392	62,993	(1,707)	(38,071)	(183,871)	1,571,653	3,496,807	(99,499)	99,499	0
20 - 54 / 54	1,797,932	86,734	67,325	(1,913)	(38,684)	(171,546)	1,713,725	3,651,486	(102,959)	102,959	0
21 - 55 / 55	1,928,969	90,204	70,638	(2,139)	(39,322)	(158,459)	1,863,301	3,813,037	(106,543)	106,543	0
22 - 56 / 56	2,066,788	93,805	75,322	(2,388)	(39,986)	(144,566)	2,021,928	3,981,806	(110,256)	110,256	0
23 - 57 / 57	2,212,891	97,388	80,259	(2,814)	(40,677)	(129,816)	2,189,892	4,158,072	(114,101)	114,101	0
24 - 58 / 58	2,367,516	100,966	85,560	(3,414)	(41,396)	(114,157)	2,367,600	4,342,250	(118,085)	118,085	0
25 - 59 / 59	2,531,019	105,342	91,063	(3,765)	(42,145)	(97,531)	2,556,110	4,535,538	(122,211)	122,211	0
26 - 60 / 60	2,704,401	109,882	96,809	(4,189)	(42,924)	(79,880)	2,756,885	4,738,387	(126,486)	126,486	0
Totals	6,772,359	(11,203,308)	163,136	(224,128)	(6,361,911)	(5,261,887)	82,845	398,558	(25,998,727)	27,525,472	1,526,746

There are three Alternate Trailways represented in addition to their base situation.

The lowest line graph is demonstrating typical financial advice.

The second from the bottom is the result of doing Wealth Shifts from the money market account, and a 15 year mortgage into the whole life policies.

The second from the top is implementing cash-flow control with Currence while maintaining the previous wealth shifts.

The topmost line graph is all the Wealth Shifts together plus choosing to elevate Discretionary Expenses at a 3% per year instead of increasing at 4% with the rest of their spending.

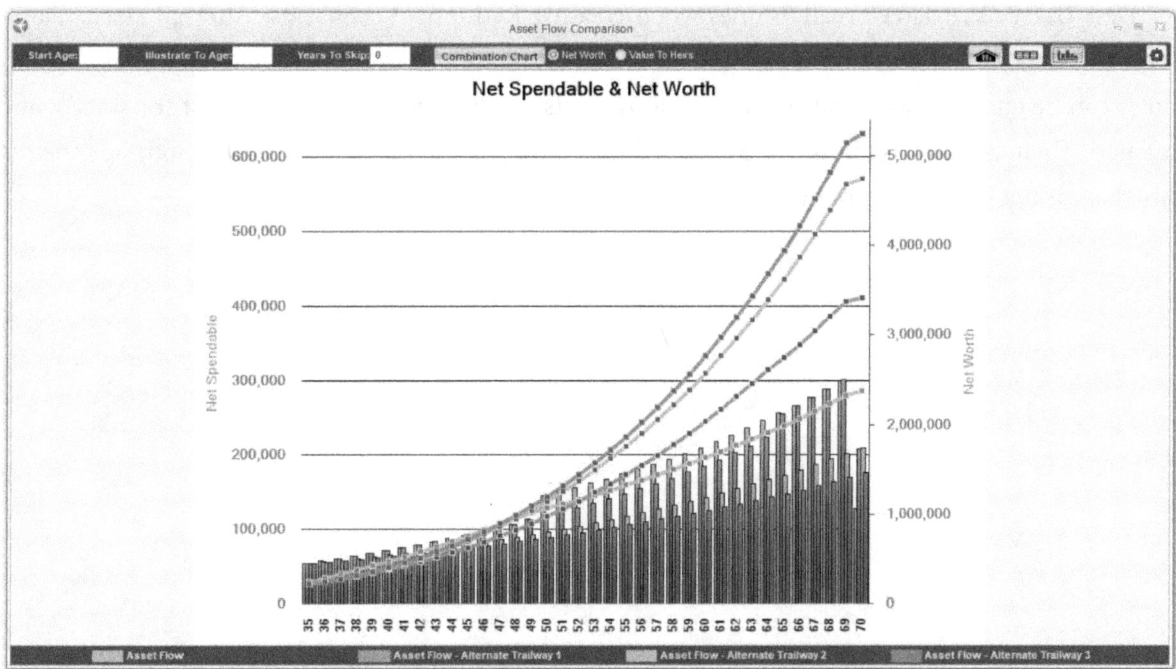

The greatest wakeup call for the clients happens after retirement. Under the typical plan they would retire at 70 with $1,292,545 in assets. But by age 81 they would be out of money (not including their house). After all the Wealth Shifts were implemented, they would have $4,082,254 in assets at retirement and at age 119 they would still have $1,665,793 in assets available. All of this was accomplished without chasing market rates of returns.

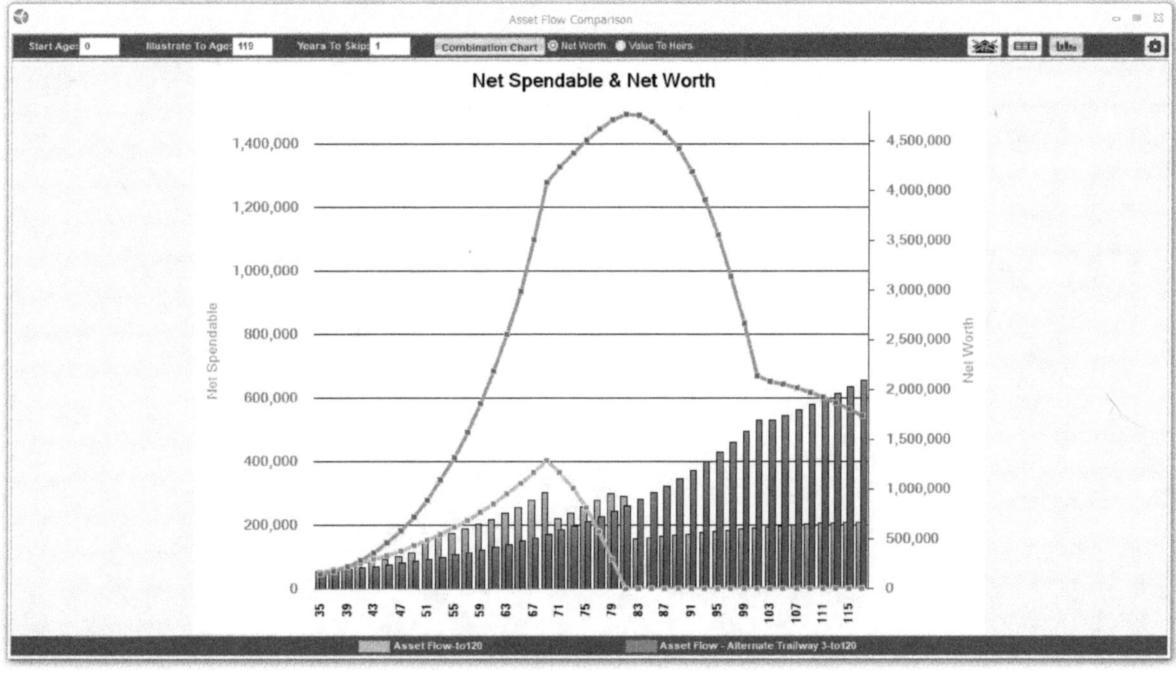

Best Uses: Asset Flow™ really shines when creating Retirement scenarios. After all assets, liabilities, incomes, expenses, and Life Insurance information are put in the calculator, a variety of cash flows can be analyzed when taken from various assets, at various times, taxed, spent (or saved), and inflated. Then, as above, graphs can be created that show the income and expenses alongside the net worth and "net to heirs" amounts.

Chapter 6: The TC Software Tools

I am passionate about this. I'm going to fight for my position. I expect you to fight for yours. That's how we get to the Truth.

In this chapter, you will learn all about the tools that enhance the calculators, make financial strategists' jobs easier, and simplify the process. We've created each of these tools intentionally based on feedback from clients and strategists. They are mostly static, behind-the-scenes tools that provide data points and other features to help clients understand the calculations. Much like having the right tools in your toolbox at home to fix a needed repair, these tools give you the precision and accuracy needed when making important financial decisions.

PURPOSE OF THE TOOLS

The bulk of these tools support a calculator or a discussion about a calculation. They are typically about one page long and provide behind-the-scenes information. They get brought into a calculator when needed to show to a client and serve in a supporting role. The one exception is the Market History chart, which has become bigger and bigger and will soon become its own calculator. It's one of my favorite tools to use!

You can access any of the tools from the same menu bar under the Tools heading.

New Instance Option

This New Instance Option tool is applicable to any calculator; it simply opens up a new calculator of the same kind without having to get rid of the data in the first one you have open. It's essentially a duplicate calculator that's empty where you can add new data and compare. For example, when you are in the Rate calculator, you can go to the New Instance Option, and it will give you another Rate calculator that you can compare to.

Case Study

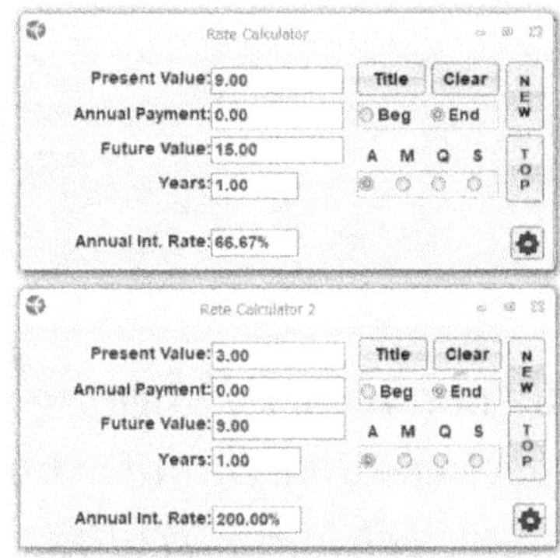

In Truth Training, we walk through a powerful concept called How Banks Make Money. The image above offers a visual snapshot of this idea.

To dive deeper into the full story, visit: https://truthconcepts.com/the-truth-about-rates-of-return-how-banks-make-money-and-more.

Notes

This tool is a small box that enables you to type a note relevant to any particular calculator and then attach that note to the calculator. This way, when they are saved, they show up together when opened again.

Notes are a really important tool for the strategist. The principle of notes is rooted in the idea that people don't think in spreadsheets. Notes are about simplifying and documenting.

You can have up to six notes at a time and can tag them to a calculator. By labeling the notes, strategists have a clear idea of what they talked with the client about. The notes stay in the client's file with everything else. Using Notes as a tool for every client is the best practice for accurate documentation.

Case Study

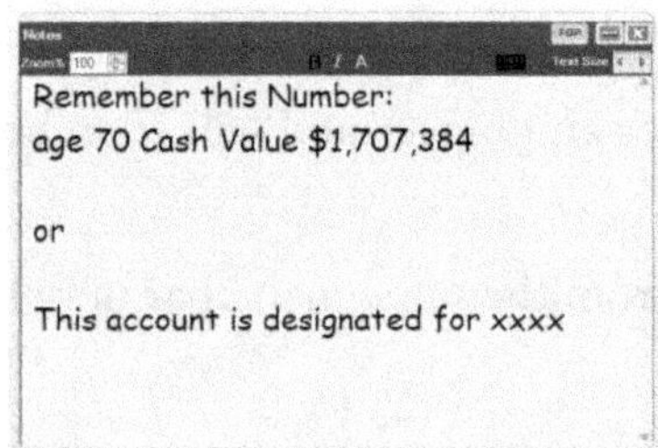

My wife Kim uses Notes extremely well. They're similar to a little yellow sticky note where you can type in a number, so when you're moving around on the calculator, that number or the words you've typed in are stuck on the screen. It's a way to show progress.

Income Tax Chart

Your average tax rate is not a helpful number.
You can only have an impact at your marginal tax rate.

The Income Tax Chart tool shows the differences between marginal and average tax brackets. It's a great tool for quickly showing clients how tax brackets work. For many people, it's an eye-opener. I use it to prove to people the Marginal Tax Bracket, which is very important since any decisions we make around taxes are at the Marginal (or last-dollar-in) bracket.

We live in a world where our taxes are based on different brackets. When you move up brackets, your tax percentage and amount paid goes up. Some people talk about only paying 10% of their income in tax. They paid this percentage because some of their income was at the bottom tax bracket. When we make a change to our taxable income, however, it happens at the margin, at the highest bracket. The bottom of the bracket has already been used, and everything else happens at the margin.

The Income Tax Chart demonstrates how tax percentages adjust. With this tool, clients can easily see, in a clear and colorful way, how the tax bracket affects their additional income and/or their additional deductions. If you click on the Canadian tools, it looks like a burst of wildflower colors because Canadians have many different rates. Canadians laugh at us when they're in our meetings and us Americans think we pay a lot of tax.

Case Study

You can see in the image below, we've selected "Married" and the year "2026" (we can also change this tool for Canadians and all their provinces, and pick a different year in the past if we want).

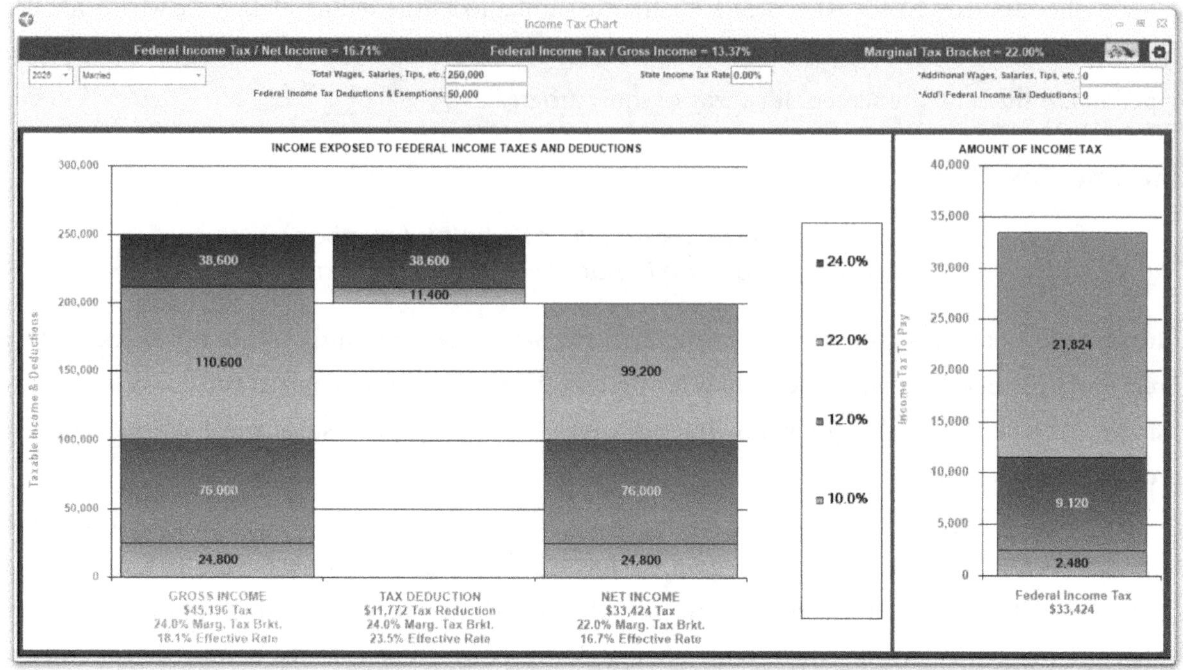

We entered $250,000 of current income and $50,000 of deductions.

Okay, so we have $33,424 of federal tax, and if I put a 5% state tax on, their federal tax due drops. Why did the federal income tax drop when I put state tax in? Because of the write-off we get on our federal taxes for state taxes. We have more overall tax that we pay, but we have less on the federal side.

You'll note the marginal brackets (middle right) of 24%, 22%, 12%, and 10%. This helps people understand how their income is taxed. Accountants often refer to the "average rate," in this example, top middle of 13.37%. Yet that is not how our income tax system functions. Our first dollars are taxed at the bottom marginal (10%), and our last income for the year is taxed at the top marginal (24% in this case). If we earn $1 million a year, our marginal bracket is 37%.

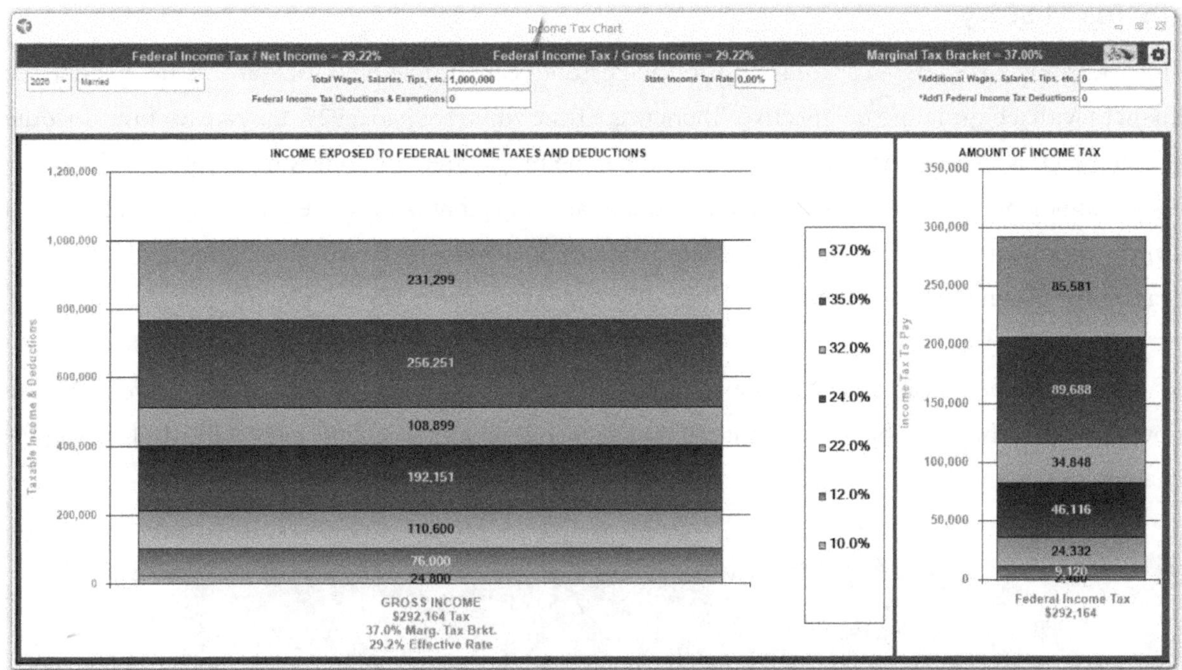
Income Tax Chart
Federal Income Tax / Net Income = 29.22%
Federal Income Tax / Gross Income = 29.22%
Marginal Tax Bracket = 37.00%
2020
Married
Total Wages, Salaries, Tips, etc.: 1,000,000
Federal Income Tax Deductions & Exemptions: 0
State Income Tax Rate: 0.00%
*Additional Wages, Salaries, Tips, etc.: 0
*Add'l Federal Income Tax Deductions: 0
INCOME EXPOSED TO FEDERAL INCOME TAXES AND DEDUCTIONS
Taxable Income & Deductions
1,200,000
1,000,000
800,000
600,000
400,000
200,000
0
231,299
256,251
108,899
192,151
110,600
76,000
24,800
37.0%
35.0%
32.0%
24.0%
22.0%
12.0%
10.0%
GROSS INCOME
$292,164 Tax
37.0% Marg. Tax Brkt.
29.2% Effective Rate
AMOUNT OF INCOME TAX
Income Tax To Pay
350,000
300,000
250,000
200,000
150,000
100,000
50,000
0
85,581
89,688
34,848
46,116
24,332
9,120
Federal Income Tax
$292,164

US Tax History

This tool shows US tax rates from 1913 to the current year. People who look at this tax history see finances with a big-picture perspective. There was a time when we had a 92% tax rate for high-income earners! Jack Nicklaus, considered by many to be one of the greatest golfers of all time, paid this on his golfing income. Ronald Reagan paid that too as an actor; that tax is largely what motivated him to switch from liberal to conservative thinking. This tool provides a history of the highest and lowest tax brackets to get an idea of what they look like over time, and where US taxes stand now.

Case Study

This tool is beneficial to lend perspective and insight into where tax percentages have been, are now, and what they may be in the future. It can help strategists and clients alike with strategizing for changes in tax rates.

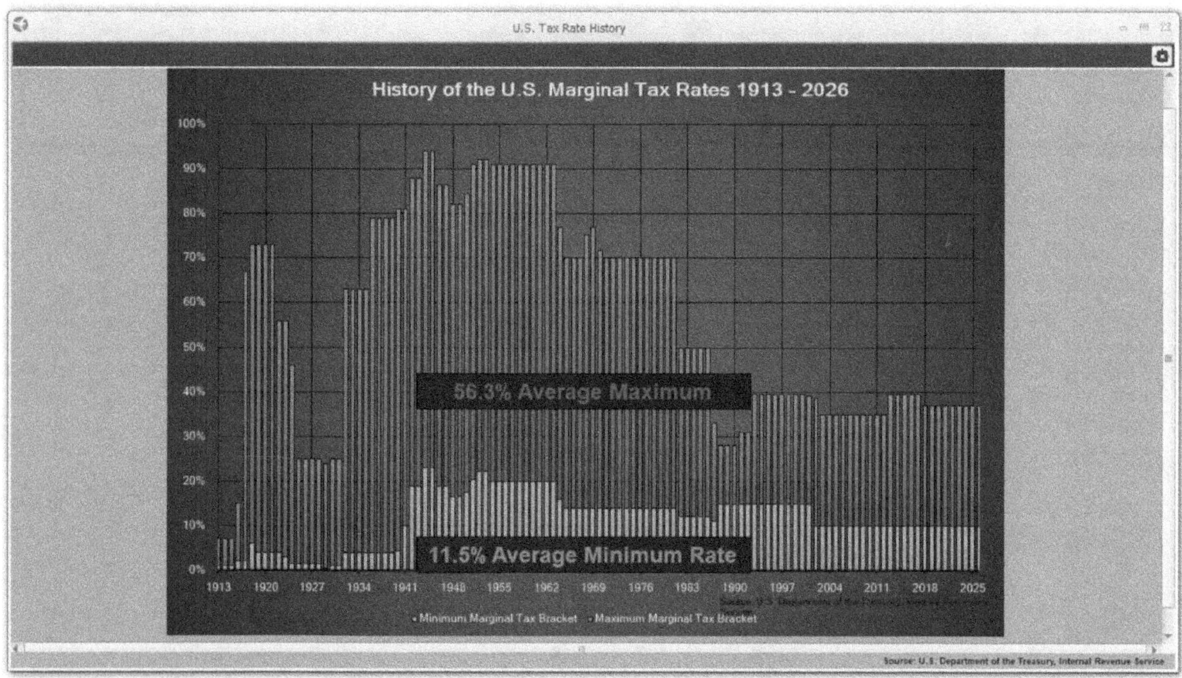

US CPI History

This tool shows the composite percentage change from 1914 to the current day's previous year. It follows the goods and services that our inflation is based on. The tool shows the Consumer Price Index and a postage stamp.

It's funny (and sad) that the federal government is trying to tell us what inflation is and that they show it low; they play around with the basket of goods and services to make it as low as possible *in appearance*. Ironically, the US postage stamp (that is government-funded) has increased beyond inflation by 4-5%.

Case Study

Use this tool to get a better understanding of inflation and how it will affect you or your client's personal finances.

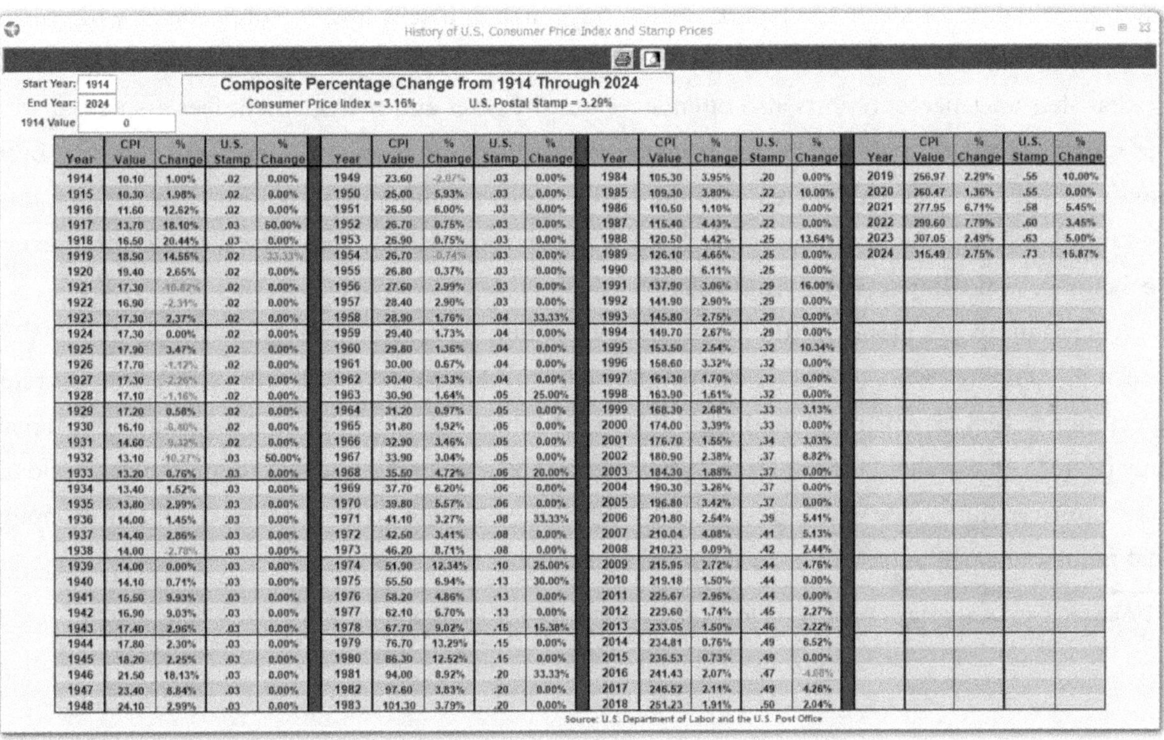

History of U.S. Consumer Price Index and Stamp Prices

Start Year: 1914
End Year: 2024
1914 Value: 0

Composite Percentage Change from 1914 Through 2024

Consumer Price Index = 3.16%   U.S. Postal Stamp = 3.29%

Year	CPI Value	% Change	U.S. Stamp	% Change
1914	10.10	1.00%	.02	0.00%
1915	10.30	1.98%	.02	0.00%
1916	11.60	12.62%	.02	0.00%
1917	13.70	18.10%	.03	50.00%
1918	16.50	20.44%	.03	0.00%
1919	18.90	14.55%	.02	-33.33%
1920	19.40	2.65%	.02	0.00%
1921	17.30	-10.82%	.02	0.00%
1922	16.90	-2.31%	.02	0.00%
1923	17.30	2.37%	.02	0.00%
1924	17.30	0.00%	.02	0.00%
1925	17.90	3.47%	.02	0.00%
1926	17.70	-1.12%	.02	0.00%
1927	17.30	-2.26%	.02	0.00%
1928	17.10	-1.16%	.02	0.00%
1929	17.20	0.58%	.02	0.00%
1930	16.10	-6.40%	.02	0.00%
1931	14.60	-9.32%	.02	0.00%
1932	13.10	-10.27%	.03	50.00%
1933	13.20	0.76%	.03	0.00%
1934	13.40	1.52%	.03	0.00%
1935	13.80	2.99%	.03	0.00%
1936	14.00	1.45%	.03	0.00%
1937	14.40	2.86%	.03	0.00%
1938	14.00	-2.78%	.03	0.00%
1939	14.00	0.00%	.03	0.00%
1940	14.10	0.71%	.03	0.00%
1941	15.50	9.93%	.03	0.00%
1942	16.90	9.03%	.03	0.00%
1943	17.40	2.96%	.03	0.00%
1944	17.80	2.30%	.03	0.00%
1945	18.20	2.25%	.03	0.00%
1946	21.50	18.13%	.03	0.00%
1947	23.40	8.84%	.03	0.00%
1948	24.10	2.99%	.03	0.00%
1949	23.60	-2.07%	.03	0.00%
1950	25.00	5.93%	.03	0.00%
1951	26.50	6.00%	.03	0.00%
1952	26.70	0.75%	.03	0.00%
1953	26.90	0.75%	.03	0.00%
1954	26.70	-0.74%	.03	0.00%
1955	26.80	0.37%	.03	0.00%
1956	27.60	2.99%	.03	0.00%
1957	28.40	2.90%	.03	0.00%
1958	28.90	1.76%	.04	33.33%
1959	29.40	1.73%	.04	0.00%
1960	29.80	1.36%	.04	0.00%
1961	30.00	0.67%	.04	0.00%
1962	30.40	1.33%	.04	0.00%
1963	30.90	1.64%	.05	25.00%
1964	31.20	0.97%	.05	0.00%
1965	31.80	1.92%	.05	0.00%
1966	32.90	3.46%	.05	0.00%
1967	33.90	3.04%	.05	0.00%
1968	35.50	4.72%	.06	20.00%
1969	37.70	6.20%	.06	0.00%
1970	39.80	5.57%	.06	0.00%
1971	41.10	3.27%	.08	33.33%
1972	42.50	3.41%	.08	0.00%
1973	46.20	8.71%	.08	0.00%
1974	51.90	12.34%	.10	25.00%
1975	55.50	6.94%	.13	30.00%
1976	58.20	4.86%	.13	0.00%
1977	62.10	6.70%	.13	0.00%
1978	67.70	9.02%	.15	15.38%
1979	76.70	13.29%	.15	0.00%
1980	86.30	12.52%	.15	0.00%
1981	94.00	8.92%	.20	33.33%
1982	97.60	3.83%	.20	0.00%
1983	101.30	3.79%	.20	0.00%
1984	105.30	3.95%	.20	0.00%
1985	109.30	3.80%	.22	10.00%
1986	110.50	1.10%	.22	0.00%
1987	115.40	4.43%	.22	0.00%
1988	120.50	4.42%	.25	13.64%
1989	126.10	4.65%	.25	0.00%
1990	133.80	6.11%	.25	0.00%
1991	137.90	3.06%	.29	16.00%
1992	141.90	2.90%	.29	0.00%
1993	145.80	2.75%	.29	0.00%
1994	149.70	2.67%	.29	0.00%
1995	153.50	2.54%	.32	10.34%
1996	158.60	3.32%	.32	0.00%
1997	161.30	1.70%	.32	0.00%
1998	163.90	1.61%	.32	0.00%
1999	168.30	2.68%	.33	3.13%
2000	174.00	3.39%	.33	0.00%
2001	176.70	1.55%	.34	3.03%
2002	180.90	2.38%	.37	8.82%
2003	184.30	1.88%	.37	0.00%
2004	190.30	3.26%	.37	0.00%
2005	196.80	3.42%	.37	0.00%
2006	201.80	2.54%	.39	5.41%
2007	210.04	4.08%	.41	5.13%
2008	210.23	0.09%	.42	2.44%
2009	215.95	2.72%	.44	4.76%
2010	219.18	1.50%	.44	0.00%
2011	225.67	2.96%	.44	0.00%
2012	229.60	1.74%	.45	2.27%
2013	233.05	1.50%	.46	2.22%
2014	234.81	0.76%	.49	6.52%
2015	236.53	0.73%	.49	0.00%
2016	241.43	2.07%	.47	-4.08%
2017	246.52	2.11%	.49	4.26%
2018	251.23	1.91%	.50	2.04%
2019	256.97	2.29%	.55	10.00%
2020	260.47	1.36%	.55	0.00%
2021	277.95	6.71%	.58	5.45%
2022	299.60	7.79%	.60	3.45%
2023	307.05	2.49%	.63	5.00%
2024	315.49	2.75%	.73	15.87%

Source: U.S. Department of Labor and the U.S. Post Office

Market History

The Stock and Bond Market History tool shows a variety of Indexes, like the S&P 500 with and without dividends during the past period of time you have identified.

You can split a portfolio between stocks and bonds and see a combined asset, plus you can add in taxes and fees that reduce balances. Additionally, you can reflect Minimums and Caps if you are discussing a product that incorporates those. People who own life insurance understand the value of its cash at 4-5%, like a fixed asset. Everybody else wants to look at money from the perspective of, "The S&P has yielded a 12% return in the last ten years, so surely I can do 10-11%." **However, averages don't equal actuals for many reasons.**

The DALBAR[3] study shows a twenty-five-year running *actual return* of 4-5% return for the average investor before tax. There's many reasons for that. The average person panics and pulls their money when the time is not ideal. The typical person buys high and sells low, the opposite of what you're supposed to do.

Statistics and market reports also often leave out the taxes and management fees associated with the returns. The other big factor is the safety, or certainty, component. These have typically been bonds. Initially, when bonds came out in the 1950s, they were thought of as non-correlated, but now we know bonds are not exactly non-correlated with the stock market. They have a ripple effect. **Every decision we make impacts everything else.**

A decision to put money in the stock market because a client believes they can yield a 10-12% return, if combined with a bond investment, actually produces a very different return. Interest rates affect money very exponentially, and even if you could make 10-12% in stocks, the actual return may only be 8.5% or less after taxes and fees. What clients often don't realize is that they're going to end up with a third of the money with that substantial drop. They actually lose ⅔ of the account by dropping that point and a half in fees, because it builds on itself over time.

---

[3] DALBAR, Inc. Quantitative Analysis of Investor Behavior (QAIB). Marlborough, MA: DALBAR, Inc., 2026.

Case Study

Market History

Years To Illustrate: 36 | Source: Pinnacle Data Corp.

First Year: 1991
Last Year: 2025
Present Value: 0
Annual Payment: 0

Combined Earnings

DJ-No Div · S&P-No Div · S&P- With Div · DJ-Corp Bond · 10Yr T-Bond · 5Yr T-Note · 1Yr T-Bill

AVERAGE ROR:	9.58%	10.50%	12.60%	4.92%	4.50%	3.35%	2.79%
Year	**Dow Jones Ind. NO Dividends**	**S&P 500 NO Dividends**	**S&P 500 With Dividends**	**Dow Jones Corp. Bond**	**10 Year U.S. T-Bond**	**5 Year U.S. T-Note**	**1 Year U.S. T-Bill**
1991	21.52	26.30	29.98	8.00	7.71	5.79	4.35
1992	4.31	4.46	7.48	4.83	7.36	5.59	3.64
1993	13.52	7.06	9.98	1.01	6.27	4.38	3.60
1994	2.18	(1.54)	1.32	(10.65)	7.85	7.77	7.12
1995	34.88	34.11	37.20	12.53	6.12	5.50	5.30
1996	24.43	20.26	22.70	(5.83)	6.63	6.07	5.51
1997	23.63	31.01	33.12	11.65	5.96	5.72	5.49
1998	15.31	26.69	28.38	9.69	5.16	4.62	4.63
1999	23.66	19.51	20.87	(3.39)	6.46	6.28	5.35
2000	(6.26)	(10.14)	(9.07)	11.02	5.43	5.07	5.71
2001	(5.38)	(13.04)	(11.85)	9.29	5.49	4.07	2.23
2002	(14.55)	(23.37)	(21.98)	10.61	5.10	2.63	1.43
2003	20.94	26.38	28.45	10.35	5.10	2.79	1.27
2004	3.07	8.99	10.87	7.00	4.84	3.40	2.71
2005	1.10	3.00	4.92	1.33	4.71	4.39	4.37
2006	15.00	13.62	15.68	3.94	4.82	4.59	4.96
2007	4.56	3.53	5.51	5.00	4.58	3.35	3.28
2008	(30.74)	(38.49)	(36.63)	1.80	3.04	1.16	0.45
2009	17.15	23.45	25.85	17.85	4.53	2.00	0.41
2010	10.27	12.78	14.89	8.44	4.23	1.54	0.30
2011	6.23	(0.00)	2.23	8.32	2.63	0.65	0.12
2012	8.19	13.41	16.00	10.88	2.56	0.57	0.15
2013	22.58	29.60	32.23	(1.23)	3.61	1.13	0.13
2014	8.46	11.39	13.63	8.13	2.47	1.34	0.23
2015	(3.84)	(0.73)	1.46	(0.41)	2.60	1.51	0.65
2016	15.94	9.54	11.85	5.70	2.86	1.80	0.88
2017	24.86	19.42	21.64	5.40	2.66	2.10	1.72

This Market History tool shows the actual return when you put in either a Present Value and/or an Annual Payment. *Note*: You can use the Combined Earnings button to get a diversified portfolio of stocks and bonds, and you can subtract taxes and fees and use the Min and Cap buttons.

Life Expectancy Tables

The Life Expectancy Tables tool goes back to 2001 (the most recent year available), showing male and female (single and joint life), standard, preferred and super preferred, smoker and non-smoker, and tells the whole truth about longevity: the longer you live, the longer you'll live. You can compare two tables side-by-side or look at the percentage chance both people will be alive (joint life expectancies). You can also simply see the life expectancy of a certain age.

Life insurance companies and many other companies use these Life Insurance Tables to judge the cost of insurance, annuity payouts, etc. All data comes from the American Academy of Actuaries. This is where all insurance companies pull their numbers from. It's helpful for people to see these numbers. We tend to look at an average life expectancy of eighty-five, but when viewed together, one partner may have a higher expectancy of living to ninety or beyond with the statistics available.

Case Study

Use these tables to determine individual or joint-life expectancy to help with life insurance work and other personal financial strategizing for the long term.

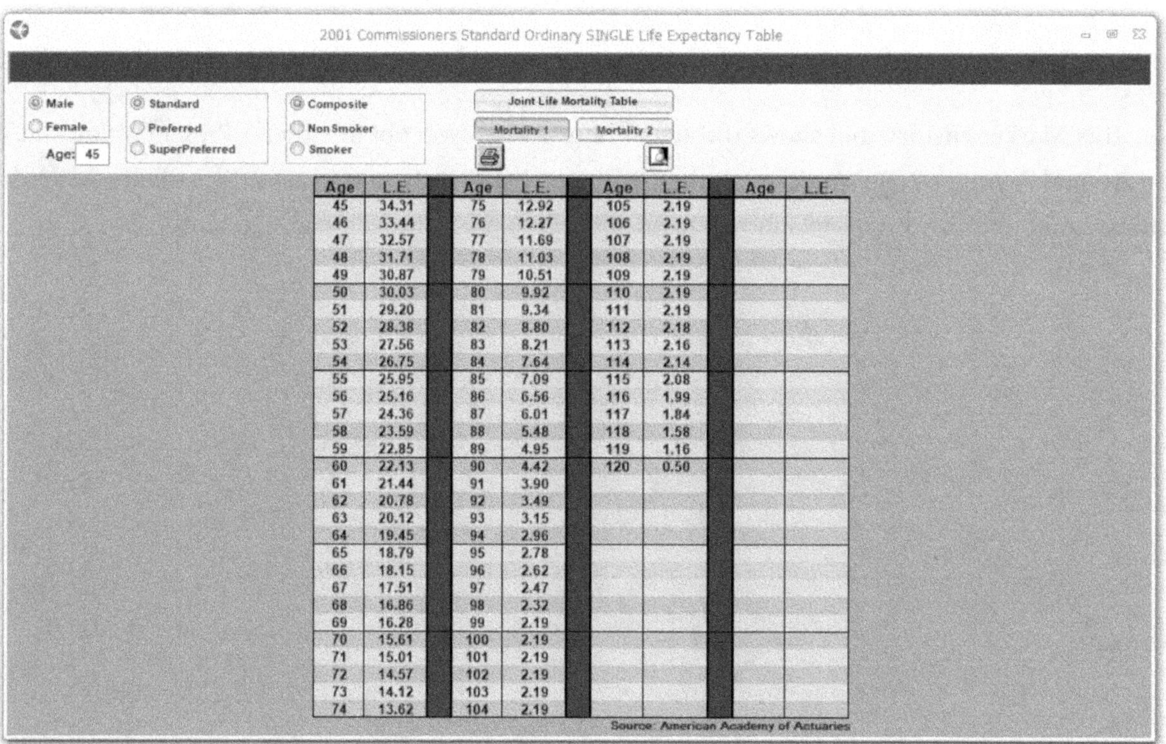

Age	L.E.	Age	L.E.	Age	L.E.	Age	L.E.
45	34.31	75	12.92	105	2.19		
46	33.44	76	12.27	106	2.19		
47	32.57	77	11.69	107	2.19		
48	31.71	78	11.03	108	2.19		
49	30.87	79	10.51	109	2.19		
50	30.03	80	9.92	110	2.19		
51	29.20	81	9.34	111	2.19		
52	28.38	82	8.80	112	2.18		
53	27.56	83	8.21	113	2.16		
54	26.75	84	7.64	114	2.14		
55	25.95	85	7.09	115	2.08		
56	25.16	86	6.56	116	1.99		
57	24.36	87	6.01	117	1.84		
58	23.59	88	5.48	118	1.58		
59	22.85	89	4.95	119	1.16		
60	22.13	90	4.42	120	0.50		
61	21.44	91	3.90				
62	20.78	92	3.49				
63	20.12	93	3.15				
64	19.45	94	2.96				
65	18.79	95	2.78				
66	18.15	96	2.62				
67	17.51	97	2.47				
68	16.86	98	2.32				
69	16.28	99	2.19				
70	15.61	100	2.19				
71	15.01	101	2.19				
72	14.57	102	2.19				
73	14.12	103	2.19				
74	13.62	104	2.19				

Source: American Academy of Actuaries

Side by Side

With the Side by Side tool, you can visualize and prove a variety of comparisons. This tool incorporates Maximum Potential, Life Insurance Values, Accumulation, Cash Flow, Distribution, and Qualified Plan Calculators. The Side by Side tool allows us to take a couple different calculators and combine them side by side, such as two life insurance policies or three Accumulation calculators. You can look at which scenario would perform better.

Case Study

Let's say we're using two Cash Flow calculators, and based on the inputs, each has a chart. With the Side by Side tool we can put both of those calculators side by side on the same chart. It's like combining two spreadsheets into one. It doesn't do its own calculations from there; it relies on the other calculators to do the calculations. It simply pulls the numbers together to more easily compare and analyze them. *Note*: the "Years to Illustrate" and "Current Age" must be put in first.

For example, we have an article (www.truthconcepts.com/can-you-compare-taking-social-security-at-different-ages) that highlights how you can use the Side by Side tool to compare numbers and decide whether to take Social Security now or later. Say Monte, a sixty-two-year-old, wants to retire now. He makes $150,000 currently, and is trying to decide if he wants to take Social Security now or later. (Note: These SS numbers are hypothetical based on BankRate's calculator, or you can use the Social Security website's .)

First, in the Cash Flow calculator, you can see that by taking approximately $25,000 of income at age sixty-two and putting it into savings at 4%, the client will have just over $3 million by age one hundred.

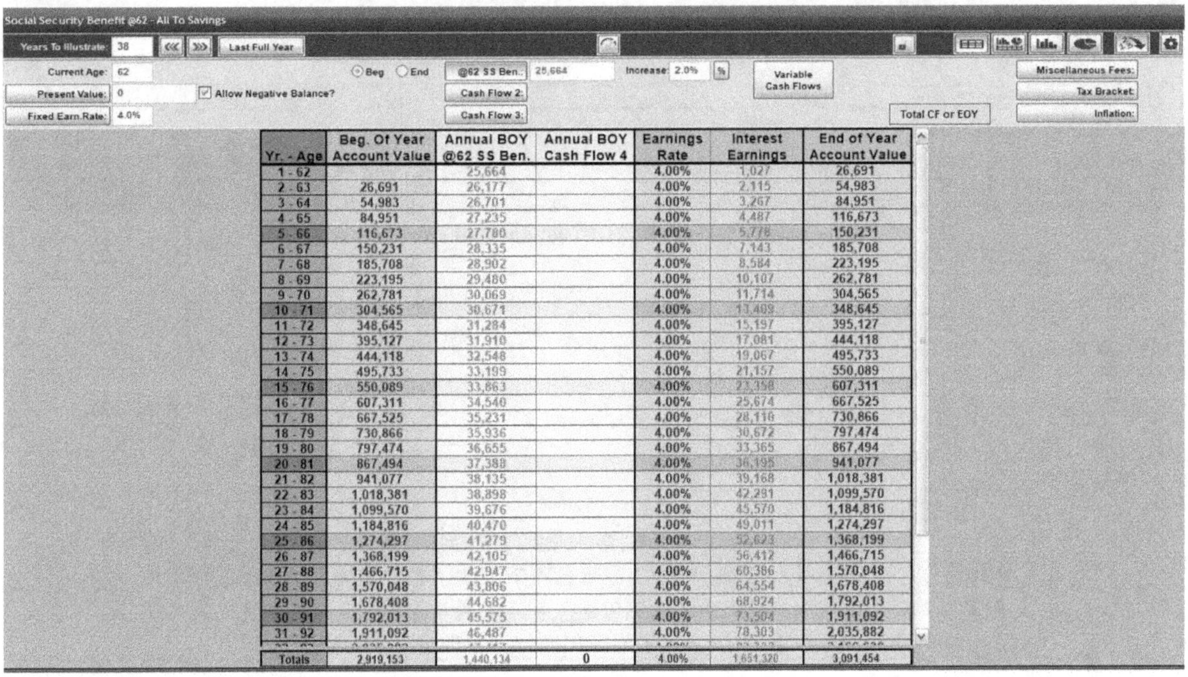

Social Security Benefit @62 - All To Savings

Years To Illustrate: 38 | Last Full Year

Current Age: 62 | Beg / End | @62 SS Ben.: 25,664 | Increase: 2.0% | Variable Cash Flows | Miscellaneous Fees:

Present Value: 0 | Allow Negative Balance? | Cash Flow 2: | Tax Bracket:

Fixed Earn.Rate: 4.0% | Cash Flow 3: | Total CF or EOY | Inflation:

Yr. - Age	Beg. Of Year Account Value	Annual BOY @62 SS Ben.	Annual BOY Cash Flow 4	Earnings Rate	Interest Earnings	End of Year Account Value
1 - 62		25,664		4.00%	1,027	26,691
2 - 63	26,691	26,177		4.00%	2,115	54,983
3 - 64	54,983	26,701		4.00%	3,267	84,951
4 - 65	84,951	27,235		4.00%	4,487	116,673
5 - 66	116,673	27,780		4.00%	5,778	150,231
6 - 67	150,231	28,335		4.00%	7,143	185,708
7 - 68	185,708	28,902		4.00%	8,584	223,195
8 - 69	223,195	29,480		4.00%	10,107	262,781
9 - 70	262,781	30,069		4.00%	11,714	304,565
10 - 71	304,565	30,671		4.00%	13,409	348,645
11 - 72	348,645	31,284		4.00%	15,197	395,127
12 - 73	395,127	31,910		4.00%	17,081	444,118
13 - 74	444,118	32,548		4.00%	19,067	495,733
14 - 75	495,733	33,199		4.00%	21,157	550,089
15 - 76	550,089	33,863		4.00%	23,358	607,311
16 - 77	607,311	34,540		4.00%	25,674	667,525
17 - 78	667,525	35,231		4.00%	28,110	730,866
18 - 79	730,866	35,936		4.00%	30,672	797,474
19 - 80	797,474	36,655		4.00%	33,365	867,494
20 - 81	867,494	37,388		4.00%	36,195	941,077
21 - 82	941,077	38,135		4.00%	39,168	1,018,381
22 - 83	1,018,381	38,898		4.00%	42,291	1,099,570
23 - 84	1,099,570	39,676		4.00%	45,570	1,184,816
24 - 85	1,184,816	40,470		4.00%	49,011	1,274,297
25 - 86	1,274,297	41,279		4.00%	52,623	1,368,199
26 - 87	1,368,199	42,105		4.00%	56,412	1,466,715
27 - 88	1,466,715	42,947		4.00%	60,386	1,570,048
28 - 89	1,570,048	43,806		4.00%	64,554	1,678,408
29 - 90	1,678,408	44,682		4.00%	68,924	1,792,013
30 - 91	1,792,013	45,575		4.00%	73,504	1,911,092
31 - 92	1,911,092	46,487		4.00%	78,303	2,035,882
Totals	2,919,153	1,440,134	0	4.00%	1,651,320	3,091,454

If he delays his Social Security to age seventy, his annual income goes from $25,664 to $46,512. However, he's playing eight years of catch-up. Which means that until age eighty-eight, the client's total account value is still less than if he took the income at age sixty-two. Beyond that age, however, his value is always greater. And by age one hundred, he has almost $3.5 million in savings.

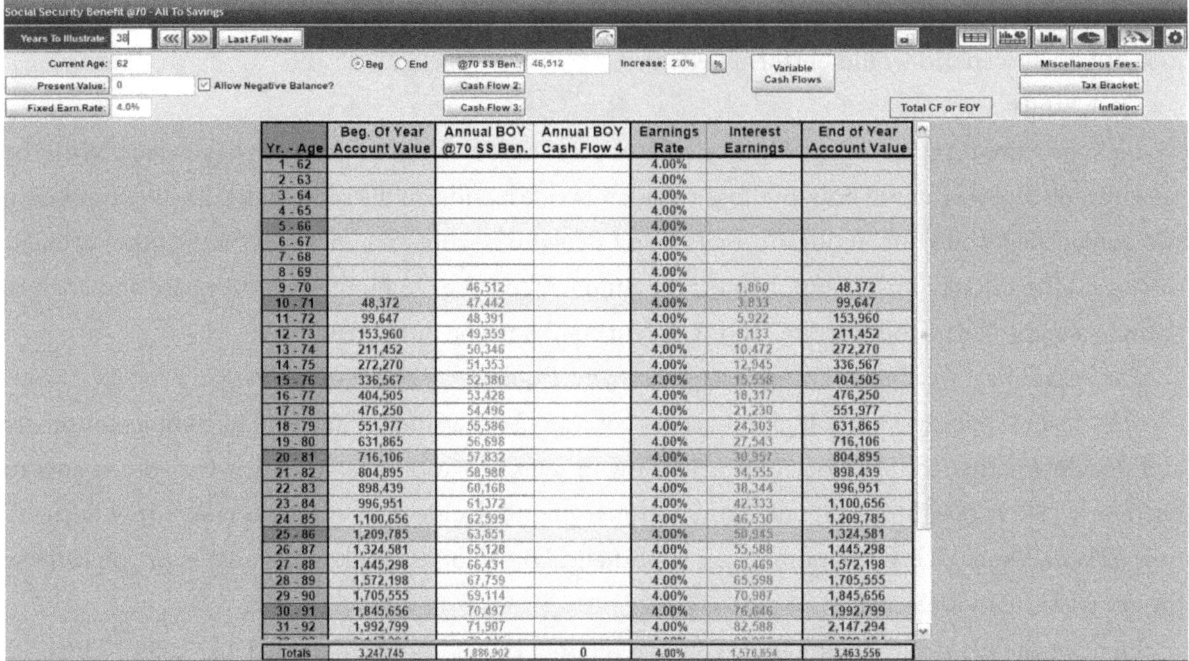

Yr. - Age	Beg. Of Year Account Value	Annual BOY @70 SS Ben.	Annual BOY Cash Flow 4	Earnings Rate	Interest Earnings	End of Year Account Value
1 - 62				4.00%		
2 - 63				4.00%		
3 - 64				4.00%		
4 - 65				4.00%		
5 - 66				4.00%		
6 - 67				4.00%		
7 - 68				4.00%		
8 - 69				4.00%		
9 - 70		46,512		4.00%	1,860	48,372
10 - 71	48,372	47,442		4.00%	3,833	99,647
11 - 72	99,647	48,391		4.00%	5,922	153,960
12 - 73	153,960	49,359		4.00%	8,133	211,452
13 - 74	211,452	50,346		4.00%	10,472	272,270
14 - 75	272,270	51,353		4.00%	12,945	336,567
15 - 76	336,567	52,380		4.00%	15,558	404,505
16 - 77	404,505	53,428		4.00%	18,317	476,250
17 - 78	476,250	54,496		4.00%	21,230	551,977
18 - 79	551,977	55,586		4.00%	24,303	631,865
19 - 80	631,865	56,698		4.00%	27,543	716,106
20 - 81	716,106	57,832		4.00%	30,957	804,895
21 - 82	804,895	58,988		4.00%	34,555	898,439
22 - 83	898,439	60,168		4.00%	38,344	996,951
23 - 84	996,951	61,372		4.00%	42,333	1,100,656
24 - 85	1,100,656	62,599		4.00%	46,530	1,209,785
25 - 86	1,209,785	63,851		4.00%	50,945	1,324,581
26 - 87	1,324,581	65,128		4.00%	55,588	1,445,298
27 - 88	1,445,298	66,431		4.00%	60,469	1,572,198
28 - 89	1,572,198	67,759		4.00%	65,598	1,705,555
29 - 90	1,705,555	69,114		4.00%	70,987	1,845,656
30 - 91	1,845,656	70,497		4.00%	76,646	1,992,799
31 - 92	1,992,799	71,907		4.00%	82,588	2,147,294
Totals	3,247,745	1,886,902	0	4.00%	1,576,854	3,463,556

Below, you can see the exact crossover point pinpointed in the graph from our Side by Side tool.

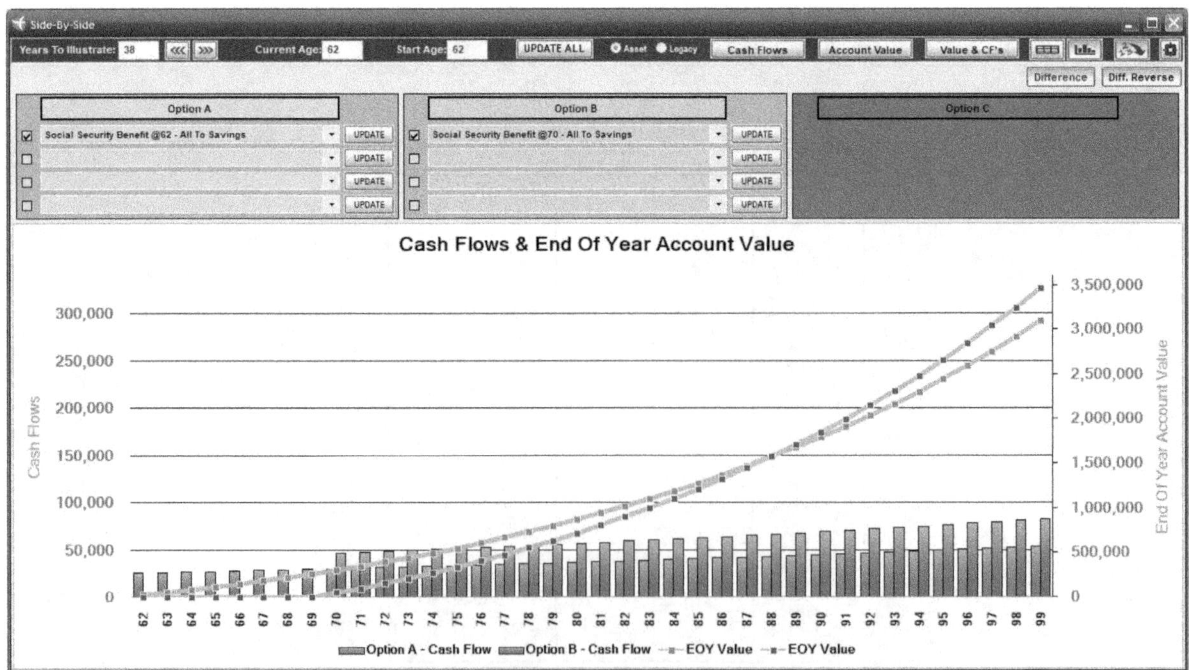

If this is the client's retirement income, why are we even viewing it as if it's savings? Well, we like to come at it from an opportunity standpoint first. This is a look at the overall opportunity of this money, assuming that he's not going to spend it. This gives us some insight into the overall impact of the Social Security money. After all, when used for income, it's going to have a different impact depending on whose wallet it goes into. This is where the assumptions come in.

So let's look at a more macro approach to taking Social Security, and assume that the client will be using this as income to pay his expenses.

Assuming the client's Social Security information all stays the same, let's imagine that he has an account at $1 million for retirement income, earning 4%. His expenses are about $50,000 when he retires at age sixty-two, yet they're increasing slowly over time. As you can see below, that account lasts him until age one hundred, with some to spare. Yet this assumes that his expenses never increase drastically.

Note: Expenses appear *green* even though it's a withdrawal because it's flowing away from the account into the client's "pocket." The Social Security income is *red* even though it's a deposit because it's flowing away from the client's pocket and into the account. If you were to toggle one or the other off, this becomes clear.

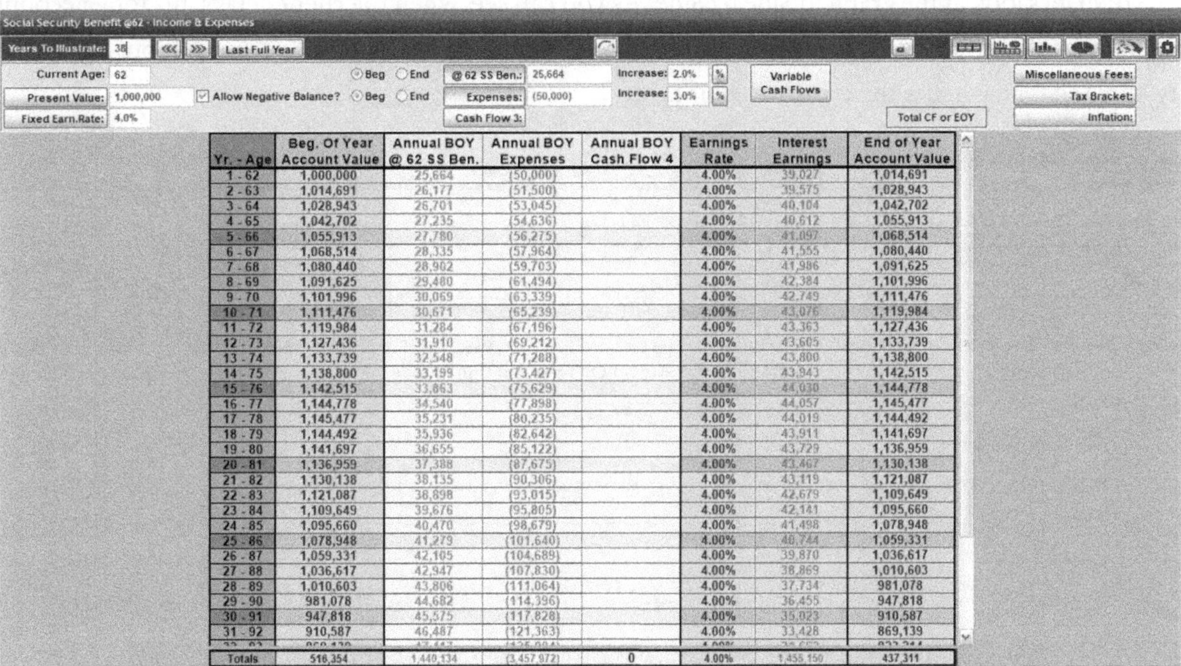

Yr. - Age	Beg. Of Year Account Value	Annual BOY @ 62 SS Ben.	Annual BOY Expenses	Annual BOY Cash Flow 4	Earnings Rate	Interest Earnings	End of Year Account Value
1 - 62	1,000,000	25,664	(50,000)		4.00%	39,027	1,014,691
2 - 63	1,014,691	26,177	(51,500)		4.00%	39,575	1,028,943
3 - 64	1,028,943	26,701	(53,045)		4.00%	40,104	1,042,702
4 - 65	1,042,702	27,235	(54,636)		4.00%	40,612	1,055,913
5 - 66	1,055,913	27,780	(56,275)		4.00%	41,097	1,068,514
6 - 67	1,068,514	28,335	(57,964)		4.00%	41,555	1,080,440
7 - 68	1,080,440	28,902	(59,703)		4.00%	41,986	1,091,625
8 - 69	1,091,625	29,480	(61,494)		4.00%	42,384	1,101,996
9 - 70	1,101,996	30,069	(63,339)		4.00%	42,749	1,111,476
10 - 71	1,111,476	30,671	(65,239)		4.00%	43,076	1,119,984
11 - 72	1,119,984	31,284	(67,196)		4.00%	43,363	1,127,436
12 - 73	1,127,436	31,910	(69,212)		4.00%	43,605	1,133,739
13 - 74	1,133,739	32,548	(71,288)		4.00%	43,800	1,138,800
14 - 75	1,138,800	33,199	(73,427)		4.00%	43,943	1,142,515
15 - 76	1,142,515	33,863	(75,629)		4.00%	44,030	1,144,778
16 - 77	1,144,778	34,540	(77,898)		4.00%	44,057	1,145,477
17 - 78	1,145,477	35,231	(80,235)		4.00%	44,019	1,144,492
18 - 79	1,144,492	35,936	(82,642)		4.00%	43,911	1,141,697
19 - 80	1,141,697	36,655	(85,122)		4.00%	43,729	1,136,959
20 - 81	1,136,959	37,388	(87,675)		4.00%	43,467	1,130,138
21 - 82	1,130,138	38,135	(90,306)		4.00%	43,119	1,121,087
22 - 83	1,121,087	38,898	(93,015)		4.00%	42,679	1,109,649
23 - 84	1,109,649	39,676	(95,805)		4.00%	42,141	1,095,660
24 - 85	1,095,660	40,470	(98,679)		4.00%	41,498	1,078,948
25 - 86	1,078,948	41,279	(101,640)		4.00%	40,744	1,059,331
26 - 87	1,059,331	42,105	(104,689)		4.00%	39,870	1,036,617
27 - 88	1,036,617	42,947	(107,830)		4.00%	38,869	1,010,603
28 - 89	1,010,603	43,806	(111,064)		4.00%	37,734	981,078
29 - 90	981,078	44,682	(114,396)		4.00%	36,455	947,818
30 - 91	947,818	45,575	(117,828)		4.00%	35,023	910,587
31 - 92	910,587	46,487	(121,363)		4.00%	33,428	869,139
Totals	516,354	1,440,134	(3,457,972)	0	4.00%	1,455,150	437,311

Assuming all else is the same, here's what happens when the client delays his Social Security income until age seventy. The difference is much more slight, and the client only ends up with a little over $100,000 more at age one hundred.

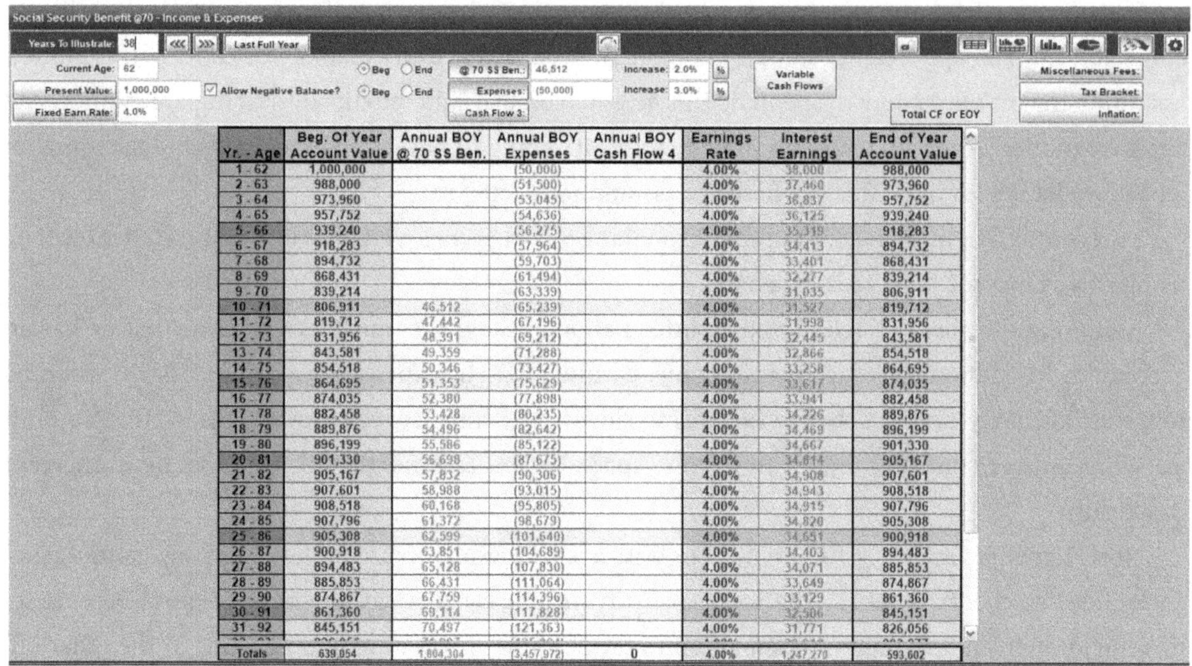

Social Security Benefit @70 - Income & Expenses

Years To Illustrate: 38 | Last Full Year

Current Age: 62 | Present Value: 1,000,000 | Fixed Earn Rate: 4.0% | Allow Negative Balance?

@ 70 SS Ben.: 46,512 (Beg) Increase: 2.0% | Expenses: (50,000) (Beg) Increase: 3.0% | Cash Flow 3: | Variable Cash Flows | Total CF or EOY | Miscellaneous Fees: | Tax Bracket: | Inflation:

Yr. - Age	Beg. Of Year Account Value	Annual BOY @ 70 SS Ben.	Annual BOY Expenses	Annual BOY Cash Flow 4	Earnings Rate	Interest Earnings	End of Year Account Value
1 - 62	1,000,000		(50,000)		4.00%	38,000	988,000
2 - 63	988,000		(51,500)		4.00%	37,460	973,960
3 - 64	973,960		(53,045)		4.00%	36,837	957,752
4 - 65	957,752		(54,636)		4.00%	36,125	939,240
5 - 66	939,240		(56,275)		4.00%	35,319	918,283
6 - 67	918,283		(57,964)		4.00%	34,413	894,732
7 - 68	894,732		(59,703)		4.00%	33,401	868,431
8 - 69	868,431		(61,494)		4.00%	32,277	839,214
9 - 70	839,214		(63,339)		4.00%	31,035	806,911
10 - 71	806,911	46,512	(65,239)		4.00%	31,527	819,712
11 - 72	819,712	47,442	(67,196)		4.00%	31,998	831,956
12 - 73	831,956	48,391	(69,212)		4.00%	32,445	843,581
13 - 74	843,581	49,359	(71,288)		4.00%	32,866	854,518
14 - 75	854,518	50,346	(73,427)		4.00%	33,258	864,695
15 - 76	864,695	51,353	(75,629)		4.00%	33,617	874,035
16 - 77	874,035	52,380	(77,898)		4.00%	33,941	882,458
17 - 78	882,458	53,428	(80,235)		4.00%	34,226	889,876
18 - 79	889,876	54,496	(82,642)		4.00%	34,469	896,199
19 - 80	896,199	55,586	(85,122)		4.00%	34,667	901,330
20 - 81	901,330	56,698	(87,675)		4.00%	34,814	905,167
21 - 82	905,167	57,832	(90,306)		4.00%	34,908	907,601
22 - 83	907,601	58,988	(93,015)		4.00%	34,943	908,518
23 - 84	908,518	60,168	(95,805)		4.00%	34,915	907,796
24 - 85	907,796	61,372	(98,679)		4.00%	34,820	905,308
25 - 86	905,308	62,599	(101,640)		4.00%	34,651	900,918
26 - 87	900,918	63,851	(104,689)		4.00%	34,403	894,483
27 - 88	894,483	65,128	(107,830)		4.00%	34,071	885,853
28 - 89	885,853	66,431	(111,064)		4.00%	33,649	874,867
29 - 90	874,867	67,759	(114,396)		4.00%	33,129	861,360
30 - 91	861,360	69,114	(117,828)		4.00%	32,506	845,151
31 - 92	845,151	70,497	(121,363)		4.00%	31,771	826,056
Totals	639,054	1,804,304	(3,457,972)	0	4.00%	1,247,270	593,602

Then let's look at the graph in Side by Side. As you can see, when the client delays, his total account value goes down before it goes back up, thanks to his expenses. And it isn't until about age ninety-three that he reaches the crossover point.

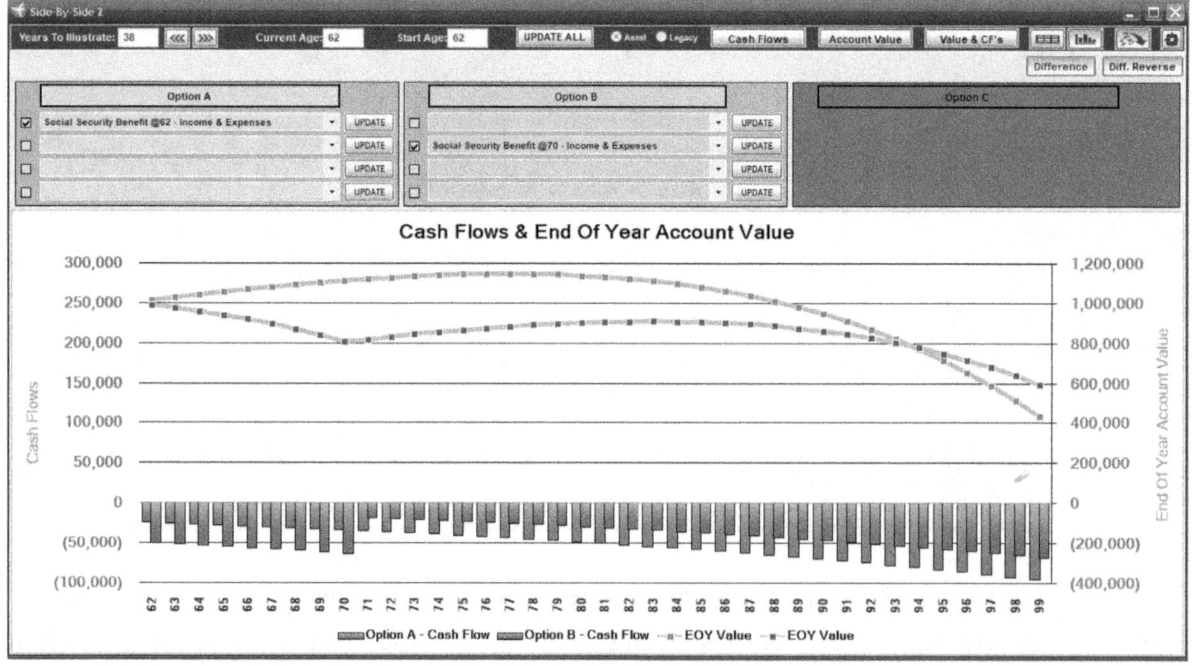

Armed with this knowledge, what is the right choice? In this instance, it's hard to say. There are a lot of assumptions happening. Based on pure mathematics, there is a marginal improvement in delaying, yet only if the client lives to at least age ninety-three (assuming he will spend the income). However, what is his personal life expectancy? Depending on that, he may not want to delay.

There's also much that can't be predicted—additional expenses in retirement, higher inflation, and taxes, etc. And if this account is correlated to the stock market, what would the results be?

What you can do, with the help of the Side by Side tool, is to help a client see the bigger picture and make choices about their finances with confidence. What if they keep working until age seventy, while they delay Social Security income? What if they have whole life insurance to use as a Cash Flow Bridge for their distribution income? Could a reverse mortgage provide additional income? Maybe they want to improve their lifestyle habits to increase their longevity. There are so many things to consider that contribute to the whole picture.

Ultimately, what gives the client peace at night? That counts for a lot as you guide your clients to make a choice.

Life Insurance Values

"If you want to turn an expense into an asset,
convert term insurance into whole life insurance."

TOM WHEELWRIGHT, CPA

The Life Insurance Values tool enables uploading of illustration values (via copy and paste) to this tool, which then calculates IRR and Annual ROR of cash value and death benefit. Then it gives you the ability to pull that information into other calculators, specifically Funding, Borrowing, Diversification, Distribution, and most importantly Asset Flow™.

This is where we put in actual life insurance illustrations; it truly is behind the scenes. It's like a holding tank to hold data and pull it into other calculators to use when needed. This tool greatly improves the effectiveness of the five calculators listed in the case study below and is critical for strategists to know how to use.

Case Study

If you're a client, the key part of this tool is being able to see the result. Some strategists work directly off of this tool with their clients, others combine it with Funding or another calculator that gives an easier way to view the background numbers.

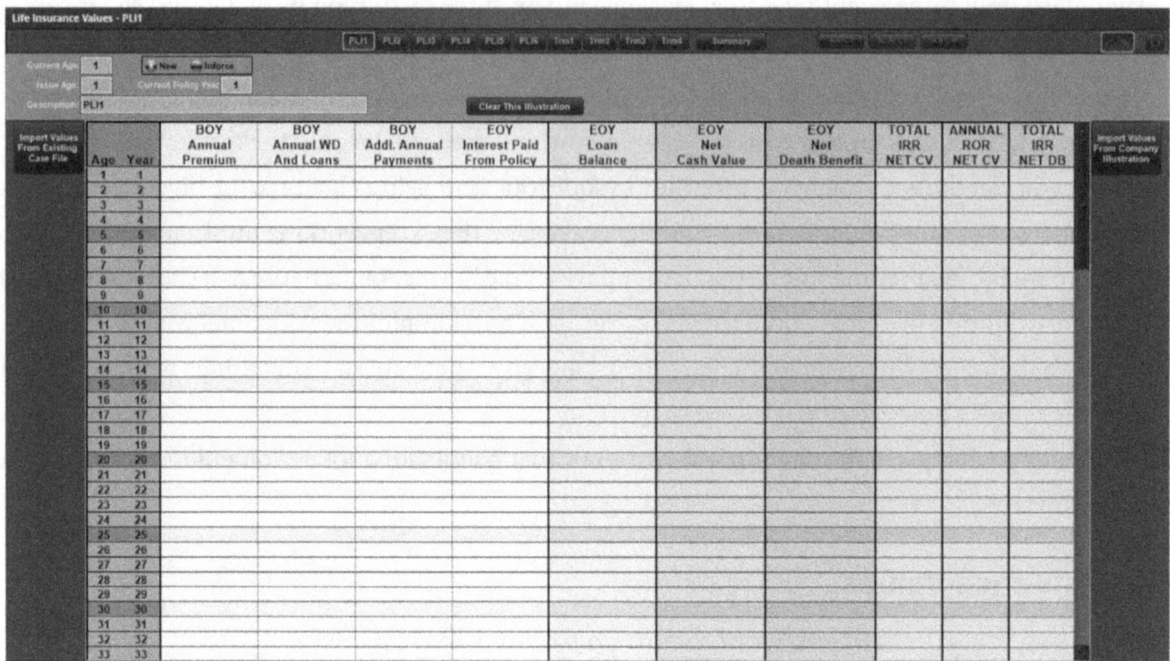

The five calculators that pull data from the Life Insurance Values tool are: Funding, Diversification, Distribution, Accumulation, Qualified Plans, and Asset Flow™. All of those calculators require this tool to be truly effective.

Now, how do we get the data in here from our illustration? That's going to depend on the insurance company you work with and the way they have their illustration software set up. Some have reports where you could send the illustration out to an Excel sheet or a PDF. Some of them allow you to copy directly off of the illustration software.

Note: if you need help converting information to input it into this tool, you can use our OCR to PDF Converter tool (listed later in this chapter). This comes in handy when the PDF is a printed picture instead of underlying numbers embedded in the PDF.

You can also see the descriptions of each of the illustrations that are saved. Descriptions are really important so you have a clue what is saved in which tab (PLI 1 PLI2, PLI3). You have six of them for Permanent Life Insurance, and four term illustrations that you can copy and paste in. And you have unlimited case files you can save.

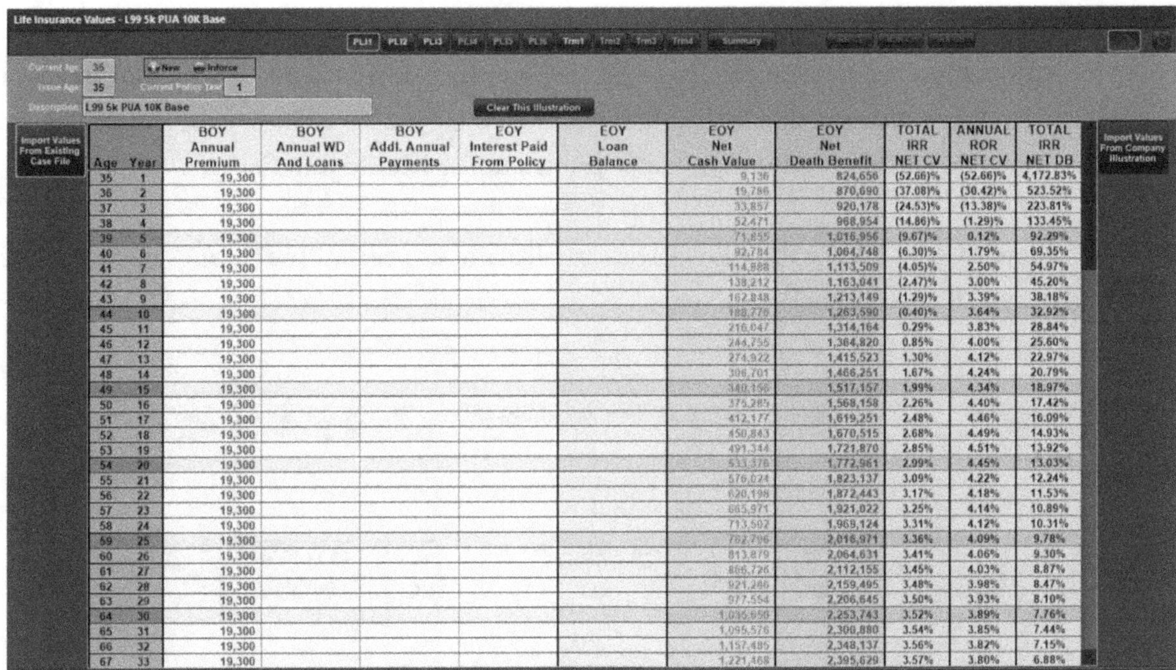

Life Insurance Values - L99 5k PUA 10K Base

PLI1 PLI2 PLI3 PLI4 PLI5 PLI6 Trm1 Trm2 Trm3 Trm4 Summary

Current Age 35 | New | Inforce
Issue Age 35 | Current Policy Year 1
Description L99 5k PUA 10K Base
Clear This Illustration

Import Values From Existing Case File

Age	Year	BOY Annual Premium	BOY Annual WD And Loans	BOY Addl. Annual Payments	EOY Interest Paid From Policy	EOY Loan Balance	EOY Net Cash Value	EOY Net Death Benefit	TOTAL IRR NET CV	ANNUAL ROR NET CV	TOTAL IRR NET DB
35	1	19,300					9,136	824,656	(52.66)%	(52.66)%	4,172.83%
36	2	19,300					19,786	870,690	(37.08)%	(30.42)%	523.52%
37	3	19,300					33,857	920,178	(24.53)%	(13.38)%	223.81%
38	4	19,300					52,471	968,954	(14.86)%	(1.29)%	133.45%
39	5	19,300					71,855	1,016,956	(9.67)%	0.12%	92.29%
40	6	19,300					92,784	1,064,748	(6.30)%	1.79%	69.35%
41	7	19,300					114,888	1,113,509	(4.05)%	2.50%	54.97%
42	8	19,300					138,212	1,163,041	(2.47)%	3.00%	45.20%
43	9	19,300					162,848	1,213,149	(1.29)%	3.39%	38.18%
44	10	19,300					188,776	1,263,590	(0.40)%	3.64%	32.92%
45	11	19,300					216,047	1,314,164	0.29%	3.83%	28.84%
46	12	19,300					244,755	1,364,820	0.85%	4.00%	25.60%
47	13	19,300					274,922	1,415,523	1.30%	4.12%	22.97%
48	14	19,300					306,701	1,466,251	1.67%	4.24%	20.79%
49	15	19,300					340,156	1,517,157	1.99%	4.34%	18.97%
50	16	19,300					375,285	1,568,158	2.26%	4.40%	17.42%
51	17	19,300					412,177	1,619,251	2.48%	4.46%	16.09%
52	18	19,300					450,843	1,670,515	2.68%	4.49%	14.93%
53	19	19,300					491,344	1,721,870	2.85%	4.51%	13.92%
54	20	19,300					533,376	1,772,961	2.99%	4.45%	13.03%
55	21	19,300					576,024	1,823,137	3.09%	4.22%	12.24%
56	22	19,300					620,198	1,872,443	3.17%	4.18%	11.53%
57	23	19,300					665,971	1,921,022	3.25%	4.14%	10.89%
58	24	19,300					713,502	1,969,124	3.31%	4.12%	10.31%
59	25	19,300					762,796	2,016,971	3.36%	4.09%	9.78%
60	26	19,300					813,879	2,064,631	3.41%	4.06%	9.30%
61	27	19,300					866,726	2,112,155	3.45%	4.03%	8.87%
62	28	19,300					921,286	2,159,495	3.48%	3.98%	8.47%
63	29	19,300					977,554	2,206,645	3.50%	3.93%	8.10%
64	30	19,300					1,035,650	2,253,743	3.52%	3.89%	7.76%
65	31	19,300					1,095,576	2,300,880	3.54%	3.85%	7.44%
66	32	19,300					1,157,485	2,348,137	3.56%	3.82%	7.15%
67	33	19,300					1,221,468	2,395,629	3.57%	3.80%	6.88%

Import Values From Company Illustration

This tool can be used to prove the effectiveness of Life Insurance when combined with other assets, usually with other calculators, depending on where the client is in the life insurance process.

It's important to note that dividend rates on companies' websites can be pretty misleading. The dividend rate is really a declared gross rate that all insurance policies will get. Yet how it's applied to individual policies is going to differ across the board, so I caution strategists and clients when it comes to quoting the gross dividend rate.

The guarantees are very similar across all companies as far as what they're willing to sign on the dotted line for and say they will absolutely guarantee.

So when you have a client who shops around and says, "Let's compare this company versus that company," remind them: There's no deal with insurance companies, because mutual companies will have very similar investment portfolios, very similar expenses, and very similar salespeople. And they have been that way for over 150 years.

In this business, the confidence of knowing that you know what you know is key. That's a big part of what the Truth Concepts software is for.

Whether you are a client or a financial strategist, knowing how to use these calculators can give you the strength and confidence you need to make intelligent, well-informed financial decisions.

In my experience, there's too much competition and not enough collaboration in the business of insurance and personal finance, and we ought to be free and knowledgeable enough to collaborate.

Printing

Using the Printing tool, each calculator can be printed on paper or copied into a Word document or an email to share with clients or add to your file. Additionally, if you have a large calculator on screen with a small one over it, that combination can be printed under File, Screen, Capture.

Case Study

Use this tool to Print and/or Print Preview each calculator as needed. The Settings button on the right is where you'll find this tool.

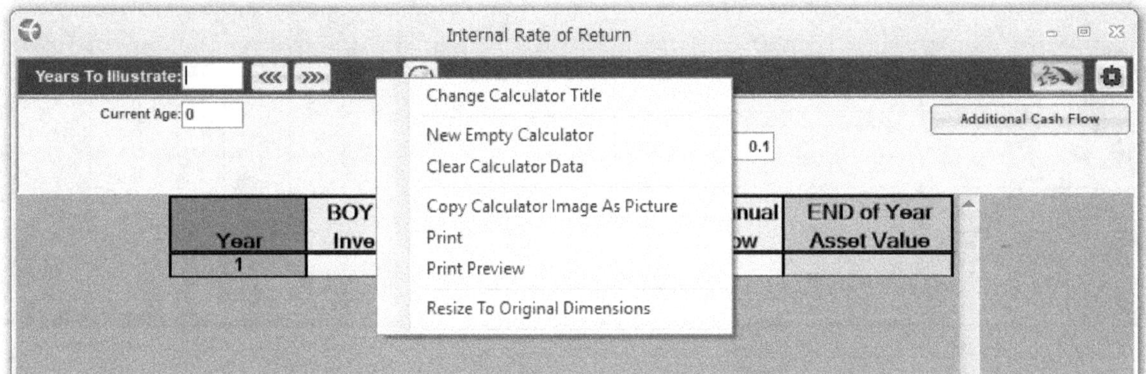

There you can see the Print Preview, and the button that will bring up another calculator. You can pull up most of the calculators, up to six of the same calculator if needed. If you do that, how are you going to remember what those calculators were for? At the very top you'll see where it says "Change Calculator Title," and you can specifically label each calculator so you'll remember what it was for later.

In a year's time, if you pull that up, that label will help you know what that calculator was telling you. Sometimes it can be helpful to leave part of the name of the calculator in there, as well as your title, such as "Cash Flow 2026," to stay organized and remember what you are looking at.

OCR to PDF Converter

Have you ever gone to copy and paste life insurance values and were unable to because the PDF isn't editable? **When you take a picture with your cell phone of any Life Insurance Illustration, this OCR to PDF Converter will switch the image to a PDF** so that you can copy and paste it into the Life Values Tool. It effectively takes an image of numbers and turns them into the actual numbers in a sheet where you can use those numbers like you would in a calculator. Some PDFs have numbers or text embedded, whereas some are just a picture of numbers.

What is OCR?

OCR stands for Optical Character Recognition. As the name implies, OCR uses software to analyze images and identify all of the characters so that they can be encoded into the PDF and therefore be copied from the document.

Until recently, OCR software has been mediocre. In other words, it hasn't been 100% accurate all the time, however, it's often better than inputting everything by hand in the first place. Recently, however, I came across some technology that combined the original Tesseract OCR engine with AI technology, which has increased the accuracy exponentially.

This new OCR technology is going to drastically improve your time inputting difficult illustrations into Truth Concepts.

One fun fact is that it's just a small tool, but it is massive in the size of data it uses. A user group maintains the core Tesseract engine of this software: 130MB. The OCR piece is 100MB of that. That's a lot of work for a computer to go through to take a graphic and turn it into an actual number!

Case Study

This OCR converter opens up all sorts of opportunities for inputting life insurance values, especially while traveling, working on joint cases, or using scanned documents.

If a client has an existing life insurance policy and we're going to analyze it, instead of manually typing in all the numbers, you can use this OCR scanner to convert the numbers. It's such a time-saver. It not only saves time, it provides accuracy. You cannot type in three columns of numbers and get them all right; there will always be some wrong due to human error.

One great example of the type of file you may use this tool for is a PDF you may get from the advanced underwriting department of a special illustration, which may just be a photograph or scan. These file types don't have the characters encoded, so you cannot copy them.

Another example is if you're traveling and have a physical copy of an insurance illustration with you, and you'd like to put it in Truth Concepts, you just snap a photo or use a document scanner, move that file to your computer, and use the OCR reader to turn that image/scan into a new PDF. If you have a life insurance illustration that has unusual formatting, you can also use the OCR reader to make a copy without the formatting.

This tool will streamline your learning curve as you input values into the Life Insurance Values tool. If you want a tutorial of how to use it, go to: https://truthconcepts.com/ocr-file-converter-tutorial.

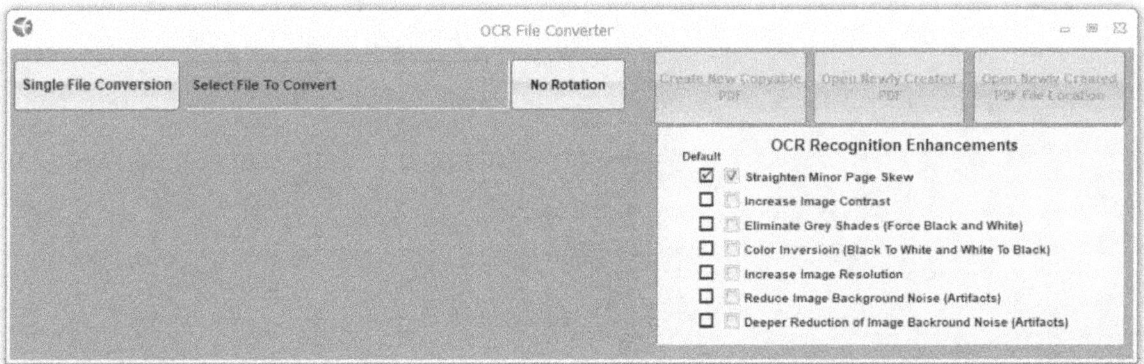

Virtual Keyboard

The Virtual Keyboard tool is helpful when using Truth Concepts on a tablet via the Online Ready To Go version **(tablets cannot do the mathematical computations as they are not technically computers).**

If you have a touchscreen on your tablet, a keyboard will pop up, and it will use that instead of a physical keyboard. It's just on the screen instead of separate from the device.

Case Study

Use this tool to optimize your freedom and flexibility if you use a tablet that you can easily take with you when traveling (if a client) or to visit clients (if a strategist). It's a simple tool that makes a big difference in the portability of the calculators!

Move All TC to Primary Display

This tool is helpful when using two or three screens and sharing Truth Concepts data files.

In my office, I've got two forty-nine inch screens stacked on top of each other, and an additional screen for Zoom on the side. They're all connected. When working with software, I'll throw calculators all over all the screens so I can see what's going on, exchange numbers, and see the impact in real time.

When you save a file like the one I was working with above, this tool saves all the data in the locations where I viewed them, so I have the convenience of not moving them around. In a standard setup without this tool, if you opened the file on a laptop with just one screen, those other calculators would just be floating out in space. This tool moves all those calculators into the main display automatically for ease of viewing.

Case Study

Use this tool to save time and access your primary view of all calculations you may have saved in a data file, regardless of how many screens you used initially.

Working on two or more screens is very helpful for copying and pasting information from one place to another, such as Illustrations to Life Insurance Values, and this tool streamlines the view after saving so you can see them all on one primary screen.

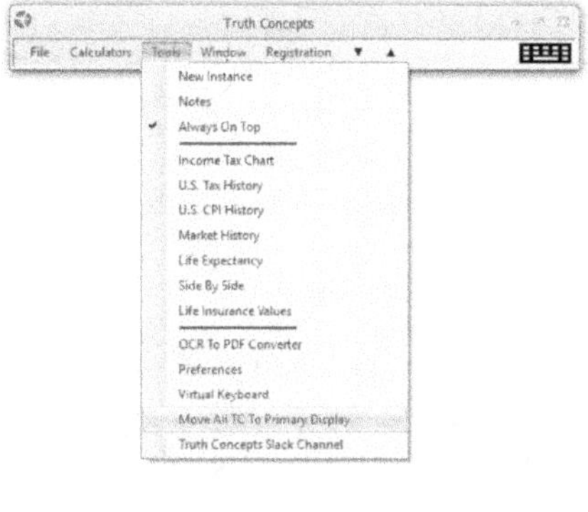

• • • • •

The tools shown above are included with the latest Truth Concepts software through a TC 360 membership. Start a free trial or learn more here: https://truthconcepts.com/free-trial.

Chapter 7: Duet of Truth: Math and Principle

Calculators can calculate numbers,
yet they can't calculate the real world.

In the world of finance, there's one thing we—clients *and* strategists—can't afford to compromise on: the truth. At Truth Concepts, we believe math is absolute. There's no gray area when you plug in the right numbers, but the human element, the assumptions and interpretations, can throw everything off. That's where we've seen the industry begin to lose integrity. And where our calculators step in to help you align math with principle, definitive numbers with personal desires.

Financial professionals often lean on partial truths, skewed inputs, or incomplete formulas to present numbers that seem right but aren't. Why? Sometimes it's a lack of understanding. Other times, it's inherited misinformation passed down from mentors or product-focused training.

The job of any strategist isn't just to run numbers. It's to ensure the numbers are *true*—rooted in proper assumptions and accurate logic—and to make sure the client takes action and gets the results. That's where the Truth Concepts calculators shine. They reveal the whole picture, not just a snapshot. With our calculators and tools, you don't need to take anyone's word for it that the numbers are true. You can prove the truth to yourself (and to your clients if you're a financial strategist).

When truth is compromised, trust goes with it. The average client today is skeptical, and rightly so. They've been burned by strategists who meant well but didn't truly understand the math behind their recommendations. The result? An entire industry out of balance. The strategists who use Truth Concepts use it because they care about the truth, and they share in the cause to *restore that balance.*

In our community, we teach financial strategists how to think, rather than what to think. With this independence, you're not reliant on gurus, sales scripts, or even us as your teachers. *You*, as the strategist, become the authority your clients can trust, not because you're persuasive, but because you're right. You also know that the mathematical calculations are only one part of the equation; principled alignment with your clients' desires and particular circumstances are essential to providing sound financial advice.

MATH IS BLACK AND WHITE—INTERPRETATION IS NOT

Because math is absolute, by itself it doesn't allow for particular situations that can't be analyzed in a mathematical format. Assessing risk is one of the biggest examples of this concept. Risk shifts for a person based on their background, education, financial circumstances, and time of life. Whether you are a client or a strategist, you can look at the different options available to you and weigh most of the risks. At least the ones that are weighable with math. There are many times when a decision isn't as much about the numbers, it's more about the mindset.

In your situation, what decision fits your principles best, knowing you may give something up mathematically? In our lives there are times where we violate what the math may tell us is the "best" solution because of a principle we're committed to. Or sometimes it is about making sure we have a higher likelihood of an end result we are aiming for. While mathematically, a financial result might be high, the results may actually be low, depending on factors like risk and timing.

An example of when you might violate the math in deference to principle is when your client is seeking peace of mind above and beyond financial gain. Sometimes peace of mind overrides mathematical equations. I tend to view peace of mind in an opposing way from most people.

Mortgage payments provide a big example of this in practice. People often get peace of mind from the idea of paying off their mortgage in full. But when they do that, they are making financially unsound decisions in an attempt to mitigate a fear they have, a misplaced fear as I see it. We see people who will strain themselves so heavily cash-wise because they're funneling all their extra money toward their mortgage. This can even cause them to take on 18%+ credit card debt! It's the *size* of the mortgage that tends to drive people to make extreme, unsound decisions in this arena. But they believe it is necessary for their peace of mind.

Even if it was mathematically better, I still wouldn't pay off my mortgage. I would hold the debt even if it would cost me. That's the beauty of understanding personal financial math in its entirety; you have to know how much a decision is going to cost you. If it's going to cost you $20,000 to make a decision, $20,000 in light of $100,000, that's a high percentage. But if it's a $20,000 cost in light of $1 million, it's a much less risky decision.

One issue we see in the industry is that there is so much hype not backed up with math that people are just following the hype they hear or see. People will say in every situation, "you should do X, Y, or Z." Instead, for best practices in aligning the math with your own principles, weigh your decision with factors like the following:

- What is your life like right now?
- What are your financial objectives?
- What are your current and future desires?

Talking these questions through with a trusted strategist can help you make the right decision for you and your family that benefits you financially and emotionally.

TO BUY OR NOT TO BUY

Car purchases are another great example of a decision where it helps to understand the math, not just the emotional appeal. Don't get me wrong, I love a new car! I love the way it smells, the new technology, all of it. However, when I run the numbers on what it costs to buy a new car, as much as I love it, that's off the list for me. I don't mind a one-year- or two-year-old car as an initial purchase. Buying gently used cars aligns my value of enjoying a relatively new car with getting a good deal so I can use the money I've saved on the purchase for investments.

Another person may say, "I love new cars too much, and that's the quality of life I am willing to pay for." But when I weigh the value of a new car against the cost, it's not worth it to me. The math overrides my desire. We have a calculator specifically for that equation.

Please understand, I'm not saying don't buy new cars; I'm just saying look at the math and the cost of that decision. Then ask yourself, is it worth that cost for the temporary pleasure I will get driving the new car? Is it worth giving up $1 million of retirement money? (This is roughly how much it could cost in the long run for that money to be used on a new car purchase instead of an investment.) How many people are aware that's what it will cost them? This is where our calculators come in handy.

It's also important to look closely at large purchases (like a car) and their wider impact on your life beyond the mathematical calculations. Buying a new car, or any new item (clothes, jewelry, furniture, etc.), can be beneficial, both financially and in reputation, depending on the business you're in. You may want to buy a new car, for example, if it boosts your income, business, and image as a result. As a financial strategist, if you drive up to someone's office in a thirty-year-old beater car, they may decide they don't want to do business with you. How do you put a number on that? You can only estimate and trust yourself to make the best decision that weighs both your values and your finances.

DECISION-MAKING FROM FEAR

Houses, on the other hand, are a purchase that I believe can be made in a financially sound *and* value-aligned way without a whole lot of interpretation. However, doing so may require a mindset shift. As I mentioned earlier, when people dump money into a house, they may *feel* peace of mind, but they're actually putting themselves in a much riskier position than putting it elsewhere. How?

First off, what I mean by "dumping money" is paying additional money towards the mortgage beyond what's required. With a mortgage, you're socking money away already, and buyers think they're building equity in the house by doing so. **Yes, you *are* building equity, but you're building it in the *bank*, not the house, and the bank ultimately decides if you get the money back or not.**

Fear drives many homeowners' decisions to pay down their mortgage. They are afraid of losing the house, but the action they take of paying it off actually makes them more likely to lose it. My wife, Kim, talks with her clients about green times and lean times. Green times are times of plenty, when money is abundant. Lean times are times where money is tight, and spending is restricted. What happens when you have cashflow problems and are going through a lean time, but you've put all your extra money toward your mortgage? Now you can't afford your mortgage payment, and you lose the house. Whereas if you accumulated the cash somewhere else, you would have the money needed to pay your monthly mortgage payment *and* get you through the lean time into a greener time.

I have found that when I make a decision out of fear, I almost always make the wrong decision. Fear puts us into fight or flight mode. The fight or flight reaction has allowed humankind to survive. In today's society, however, that fight or flight reaction can be destructive, especially when it comes to personal finances. Our fear, ironically, often causes what we're afraid of to happen. I believe in the power of mindset heavily, but I also think the results of a person's mindset are largely due to their actions. Someone might say, "They were so focused on their fear of losing the house; that mindset caused them to lose the house." No, I believe something tangible happened in such a circumstance. Their fear (mindset) caused decisions (actions) that ultimately brought about losing their house (result).

Therefore, changing our mindset and making financial decisions from a place of calm confidence will typically yield decisions and actions that bring about positive growth. Choosing to work with a strategist experienced in navigating all the emotions and myths around money and personal finance can be hugely helpful. It can be a tough road to travel down without a guide.

DECISION-MAKING FROM PRINCIPLE

We've been working on a new calculator on debt management which has sparked some debate. The debate is between me, my wife Kim, and a group advocating for using "velocity banking." We discovered this group is not always telling the truth about certain aspects. When we showed some of the results from our calculator, the moderator of the group asked me, "What would you do in this situation?" That's an opportunity to make a decision from principle: defining my thought process and action steps with integrity, regardless of the numbers.

Sure, I can state the mathematical facts, like, "In this scenario, using a HELOC with a variable rate versus a mortgage with a fixed rate shows you'll have $1,000 more in thirty years." Yet, along the way, you'll have much less cash on hand. In a situation like that, I would take a little less of a loan to be in a better cash position, knowing in the next thirty years, very little will play out the way I expect it to. There will be opportunities and hardships, and I will need cash to get me through it. That's what I would do, but it may not be what you would do. That's an example of me acting from my own individual perspective and principle.

Principle, when it comes to personal financial decision-making, refers to one main question: what do you (the individual client) hold in order of importance? Is your priority having a possibility of getting a bigger number in the future? Or having less risk? Regardless of your individual principles, the math will tell us the pure math every time. And without personal finance math, we can't make educated decisions that align with our principles.

A while ago I knew someone with a family history of smokers who was very much against smoking because of what it had done to their family's health. They were invested in a fund, and part of the fund was with Phillip Morris and other cigarette companies. When they discovered this, they wanted out of the whole fund because it violated their principles, regardless of the financial gain they could have achieved staying in. The returns were good. The fund was growing, but it violated key principles in their life. They opted out.

THE PRINCIPLE OF LEGACY

Principles are often passed down from generation to generation. When we're looking at the principle of legacy, it's important to consider: do you want to pass on a legacy? And if so, what is it? How much is it? What matters to you?

Passing on a legacy, a real legacy, is not just about the money. People hear the word legacy in the personal finance space and tend to think trusts, life insurance, and other similar legacy products. That's not what legacy really is. The money simply allows for the real principles to get passed on: your standards of what you expect your family and community to look like in the future.

There's so much good that people have to pass down in addition to money: they can write a letter, share failures and lessons learned, share items or hobbies they loved, and more. The lack of money, however, can cause the opposite of what you want to happen when leaving a legacy. If you're broke and out on the street, it's hard for your kids to listen to whatever legacy you leave and believe you in what you do and say. This is where having the money to leave to your family is not about the passing on of money; it's about having integrity so your voice has merit. Money is simply one key piece in that legacy scenario that plays multiple roles and reinforces your values.

Money does not bring happiness directly, but it does allow for the opportunity to bring happiness to yourself and others. Without it, living becomes a lot more difficult. Money's neither good nor bad in and of itself; what it pays for can bring about good or bad results and experiences, depending on what we do with it. As with anything in life, decisions about money are all about moderation and balance. As the ancient philosophers Aristotle, Plato, and Socrates taught, virtue taken to an extreme can become a vice. Balance is that magic "mean in the middle" that helps us weigh whether our decisions are aligned with our values.

Defining values and principles makes up a big part of a financial strategist's role with their clients. Leaving a legacy feels far off for many young people who are just starting to invest. The only way they tend to understand it is when tragedy strikes. Generally, young people feel invincible, as if they'll never die or become disabled. However, when they turn a certain age, (usually mid-fifties to sixties), all of a sudden legacy becomes more important than eating. If we could somehow get a message across to younger people that they can find meaning and value in thinking about their legacy *now* when they're young, that could make a huge difference in their lives and financial gains. Think about the stress relief for their future self, how much they could prevent worrying about that later on.

CONNECTING NUMBERS TO REAL LIFE

One of the most common mistakes strategists make is presenting numbers that don't connect with their clients' lives, whether they are young, elderly, or somewhere in between. Spreadsheets are sterile; they don't evoke action. But when strategists tie those numbers to their client's goals—freedom, legacy, time with family—those same figures become fuel for change.

The Truth Concepts calculators help you—client and strategist—*understand* the principles deeply enough that you can speak the truth about your personal finances clearly, confidently, and contextually—even without the screen.

UPHOLDING EXCELLENCE: TRUTH CONCEPTS STANDARDS

To truly elevate the quality of financial advising, Truth Concepts operates by seven non-negotiable standards that serve both math and principle. They are so important that I opened the book with them, and I'm going to repeat them again here. These are best practices and the backbone of our calculators, training, and entire philosophy. Here's what they mean and why they matter:

1. Use *Financial Math* Formulas & Calculators–Not Simple Grade-School Math Which Ignores Time

Time affects money in powerful ways, for better or worse. Too many strategists rely on oversimplified math that ignores time value, which leads to inaccurate conclusions. Our software is built around true financial mathematics—compounding, discounting, amortization—so you see the *real* impact of every dollar over time. This way, clients can think about how their choices will impact their bottom line today *and* forty to one hundred plus years out.

2. Always Compare Strategies Using *Equivalent Cash Flows*

Comparing apples to oranges? That's a fast track to confusion. You must measure strategies with the same cash flows—timing, amount, and frequency—to see which truly performs better. The Truth Concepts tools standardize this process, making sure every comparison is fair and accurate.

3. Measure Both Opportunity *Cost* (What You Give Up) *and* Opportunity *Gain* (What You Earn)

It's not enough to look at ROI. You also need to measure what you *could have* earned elsewhere with those same dollars. We factor in the *net cost of money* to show both sides of the opportunity—what you lose *and* what you gain.

4. Use the *Actual* Internal Rate of Return (IRR) Over Time, *not* the Misleading *Averages*

Average rates lie. A portfolio that drops 50% and gains 50% doesn't break even, even if the "average" return says 0%. We help you uncover the *actual IRR*, showing the true performance of a financial strategy over time—because real life isn't average.

5. Consider the *Ripple Effects* of Every Financial Decision–Nothing Exists in a Vacuum

Buy a car, fund a policy, take a loan—every decision affects other parts of your financial life. We show the interconnected impact of each decision, helping clients think about the "big picture." This holistic view helps prevent costly oversights.

6. Avoid *Paltering*–Don't Let True but *Irrelevant* Facts Lead to False Conclusions

Facts can be dangerous when misused. Just because something is true doesn't mean it matters. We equip strategists to spot and avoid *paltering*—the practice of misleading with technically correct but irrelevant data. Truth Concepts helps you keep the .

7. Accurate Strategies Require Both Accurate Math *and* the Correct Formula

There are many times when financial analysis has accurate math, but the wrong formula was used so the results are irrelevant. For example, you can't add up interest costs over time (cumulatively) without impacting that stream of interest payments with the time value of money (an interest rate, compounded). The total interest paid on a loan is just a fun fact. It is a meaningless calculation, mathematically correct, yet misleading.

BUSTING MYTHS

In this section, we'll address common financial myths and oversimplifications that obscure true understanding. These are myths that both clients and strategists mistakenly believe—until they know better.

You'll see from the myths below that you can tell a lie (or simply an untruth) in a sentence, yet it often takes a whole paragraph to tell the truth. How do we get rid of the gimmicky, incorrect math and quick soundbites? We must learn and share the information below with others. Bust the myths and make better-informed choices!

Myth 1: It's all about Rate of Return.

As Standard D states above, the *actual* rate of return has a lot to do with time. Instead of accepting what you are told are the average rates of return, use our Rate Calculator to calculate the necessary rate of return to get from point A to point B over a specific period of time. This calculator helps you determine your IRR (Internal Rate of Return), instead of just the average rate. That way you are taking into account time and contributions as well as the rate of return. You can also use our Cash Flow calculator and Market History tool to estimate more detailed, complex scenarios and make better-informed decisions.

Myth 2: Rate of Return has nothing to do with it.

You'll hear both sides! It's important to examine: what does ROR (rate of return) look like for the big picture? Rate of return (or rate of cost), especially matters when it comes to debt. Knowing the interest rate of a loan should drive our decisions on whether we pay cash or not, based on the rate we can earn versus the rate we have to pay. That is a critically important point: it's not the size of the debt that matters; it's the rate of return (or in this case the rate of the cost) on the debt that determines if it's good debt or bad debt.

Myth 3: You can add or subtract interest rates to determine efficiency.

Interest rates work exponentially over time. They don't function in a linear fashion. You must use a financial calculator when working with interest rates in order to tell what is really going on. For example, 5% is not 1% better than 4%; it is 25% better. Sometimes converting the interest rate into a dollar figure helps. $500 is 25% more than $400.

Myth 4: You pay more interest at the beginning of a loan than you do at the end of a loan.

While this statement is true, and a higher percentage of the payment initially is interest (whereas the last payment is mostly principal), the reason this is true is because the interest is based on the *amount* of the loan. You're going to have a higher amount of interest on a loan with a higher balance. What people hear and take away from this is that loans are constructed in a way that first you pay all the interest, and then you pay all the principal. That's not the way it works. Paying more interest in the beginning is a function of there being a bigger balance.

Myth 5: You don't have to pay life insurance loans back.

Technically you don't have to pay the loan back to the life insurance company because it's on your terms, but if you don't ever pay the loan back, it will destroy the policy. Strategists may say that your death benefit will pay your loan back so people hear, "This is free money!" They think, "We can just borrow and never pay it back!" You don't *have* to pay it back, but there are major consequences if you do not. Interest is charged every year because you are using the life insurance company's money. Your cash value is still sitting in your policy.

Myth 6: Paying cash eliminates an interest cost.

You never truly get outside of interest. **When you understand how opportunity works, you realize there's a *negative* opportunity when you pay cash for something.** There are positive and negative numbers for a reason. In early elementary school, you couldn't go below zero in math. But in third grade the teachers said, "Guess what? There are negative numbers!" Negative numbers are the basis for how negative opportunity works. Negative opportunity compounds in the same direction, for the same reason. The fact that we paid cash didn't mean we avoided an interest cost. There's an interest cost on *everything* we buy. Period. We either finance it directly with a financial institution (with a loan, typically via credit card), or we finance it with our *future* cash.

This myth also brings up an example where it makes sense to violate the math. If you were earning 5% and your banker was charging you 8%, it would be cheaper to withdraw cash. But I would argue your quality of life is better paying the 8% because you'll guarantee to pay it instead of demolishing your savings account. This is a perfect example of where quality of life outweighs the literal math.

INTEGRATION OF MATH AND PRINCIPLE

Math and individual principles must work together for sound financial advice and decision-making. Through working with the Blueprint Process by Tammi Brannan, I've learned that one of my tower parts (core ways of being) uses principle to narrow the field and pull in all the facts. I have an idea of the way personal finance math works in a lot of different scenarios. **And I'm always open to exploring and ensuring that in *this* particular situation, the math still makes sense.**

Sometimes situations change, and that can change the math. Rather than having a broad stream of testing every possible outcome, I test the specific scenarios we're making a decision about. The math might say a decision will cost me a certain amount to go down one road, but I always have to ask: "Will it cost me more than how far my principles are willing to stretch?" If so, it's not worth any amount of savings or income that could come. If it compromises my principles, it's a deal-breaker.

When we talk about cars, for example, as mentioned earlier, people have no idea that a $30,000 brand-new car, trading it in every four years for thirty years, will cost them over $1 million in their lifetime. As we work with the numbers in the calculator, we can see that by changing the trade-in timeframe from every four years to every six years, we increased the money available at the end by $700,000.

The average person at retirement now has about $300,000. Is it worth that extra $700,000 to have a new car every four years versus every six? If we don't know the math, how can we make that decision? There's no way a person can conceive of that decision costing them that much money unless they're looking at the math. They see it as only $280,000 worth of cars. It's really the interest they're paying and the time value of money that increases that number so dramatically. This is where a person's principles must come into play in order to integrate them with the math so that a decision can be made that aligns with them both.

CASE STUDIES AND INSIGHTS

Clear, truthful financial guidance is priceless and, unfortunately, rare. We see examples of famous or well-known celebrities in the financial space giving advice that, when examined, is often not clear, not truthful, or both. Yet people follow it because they trust someone they have seen or read so many times before. **It's essential, especially in personal finance, that you do the math yourself, understand how it applies to your situation, and align your principles with the math to create the life you want.**

Sometimes with thought leaders in the personal finance space, like Dave Ramsey, followers can get literal about their message. Dave Ramsey personally got himself upside-down on real estate debt and went bankrupt. As I see it, his strategy caused the bankruptcy to happen, but he blamed it on his debt, which led to his one big message: get rid of debt.

One time we attended a church on graduation day, where people were graduating from the Dave Ramsey program. During the graduation, people who had gone through the program came up to give a testimony. Up front they all said it was the most freeing, greatest thing in the world that's happened to them. "We used to cook dinner all the time, now we go out almost every night." Translated in a truthful way, mathematically, they're blowing the money they would've saved. Before, they were saving money and paying off debt. Now, because they're paying cash, they think they don't need to make payments. Actually, those payments need to go back into their bank account; otherwise they'll be at zero in the future. They may be better off for having paid off debt per Dave Ramsey's program, but this is only true if they invest the money they saved once the debt is paid off. It can be difficult for people to think in mathematical terms like this. I do it quickly and effectively, but I'm aware I am the exception.

In the 1980s, A.L. Williams (now Primerica) promoted his own marketing message in the personal finance space that many people took to be true, also as a result of a personal experience of his. His dad died with a small whole life policy, and his strategist had not added the term insurance to insure his dad's Human Life Value. Because there wasn't any term insurance (in addition to the whole life) when his dad died early, his family was left with no money. Therefore, Williams' message became all about term insurance and advised that you should *never* have whole life insurance. He is the one known for the axiom, "Buy term and invest the difference."

Lastly, I'll share an example that has to do with taxes and twisting the truth. Nelson Nash, founder of the Infinite Banking Concept, tells the story of an eighteen-wheel trucking company that boasts on the back of their trucks, "This truck paid $X in taxes last year." The reality is they didn't pay any of those taxes. Nash brings to light that the truth of the matter is that the people who bought their products pay the taxes.

Corporations don't pay tax. That's why, economically, you'll hear legislators say, "We're going to increase corporate tax and lower income tax." But corporations don't actually pay tax. They send in the money they've collected. Whenever the government raises taxes, it's a tax on all the people *buying* the products. The corporations simply raise the cost of goods to the people.

Overall, people choose their principles based on their experience, their level of knowledge, and their interpretation of that knowledge. People often think, as the creator of the Truth Concepts calculators, that I'm "all about the math." Yes, the math has to be right. However, it's not our sole decision-maker. Principles must be taken into account. But we can't follow our principles intelligently *without math*. What fits us and our family best at that time of our lives? Some of the words a financial strategist should not use with clients are "always" and "never." When it comes to interpretation of principles, it all depends.

The book *Math-Ish* by Dr. Jo Bealer brings to light the consequences of math done badly or incorrectly, as well as encourages us to interpret math from diverse perspectives. It also emphasizes recent research in the past ten years that shows that "there is no such thing as a math brain, and all brains are constantly developing, connecting, and changing." (*Math-Ish*, p. 224) This encouraging finding helps those of you who may feel anxious about math to give it another chance, and to take a positive attitude toward learning math. Especially when you see how math applies to your finances and life, you may feel motivated to learn more and gain a deeper understanding of how the numbers work.

APPLYING MATH AND PRINCIPLES TO FINANCIAL ADVICE

Integrity in both numbers and principles is key when applying mathematical knowledge. Financial strategists have an obligation to their clients to be truthful about the math and to listen to their clients' perspectives.

When it comes to personal finance, how a decision applies to an individual is different for each person. At a cocktail party, as soon as people find out you're in finance, they ask, "What should I invest in?" How can you ever guess? The answer across the board is, "It depends." But the person asking then feels like you're hiding something or that you must be a salesperson. So some financial strategists will give an answer, but there's no way it's done with integrity. Strategists who do their job well will say, "Let's meet and we'll discuss it." The truth is, we need a way to be able to say, "I could tell you something, but it would be wrong. If you want an accurate answer, I need more data."

There are three main applications of the calculators that help you incorporate math with principle:

The first is for *you*. It's the game of personal competence: knowing what's right and knowing that you know it. That is done through objective analysis, through direct math.

The second is the strategic use—solving problems for clients. Are clients getting what they want to accomplish? And are you helping them do it with the proof in the back of your head?

The third is for communicating with a client. Humans are not wired to understand math. That is why we are adding graphs to all the calculators and have made them as user-friendly as possible.

In human relationships, there's natural resistance when there are two opposing forces. We naturally resist when there's no assistance. **Calculators can be that third-party resource that assists and is not polarizing.** Other times, the calculators can cause polarization.

Preaching the gospel to people by telling them what they're doing wrong when they don't think they're doing anything wrong is not going to get you very far. Using the calculators to prove you're right and they're wrong is definitely not going to help. Again, know yourself, know your client, and know your material so well you don't have to prove things mathematically all the time. The calculators are there as a support, to show the math that supports your story. Over time, it's essential that you find a way to have a conversation with your clients so that you can help them see a different way of thinking and doing things without pushing the math on them.

You'll want to know yourself and know your client to determine *when* and *how* to show the calculators. It also helps if you agree with our seven Truth Concepts Standards. There's no universal solution, no one perfect product, and no perfect calculator. There are principles, and then there is the application of those principles to a person's life. It's vital you understand their life, what they're trying to accomplish, where they're at, and then help them get closer to where they want to be with as much certainty as possible.

Chapter 8: Becoming a Conscious Calculator

It is time to turn your brain on.

In this final chapter, you will learn to synthesize the calculators, tools, and insights from the book into your own financial understanding. I'll share practical tips to enhance your financial literacy, competency, and analytical capabilities. You'll learn to build your own integrated financial strategy using the Truth Concepts calculators and standards.

Whether you're a financial client or strategist, you'll walk away inspired with the knowledge and confidence you need to improve your own conscious calculations.

EMPOWERMENT THROUGH KNOWLEDGE

Sometimes we are unclear on what to do financially because we don't have the right knowledge to make the best decision. The good news is that there are mathematical calculations that will tell you the most efficient thing to do. However, financial decision-making is rarely as simple as following a calculation. Sometimes we need to make a different choice for our own personal satisfaction, quality of life, or for a big-picture reason, like risk. But if we don't know the *cost* of making a different decision than what the calculator tells us, it is impossible to make the best decision we can.

Cars are the best example of this concept. Most people look at their cars as an expense of $X per month. They say, "It's easy; we'll just keep paying it." But when you actually look at the long-term numbers in a calculator, you might see that it will cost you $2 million over thirty years! You may not really like cars all that much. You may prefer to use that money on something else. But you wouldn't know this if you didn't see the long-term numbers.

On the flip side, other people will pinch dollars and cents here and there to save money, but is it really worth it? If you do the math in the Truth Concepts calculator and find your time is more valuable than the money you're saving, you may change your decisions around saving those dollars. **The math is your measuring stick for how close you are matching your financial decisions to your own principles and values; without the math, you're just guessing.**

Some people, like my wife, Kim Butler, are primarily conceptual people who do not look at the numbers first. Now, because she knows the numbers quickly and easily, it helps her be conscious of the potential for misleading misinformation. Even if she is not able to calculate the numbers in the moment for herself or with a client, she is now *conscious* that there's a potential for misinformation as it relates to anything that has to do with money. She knows the concepts must be verified by the calculations.

If you're a strategist, using calculators like ours is part of your job. It's important that you use the calculators enough to be familiar with them and eventually know what the answers will be. When you have a good sense of what the numbers are, you become a more well-rounded and trustworthy strategist to your clients. To identify blind spots you may have as a financial strategist, check out this article: https://truthconcepts.com/7-blind-spots-of-financial-advisors.

On the client side, I believe in greater self-reliance. Our calculators can help with this. At the same time, we have so much information coming at us now, and it can be confusing. Some people are naturally wired to know and care about the numbers; others are not. If you're not wired that way, you must be able to trust that your strategist is doing what they need to do.

Does your strategist know what they're talking about? Can they prove it with calculations? If your strategist is doing their job correctly, they should be able to explain what it is that you're doing with your money conceptually and numerically. Unfortunately, as I've mentioned earlier, in the financial industry the more complicated they make a financial decision, the more sexy it seems. Honestly, it probably comes across as complicated because the strategist doesn't fully understand it. Some things *are* difficult to explain. Simplicity is key. Your strategist must be able to explain it to you like they would to a kindergartner. The better the strategist knows the financial information, the more simply they can explain it.

BUILDING TRUST

One of the most important conscious calculations on the client side is: Who am I going to trust? Who knows how to do the math and has my best interest in mind? One client we were working with early on was very analytical, having come out of the finance world. Our colleague John Baker told us, "You'll need to work hard at this." But in actuality, our initial conversation lasted just a few minutes. The client asked me a couple of questions, I showed her the math, and she said, "Okay, do whatever you need to do." **As soon as she saw the mathematical proof one time, she was confident in our financial suggestions.**

This experience brings up the importance of trust between strategists and clients. Strategists often don't need to back up every single decision over time with calculations as they build more trust. But using the calculators consistently in the beginning and showing the math helps strategists build that trust over time.

The other place the calculators come in handy is in showing the numbers for situations clients see in the media and other places, the "everybody knows this," but it's wrong data. Those are often the hardest to educate a client on because the beliefs are deeply ingrained. Clients, and sometimes strategists, must make a complete paradigm shift. When countering social norms, showing the math really helps, but it can also really hurt.

People need to be sincerely open to realizing that there are just as many things that are not true as there are that are true. Nobody wants to be wrong. Subconsciously, we put up barriers when somebody challenges something we believe to be true. That can create arguments. From the client side, we need to be open-minded. Do we want the best for our family, even if it means admitting we might be wrong? We must be willing to examine the numbers, be wrong, and change our minds.

However, the strategist can't be in the business to prove clients wrong. If they go in hard with the math on the calculators right off the bat, that may be a huge turnoff to clients. My friend Vince D'Addona says, "If you call the people your clients admire 'idiots' and knock the ideas they've bought into, you will create a bar fight, not a mutually beneficial relationship. Then you haven't helped your client or yourself."

Strategists must have empathy for the client. It's a hard thing to do. And lacking empathy or proving clients wrong is often not something strategists do consciously. **This is why we're bringing attention to the idea of conscious calculations: build trust with your clients, then show them the math that will help them reach their goals.**

It doesn't matter what the numbers show if, as a financial strategist, you can't build trust first. Every decision we make is emotional. If we don't understand the human psychology side of our financial decision-making, we're not going to be effective strategists. Contrary to what some may believe, it's not selfish to be focused on your clients' emotions in order to sell them the right solutions. It's actually the most unselfish thing you can do. If your client doesn't implement your ideas that are aligned with their best interests, their family (and generations after them) doesn't get helped. We owe it to our clients to understand them. It's not just about selling things to them, or throwing numbers or calculations at them. It's about making an impact in their life.

CALCULATORS CREATE CONFIDENCE

You do not want to overwhelm clients with calculators. The calculators actually need to be treated as a backup tool with clients. The calculators support the narrative, the conversation, with a client. You may use a calculator to demonstrate to clients, "This is what I'm talking about in the big picture; this is the math that says it's true." The calculators give you, as the strategist, confidence and a financial backbone for your conversation.

The calculators can also be used as an educational sales tool. There is a line I really like and recommend from the strategist side when a client says something directly, such as, "I love qualified plans!" Rather than being judgmental as the strategist, say, **"Cool, would you like to see how that works?"** They'll naturally say yes, and then you can say, "Okay, let's just run this through the calculator." Show them the numbers and then ask, "Is that what you hoped to see?" If not, then you can say, "Would you like to see something different?" This opens the door to a paradigm shift and the opportunity to show them alternatives that might better suit their needs.

Asking questions is a huge part of our process. It sets me apart from so many other calculator gurus in the industry. I've been in the field and spent five years working with clients, on top of thirty years behind the scenes, so I know what it's like to educate them on ideas that are not necessarily mathematical. Because personal finance deals with numbers, there has to be math involved to a certain degree. The numbers help you tell not only the whole truth but also a truth that a person can assimilate into their lives and see the practical application. Remember, though, even when people say they're analytical, they're still making emotional decisions.

My friend Vince also says it's critically important for a financial strategist to understand that they should never answer statements with their own statements. We do that as humans all the time. Someone says a statement such as, "I like this," or, "I don't like this." As a strategist, don't answer that with your own statement. Instead, ask the client a question. Strategists often want to answer every statement a client makes, but they would make many more sales and a bigger impact on their clients' lives if they asked more questions.

Listening is key in empathizing with your clients and understanding their situation and willingness to learn about new financial possibilities. Strategists often want to "fix" the client's situation when the client is not ready to face what needs to be fixed yet. A short video on YouTube, *It's Not About the Nail* by Jason Headley (https://www.youtube.com/watch?v=-4EDhdAHrOg), is well worth the watch for both clients and strategists and really demonstrates this part of human nature. It shows how strategists must have patience and practice active listening with their clients. **People often just want you to be with them and acknowledge that their opinions are valid.**

As a client, you have to rely on other people. There are some who are hardcore in the industry and say it's your responsibility as the client to know and manage your own finances. But I think as the client, your job is actually to make your strategist prove their financial decisions to you. If they can't, that shows there's a lack of knowledge. As my wife Kim says, "That's why I wrote all the books I wrote (eleven to date) with Todd's calculators. The proof is there in the books."

Kim was utterly amazed at the confidence she developed in her voice because of the calculator work she's done for so many years. It's transformative for strategists. It gives your voice so much strength. With the calculators, you know that you know what you know.

The son of Gary Smalley, a Christian speaker and proponent of family values, spoke in one of my classes. He's a longtime teacher, and he says, "What's really interesting is the difference between the grades that happen: who makes As, Bs, and Cs. The difference between the As and Bs is not a lack of knowledge. What happens with the Bs is they haven't studied enough to know they know what they know. They get into a test, and then they question themselves. They know the answer, yet they doubt themselves and put the wrong answer down. That's the difference between knowing something and knowing you know it. It's confidence."

DEVELOPING ANALYTICAL SKILLS

One of the biggest pieces of advice I give clients for developing their financial analytical skills is keep working at it. Be persistent! Your personal finances thrive when you see them as your second career or business. My wife, Kim, says, "Money isn't everything, but money affects everything that matters." Personal finance is not a set-it-and-forget-it space. Too many people think, "Oh, someone will take care of it: the government, my strategist, my parents . . . " Take charge of your finances today and commit to working on your own analytical skills. Our calculators can help you expand your financial knowledge significantly.

In the end, it's not about the money, it's about *what the money does*. That's the distinguishing difference. The King James Version of the Bible, I Timothy 6:10, says, "For the love of money is the root of all evil . . . " Ultimately, analyzing your personal finances is not about loving money; money is just a thing. What do you want to *accomplish* with your money? A three with a bunch of zeros behind it doesn't mean anything. What you do with that amount of money for yourself and your community is what matters.

One of the first steps to improving your analytical skills is to ask yourself: **What is it that I want to accomplish?** Forget the money. Focus on what you want to accomplish. I think people often struggle with savings because they don't have anything on the horizon they want to accomplish. If they're just taught to pile up money but they don't have a purpose, it won't be meaningful.

You need to have a reason to save or invest. That's where you have to start. What do you want your life to look like five years from now? Ten years from now? Fifty years from now? People get afraid and discouraged, thinking, "It takes too much money to do what I want to do." Push that discouraging thought off the table and just entertain the idea. **What would you need to create to make your vision happen?**

Money just amplifies who you are. If you're a gracious, patient person, money will make you more of that. If you're a belligerent, impatient blowhard, money will make you more of that. So a second question you might ask yourself as you're developing your analytical skills is: **Who do I want to become?**

When we think bigger about what we want to accomplish and who we must become to do that, it's amazing to see how we can make the impossible possible. I believe some of our creation is driven by our communication with a higher being. But I also think some of it is that we start to see opportunities we wouldn't otherwise. Our vision changes and broadens. Those opportunities may not have meant anything before because they didn't apply to what we're doing. But now? Possibility and opportunity matter.

If you don't develop the first piece of financial analysis, finding meaning and purpose, you can't do the second piece of actually analyzing the numbers. Not long term. And not well. You will burn out. It's also great to know yourself using a tool, such as the Kolbe profile or the Clifton StrengthsFinder questions. When you know your strengths and natural skills, you might find that while you can do the calculations, you won't. Again, that is where a strategist or financial strategist can be so helpful. Your timing or strategy for financial analysis might look different depending on your Kolbe profile, your strengths, and your own curiosity and interest level, which often vary at different times in your life.

For my wife, Kim, a purpose higher than just being analytical helps her be analytical. Also, a strong sense of responsibility and self-reliance helps her be analytical. She says, "As a human being on this earth, it helps me be a good steward of money. My goal has never been to be analytical, but I need to know how to analyze. From a strategist standpoint, I show up at training once or twice a year, so it's constantly fed into me even though it's not my natural strength. Layer upon layer of education will help you get over that hump enough to be a professional in my profession. When Todd and I first met, Todd was the computer guy in the back of the room, and Norman Baker was at the front, and I attended those sessions every year for ten years. I needed to immerse myself in that learning. Get on a plane, get to a hotel, focus on it for three full days."

As you continue developing your financial analysis skills, choose the learning methods that work best for you. Use this book as a reference, attend live training sessions, and explore the Truth Concepts blog (https://truthconcepts.com/blog) and YouTube channel (https://www.youtube.com/channel/UCROid71u3qYVgN7KBySZBvg) for additional insights.

CREATING A PERSONAL FINANCIAL STRATEGY (FOR CLIENTS)

I prefer the term "financial strategy" over "financial plan" because the idea behind a "plan" is both limiting and likely to fall short. It's somewhat in the range of goals. Goals are limited by nature and can be a bad thing to have because of that. The problem with a goal is that when we accomplish it, we stop. However, a strategy is open-ended, opportunistic, and we're doing all we can. There is no endpoint, just a pivot to a new strategy or an additional branch of a current strategy. A financial strategy helps you look at a horizon you're driving toward, while at the same time actually doing what can be done in the next one to three years. A plan or goal can create a roadblock that you hit when it's accomplished. It limits your capability and drive instead of expanding your possibilities.

When designing your personal financial strategy, focusing on what you can do today and in the next one to three years is critical. While you want to also have an idea of what you are working toward, too often in personal finance, we try to start with the end in mind and that is very difficult to do.

Your job as a prospect or client is to figure out how you learn best. Do you like to read, listen, watch, or get your hands involved? Then find a way to learn some basic areas around personal finance. As shared earlier, money may not be everything to you, yet it affects everything that is important to you, so you'll want to treat it seriously. So many personal and family challenges would either not happen at all or be easily solved if more people had a basic level of financial competency. Additionally, try to be aware of your own biases and decide to be as open-minded as possible as you go through the learnings.

Financial analysis is often done in a vacuum, with conditions we know will be different down the road. Did anybody see 9/11 or COVID coming? We have many possibilities that could occur, yet most people's strategy or plan is predicated on everything being the best it can be all the way out. That's not a thorough strategy that takes all situations into account. Having a strategy that works in all situations may not end up with as much money in the future, yet you can be confident your life will work no matter what obstacles pop up along the way.

First off, we have some intangible things that must be thought about: risk and emergencies. As everybody knows, cash is not going to be a great investment, and it's not designed to be. From the standpoint of rate of return, cash is at the low end of the scale. But cash enables everything else to make it through the hard times. Cash can help you from losing real estate, or it can put you in a position to be capable of buying real estate or a business that you might not otherwise have been able to. Cash can help you sustain a job loss or a medical event. Yes, it's important to try to get as good of a return as you can, but it's equally important to understand cash from the perspective of opportunities and emergencies. We need to consider these factors during our calculations so we have the most likely potential for success.

There are certain things we may choose to override the obvious math on because of the bigger picture we see. A good example is qualified plans, your 401(k), 403(b), IRA, etc. Could there be tax advantages if everything worked just right? Yes. But the fact that the money is locked up and you can't use it along the way is a serious limiter. You'll want to ask yourself the question: Would you rather take less in the end to have access to the money in the present? You don't know what opportunities you might be missing. And you have to consider all the things you can't do because your money is tied up in a government-sponsored program. Plus, much of it can't be analyzed mathematically because there are too many elements to it.

For example, qualified (or retirement) money can't buy investment real estate, life insurance, solve emergencies, or take advantage of a business opportunity. That's not included in such a linear calculation. Most assets are such that the best you can hope to get out of them is whatever the linear calculation shows, without a hiccup.

There are other assets that require a bigger-picture view, and while you can analyze one or two aspects of them individually, it is difficult to analyze all of the aspects of each and almost impossible to analyze them in light of each other. Investment real estate and whole life insurance are good examples of assets that must be looked at from a big-picture standpoint, not just a linear calculation. This is an example of looking at more than just the straight numbers.

Strategy involves looking at both your tangible numbers and your intangible vision. If we're running around the base of a mountain with no strategy for the climb, we won't get anywhere. Once we establish our strategy, we have to break it down into achievable steps, or some may say, goals. Treat the end of your goals like the horizon (your strategy) rather than the peak of the mountain (a more limiting endpoint). Each step is essential for a successful mountain-climbing trip, both up and down the mountain. Your finances are no different. **And I find the "down the mountain" part is often overlooked. A trip is not successful if you don't make it down.**

It's not the big pile of money at the peak you're after. That would be simple accumulation. It's all about what you do on the way down (the second half of your life). Why are you saving money? Why are you doing without current trips with your family to save for a later, unknown goal? Why are you eliminating quality time with the people you love to pile up money? Is it just because you want $X in the future? Because you want money in retirement or for the distribution years? I have never liked the word "retirement" because it means "to take out of service." I want to be in service my whole life, and I've found most other people do too.

To revisit the reason you might be going without now: Is it strictly for the distribution phase (going down the mountain), yet you don't even know what that looks like? Strategists will calculate the average person needs $X by the time they retire, but they don't typically look at all the details and the journey down the mountain. We don't know completely what it will look like, but we've got to have some vision, some way of giving what we want to do a fair shot. If our strategy doesn't work in perfect conditions, it definitely won't work in less-than-perfect conditions. There are many factors to consider.

One factor to always keep in mind is what I mentioned earlier: we make decisions from an emotional place. For example, when paying a mortgage, that decision is largely driven by emotion, most commonly, fear, which is almost always the wrong emotion to make decisions from. Our fight or flight reaction got us here, to where we are in the universe. But it's not ideal for financial strategies.

With home mortgages, we often focus on the problem, and our analysis of just the numbers limits our ability to see the big picture. If I can borrow money at 3% but make 6%, I would, but with home mortgages, it's the opposite when people are trying to pay down their mortgage. When looking at the pure numbers, it doesn't make sense to prepay or pay down a mortgage. If we can put aside the emotion and let logic rule here, it will help clients make a good decision about their mortgage payments. It can be tough for strategists to be patient with their clients on the mortgage topic.

Fear can cause people to make extreme financial decisions (like pouring extra money into a house to get it paid off faster). But then, if an event you're afraid of happens, you won't have the cash flow to make the house payment, and you won't have the cash either, so you may ironically lose the house. You may have all the equity in the world, but if you can't show that you have income to cover the payment, a bank will not let you take money out of the house, which makes it a dead asset. Let's understand this is a possibility and do what we can to mitigate risk and have cash available for emergency situations, *not* have it locked up in the walls of our home.

The main thing we want to make sure of when developing our financial strategy is that we're not putting money into a risky environment. We want it in a safe, liquid space (regardless of what the stock or real estate market does) where it can earn a reasonable rate of return. For a lot of people, whole life insurance cash value would be a good place to put extra money, but a high-yield savings account also works. Anything that has guarantees and liquidity.

If people pay attention to the math, that can influence their emotions but ultimately all financial decisions are still emotional decisions. This is why we need strategists. A good friend of mine, Michael Isom, says, "I understand your objective; what if we could do that with a different method?" I would encourage strategists to use language like this to speak with their clients. The marketplace preys upon clients with emotional ads; they know how to influence our emotional decisions. Ads don't talk to you about logical reasons to buy things. They play to the emotional side. It's effective for the companies selling the products, but it's not necessarily effective for the consumers or clients.

I'll end this section on financial strategy with a story. Let me set the stage. Plenty of people in 2008 and 2009 lost their houses. Foreclosures were happening because it was to the bank's advantage. Banks do not want real estate on the books; that is not their area of expertise. When you've got a ton of equity and the bank can turn around and sell that house at a fire sale, they are going to be much quicker to move to foreclosure. If something has a lot of equity in it, banks are okay with it because it's easier for them to sell.

There were two families: Family A prepaid, added extra principal, and built up equity in their home; Family B did not. The adults in both families lost their jobs in the real estate crash of 2008, and here's what happened. Family A believed: If we pay more money into our equity (against our mortgage), our equity is earning a rate of return. Family A put 20% down on a mortgage, paying over fifteen years. But Family B bought a house on the same block, and they got a special deal with nothing down and an interest-only payment. Family B was not growing equity at all. Twenty years from now, whose house would be worth more? They're the same! When the crash happened, which family do you think had enough cash to continue making their mortgage payments? Which one got a foreclosure notice?

House value grows whether it has debt on it or not. People sometimes think interest is a huge, horrible thing, and they need to get rid of it as soon as possible. They believe it's a fact that if you pay more interest, you pay more cost. But with the element of time, more interest over time is not necessarily more cost.

People lost houses in the Great Depression even though they were making payments on those houses. The banks can't take houses like that anymore, but a lot of that fear still permeates society. People like the ones in Family A believe, "I'm rid of the bank when the house is paid off. I better pay as much as I can." But people like those in Family B, who prioritized cash flow over paying off their mortgage, fared much better in such a risky housing market.

ENCOURAGEMENT FOR FINANCIAL STRATEGISTS

Educating clients with empathy, bringing clarity to financial decision-making, and doing it all by forming a connection that will last through financial ups and downs is the basis for being a trusted financial strategist. When it comes to working with calculations, the more you know the numbers, the less you need to show them. Your confidence speaks for you. This can be scary because then strategists might think, "If I'm not going to show it, I'm not going to invest any time in it." But the opposite is actually true: the more you know it, the more you are prepared to prove it, and the less you need the calculators.

Even though I know the numbers backward and forward, I'm still going to show the calculators because I'm an 8 Implementer on the Kolbe Index; it's my MO to show. I'm going to show the numbers in a way that supports the narrative though. The calculators can't stand alone; they have to be supporting instruments for the larger conversation. I know my calculators use fifteen decimal places, yet that doesn't mean you care. Your strategist must find out what *you* care about.

A friend of mine keeps coming back to my seminars, and the last several times when I asked him why he keeps coming back, he said, "The more I come, the less I need the calculators." My wife, Kim, says the same thing. She's not numerically or technologically minded, but because she attends my seminars over and over, she has greater confidence when she speaks with clients about the numbers.

Do you need to learn calculators? Yes! So you don't need them in the end! It's a contradictory statement, but it's true. Unfortunately in the financial industry, people are doing the opposite: not learning the math, getting by without knowing how it works, and then their clients ultimately suffer. But when clients do figure that out, they leave and find a strategist who knows the numbers that they can trust.

My advice to a new strategist? Whether it's the Truth Concepts calculators or other truthful financial calculators, get an education in that area. I guarantee you didn't learn it in school. You're not getting it from financial institutions either (they used to have thorough education, but it's quickly going away and almost non-existent now).

One of the young guys in the industry (whose dad is also in the business) took a higher-level financial class in college. Because he knew the software, he got into a big argument about the fifteen-and thirty-year mortgages because the professor didn't know anything about opportunity cost. Opportunity cost and time value of money are so foreign to people who only use basic calculators. Too many financial strategists use those basic calculators alone and make mistakes because of it. A financial calculator (available online or for free at https://truthconcepts.com/five-financial-calculators) is a helpful tool, yet it takes a bit of learning to use it properly.

A lot of people look at opportunity cost as a phantom element . . . thinking, "It's not real money because I didn't really have it." Or how can I have interest on money I lost, that didn't even exist? But another way to look at it is that the opportunity cost is just *negative opportunity*. You can't have one without the other, an opportunity without the opportunity cost. It's like a negative number.

All of our calculators deal with opportunity cost. It's really just a future value calculator. In its simplest form, it's just the future loss: taxes, term insurance premiums, anything that will have no value in the future. You spent $1 to pay the tax or buy the insurance, and then you lost the opportunity for that $1 to earn interest in the future. These are dollars that, if we didn't have that risk or have to pay that tax, could go somewhere else. We obviously can't get around having home insurance, car insurance, and paying taxes. We'd have to have the value of our house sitting doing nothing as an asset just in case, but instead we can pay an insurance company to rent that whole amount to avoid risk. And we pay taxes so we have roads to drive on and policemen to help keep us safe.

This year's premium, or this year's tax bill, compounded out at whatever earning rate we can make, is the opportunity cost for that dollar. That is the loss for making that payment. With a future value calculator, you can calculate opportunity cost like this very quickly.

Opportunity cost requires a mindset shift for many strategists. Financial strategizing is so much more comprehensive than a lot of the industry makes it out to be. That's where the fallacy is. To follow the typical financial solutions and actually have them work out for you, you have to earn unreasonable rates of return that can't happen in the long term. Or you must save unreasonable amounts of money that you do without in the present and are miserable because of it. When you start to understand the full cost of all of those decisions and what happens when you have an exponential curve with time, you start to see that incremental small shifts today make big shifts in the future. **A healthy financial strategy requires talking about a long-term timeframe, yet making decisions and taking actions today.**

At the Currence conference where I presented recently, we showed a major curve from the money you put in (small amounts) that actually makes a huge difference in the long run (even though in the short run it might not look like much). Dave Mozeika, CEO of Currence, uses the term "layering." I use "ripples." Either way, it means that when you make one change, it frees up another change and starts a circular pattern that expands. Currence is a structure that creates accountability for clients and Income Under Management™ for Strategists.

Shifting someone from a fifteen-year mortgage to a thirty-year mortgage is one example where Currence can be extremely valuable because the difference in those two payments must be saved. This fifteen-year versus thirty-year mortgage discussion is a good example of a learning point the Truth-Concept calculators show. If interest rates and opportunity are the same, the two mortgages cost the same. But with a thirty year mortgage, we have more free cashflow upfront.

The key is having a structure like Currence to take advantage of it. If we understand the exponential curve (the hockey stick-like route that saved money makes, starting very slowly and gaining greater and greater ground over time), then we know how beneficial it is to get cash saved in the early years instead of spending it. Currence shows the momentum and enables us to then create another income engine. The cash flow just starts feeding off itself if we understand how all those pieces work together. Now those incremental changes can have a massive impact over time.

Many financial strategists, or strategists I train, have experience getting trained from financial institutions. These strategists still work with the same products the financial institution sells, yet it's the strategies that vary. Products are things you buy; strategies are things you do. My calculators help us look at the strategies. Examine A and B (two different strategies) and ask: What's better for the client?

So much of financial strategist training comes from financial institutions, and guess who that is designed to benefit? My calculators help us remove the numbers from any bias and look at all the options. The financial strategist has to really seek truth, be open-minded, and seek learning, because most of what they learn from the financial institutions will serve the financial institution best. It's not about sales hype; it's about full financial efficiency that's both measurable and provable.

That's the beauty of having the right strategy in place; you don't have to sell it. When we start with the math and say, "This is with this strategy, and this is without it," it's pretty straightforward. It could resonate in a different way depending on the client's situation, but we have to start from an objective truth basis where the math tells us the results. The time element is what makes personal finance so difficult for people; it's a pretty different setup of calculations once we enter time. Everything changes, and we can't use basic addition, subtraction, multiplication, and division. Not only do most people not like regular math; they *really* don't like financial math.

Money by itself is not mathematical. You can't put emotion in math; it's unbiased. Yet people are biased, as are the decisions they make with their money. Whether we like it or not, we all carry our biases and filter what's been said through our biases.

Your job as strategists is to get to a place of objectivity and understand that there are other factors surrounding the decisions clients make that are just as important as the numbers. What if you have a client who's always had a dream of having a cabin in the woods? Maybe it doesn't make financial sense, but it binds their family together and the benefit to them outweighs the financial math. When you're helping them make the decision, though, it's important to look at the math so you know if it's worth it to follow one path or strategy over another.

Using another example, I love a new car, but I don't love a new car enough to have $2 million less in retirement/distribution assets. The joy I get from having a new car is not worth what I give up in the future. If I didn't know what that cost was in the future, I would do what many other people do and just trade in cars every two to three years for new ones. But my decision about new cars doesn't mean it's wrong for somebody else. We need to have all the facts to help make that decision.

Using another analogy, most people using grade school math and a regular calculator say two plus two equals four. However, applying financial math principles and the element of time, if you put two oranges together with two more oranges on a table, is that four oranges thirty years from now? No, because they could roll off the table, or their seeds could plant trees and produce much more for years to come. Or they rot, and they're gone. Money has all these other variables to consider—taxes, fees, opportunity costs, and time—like the oranges. We have to know the variables and figure out how we can make the best financial decisions that align with our clients' strategy and their hearts.

Lastly, the biggest thing I tell strategists to remember when working with clients is that nobody likes to be wrong. If you approach a client to discuss their financial decisions or strategy, it doesn't matter how much proof you have. They will likely move into fight or flight, and with a pushy attitude, you force the client into defending their position.

The way you communicate determines whether it's going to be a fight that everybody loses or not. The truth is the truth, but trying to beat somebody up with a calculator or numbers will never bring you success. Remember to ask questions like: Would you like to see what your strategy looks like? Is that what you hoped for? Would you be open to some alternative suggestions?

It's not about proving to a client that they're wrong. Most strategists fall into one of two categories:

1. Using the software as too big a piece of their narrative, trying to prove clients wrong, or
2. Not using it enough and communicating information that's not true to the client.

I encourage you to have empathy for the client and do what it takes to get them to a place of understanding what you're showing them in a truthful way. And to know your numbers, even if you choose not to show them every time.

Epilogue: Nothing Is Truer Than Truth

The name of my software, Truth Concepts™,
is actually quite binding.

There is a Latin motto, "Vero Nihil Verius." It means "Nothing is truer than truth." This is the principle Truth Concepts and this book are based on. Yet, in closing, I would like to examine how we define "truth" and implement true conscious calculations in personal finance while also integrating the human element of emotion.

Math is black and white. There is no gray in math. It is either true or not true. However, humans are emotional beings. That's one area where the gray in financial math comes from. The other one is when people use the right numbers but the wrong formula. (See example below.) We have to take the black and white (and get rid of the gray), while we also coordinate with our hopes and dreams as individuals. We want to use math to the best of our ability, while also still having the enjoyment of life. What are we here for, if not to live and serve?

When we can use the calculators to understand the whole truth and full cost of some of the things we do in life, we can prioritize those things that are really meaningful to us and reduce or eliminate the things that aren't. Then we can have more money for the things we enjoy and that bring us fulfillment. We have to take care of the present *and* the future. How do we cover things that are really important? And how do we eliminate the unconscious costly things (including hidden fees, taxes, and opportunity costs) that have an impact in the end and cause us to make irrational decisions in the moment?

BEYOND FIGHT OR FLIGHT

In our long history as humans, we have been creatures of fight or flight. In caveman days, that was beneficial and necessary for our survival. In today's world, when we make decisions out of fear, especially in regards to money, we're almost always wrong.

When we can release stress over money and free our minds to actually think clearly, what might we come up with to make our financial world even bigger? When we're stressed over money, it's like we're locked in a box, and our habitual, often unconscious, decisions keep us there. While money isn't everything in life, the lack of it is seriously destructive to our wellbeing and our capacity for serving others and living every part of life.

Truth Concepts, our name, came about as one of those fight or flight decisions. In a single meeting, I said, "I like that!" But the thing is, it's a binding name; whatever we talk about better be truthful since it's part of the name! That really drives the analysis I do in the background of every calculator: checking the facts, reversing equations, and making sure everything comes back the same with numerous iterations.

I'm willing to be wrong in order to be right, but I don't want to be wrong if I can help it. I will go so far as having ten decimal points (or more!) on almost all of the calculators. One of my favorite quotes to say is: "There is no 'about' in construction." The same is true in financial math. **There is no "about" in financial math.** Many people want to round and not include all the decimal places, but if you don't have them all, the numbers won't work out cleanly and accurately. We are after the truest truth.

FORMULAS THAT LEAD TO THE TRUTH

To confirm our calculators' numbers are right, I use an HP12C to backcheck everything. The answers are not approximately right; they're *right.* A strategist came to me once and said, "I've got all these Excel spreadsheets I've been using for years, but using your calculators would help me know that all my ripples are right." Think back to the previous chapter and the ripple effect of every calculation and decision. If you don't have your numbers right and you're off by a degree, it can make a profound difference in the long run on calculations for your financial future. If you're going to go to the moon and you're off by a degree, you've missed it by a galaxy.

The formula you use must be right, it must lead you to the truth. I'll share a story to demonstrate the value of using the correct formula in financial math. You may have heard it before. It's about three hungry guys and a pizza.

Three friends were all playing cards and were all hungry, so they decided to buy a pizza. They each threw $10 into one pot for a $30 pizza. Upon delivery, the pizza guy says, "I'll give you a $5 off coupon," and proceeds to give a dollar back to each of the three friends and keeps a tip of $2.00. But if you do the actual math, 3 x 9 = 27 + 2 (for tip) = $29. Where did that last $1 go?

The answer is that they paid $25 for the pizza + $2 to the delivery guy = $27 total. Then they each got $1 back. $30 should not even be part of the equation. They each contributed only $9 (since they each got $1 back from the $10 they originally put in.) $9 x 3 = $27 - $25 for the pizza, - $2 for the tip =$0. But $30 - $27 - $2 does equal $1. It is the correct math, yet the wrong formula because it has nothing to do with the issue at hand, which is the pizza cost $25 and they left a $2 tip.

We see this in the financial world all the time. It often happens when people are asking questions about their mortgage and somebody shows them accurate math with an inaccurate formula. It can be extremely misleading. If you're a strategist, as the messenger, you're painted as the bad guy when the numbers don't line up because you used a formula that doesn't work for that scenario. And it's even worse if the clients discover the correct formula to lead them to true numbers *after* the decision has been made and the transaction has already happened.

TRUSTING FINANCIAL MATH AND MENTORS

Before meeting Norman Baker, I was well on my way to getting a biology and chemistry degree. Can you imagine? No thanks for me. Yet studying those hard sciences did teach me to think very critically about any type of equation. The biggest impact is **knowing that in any scientific equation you are testing, you can only change one variable at a time**. Thanks to having Norman as my mentor, I trust the financial math I do and think through every calculator I create with keen eyes. Norman was a truly great financial strategist, our partner in "telling the whole truth about money," the co-founder of Truth Concepts, and our friend.

As I mentioned earlier in the book, I began working with Norman when I was only in my twenties. He needed someone to help with computers and other technical aspects of the business. In time, I learned to develop calculators and software. Norman and I embarked on a project to develop calculators that could prove the validity of various financial strategies. Norman had heard a few strategists making statements that went against "common financial wisdom," and he thought the calculators would show that they were mistaken.

Ironically, some of the concepts that Norman and I set out to disprove ended up being correct!

Concepts we actually proved right instead of wrong included:

- A fifteen-year mortgage, a thirty-year mortgage, and paying cash all have the same total cost when you consider the opportunity costs.
- You can't avoid interest *costs* by paying cash–only an interest payment.
- 0% car financing does *not* mean you'll pay the same as cash.
- *Average* rates of return aren't the same as *actual* rates of return.
- "Buy term insurance and invest the difference" doesn't work unless you die early.
- Mutual fund fees total up to much more than the advertised 1% a year.
- Whole life insurance doesn't have a poor rate of return, and it isn't more "expensive" than term life insurance in the long run.
- If banks borrow at 3% and loan at 6%, they're not making a 3% profit, but a 100% profit!

- Retirement plans only defer tax, and much of any match or government benefit often gets eaten up in fees.
- A family buying new cars every few years will spend over $2 million during their lifetime, opportunity costs being considered.
- Paying the tax (and calculating the opportunity costs) on taxable accounts during a lifetime can completely destroy all the earnings on liquid cash.

When the calculators showed "the whole truth" about these concepts and others, Norman changed his whole business to reflect the new truths he was learning. His open-mindedness and ability to change his philosophy based on what he knew was best for his clients are something we still strive for each day.

Years later Norman helped us prepare to launch Truth Concepts, and unfortunately, he was not around to see it fully realized. Yet in spite of his physical absence today, his leadership, character, and vision live on.

Another mentor I have learned from over the years is Dr. Wade Pfau. I've had conversations with him at meetings, and at Truth Concepts we definitely back up what he says, and his data backs up what we say. He's all about exposing the whole truth around the "sequencing of returns risk" and what happens to your income, especially during the distribution phase. Instead of being in a position to consistently create income, he points out what actually happens when, during the down years, you're withdrawing money and how much of a disastrous impact those down years have.

If you have a stock or mutual fund that is down and you are still having to take income from that account, it can devastate your portfolio. People get to retirement and hope that averages will work, and when they don't, they struggle. Dr. Wade Pfau addresses this, has inspired me to create the proof in Truth Concepts (known as the Cash Flow Bridge), and has validated much of the work we do with financial strategists. We are grateful for his wisdom and to have him as a colleague in the personal finance industry.

If you would like the *Cash Flow Bridge Report*, the long version is at https://bit.ly/4u2QtJE or the QR code below.

And a shorter version is known as *Paydown Permission* available at https://bit.ly/3RJEq6n or the QR code below.

STRATEGY WITH SIMPLICITY, INTEGRITY, AND PREPARATION

"Everything should be made as simple as possible, but not simpler."
ALBERT EINSTEIN

One of the primary jobs of the strategist when it comes to looking at a long-term strategy is understanding the math and the details behind it. But simplifying those details for the client so they understand them is another thing altogether. That doesn't mean brushing over and rounding numbers so your formulas are not accurate anymore. It *does* mean understanding the accuracy, and being able to communicate it so it's digestible to the average person.

In the personal financial world, the more complicated a solution is, the more revered it often becomes. I believe if it's too complicated to understand, it's questionable as to whether it really works. Simplicity is key to good financial advice and leads to a relationship between strategist and client that is transparent and has integrity.

The Boy Scouts' motto is "Be prepared." For me, that always meant having backups for backups. For example, when we went on camping trips, we always took small amounts of things because we carried everything we might need. Later, I would go camping with a cousin or uncle who had forgotten certain things, and I would say, "That's okay, I've got it." We learned that core lesson of being prepared from enduring tough circumstances when we were *unprepared* and didn't have a good time (like wishing we had packed an extra pair of dry socks!).

Each calculator I have developed is a form of preparation for the person who uses it. When we're talking with clients and trying to get them over a hump of understanding, and they bring something out of left field that we need to address, that's where the calculators can help. We're not trying to fool somebody into believing what we're talking about. We're trying to explain it in a mathematical way that is based on more than our opinion.

We say, "Let's actually look at the numbers." The numbers have to be right. If they are right, then they don't matter, and they are not the focus. In the same way, when you're camping, if you have a backup set of dry, waterproof matches somewhere when rain gets your first set wet, you can actually have a fire and not focus on the matches you don't have, or that you're cold, wet, and fireless. When you have the matches, just like the right numbers, you don't think about them. But when you don't have them, you would trade everything you have for a dry match.

A Lesson from Boy Scouts

The first time I learned the lesson of being prepared in Boy Scouts, I was twelve years old, and we took a weekend scout trip to Grandbury, Texas. It was a warm, sunny day, and we played games in groups, jumping back and forth over a ravine the whole day. That night, we built a big fire and all performed skits. Then we tucked into our sleeping bags and went to sleep.

In the middle of the night, a storm came rolling in that dropped the temperature to forty degrees.

The rain and wind blew so hard that they folded and bent the poles of our tents (these were poles that had withstood over thirty years of use). We packed up our things as quickly as we could and crossed the ravine, now a raging river. We had to hold hands to make sure we didn't get washed down the river. Steeling ourselves against the storm, we trekked to an old wooden-floored, one-room schoolhouse. As we tried to light a fire for light and warmth, wet match after wet match fizzled out. With the very last match, we finally got a fire started inside the old schoolhouse fireplace.

That experience taught me to always carry waterproof matches. Sometimes, it's just inconvenient not to have matches; other times it can be life threatening. I have learned to heed a warning from the small lessons so that when I have big lessons, I am prepared.

In the same way I always carry waterproof matches, I designed the calculators so they can all be backed up or proven by another calculator. We get the same answers from different calculators. Sometimes a calculator is solving one problem (A + B = C), while another calculator may be calculating C - B = A. They both come out with the same answers, just in a different order.

The Value of Backups

When I was in school, I would always get in trouble in math class for rushing through answers. After getting in trouble from teachers enough times, I finally learned to slow down and calculate the equation in a different way. By rearranging the equations and answers, and making sure the numbers worked all the way around, I finally learned not to make silly mistakes by rushing through to the answer. That's what I do with the calculators as well. I back-check with other calculators and make sure everything comes out correctly, down to the penny plus 10 decimal places.

One calculator might show big, deep calculations. I have another calculator that can prove the same results in a simple way. It's instructive to anyone looking at the calculators to know that whatever it is you're proving can be proven and backed up, and you can have confidence that it is accurate.

From a backup standpoint in personal finance, most people turn to debt. Having access to borrow is a huge opportunity, but we want to go to the cheapest backup source first. If our goal is efficiency, the rate we're being charged is a critical piece to determine which direction we go. Another critical piece is the ease of getting that debt. There may be times we pay a higher rate of interest because the loan is easier to get. **The other back up is liquid cash, available to solve emergencies and take advantage of opportunities.** People don't realize the value of cash.

On our property, we have a farm truck and a regular truck. Both trucks have a full set of tools in them because I want to be prepared. I guess you could say I was a go-go-gadget man before go-go-gadget was a thing! Having backups for the backups is the main way I stay prepared for anything. During a recent power outage, we needed one of our backups. We have solar power and a generator, plus the generator has batteries, *and* we have a backup generator. In this last storm, we were so thankful we had the backup because I had fuel issues with the main generator, and we survived for six days using the backup generator! As my wife, Kim, says, "If Armageddon comes, the neighbors know it's the Langford house that they'll go to."

Solar typically covers the power backups we need at our house, which is effectively free since we have all the equipment in place. We have batteries we can pull off of as well. The next cheapest place is the grid. Then we have generators as a backup, and I'm willing to lean on them for a short period of time, but they are the most expensive option.

People may have cash doing double duty (like solar), but then also have a backup of an equity line of credit on their house (like the grid), and maybe, lastly, on credit cards (like generators). If you get to a place where you need it, the bank is likely *not* going to lend you money then. Prepare and have those backups available *before* you need them.

We have solar because when the grids go down, we're stuck. While solar might not be available on a stormy day or when iced over, **cash is always available**. When we look at cash as strictly a rate of return, there's no reason we should have it. But everything else we have is in danger if we don't have cash because *things will not go as planned*. The cost of that is selling something at a fire sale because we didn't have cash to get us over the hump.

When you think of cash, you have to *think of the certainty that comes along with that cash*. You can immediately take care of a problem or take advantage of an opportunity instead of having to sacrifice an asset, and that might have a huge impact long term. Everyone wants to boil things down to a rate of return, but cash doesn't play into that. In 2008-2009, the people who had enough cash to weather the real estate storm fared well. Cash in these extreme circumstances is like the waterproof matches.

Preparation Gives Peace of Mind

As the saying goes, "When man plans, God laughs." Planning mathematically can be tempting, but there are too many variables in personal finance. Preparation, on the other hand, enables us to look at everything clearly ahead of time, and be thorough and holistic in our approach—without planning. To be prepared for a "black swan" event, you need to have cash. Cash gives you the preparation needed for almost any situation. It's necessary to be prepared to shift, knowing things are not likely to go according to plan.

After I needed the waterproof matches while camping the first time, I brought them every trip. But I never used them again. However, having them there in my pack, being prepared, gave me peace of mind and allowed me to make decisions from a calm place.

When financial crises occur, backups are critical for the client to have in place. For the financial strategist, being prepared means having the calculators and tools available to quickly address the clients' concerns. To truly meet the clients' needs, strategists need to be prepared to field any questions that may come their way. When a financial strategist doesn't know an answer and isn't sure how to get it quickly, they can say, "Great question! Let me get my team together, we'll discuss it, and get back to you."

Being prepared as a strategist means doing the work so you have the knowledge and tools to wing it in a client meeting (you've got your waterproof matches!). **The only way to *not* focus on the numbers and instead be focused on the client is to *know* the numbers so well that you don't have to show them every time (they simply become automatic).** If needed, you can use the calculators to prove things numerically, mathematically. They will help you be prepared for any questions that may come up.

I hope you have discovered some of "truth's simplicity" in this book, and that you have learned more about how to do your own conscious calculations with integrity when it comes to personal finance. Whether you are a client or a strategist, there is much to be gained when we are prepared, know the numbers, connect with empathy, and find financial solutions that expand our dreams of what's possible—for ourselves and for generations to come.

Appendix

TODD'S LLAMA SHED

Todd's Llama Shed he built with his children that will still be standing decades into the future.

A BEHIND-THE-SCENES INTERVIEW WITH TODD

Q: What were the best lessons you learned as a teenager?

A: One of the best lessons I've learned that's helped me think through things logically was while I was programming in college: A computer is never wrong. I could enter whatever I wanted, have a temper tantrum, or go off the deep end, but I would always see that the computer was right. Anytime things went wrong, it was human error. It's logical. Instead of getting mad that the computer didn't do what it was supposed to, it's best to just check where the human error is.

I have an 8 Implementor in Kolbe which means I like to use my hands. I grew up working on cars. People ask me, "How did you figure that out as a kid?" I had to! I was either walking or working on cars to be able to have transportation. Computers for me were like working on cars without getting my hands dirty.

Going back further, two important lessons I learned from my dad were to put things away and to have a good work ethic. He would inspect my work on a car and make sure I had done the right thing and gotten all the pieces done correctly. I'd say, "But I got paid, it's done."

Then he'd say, "It doesn't matter. What matters is that you did it right." That was the best lesson for having a good work ethic.

We use software to find out the absolutes and do things right. While yes, I'm teaching a software class, and yes, I sell software that is mathematical, I know that is not the end-all, be-all. So I ask advisors, "What is your purpose? Why do you exist?" If a computer can do your job, you have no place. If you're not creating value, your life in this industry is short-lived. You need to be someone who can apply math to the real world outside of the "laboratory" we get with the computer and calculators.

Q: What were your biggest turning points growing up?

A: When I went to school, I was horsing around and didn't go to class nearly as often as I should have. When I was finally ready, I did. School's easy when you just apply yourself. It was amazing to see the difference when I applied myself at twenty-one or twenty-two. It was a combination of age and awareness. I just knew it was time to get serious.

I realized from that experience that education is a decision. You may not be ready, but you have to decide whether you're going to do it or not. The in-between limbo doesn't help anyone. So many things in life are that way. Just decide to do it. Then you'll find out if it's for you or not.

Q: What values and beliefs were you raised with that helped you the most?

A: I was raised to do the right thing, even when nobody else is. It's really about you, not what other people are doing. Follow the golden rule. How would you like it if someone did this to you?

Thinking of others is important. One of my big pet peeves is when people don't put the cart back at the grocery store. It amazes me that people have no qualms about leaving a cart in a parking space. It points to a lazy work ethic.

My Kolbe Index is: 6338 - 6 Factfinder, 3 Follow Through, 3 Quickstart, 8 Implementor. Sometimes my low Follow Through is helpful because when you follow the norm and it doesn't work, going about it in a different direction and trying something new can be helpful. The downside is I'm always creating something new, or having to go through the learning process of something new because even if I've done it in the past, I never do it the same way.

When we had an issue with the software and one of the tools, if I'd done everything the same way, I could've changed just a couple of lines of code. But no, I had to go through every line to find the problems. However, overall it helps me solve problems where others might say "No, it can't be done." I say, "No, it can't be done *that way*." I have an ability to overstep, find a way through, go around, etc. It has enabled me to create things in the software and on our farm that appeared that they couldn't be done. It pairs well with my growth-oriented mindset. My brothers have this mindset and innovative skillset too, and we collaborate well on projects. That's my 3 Follow Through at work, along with the 8 Implementor.

Another belief I was raised with was that more than one thing can go wrong and to be alert to all the issues. With cars, we didn't have money for parts, so we had to figure out what the issue was, troubleshoot it, and fix the part. Sometimes we would realize something else was the problem. I have come to find out with age that more than one thing can fail at the same time. I used to think things were binary, but now I know there can be multiple answers and challenges.

Somehow, humans can rationalize and store conflicting ideas in their head. Everybody thinks they are unique. Also, when they present something and push stuff out there, they think everybody thinks the way they do. Somehow in their minds, they're not in conflict about that. For the most part, everybody receives things a different way. You're going to have failure if you assume everything you put out there is exactly the way other people think.

Most people don't make decisions based on math. I do, but I know that's not normal for most people. I try to use that for me internally, but not push the numbers on other people. Numbers may sway their thinking a little bit, but numbers are not usually the decision-makers.

I have to be careful because in class, every decision, financially or otherwise, is an emotional decision. I use math to help with emotional decisions. I don't want advisors in class to throw the calculator or computer in front of a client to make the final decision. It's an assist: it helps them make the final decision.

Q: If you were to talk to yourself as a kid, what would you say?

A: Get serious early on. I would not have wasted time in school that should not have been wasted. It's not hard; it's all about making a decision. For me, looking back, being more serious early on would have made a difference.

When you're young, you don't realize time is not forever. Time moves pretty slowly and it feels like you have all the time in the world. Now there are lots of things I want to do, think about, and explore from a knowledge standpoint, and there's not as much time for it.

You can take this search for knowledge too far and not enjoy life. But you can also waste a lot of time. I enjoy learning about things and doing research, but the tools were not available to me early on. One of the things we did when I was a kid (I grew up in Houston) was figure out the bus schedule to ride the city bus to the library to dig out books that held old information and were sometimes not usable anymore. I would also dig out the yellow pages and call places.

I went to a Lutheran junior high during the same time the band Kiss came out. I had a few friends who loved them, and we put on student concerts at one of their houses. We talked the school into letting us do a concert at the school, and we decided we needed to make smoke, so I figured out how to make smoke bombs with black powder. In the process, we burned a hole in the stage and got in so much trouble! My 7th grade teacher stuck his neck out for us and he got in a lot of trouble when we burned the stage. He looked at us and was so disappointed. Though what I did was inventive, the lesson I would have taught my young self would have been to get serious!

Q: What advice do you have on relationships, money, and health?

A: It's funny to think of the old adage that "Money is not everything." But one of my wife Kim's quotes extends that adage to "Money is not everything, but it affects everything we do." I think when it comes to relationships, happiness, and being confident, money impacts all of those things. You can't *buy* them, but without money, you can have a negative response in all of those areas. Money affects both our health and our ability to produce.

How much does money affect our mental perspective? Especially if we're unsure about where it is? A lot of people have not worked with an advisor to see a path or a solution. Many people push it out of their mind. Or they stress over it. The act of being concerned about their money causes them to never be able to get to that place where they have enough and they can comfortably shift the amount of time they're working. Maybe it's a matter of not wanting to work in a paid job, maybe they want to do volunteer work and want to know they have enough money to do that, or they simply want to have a choice about what they do and be confident in that choice.

I think without confidence in relationships you end up in the same stressed-out situation; it wears on your health and your ability to produce. I wish there was a way to measure the impact of confidence and certainty on all of these areas. There's no way to measure it or the real impact. Years ago, a friend of mine, Les McGuire, wrote an article on this topic titled "The Economic Value of Certainty" that explores this idea further (https://themoneyadvantage.app.box.com/s/8pd9mggmm7sbj9cy3isurql9q16gwiv4).

Q: What was the hardest thing you ever accomplished and why?

A: Physically, the hardest thing was pulling wire at our house. We rearranged where the power was coming in, and I didn't want to tell the electric company we were setting up solar because they weren't in support of it at the time. So we dug and laid a four-inch pipe for almost four inches of wire, 350 feet. We had all the wire, and it was so heavy we had the tractor pulling spools! We were trying to push, and Kim was pulling on the other end with a winch. Plus we had an electrician helping. My brother

Ken called and we said, "We're dying trying to pull this wire!" It was over 100 degrees, hot, trying to get wire pulled, not sliding, and they said, "I'll come by and help." We finally got it done!

Mentally, the hardest thing I've done was public speaking. I avoided all communications classes in school and was not about to speak in front of people. But one day, my mentor Norman was sick, we were in the middle of a class, and I just had to make it happen. It turned out I didn't mind doing it as long as I knew what I was talking about. When Kim met me, I was the quiet computer guy in the back who didn't say anything to anybody. Today, while I still don't love it, I can confidently speak in front of rooms full of a few hundred people!

Q: What's your biggest business success?

A: Truth Training, our live 3 day classes, are my biggest business success, the training of financial logic to financial strategists. Between the strategists and the client, there has to be interpretation of the numbers. It is personal finance and while money doesn't always act like math (for example, when average does not equal actual), we must be able to do the math around money. Those 3 days demonstrate that from every angle possible over most products and every wealth shift we have listed in the Appendix.

Q: What were the best business lessons you learned?

A: Keep going. Keep pushing. You hear people say things like, "We tried it umpteen times in different ways, and on the 500th try, it worked!" Ask yourself: What's the logic behind continuing on versus shifting to something else? I think when it's a passion you have, you've got to keep going as long as you can.

Q: What are you most proud of in your life?

A: I'm most proud of my ability to figure things out. Working on problems until they are solved. Not accepting it can't be done. There are some things that can't be done, but usually I've extinguished every other possibility and workaround by that point. There are times you have to figure out if something is not worth it. That's a big difference.

Q: How do you want to be remembered?

A: For providing value and doing the right thing.

FIVE FINANCIAL CALCULATORS

To get access to these calculators, sign up for a free 30-day trial of Truth Concepts™. This will get you access to the entire software suite for your trial period, including our larger, more specialized calculators. Then, when your 30-day license is up, instead of paying to renew, you can simply hit "Continue" on the Registration window to disable everything except for these five financial calculators, as well as the IRR Calculator (Internal Rate of Return), for your personal use.

https://truthconcepts.com/five-financial-calculators

List of Calculators and Tools in the Truth Concepts™ Software

CALCULATORS

0 **BASIC CALCULATOR:** For grade school math

1–5 **FINANCIAL:** Future Value, Present Value, Payment, Interest Rate, and Time Period for financial math

6 **INTERNAL RATE OF RETURN:** IRR for varying stream of payments and withdrawals

7 **LOAN ANALYSIS:** Calculates amortization schedules, and the benefit of paying back loans under various scenarios (like comparing a fifteen- and a thirty-year mortgage). Also allows you to pay the loan back at different rates and compare two loan scenarios for deductible and non-deductible loans

8 **BORROWING STRATEGY:** Illustrates the principles of banking (borrowing and paying back) with varying interest rates, strategies, and money sources

9 **REVOLVING CREDIT:** Enables you to prove which is the most economical way to pay down or off consumer debt. Snowball, Avalanche, or Cash Flow based methods are all demonstrable

10 **MAXIMUM POTENTIAL:** Shows a person's focus should be on saving money rather than seeking a higher rate of return as it identifies full capability, then reduces it by taxes, debt service, lifestyle, and inflation

11 **AUTOMOBILE PURCHASES:** Shows the "true" cost of paying cash for automobiles

12 **EDUCATION COST:** Demonstrates the major impact on parents' assets and cash flow that paying for high school and/or college has; can also calculate education "need"

13 **FUNDING ILLUSTRATION:** This calculator allows the user to compare life insurance illustrations (with or without loans) to an alternate investment with identical cash flows

14 **REAL ESTATE ANALYSIS:** In-depth real estate calculations and analysis for any investment real estate, allowing you to show the actual rate of return a property is earning

15 **QUALIFIED PLAN:** Graphic overview of the whole truth about qualified plans, picturing the costs to fund them, the management fees that erode them, and how ineffective the match and tax-deferral really are. It shows clients why *not* maxing out their qualified plan may be the best strategy

16 **CASH FLOW:** Provides for up to three different and varying payment and withdrawal streams with varying annual earnings rates, shows an "average" versus "actual" ROR (rate of return)

17 **ACCUMULATION:** Shows effectiveness of money growing (taxable, tax-deferred, tax-deductible, and/or tax-free), and it has multiple variable payment and withdrawal columns, the ability to vary the earnings rate, and the ability to add term insurance and other costs

18 **DISTRIBUTION:** Shows money coming out of an account with varying interest rates. It allows for taxable, tax-deferred, tax-deductible, and/or tax-free accounts. It compares two different strategies for distribution

19 **DIVERSIFICATION:** Shows the outcome of transferring assets from savings accounts and money markets into permanent life insurance and how that reduces the taxes, term insurance costs, and risks along the way. It helps clients understand how life insurance increases both their asset base while alive and the net to heirs upon death

20 **FUTURE REQUIREMENTS:** Retirement planning calculator used to show the ROR necessary to have sufficient retirement income with or without consuming assets

21 **TERM CONVERSION:** Demonstrates term conversion strategy over the life of the client

22 **ASSET FLOW:** The "all-in" calculator that demonstrates any person's entire financial life. It can be used simply with just a few assets, combined with insurance, or in a complex fashion like a retirement plan or a financial plan

TOOLS

23 **NOTES:** This small box enables you to type notes relevant to any particular calculator and then attach that note to the calculator so when saved, they come up together

24 **INCOME TAX CHART:** Shows differences between marginal and average tax brackets

25 **US TAX HISTORY:** Shows tax brackets from 1913 to the current year

26 **US CPI HISTORY:** Composite percentage change from 1914 to the previous year

27 **MARKET HISTORY:** S&P 500 with and without dividends from 1937 to current, updated annually and Dow Jones Industrial from 1901 to current, updated annually. On all three columns, you can get an average and an actual as well as the year-by-year historical return

28 **LIFE EXPECTANCY TABLES:** 2001 (the most recent year available) male and female (single and joint life), standard, preferred, and super preferred, both smoker and non-smoker. Tells the whole truth about longevity: the longer you live, the longer you'll live. You can compare two side-by-side or look at the percentage chance both will be alive or just see the life expectancy of a certain age

29 **SIDE BY SIDE:** Visualize and prove a variety of comparisons in this flexible tool which can incorporate Life Values, Accumulation, Cash Flow, Distribution, and Qualified Plan Calculators

30 **LIFE INSURANCE VALUES:** Enables uploading of illustration values (via copy and paste) to this tool, which then calculates the IRR and ROR of cash value and death benefit and then gives you the ability to pull that information into other calculators

31 **PRINTING:** Each calculator can be printed and copied into a Word document or an email to share with clients. Additionally, if you have a large calculator on the screen with a small one over it, that combination can be printed under File, Screen, Capture

32 **OCR TO PDF CONVERTER:** Take a picture with your cell phone of any life insurance illustration, and the converter will switch it to a PDF so that you can copy and paste it into the Life Values Tool

33 **VIRTUAL KEYBOARD:** Helpful when using TC on a tablet via the Remote Desktop feature (since tablets cannot do the mathematical computations as they are not technically computers)

34 **MOVE ALL TC TO PRIMARY DISPLAY:** Helpful when using two or three screens and sharing TCdata files

LIST OF PRODUCTS AND STRATEGIES USED BY FINANCIAL STRATEGISTS

Products

Car Insurance
Home Insurance
Liability Insurance
Disability Insurance
Term Life Insurance
Whole Life Insurance
Investment Real Estate
Managed Money
Index Funds
30 year Mortgages
Wills and Trusts
Private Placements
Peer to Peer Lending
Reverse Mortgages
Single Premium Immediate Annuities
Deferred Annuities

Strategies

Have high deductibles on car and home insurance
Save 20% of your gross income
Pay dividends and short term capital gains in cash for all non-IRA money
Fund retirement plans to match level only
Use 30 year mortgages and no pre-payments
Borrow against Life Insurance for Emergencies and Opportunities
Focus on Cash Flow, not Net-Worth

Pay Down accounts while in "spending phase"
Keep working, don't retire, take free days along the way
Pay back interest on borrowed money
Give to charity to keep money moving
Maintain a Currence Reservoir for accountability
Review all legal documents at least every 5 years

LIST OF WEALTH SHIFTS

Purpose—What defines a successful Financial Advisor or Strategist is their ability to shift wealth in someone's financial statement and move them closer to their financial targets and outcomes with even more certainty.

Ideally, you want your finances to both grow and be protected. Many people see these two aspects as opposing goals, yet with the right financial products (things you buy) and strategies (things you do) you can implement these Wealth Shifts below and get both. Focus on a few at a time, and note many of the shifts just require simple paperwork or online check boxes.

For example, if you have mutual funds that are taxable, you can ask the brokerage house to send you the dividends and capital gains in cash with a simple form or check box. Think about it like taking the cream off the crop every quarter. Then you can use that money to improve protection with a liability umbrella or a life insurance policy. The following Wealth Shifts, split up into 8 sections, list the action first, and then the benefit.

CASH FLOW SHIFTS

ADDITIONAL MONEY ADDED

Redirect additional monthly cash flow into a properly structured whole life policy instead of allowing it to accumulate in low-efficiency savings or spending accounts. Doing so increases the amount of capital compounding inside a tax-advantaged environment while improving liquidity and long-term financial control.

EXPENSE OPTIMIZATION

Reduce unnecessary or inefficient expenses and redirect the recovered cash flow toward an emergency fund or high-efficiency assets such as properly structured whole life insurance. Doing so converts money that was previously disappearing into consumption into capital that can solve emergencies and take advantage of opportunities.

PAYCHECK WITHHOLDING SHIFT

Adjust paycheck tax withholding to reduce large annual tax refunds and increase monthly take-home cash flow available for protection or growth. Doing so converts idle money previously held by the IRS into capital that can begin compounding and working immediately throughout the year.

401(K) SHIFT FROM MAX TO MATCH

Reduce 401(k) contributions from the maximum level down to only the employer match and redirect the freed-up cash flow to a properly structured whole life policy. Doing so increases control, liquidity and use of money while building tax-advantaged capital without the access restrictions and future tax uncertainty of qualified plans.

401(K) DELAY

Delay beginning 401(k) contributions early in a career and redirect those initial savings years into building a strong liquidity foundation with properly structured whole life insurance. Doing so allows capital to accumulate in a flexible system first, improving long-term financial efficiency and funding opportunities later.

PAID-UP ADDITIONS SHIFT TO BASE PREMIUM

Shift life insurance contributions from excessive Paid-Up Additions toward a stronger base premium for the next policy within your portfolio. Doing so increases the long-term guaranteed growth and dividend base of all your policies while maintaining strong liquidity and improving long-term policy efficiency.

EDUCATION SHIFT

Redirect a portion of traditional college savings toward building family capital using properly structured whole life insurance. Doing so creates flexible funding that can be used for education or other opportunities while preserving long-term capital that would otherwise disappear through direct education spending.

INSURANCE OPTIMIZATION

PROPERTY & CASUALTY OPTIMIZATION

Review and optimize property and casualty insurance coverage to eliminate redundant policies and inefficient premium structures. Doing so frees up unnecessary premium expenses that can be redirected toward a liability umbrella or other protection products.

INCREASING DEDUCTIBLES

Increase insurance deductibles where appropriate to reduce ongoing premium costs. Doing so lowers long-term insurance expenses and redirects the premium savings into improved or additional protection thereby increasing the overall efficiency of the financial system.

TERM INSURANCE PREMIUM RECAPTURE

Replace long-term term life insurance strategies with properly structured participating whole life insurance where appropriate. Doing so converts insurance premiums that normally expire with no value into premiums that build an asset and a death benefit that is guaranteed to pay out at death, no matter the age. Please note: all income earners should keep total death benefit levels at or near Human Life Value so many times keeping term insurance in place is required.

IUL/VUL ADJUSTMENTS

Evaluate existing IUL or VUL or Universal policies and reposition them when appropriate toward more stable and predictable insurance structures. Doing so reduces exposure to market volatility and policy performance uncertainty while improving the long-term reliability of the capital accumulation and protection strategy.

EXISTING ASSET SHIFTS

INTEREST ONLY

Reposition interest income generated from existing assets into a properly structured whole life policy rather than allowing it to accumulate inefficiently in taxable accounts or be consumed. Doing so converts passive interest flow into capital that compounds in a tax-advantaged environment while remaining accessible for future opportunities.

BALANCE PAYDOWN

Reallocate excess balances sitting in low-efficiency savings or investment accounts into high-efficiency capital structures such as properly structured whole life insurance. Doing so preserves liquidity while repositioning idle capital into an environment designed for long-term growth, stability, and financial control.

401(K) SHIFT VIA 72T

Utilize IRS Rule 72(t) to begin structured distributions from qualified retirement plans prior to traditional retirement age. Doing so can reposition tax-deferred assets into more flexible environments while improving access, liquidity, and long-term tax diversification.

INTEREST, DIVIDEND, AND CAPITAL GAIN SHIFTS

Redirect interest, dividend, and capital gain income that would normally be consumed or reinvested inefficiently into high-efficiency capital accumulation structures. Doing so converts passive investment income into capital that compounds predictably and without tax while remaining accessible for future opportunities.

LOANS / DEBT SERVICE SHIFTS

CREDIT IMPROVEMENT

Improve credit profile through disciplined payment history, debt management, and credit utilization adjustments. Doing so increases borrowing efficiency by qualifying for lower interest rates and improved lending terms across future financing opportunities.

LOAN REFINANCE

Refinance existing loans when interest rates or loan structures can be improved. Doing so reduces interest expense and monthly obligations while freeing additional cash flow that can be redirected toward capital-building assets and more protection.

LOAN OVERPAYMENT

Evaluate whether excess loan payments should instead be redirected toward building liquid capital reserves. Doing so preserves access to capital while allowing dollars to compound rather than becoming trapped as inaccessible equity.

LOAN PAYOFF

Eliminate high-interest consumer debt when interest costs exceed reasonable capital accumulation opportunities. Doing so reduces financial drag on the system while improving overall cash flow efficiency.

PAYMENT NEGOTIATIONS

Negotiate loan terms, payment structures, or interest rates directly with lenders when possible. Doing so can reduce monthly obligations or interest expense, improving cash flow and overall financial efficiency.

CREDIT SCORE OPTIMIZATION

Optimize credit score through responsible credit utilization, payment timing, and account management practices. Doing so improves access to favorable lending terms and lowers borrowing costs throughout a lifetime of financial activity.

HELOC OVERHAUL

Restructure existing Home Equity Lines of Credit to improve interest rates, payment flexibility, or lending terms. Doing so increases borrowing efficiency while maintaining access to equity capital when needed.

CASH-OUT REFINANCE

Refinance real estate to extract equity while securing improved loan terms when appropriate. Doing so converts trapped home equity into accessible capital that can be repositioned into more productive financial environments.

REVERSE MORTGAGE

Utilize reverse mortgage structures strategically in retirement to access home equity without mandatory loan repayment during the homeowner's lifetime. Doing so converts illiquid housing equity into usable cash flow while allowing homeowners to remain in their homes.

BUSINESS OWNERS' SHIFTS

401(K) MATCH BY COMPANY

Shift retirement contributions that appear to come from the company, yet are actually the owners money into accounts the owner controls, are liquid, and usable by the owner and the business. Doing so can improve the business's ability to solve emergencies and take advantage of opportunities.

Employee Stock Ownership Plans (ESOP)

Establish an Employee Stock Ownership Plan to allow employees to participate in company ownership over time. Doing so can create tax advantages for the business owner while providing a structured ownership transition opportunity.

CHARITABLE REMAINDER TRUST (CRT)

Transfer highly appreciated assets into a Charitable Remainder Trust while retaining an income stream during life. Doing so reduces immediate capital gains exposure while supporting long-term charitable goals.

BUSINESS ENTITY SHIFT

Evaluate whether the current business entity structure remains the most tax-efficient option for the company's size and profitability. Doing so can reduce tax exposure while improving flexibility in compensation and profit distribution.

EXIT / LIQUIDITY STRATEGIES

Prepare a structured exit approach for business ownership through sale, succession, or internal transfer. Doing so improves the likelihood that years of business equity translate into usable retirement capital.

EXECUTIVE COMPENSATION

Implement executive compensation structures designed to reward key leadership while improving tax efficiency for the business. Doing so strengthens leadership retention while aligning incentives with long-term business performance.

EMPLOYEE BENEFITS

Optimize employee benefit structures to improve value while managing employer cost and liability exposure. Doing so enhances employee retention while improving the overall efficiency of compensation packages.

INSURANCE EVALUATION

Evaluate existing business insurance coverage to confirm appropriate protection against operational, liability, and ownership risks. Doing so protects the enterprise while preventing unnecessary or redundant premium expenses.

CAPTIVE INSURANCE

Establish a captive insurance company when appropriate to manage insurable business risks internally. Doing so can improve risk management while potentially creating tax and capital accumulation advantages.

REAL ESTATE SHIFTS

CHARITABLE REMAINDER TRUSTS

Transfer appreciated real estate into a Charitable Remainder Trust while retaining an income stream for life. Doing so can defer capital gains taxes on the sale of the property while converting highly appreciated assets into diversified income-producing capital.

PROPERTY LEASEBACKS

Sell real estate owned by a business or individual and lease the property back from the new owner. Doing so unlocks trapped equity in the property while allowing continued use of the real estate for business or operational needs.

DEPRECIATION ADJUSTMENTS

Review real estate depreciation schedules to ensure allowable depreciation deductions are being fully utilized. Doing so can increase current tax deductions while improving the overall after-tax efficiency of the real estate investment.

COST SEGREGATION

Conduct a cost segregation study on qualifying real estate to accelerate depreciation of certain building components. Doing so increases early tax deductions and improves near-term cash flow while maintaining the long-term value of the property investment.

RELOCATION

Relocate primary residence or business operations to a more favorable tax or economic jurisdiction when appropriate. Doing so can significantly reduce ongoing tax exposure while improving overall financial efficiency over time.

TAX SHIFTS

TAX STRATEGY (VIA WEALTHABILITY OR YOUR CPA)

Engage a proactive tax professional to identify deductions, credits, and structural opportunities that may currently be overlooked. Doing so can reduce lifetime tax exposure while allowing more capital to remain working inside the financial system.

TAX REFUND

Adjust tax withholding so excess payments to the IRS are minimized and monthly take-home cash flow increases. Doing so converts money previously held by the government into capital that can begin compounding throughout the year.

EMPLOYMENT SHIFT

Reposition income sources between W-2 employment, business ownership, or consulting structures when appropriate. Doing so can unlock tax deductions and structural advantages not available through traditional employment compensation alone.

INVESTMENT LOSS / PASSIVE LOSSES

Harvest investment losses or utilize allowable passive losses to offset taxable gains or income when appropriate. Doing so reduces current tax liability while improving overall portfolio efficiency.

WASH SALE

Carefully sell and repurchase investments within IRS guidelines to maintain market exposure while realizing allowable tax losses. Doing so can reduce taxable gains while keeping long-term investment positions intact.

INSTALLMENT SALE

Structure the sale of appreciated assets using installment sale treatment to spread taxable gains over multiple years. Doing so reduces the immediate tax burden while creating a predictable income stream over time.

HIRING CHILDREN

Hire children within a family business for legitimate work performed and compensate them appropriately. Doing so shifts taxable income into lower tax brackets while teaching financial responsibility and work ethic.

RESEARCH AND DEVELOPMENT CREDITS

Claim available Research and Development tax credits when business activities qualify under IRS guidelines. Doing so directly reduces tax liability while encouraging innovation and reinvestment into business growth.

CONSERVATION EASEMENTS

Donate qualifying land development rights through a conservation easement arrangement. Doing so can generate significant charitable deductions while preserving land for environmental or agricultural purposes.

LEGACY SHIFTS

CHARITABLE GIVING

Direct charitable contributions through structured giving vehicles rather than simple cash donations. Doing so can increase the impact of charitable gifts while improving tax efficiency for the donor.

TRUSTS

Transfer assets into appropriately structured trusts to manage ownership, control, and distribution across generations. Doing so protects family assets while improving estate efficiency and long-term wealth transfer.

PRIVATE INSURANCE

Establish properly structured life insurance designed to provide tax-efficient liquidity at death. Doing so creates immediate estate liquidity for heirs while protecting family assets from forced liquidation.

What Is Next for You?

If you are a Financial Strategist and want more proof as to how these work, join Todd Langford and the TruthConcepts.com team at a live training. Additionally you can take a look at the suite of calculators available for 30 days free at https://truthconcepts.com/free-trial.

If you are an investor, you may also want to look at the above free trial, or if you want personalized help, reach out to Katie@TruthConcepts.com and she can connect you to a Financial Strategist who uses Truth Concepts and can help.

FINANCIAL ACRONYMS FOR PROFESSIONALS

Here's a comprehensive list of terms you might come across as a financial professional.

TC: Truth Concepts

BOY: Beginning of year

EOY: End of Year

IRR: Internal Rate of Return

ROR: Rate of Return

PUA: Paid-up Additions

PLI: Permanent Life Insurance

IUL: Indexed Universal Life (insurance)

EIUL: Equity Indexed Life (insurance)

VUL: Variable Universal Life (insurance)

UL: Universal Life (insurance)

WD: Withdrawal

CV: Cash value

DB: Death benefit

YRT: Yearly-Renewable Term (insurance)
CG: Capital gains
CRT: Charitable Remainder Trust
DST: Deferred Sales Trust
WL: Whole Life (insurance)
CD: Certificate of Deposit
IMO: Independent Marketing Organization
FMO: Field Marketing Organization
NMO: National Marketing Office
MGA: Managing General Agent
GA: General Agent
BGA: Brokerage General Agency
PPGA: Personal Producing General Agent
CFB: Cash Flow Bridge
VB: Volatility Buffer
ETF: Exchange Traded Funds
FDIC: Federal Deposit Insurance Corporation
FRB: Federal Reserve Board
IRA: Individual Retirement Account
REIT: Real Estate Investment Trust
SEC: Securities Exchange Commission
TSA: Tax Sheltered Annuity
SPIA: Single Premium Immediate Annuity
MEC: Modified Endowment Contract
LLC: Limited Liability Company
P&L: Profit and Loss
YTD: Year to Date

REFERENCE LINKS

Truth Concepts Standards: https://truthconcepts.com/the-truth-concepts-standards
Seven Blind Spots of Financial Strategists: https://truthconcepts.com/7-blind-spots-of-financial-strategists
Currence: https://strategist.livecurrence.com/offer?code=pem20
This is an affiliate link. All proceeds go to the non-profit Prosperity Economics Movement at ProsperityEconomics.org, designed to teach financial competency.
Funny Financial Literacy Videos: https://truthconcepts.com/funny-financial-literacy-videos

About the Authors

Todd Langford is the founder and creator of Truth Concepts™ financial calculators. His love for numbers and desire for integrity in the personal financial space inspired him to create calculators that cut the pretense and get straight to the Truth. Todd believes in making decisions from principles first, then checking those principles with the facts.

This technical, straightforward, and earnest thinking sets the tone for much of Todd's work. Driven by a desire to understand how all things function and to make meaning out of data, Todd continues to up-level the calculators, as well as his own personal technology, evidenced through his personal solar panel network (https://www.youtube.com/watch?v=MWymMBsug6Q)

In all things, Todd asks, "How could it be even better?" Then he brings forth the Truth to be as loud (or louder) than the lies, and to inspire people to seek more Truth.

With a Kolbe™ profile of 6338, Todd is on a strong quest for detail, and as an initiating implementor, he lives fully in the present. Any time he is asked, "How long will you be?" His answer is always, "As long as it takes." Driven to build lasting results, he enjoys working with his hands and feels like programming a computer is like working on cars without getting his hands greasy.

His strengths (from Clifton StrengthsFinder) are: Maximizer (stimulates excellence and transforms strong to superb), Futuristic (inspired by the future and inspires others with vision), Achiever (stamina, works hard, satisfaction in being productive), Focus (takes a direction or makes a decision, prioritizes, and acts), and Individualization (intrigued by each person's unique qualities). These are evident in his house, on his farm, and in his interactions with his TruthConcepts 360 members.

Contact: Katie Fitzgerald (assistant), 903-822-4133, TruthConcepts.com

LinkedIn: LinkedIn.com/in/TruthConceptsSoftware

Facebook: Facebook.com/TruthConcepts

YouTube: YouTube.com/user/TruthConcepts

Kristen Joy Hugins is the founder of Joyfull Communications, where she and her team write and edit human-made books, newsletters, and marketing copy. With over twenty years of experience crafting content for businesses and nonprofits, she officially launched her own firm in 2022 and brings a wealth of cross-industry expertise to her work. Kristen is the Co-Author with Kim Butler of *Busting the Scarcity Mindset: Your Guide to Becoming a Prosperity Thinker*, and Contributing Author and Editor of the *Six Figure Chicks* book series. She also runs Authors in Action, an online community for authors seeking guidance, accountability, and connection as they write.

Based in Phoenix, Arizona, where she also dances with Movement Source Dance Company, Kristen is a proud mom to two teenagers. She loves to travel, hike, snowboard, and spend as much time outdoors as possible. A lifelong learner and adventurer, Kristen brings her vast experience to every project through her creativity, rich storytelling, and strategic insight.

With a Kolbe profile of 7762, Kristen gathers and organizes information systematically, and she is a natural strategic planner, looking at the big picture before organizing the smaller steps for any project. Her strengths (from Clifton StrengthsFinder) are: Achiever (stamina, works hard, satisfaction in being productive), Responsibility (psychological ownership of what she says she will do, committed to stable values), Learner (great desire to learn and continuously improve), Input (collect and archive information, ideas, artifacts, or even relationships), and Harmony (looks for consensus, seeks areas of agreement).

Contact: 480-712-3959, JoyfullCommunications.com

LinkedIn: LinkedIn.com/in/KristenHugins

Facebook: Facebook.com/Kristen.Hugins

Instagram: Instagram.com/k10joy

www.ingramcontent.com/pod-product-compliance
Lightning Source LLC
LaVergne TN
LVHW081402110826
845149LV00010B/1642

* 9 7 9 8 9 9 4 0 9 9 4 6 9 *